THE EUROPEAN
AND THE INDIAN

THE EUROPEAN
AND THE INDIAN

*Essays in the Ethnohistory
of Colonial North America*

JAMES AXTELL

New York   Oxford
OXFORD UNIVERSITY PRESS
1981

Library of Congress Cataloging in Publication Data

Axtell, James L
The European and the Indian.

Includes index.
1. Indians of North America—Cultural assimilation
—Addresses, essays, lectures. 2. North America—
Civilization—Indian influences—Addresses, essays,
lectures. 3. Indians of North America—History—
Addresses, essays, lectures. 4. North America—
History—Colonial period, ca. 1600-1775—Addresses,
essays, lectures, I. Title.
E98.C89A9   970.004'97   80-25084
ISBN 0-19-502903-8
ISBN 0-19-502904-6 (pbk.)

Printing (last digit): 9 8 7 6 5 4 3 2 1

Printed in the United States of America

For Susan
Chief of the state of grace

Preface

SOME BOOKS OF ESSAYS ARE MADE BY THEIR AUTHORS OR PUB-
lishers; others make themselves. This collection virtually
made itself as I explored the intercultural history of colonial
North America during the past decade. Although the ten
essays included here were written over a ten-year period,
eight were written in the past five years, two especially for
this volume. They show, I think, a consistency of method and
focus as well as a commonality of subject.

The method and focus are provided by ethnohistory, a
common-law marriage of history and anthropology that remains unconsecrated by the constituent disciplines but is increasingly resorted to by their practitioners who face certain
kinds of problems and questions. Originally, ethnohistory
was shaped by anthropologists who needed to answer historical questions about the many western and midwestern Indian
tribes who were pressing land claims before the Indian
Claims Commission after its creation in 1946. The applica-
tions of ethnohistory spread unevenly to the study of eastern
tribes as well, but were accelerated after 1971 when the Native American Rights Fund was founded to represent Indian
tribes in legal actions and again after 1975 when the tribes

in the original thirteen colonies won the right to seek legal redress of past injustices in federal court.

Almost simultaneously, frontier and colonial historians began to discover the necessity of considering the American natives as real determinants of history and the utility of ethnohistory as a way of ensuring parity of focus and impartiality of judgment. As a result, the history of Indian-white relations has been revolutionized by ethnohistory in the past decade, as I showed in "The Ethnohistory of Early America: A Review Essay" (*William and Mary Quarterly,* 3d ser. 35 [1978], 110-44). Most of the tough and interesting new questions have been limited thus far to the Indian cultures, but ethnohistorians can be expected to achieve another breakthrough in understanding when they ask the same kinds of elemental questions about colonial culture, which their colleagues in social history are already beginning to ask.

This collection, then, may be regarded as a casebook in ethnohistorical method which differs from its few predecessors in providing examples of several kinds of ethnohistorical questions, sources, problems, and answers, in being written by an historian rather than an anthropologist, and in focusing equally on the European as well as the Indian side of the colonial frontiers.

These essays are also held together by a sustained interest in the social and cultural interactions of the various peoples in the greater northeastern quadrant of colonial North America, particularly the French, English, and Indians. Elsewhere I have argued that American historians should cultivate "A North American Perspective for Colonial History" which would encompass not only all the European colonies in North America and the Caribbean—French, English, Dutch, Spanish, and Swedish—but the continental mother countries, Africa, and the Atlantic shipping lanes as well. I urged that we rid ourselves of anachronistic political boundaries and pay closer attention to historical geography and to the borderless histories of trade, warfare, disease, exploration, settlement patterns, conversion, and acculturation, all of which revolved around the still-neglected Indian peoples of America. In a brief scenario of what colonial America would have looked like in the absence of the native Americans, I suggested that "without the Indians America would not be America as we know it" (*The History Teacher*, 12 [1979], 549-62, at 558), a theme pursued at greater length in Chapter 10 below.

In retrospect, the value of ethnohistory and the logic of a North American perspective seem patently obvious, but at the beginning of my historical training neither was perceptible. "Colonial America" meant, much as it does today, the thirteen English mainland colonies, and in our textbooks Indians were more invisible than blacks, who were just beginning their slow march toward social and historical dignity. Nor did I yet have questions that required self-education beyond the curricular status quo. Although I had grown up in arrowhead-rich Iroquois country, been elected as a Boy Scout to the secret "Order of the Arrow," and like most kids stalked "big game" and "hostiles" in semi-silent deerskin moccasins, I brought no consciousness of or interest in Indians to college or graduate school. I discovered Indians, ethnohistory, and a North American perspective only when the books and articles I wanted to write couldn't be written without them. Once I had articulated my felt needs, answering them was not difficult. The sources for Indian history can be found in the printed records familiar to traditional colonial historians. Getting the most out of them, however, and putting them in proper focus required the use of ethnohistory. In 1972 I attended my first meeting of the American Society for Ethnohistory, where to my pleasant surprise I found a number of scholars who knew not only the documentary sources I was working with but a variety of anthropological techniques for extracting and analyzing information from them of which most historians, including myself, were totally unaware. They were also familiar with a number of other sources that historians were largely strangers to, such as archaeological remains, museum collections, and dying languages. Subsequent A.S.E. meetings and the smaller Iroquois and Algonquian conferences in the United States and Canada have served as the main classrooms for my continuing education in the methods, sources, and rewards of ethnohistory.

I arrived at a North American perspective in fits and starts largely from an early acquaintance with England and a later one with Canada. While a junior at Yale, I came to realize that colonial America (which I still took to be synonymous with the English colonies) could not be understood without a close familiarity with Tudor-Stuart England. So for the next four or five years I concentrated on English history to prepare for an eventual return to colonial history, which helps to explain my Cambridge doctorate and the subject of my first book, John Locke. A few years later my family and I began to take the measure of the spacious geographical beauty and enchantment of eastern Canada and Maine, a happy process that coincided with my tardy discovery that the histories of New France and New England were intertwined throughout the colonial period. Added to the simultaneous illumination of my blind spot about Indians, these (I can now see) related dawnings led inexorably to the full version of "A North American Perspective," which I adumbrated in 1979, and to this collection.

Williamsburg, Va.   J.A.
March 1981

Acknowledgments

GRATEFUL HYPERBOLE ASIDE, THIS BOOK WOULD NOT EXIST without the generous support of two great national resources: the National Endowment for the Humanities and The Newberry Library. Without the two consecutive years of intellectual freedom made possible by their fellowships, I could not have conceived, much less researched and written, the majority of essays in this volume. Nor would I have benefited from the stimulation and friendship of the unique Newberry community, particularly Bill Towner and Dick Brown. My debts to Fritz Jennings began to accumulate long before his or my tenure at the library, but he and the fellows of the Center for the History of the American Indian broke many trails through our year of discovery.

I am also indebted to the American Council of Learned Societies and the College of William and Mary for summer research grants which enabled me to complete two of the essays. The college contributed still more. *The William and Mary Quarterly,* under the able editorships of Thad Tate and Mike McGiffert, first published three of the essays, and three others were improved by spirited exchanges at the monthly colloquia of the Institute of Early American History and Culture. My colleagues in the History Department, particularly Tom Sheppard and Ed Crapol, have been not only congenial but supportive in many ways.

Authorship is a lonely business in the beginning and at the

end: only you can write what you have to say and only a fool would stand with you when the reviews appear. But in between the "community of scholars" becomes palpable and friends and colleagues generously allow themselves to become implicated as sounding boards, critics, and editors. Over the past several years I have been the grateful recipient of suggestions, criticisms, and encouragement from Bob Berkhofer, Tim Breen, Bill Fenton, Cornelius Jaenen, John Juricek, Nancy Lurie, Ed Morgan, David and Alison Quinn, Neal Salisbury, Bill Simmons, Bill Sturtevant, Bruce Trigger, Alden Vaughan, Wid Washburn, and Mike Zuckerman. With such formidable help, it is tempting to say that any errors of fact or interpretation the reader may detect are likely to be theirs—tempting but, alas, not accurate.

The next two people are somewhat harder to thank because of the special kind and amount of help they have given. Jim Ronda has been a long-standing, long-suffering friend as well as the kind of frank and fair critic every writer should have. His boundless energy, thoughtfulness, and passionate concern have been an inspiration and a challenge to every essay in this collection. Although Bill Eccles has read and improved much of my work on colonial North America, I am more grateful for the example of his impeccable scholarship, high standards, and gracious style. Mentor and friend, he constantly renews my faith in, and rekindles my excitement for, the profession and learning of history.

It is impossible to do justice to the time, thought, and care that my wife Susan has lavished on these essays and their author. More than anyone else, she has allowed me to unite my avocation with my vocation, forced me to distinguish between the right word and nearly right word, and somehow kept Spinoza's faith that "all excellent things are as difficult as they are rare." For her infinite dedications I return the inadequate one above.

J.A.

Contents

It is said that the American is the perfect mean between the European and the Indian.

Moreau de St. Méry

The
Ethnohistorical
Approach

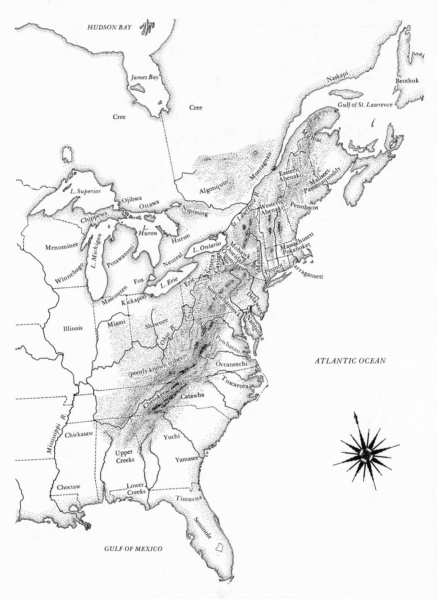

The Eastern Woodland Tribes
(At the earliest stages of European contact with each tribe)

most successful practitioners members of the anthropological tribe, but the initial definitions of ethnohistory reflected the anthropologists' recent experience in Indian claims work and their own disciplinary habits. They tended to see ethnohistory as the use of written documents only for the study of special people—"primitive" people—that is, the use of non-anthropological evidence for their own anthropological purposes. Understandably, ethnohistory was considered an exclusive "sub-branch of ethnology" or "sub-discipline of cultural anthropology."[1] If an historian wished to practice ethnohistory, he virtually had to undergo a rite of passage in which he transferred his professional identity and fealty to anthropology.

Today, however, historians with a bent for ethnohistory no longer feel obligated to alienate themselves from their own discipline. Indeed, their numbers and their contributions to the field have grown to the point where their anthropological colleagues must sublimate their feudal tendencies and admit that since history is half the essence of ethnohistory, historians are invaluable partners in its definition and practice.

Since the symposium on the nature of ethnohistory in the American Society for Ethnohistory's 1960 meeting at Indiana University, the definition of ethnohistory has been broadened and refined by a variety of practitioners.[2] Historians and anthropologists now have no difficulty agreeing that ethnohistory is essentially *the use of historical and ethnological methods and materials to gain knowledge of the nature and causes of change in a culture defined by ethnological concepts and categories.*[3] Whether we consider ethnohistory a form of cultural history or a sub-discipline of cultural anthropology, we can agree that it represents a union of history and ethnology, whose purpose is to produce scholarly offspring who bear the diachronic dimensions of history and the synchronic sensitivity of ethnology. Each partner may use the other for his own purposes, but as long as the marriage works and precocious progeny result, we should not only countenance the union but encourage our disciplinary colleagues to go forth and do likewise.

That historians and anthropologists can share the new definition of ethnohistory without fear of subinfeudation should be clear from a brief look at its elements. The first element is the subject of study—culture. Like anthropologists, ethnohistorians ideally focus on the whole culture of an ethnic group or society as a developing entity over time and space. Even when they lay particular stress on one aspect of the culture, their analysis is still ethnologically oriented by their assumption that no part is to be understood without reference to its place in the whole. While there is some disagreement about the nature of culture, most anthropologists seem to agree that culture is *an idealized pattern of meanings, values, and norms differentially shared by the members of a society, which can be inferred from the non-instinctive behavior of the group and from the symbolic products of their actions, including material artifacts, language, and social institutions.*[4] The concept assumes that the members of a society behave in patterned ways. The task of the ethnohistorian is to determine just what the patterns are in a particular society over time and how the individual parts—whether actions, beliefs, or artifacts—together constitute the functional whole.

Both history and anthropology—as they are actually practiced—tend to focus on one society or culture at a time, and ethnohistory shares the same tendency. Indeed, the consensual definition of ethnohistory is barely distinguishable from that of the branch of anthropology known as historical ethnography—the reconstruction of the ethnographic past of a single culture. But many, perhaps most, of the historians who have taken to ethnohistory in recent years have come from the study of frontiers, in which a two-culture focus is a necessity as well as a virtue. It is there—in the reciprocal relationship between two or more cultures in contact—that historians have found the greatest utility and most distinctive contribution of ethnohistory.[5] By emphasizing that each culture must be understood in its own terms as these change over time, ethnohistory ensures that the history of the frontier will cease to be (in one traditional historian's words) the short "pathetic" story of the "inevitable" triumph of a "booming" white "civilization" over a "fragile" "primitive" culture.[6]

The second characteristic of ethnohistory is its emphasis on sociocultural change, an emphasis it shares with history and with some anthropology. American anthropology began with the synchronic structural study of Indian tribes in the "ethnographic present," as if the cultural patterns found in the nineteenth century accurately mirrored pre-Columbian patterns. Today, the "ethnographic present" has found valid new uses so that the old mistaken assumption has given way to the use of the "direct historical approach," a technique originally devised by archaeologists to reconstruct the culture history of a group by working backward from identifiable historic sites to proto- and pre-historic manifestations of the same culture.[7] Uniting archaeology, ethnology, history, and linguistics, this diachronic approach has generally become known as ethnohistory. Its primary aim, like that of history but unlike that of the functionalist school of social anthropology (which prefers static synchronic analyses of a society's interrelated parts), is to gauge the degree of change that occurs in cultures and to comprehend the historical factors involved in and determining change.[8] This goal can best be achieved in the long perspective of history because it allows us both to detail specific changing variables (because of the time depth) and to control our comparison of variables (because the same cultural tradition is under study).

At the same time, since change and persistence are but two aspects of the same process, ethnohistory offers the best opportunity for "testing theories of pattern growth and decline, for demonstrating cultural change, and for explaining stability."[9] Such a service is of considerable value to both history and anthropology because historians tend to assume too much change and anthropologists too little, especially in the cultural study of small societies.

The third aspect of the ethnohistorical approach is the use of historical and ethnological methods and materials. In the infancy of ethnohistory, "historical materials" were usually equated with written documents, a natural reduction in light of conventional practice. Today, the documentary record of cultural history is seen even by traditional historians as encompassing a far greater variety of sources than books and manuscripts. Both historical and anthropological practitioners have discovered the utility of maps, music, paintings, photographs, folklore, oral tradition, ecology, site exploration, archaeological artifacts (especially trade goods), museum collections, enduring customs, language, and place names, as well as a richer variety of written sources.

Despite their newfound wealth of sources, ethnohistorians still rely primarily upon the written record, largely from the pens of non-native Western observers. These sources, of course, require the rigorous criticism customarily applied by historians but often neglected by anthropological practitioners in the past. Equally necessary is the evaluation of these sources from an ethnological perspective. Ethnohistory differs from history proper in that it adds a new dimension—"the critical use of ethnological concepts and materials in the examination and use of historical source materials."[10] For ethnohistorians have learned from their field experiences to evaluate the reliability of documentary "informants" for their own purposes and beyond the methods of ordinary historical assessments. They can bring to bear "special knowledge of the group, linguistic insights, and understanding of cultural phenomena" which allow them to utilize the data more fully than the average historian.[11]

The ethnohistorical strategy is to remain rooted in historical concreteness, eschewing large generalizations until sufficiently detailed groundwork has been laid. Like most historians, ethnohistorians are interested primarily in low-level, fact-specific generalizations which can be cautiously compared with similar hypotheses about other cultures in similar states of organization and development. They find—again like most historians—that the detailed, long-range plowing of one culture yields more theoretical fruit than the scratch-hoeing of a vast area of different soils.[12]

For ethnohistorians working in frontier studies, the social sciences, particularly anthropology, offer an abundance of theory about acculturation and the related processes of social change, revitalization, diffusion, innovation, conversion, and socialization. This body of theory provides working hypotheses, avenues of approach, and problem areas to be refined and tested by ethnohistorical analysis of specific cultures. Such detailed studies, in turn, can generate more accurate generalizations and hypotheses about social stability and change, which is no mean service in a day of theoretical consciousness.

Although historians and anthropologists share a theoretical understanding of ethnohistory and its general methodology, it is clear from their respective contributions to the literature that they sometimes differ in style and orientation. If, as William Fenton suggests, "a lot of what we call theory is a rationalization for kinds of experimental or research situations," then historians can be expected to make a larger contribution to the ongoing discussion about the nature of ethnohistory and how it can be pursued most fruitfully.[13] In the past few years a distinctive "historical" style has emerged which offers some new possibilities or, perhaps more accurately, some new emphases to students of ethnohistory.

The ethnohistorical study of cultures can move both forward and backward in time. Anthropologists usually work back from the cultural knowns of the present to the unknown past. This approach, which Fenton has called "upstreaming," rests on three assumptions: (1) that major patterns of culture remain stable over long periods, producing repeated uniformities; (2) that these patterns can best be seen by proceeding from the known ethnographical present to the unknown past, using recent sources first and then earlier ones; and (3) that those sources that ring true at both ends of the time span merit confidence. For most anthropological practitioners, "the essence of the ethnohistorical method is distilled from concepts arrived at in working with the cultures of living societies in the field."[14]

Historians, on the other hand, tend to work with the flow of time, "downstream" from the past toward the present. While they are willing to use the abundant ethnographic literature for clues to significant cultural facts and patterns, as checks on weak historical documentation and as documents in their cumulative evidence, by adhering to chronology they attempt to minimize the risk of anachronism and its attendant evils—special pleading, glorification of the present, and ethnocentrism.

Although personal experience is usually superior to vicarious experience, historians need not feel unduly sensitive about their lack of personal research among contemporary tribal cultures. Often the descendants of their historical subjects no longer survive, or, if they do, have lost much of their historical cultural character. Moreover, as E. E. Evans-Pritchard observed, it is sometimes forgotten that the anthropologist "relies on direct observation only in his role as ethnographer" in one or two cultures, and that when he begins to make comparative studies for theoretical purposes, "he has to rely on documents, just as the historian does."[15] At the same time, most historians have done something akin to field work by living in contemporary and studying both contemporary and historical Western cultures, experience that is not to be dismissed lightly when ethnohistory frequently, perhaps optimally, deals with the contact of two or more cultures in a colonial setting.

Historians also differ from their anthropological colleagues when their sources on a particular group run dry, grow sparse, or become insolubly clogged with ethnocentric bias. In such situations many anthropologists turn to general ethnological theory—for example, on band societies, peasants, Stone Age economies, ecological adaptation—or to abstract models of sociocultural change. Most historians, however, look to two historical sources: descendant cultures of the earlier group, on the assumption that major patterns of culture remain stable over long periods, and relative cultures in the same general culture area, preferably in the same period, which may be expected to share cultural traits.[16]

All ethnohistorians face the literary problem of how artfully to blend synchronic analysis with diachronic narrative and description. The sequence of change must be shown in detailed narrative, but the causes of change must also be analyzed. Since cultural change cannot be understood without knowing what aspects of the culture persisted unchanged, some synchronic analysis is required either of the whole culture early in the narrative or of its constituent parts throughout.

Historians, traditionally preoccupied with the demands of chronological narrative, tend to forgo the functional analysis of the whole culture except, perhaps, in a brief introduction. Commonly, they begin with a narrative of the events leading to change, interrupting the flow only long enough to analyze the aspects of the culture that change, seldom those that persist. In other words, the ethnohistorical work of an historian tends to be divided into chronological sections, with synchronic analysis added within the sections where necessary. This structure has the advantage of immersing cultural analysis in a steady narrative flow that attempts to convey the passage of time and events as they actually occurred. If it is successful, readers are carried much closer to the past than they would be by a more analytical style.

Anthropologists, on the other hand, traditionally devote a major portion of their work to synchronic analysis in an attempt to reconstruct general cultural patterns and the relationship of the culture's parts to the whole. Their works are often organized topically by constituent cultural parts, each topic receiving chronological treatment in its separate place. In recent years, however, several anthropologists have written ethnohistories that bear a strong resemblance to the work of their historical colleagues. Anthony Wallace's *Death and Rebirth of the Seneca,* Bruce Trigger's *Children of Aataentsic,* and James Clifton's *Prairie People* feature strong chronological narratives endowed with sensitive and sweeping analysis of cultural patterns and functions.[17] By meeting the narrative obligations of the historian, they have produced enduring works of historical art as well as models of anthropological acuity.

Although historians seldom do field work, they seem in some ways to be more engaged with the present than do anthropologists. Many of the subjects they select emerge from contemporary problems that have historical roots or from present interests that have analogues in the past. More than most anthropologists, except the practitioners of "applied anthropology," historians write for their own generation, addressing its questions and concerns about the past. They believe that the meaning of an event is perpetually open to revision, that its meaning for successive generations will differ from its contemporary meaning or its causes. For historians the commonplace that "each generation must rewrite the histories of its predecessors" is the simple truth, however frustrating it might be to their scholarly quest for immortality.[18]

By contrast, most anthropologists in practice act as scientists interested in achieving timeless explanations of cultural uniformities. Understandably, most of their data come from living cultures experienced at first hand. Their interest in past cultures tends to be less intrinsic, as it is for most historians, than instrumental in providing additional data for their working hypotheses. Even after recognizing the difference between *emic* and *etic* explanations, few anthropologists will admit that their cultural theories might be valid for only a limited time and perhaps only their own culture.

Yet to the extent that anthropologists assume the role of ethnohistorians, they must admit the possibility, even likelihood, of such a humbling fate. By committing themselves to serving the larger audience of history, they must be prepared, like their historical colleagues, to interpret the past for their contemporaries. They must not only explain the cultures of the past in their own terms, but lead their contemporaries to responsible answers to their urgent questions about their place in time and space, about their own cultural roots and realities. By providing an accurate narrative-analysis of cultural change in the past, ethnohistorians help the present generation to understand its own cultural origins and thereby to cope with the present, without pandering to the popular demand for panaceas or prostituting their scholarly ideals.

Finally, historians differ from anthropologists by allowing that moral criticism of the past is not only possible but desirable. They assume that if people have purposes, motives, and intentions, they are perforce moral beings and suitable subjects for moral criticism, largely by the standards they set for themselves. But the historian's aim is not to chastize the actors of the past, who are mortally incorrigible, but to let himself and his contemporaries be judged and instructed by the past.[19] The central issue in moral criticism for most historians "is not whether something had to happen, but whether it has to happen again."[20] They are simply concerned that what we approve by our silent consent in past conduct will be repeated in the future. As students and teachers of one of the humanities, they are not willing to separate their every-day moral lives from their professional lives, as most scientists can (though less and less easily) when dealing with nonhuman nature.

It should be emphasized that moral criticism or judgment is not to be confused with moralizing, which means to furnish with overt moral lessons, as in a sermon. "History is a preceptor of prudence," said Edmund Burke, "not of principles," and most historians would not dissent.[21] They do not feel compelled—or free—to ramble over the past handing out assignations of "guilt" and "innocence," "good" and "evil." When moral criticism is called for, which it rarely is, the historian need not and should not be obtrusive but merely descriptive, using the normative language of everyday speech. Eschewing the antiseptic, often technical vocabulary of scientific objectivity, "the [ideal] historian," as John Higham has written, "commits to moral criticism all the resources of his human condition. He derives from moral criticism an enlarged and disciplined sensitivity to what men ought to have done, what they might have done, and what they achieved. His history becomes an intensive, concrete reflection upon life, freed from academic primness, and offering itself as one of the noblest, if also one of the most difficult and imperfect, of the arts."[22]

Ethnohistorians face their most difficult problem when they treat the contact of two cultures, each with its own value system. For they must not only judge the conduct of each people "by their success in acting in accordance with the ideals they have chosen" themselves, but "recognize the conflicting value setting."[23] They must not only see the ethnocentric biases and motives in each culture, but understand the reasons for them. If this duty is performed fully and well, moral criticism beyond that provided by our value-laden vocabulary is seldom necessary. The past will be cast in its own light, and the lessons for the present will be clearly but subtly drawn.

The rub, of course, is to ensure that each culture is treated with equal empathy, rigor, and discernment. If we are to understand the total contact situation, we must fully understand the motives and actions of both groups. But as Bruce Trigger has warned, mere sympathy may not be enough because sympathy does not always lead to understanding, and without a clear understanding of people's motives, respect is impossible.[24] Bleeding-heart nativism will alienate the intelligent reader as quickly as anticolonial iconoclasm; neither approaches the standard of ethnohistory.

In the past several years, the advent of the new "Social History," which takes many of its models from the social sciences, and the growing anthropological awareness of the historical dimensions of culture have created many exceptions to the foregoing generalizations about the two disciplines. Many historians practice what can best be called "retrospective cultural anthropology," and many anthropologists—more than formerly, at least—pursue what is still called "historical ethnography."[25] Similarly, although the differences between the historical and anthropological styles of ethnohistory have been accentuated, much recent work exhibits a happy convergence of styles, blending the strengths of each into a distinctive hybrid. It is a style strong on narrative, causative analysis, and chronology, but no less sensitive to cultural nuance and the need for impartiality. Remarkably, the books and articles written in this style give little or no clue to the departmental affiliation of their authors. Perhaps we are closer to realizing the ideal and method of ethnohistory than we think. If so, I would like to think that the recent contributions of history are in no small way responsible.

CHAPTER TWO

The Unkindest Cut, or Who Invented Scalping? A Case Study

IN 1975 I BECAME INTRIGUED BY THE INCREASINGLY POPULAR SUGGES-
tion in non-Indian literature and the Indian press that the
"white man" had taught the Indians how to scalp in the colonial
period through the use of scalp bounties, an assertion found
more frequently in polemical than historical contexts. Having
read most of the sixteenth- and seventeenth-century sources on
eastern Indian warfare, I was skeptical that the proposition would
hold water. I suspected that some serious logical slippage was
occurring between the correct assertion that European colonial
governments encouraged friendly Indians to kill and scalp enemy
Indians, and the conclusion that the Europeans therefore taught
the Indians *how* to scalp each other.

Thanks to a chance meeting on a bus with William Sturtevant
of the Smithsonian, I discovered that I was not alone in my
skepticism and that we both had been collecting expressions of
the new myth for some time. Whereupon we agreed to co-author
an article, which finally appeared in the *William and Mary Quarterly* in July 1980. The delay was not entirely due to procrastina-
tion. After swapping notes, I wrote a first draft to read at the
1975 Iroquois and Algonquian conferences, where its title
spawned several bursts of outrageous punning but its message was
well taken. Then in April 1977 *American Heritage* published a
short summary of our historical argument, including some strik-

ing pictorial evidence of the Indians' priority of invention. I presented the paper at several colleges over the next couple of years, and during that time, fresh expressions of the myth came to light and our ethnohistorical data against it mounted. By the summer of 1979 we decided to wrap it up and publish the full refutation, which we did after Bill had rewritten several key sections on the linguistic and archaeological evidence. I am grateful for his ready permission to reprint a somewhat abbreviated version of our truly joint effort under my name alone.

I am the more grateful to Bill for the ethnological skills he brought to our analysis. What resulted from our collaboration was, I think, a fairly complete model of ethnohistory as a marriage of the methods and materials of both historical and anthropological disciplines. Because of our academic training in hermetic departments, few ethnohistorians are masters of the full repertoire of concepts, methods, and literary techniques offered by the two disciplines. But the ideal exists for us to seek. Perhaps collaboration is the easiest way to reach it.

THE TRADITIONAL WISDOM OF AMERICAN HISTORY ASSERTS that the "savage" Indians scalped "civilized" whites in their resistance to the "taming" of the continent. Accordingly, when the invasion of North America began, the Europeans were innocent of the practice, and though they eventually adopted it for their own bloody purposes, their teachers were still Indians, who had invented and perfected the art. Increasingly in recent years, this traditional wisdom has been assailed as a serious distortion. When advocates of the Indian cause, native or white, engage their opponents in court or print, they frequently arm themselves with a new version of scalping's ignoble history.

The new version was born perhaps in 1820 when Cornplanter, an Allegany Seneca chief, grew despondent over the disintegration of his nation. In a series of visions the Great

Spirit told him that he should have nothing more to do with white people or with war, and commanded him to burn all his old military trophies, which he promptly did on a huge pyre of logs. The reason, as Cornplanter told it, was that before the whites came, the Indians "lived in peace and had no wars nor fighting." But then "the French came over," followed closely by the English, and these two nations began to fight among themselves. Not content to wage their own battles, each tried to involve the Iroquois. "The French," said Cornplanter, "offered to furnish us with instruments of every kind and sharp knives to take the skins off their [enemies'] heads."[1]

We next hear the new history of scalping in 1879 when Susette La Flesche, a spirited daughter of a famous Omaha family, was interviewed by a newspaper reporter on the Chicago stop of her national tour to advocate justice for Indians. When she protested the United States Army's wholesale killing of Ute men, women, and children in a recent encounter, the reporter shot back, "But you are more barbarous in war than we, and you shock the public by the acts of atrocity upon captives and the bodies of the dead." "Scalping, you mean, I suppose," countered the young woman. "Don't you know that the white man taught Indians that? It was practiced first in New England on the Penobscot Indians. The General Court of the Province of Massachusetts offered a bounty of forty pounds for every scalp of a male Indian brought in as evidence of his being killed, and for every scalp of a female or male Indian under twelve years, twenty pounds."[2]

Cornplanter's and La Flesche's rejections of the traditional wisdom of scalping are significant not only for their chronological priority but because they consecrated the polemical marriage of scalp bounties with the invention of scalping in the "new wisdom." In 1968, for example, the literary critic and moralist Leslie Fiedler asserted that scalping "seems not to have been an Indian custom at all until the White Man began offering bounties for slain enemies." And environmental writer Peter Farb, putting his finger on New Netherland's Governor Willem Kieft instead of the Massachusetts legislature, remarked that "whatever its exact origins, there is no doubt that [the spread of] scalp-taking . . . was due to the barbarity of White men rather than to the barbarity of Red men." In the following year Edgar Cahn and the Citizens' Advocate Center, citing Farb as their sole authority, more confidently but even more ambiguously concluded that "contrary to Hollywood's history book, it was the white man who created the tradition of scalping."[3]

To counter the baneful effects of Hollywood westerns, the new wisdom was taken up by the powerful media of the East, among them NBC television and *The New Yorker* magazine. The week before Christmas in 1972, several million viewers of "Hec Ramsey" received a mini-lesson in history from the show's star, Richard Boone, when he carefully explained to a sidekick that the Puritans (of New England presumably) taught the Iroquois (of New York presumably) to scalp by offering them bounties for enemy hair. And when Ray Fadden, the curator of his own Six Nations Indian Museum in the Adirondacks, asked a reporter from *The New Yorker* if he knew that "scalping, skinning alive, and burning at the stake were European barbarian inventions, forced on Indian mercenaries," nearly half a million readers heard the rhetorical answer.[4]

White friends of the Indians have been the most frequent advocates of the new wisdom in print, so it is not surprising that when several were called as character witnesses for Indian culture in the trials resulting from the American Indian Movement occupation of Wounded Knee in 1973, they used it in their testimony. Alvin M. Josephy, Jr., the author of four books on the American Indians, testified at the trial in Lincoln, Nebraska, that "scalping was not originated by Indians. Poachers in England had their ears cut off. Europeans had the habit of taking parts of the body in war. The Dutch gave rewards for Indian heads even before there was open warfare in their area of colonization." In a refinement of Peter Farb's earlier attribution, he said that "Indian heads were put on pikes there very early, but people got tired of lugging in the heads so soon they just brought in the scalp to show that they had killed an Indian."⁵

Yet white advocacy has carried the new wisdom only so far. One of the political assumptions of the current Indian movement is that Indians should do their own talking and write their own history in order to help them gain control of their own destiny. Accordingly, when Vine Deloria issued his "Indian Manifesto" in 1969 under the pointed title of *Custer Died for Your Sins,* he soon became for many people the leading Indian spokesman. Not surprisingly, in a book filled with effective sallies against white America's treatment of native Americans, he employed the symbol of scalping. "Scalping, introduced prior to the French and Indian War by the English," he accused, citing a 1755 Massachusetts scalp bounty, "confirmed the suspicion that the Indians were wild animals to be hunted and skinned. Bounties were set and an Indian scalp became more valuable than beaver, otter, marten, and other animal pelts."⁶

Perhaps the latest and probably the most bizarre episode in the historiography of scalping took place in a church in Flint, Michigan, on September 7, 1975. Bruce C. Thum (alias "Chief Charging Bear"), an evangelist and self-styled three-quarter Oklahoma Cherokee, demonstrated "how the Indians scalped the white man" to the morning Sunday school classes "from toddler age through sixth grade." When confronted by an angry group of Indian demonstrators and parents, Thum lamely explained that "scalping came originally from Europeans" and revealed that "he had been giving such demonstrations for more than a quarter of a century, and this is the first time his demonstration had sparked any protests." His manager added: "Anything you can do to get children to Sunday school today, you have to do."[7] The Indian demonstration prompted *The Flint Journal* to print an apology for running an offensive advertisement for the affair the previous week. Calling for an end to racial discrimination, especially in the public media, the editorial lent its weight to the new wisdom. Such a crude charade as Thum's, it said, "perpetuates the myth that scalping was originally or even essentially an Indian practice when the truth is that it was a European practice as punishment for crimes, was brought to America and used by both the British and French as proof of slayings to collect bounties offered by each side. It was only later adopted by the Indians in retaliation."[8]

The new wisdom about scalping would not warrant scholarly attention if it were only an intellectual fad or if its proponents constituted a mere handful of obscure eccentrics like Chief Charging Bear. But it has had a long life and refuses to die, and its proponents include historians and anthropologists as well as Indians, critics, and editors. More important, the new wisdom is seldom argued in the bright light of controversy, where scholarly—and commonsensical—suspicions might be raised. Rather, it is insinuated into the public consciousness through seemingly disingenuous references dropped in discussions of Indian affairs or history. When the speakers are Indians, no matter how qualified to speak of Indian or colonial history, the statements are invested with even greater credibility. National television programs and newspaper articles that circulate via the major wire services propagate the new wisdom to such huge audiences that it has become traditional wisdom in its own right and demands a fresh appraisal.[9]

The new myth is understandable as a product of Indian activism and white guilt feelings. However, the factual basis for the novel concoction seems to have been non-existent in the late 1960s—or, for that matter, at any other time in the twentieth century. For in 1906 Georg Friederici published in German a thorough study of the distribution and history of scalping in North and South America, a study that, although it did not use certain kinds of evidence, proved beyond a doubt that scalping was a pre-Columbian Indian practice.[10] Recognizing the value of this work, the Smithsonian Institution published a sixteen-page English summary in its *Annual Report* for that year.[11] At the same time, James Mooney was incorporating Friederici's results into his article on scalping for Frederick Hodge's *Handbook of American Indians North of Mexico,* which was published in 1910.[12] From then on, Friederici's researches were drawn upon by the two leading encyclopedias used by Americans. The famous eleventh edition of the *Encyclopaedia Britannica,* published in 1910-11, made clear that scalping was a pre-Columbian practice, as did the edition of 1967, which contained a new article by William Sturtevant.[13] Likewise, the 1963 edition of the *Encyclopedia Americana* cited Friederici and Hodge's *Handbook* to prove that scalping was originally practiced by the "savage and barbarous nations of the eastern hemisphere . . . and later by the American Indians residing principally in the eastern United States and the lower Saint Lawrence region."[14] Thus if the modern promoters of the new history of scalping had turned to the standard works of reference in the course of their researches, they would have come face-to-face with a wall of evidence to the contrary.

The evidence for pre-Columbian scalping takes many forms. The first and most familiar is the written descriptions by some of the earliest European observers, who saw the Indian cultures of the eastern seaboard in something like an aboriginal condition, largely or wholly unchanged by white contact. On his second voyage up the St. Lawrence in 1535, Jacques Cartier was shown by the Stadaconans at Quebec "the skins of five men's heads, stretched on hoops, like parchment (*les peaulx de cinq testes d'hommes, estandues sus des boys, comme peaulx de parchemin).*" His host, Donnacona, told him "they were Toudamans [Micmacs] from the south, who waged war continually against his people."[15]

In March 1540, two of Hernando De Soto's men, the first Europeans to enter the Apalachee country in west Florida, were seized by Indians. The killers of one "removed his head (*cabeza*), or rather all around his skull (*todo el casco en redondo*)—it is unknown with what skill they removed it with such great ease—and carried it off as evidence of their deed." A lost manuscript by an eyewitness described an occasion when the Apalachees killed others of De Soto's men, "and they cut off the crown (*la corona*) of each Spaniard, which was what they valued most, in order to carry it on the limb of the bow they fought with."[16] In 1549 at Tampa Bay local Indians killed a missionary, one of whose companions wrote immediately afterwards that a Spaniard, rescued from these Indians among whom he had been captive since the De Soto expedition, told him, "I even saw the skin of the crown (*el pellejo de la corona*) of the monk, exhibited to me by an Indian who brought it to show," adding that he himself "had held in his hands the skin of the head (*el pellejo de la cabeza*) of the monk."[17] In 1560 a party from the Luna expedition reached the Creek town of Coosa ("Coça") on the Alabama River, and accompanied local warriors on a raid on the enemy town of the "Napochies." They found it abandoned, but in its plaza was a pole—certainly to be identified with the war pole of later Creek towns, known to be associated with scalps—which was "full of hair locks (*cabellos*) of the Coosans. It was the custom of the Indians to flay the head of the enemy dead, and to hang the resulting skin and locks (*pellejo y cabellos*) insultingly on that pole. There were many dead, and the pole was covered with locks." The Coosans, much angered at "this evidence of affront" and reminder of "all the previous injuries" done to them, cut down the pole and carried off the scalps (*los cabellos*) in order to bury them with proper ceremony.[18]

These first accounts from the lower Southeast are consistent with the details described and illustrated by Jacques Le Moyne de Morgues from his firsthand observations in 1564 while accompanying Timucua warriors on raids near Fort Caroline on the St. Johns River in northeastern Florida. He wrote,

> In these skirmishes those who fall are immediately dragged out of the camp by those entrusted with this responsibility, and they cut the skin of the head down to the skull (*capitis cutim ad cranium*) with pieces of reed sharper than any steel blade, from the brow in a circle to the back of the head; and they pull it off whole, gathering the hair, which is still attached to it and more than a cubit long, into a knot at the crown; and what there is over the brow and back of the head they cut off in a circle to a length of two fingers, like the fringe around a skullcap; on the spot (if there is enough time) they dig a hole in the ground and kindle a fire with moss. . . . Having got the fire going, they dry the skin (*cutim*) and make it hard like parchment . . . and with the head skins (*capitisque cutim*) hanging from the ends of their javelins they triumphantly carry them off home.

On returning to the village they placed the enemies' legs, arms, and scalps (*"capitisque cutim"*) "with solemn ceremony on very long stakes which they have fixed in the ground in a kind of row" for a subsequent ritual.[19]

Then for almost forty years the European exploration and settlement of eastern North America subsided into insignificance. Not until Samuel de Champlain re-explored the Canadian and New England coasts in the early years of the seventeenth century did scalping find another memorialist. In 1603 Champlain was invited to feast with the Montagnais sagamore Anadabijou and his warriors to celebrate their recent victory over the Iroquois. When they ended the feast they began to dance, "taking in their hands . . . the scalps (*testes*) of enemies, which hung behind them. . . . They had killed about a hundred, whose scalps they cut off, and had with them for the ceremony." Their Algonquin allies went off to celebrate by themselves. While the Algonquin women stripped naked except for their jewelry, preparing to dance, Tessouat, their sagamore, sat "between two poles, on which hung the scalps (*testes*) of their enemies."[20]

The correctness of translating "*testes*" as "scalps" rather than "heads" becomes clear from Champlain's account of his famous battle in 1609 with the Iroquois at the side of his Montagnais, Huron, and Algonquin allies. When the fighting ended, the victors proceeded to torture an Iroquois prisoner. Among other indignities, wrote Champlain, "they flayed the top of his head (*escorcherent le haut de la teste*) and poured hot gum on his crown." When he was dead, they severed his head, arms, and legs, "reserving the skin of the head *(la peau de la teste)*, which they had flayed, as they did with those of all the others they had killed in their attack." Upon returning to the St. Lawrence, Champlain was invited by the Montagnais to Tadoussac to see their victory ceremonies.

Approaching the shore each took a stick, on the end of which they hung the scalps (*testes*) of their slain enemies with some beads, singing . . . all together. And when all were ready, the women stripped themselves quite naked, and jumped into the water, swimming to the canoes to receive the scalps of their enemies which were at the end of long sticks in the bow of their canoes, in order later to hang them round their necks, as if they had been precious chains. And then they sang and danced. Some days afterwards they made me a present of one of these scalps as if it had been some very valuable thing, and of a pair of shields belonging to their enemies, for me to keep to show to the king. And to please them I promised to do so.[21]

At the same time Marc Lescarbot, a lawyer, was describing in markedly similar terms the scalping customs of the Micmac near Port Royal. "[O]f the dead they cut off the scalps [*têtes*] in as great number as they can find, and these are divided among the captains, but they leave the carcass, contenting themselves with the scalp [*peau*], which they dry, or tan, and make trophies with it in their cabins, taking therein their highest contentment. And when some solemn feast is held among them . . . they take them, and dance with them, hanging about their necks or their arms, or at their girdles, and for very rage they sometimes bite at them."[22]

When the Recollect missionaries penetrated the Huron country, they, too, found elaborate customs associated with the practice of scalp-taking. In 1623-24 Gabriel Sagard noted that after killing an enemy in combat, the Hurons "carry away the head [*teste*]; and if they are too much encumbered with these they are content to take the skin with its hair [*la peau avec sa chevelure*], which they call *Onontsira*, tan them, and put them away for trophies, and in time of war set them on the palisades or walls of their town fastened to the end of a long pole."[23] The Iroquois in New Netherland put scalps to similar use. When the Dutch surgeon of Fort Orange journeyed into Mohawk and Oneida country in the winter of 1634-35, he saw atop a gate of the old Oneida castle on Oriskany Creek "three wooden images carved like men, and with them . . . three scalps [*locken*] fluttering in the wind, that they had taken from their foes as a token of the truth of their victory." On a smaller gate at the east side of the castle "a scalp [*lock*] was also hanging," no doubt to impress the visitors.[24]

The Powhatans of Virginia felt a similar need in 1608. According to Captain John Smith, Powhatan launched a surprise attack on the Payankatank, "his neare neighbours and subjects," killing twenty-four men. When his warriors retired from the battle, they brought away "the long haire of the one side of their heades [the other being shaved] with the skinne cased off with shels or reeds." The prisoners and scalps were then presented to the chief, who "hanged on a line unto two trees . . . the lockes of haire with their skinnes. And thus he made ostentation of as great a triumph at Werowocomoco, shewing them to the English men that then came unto him at his appointment . . . suppos[ing] to halfe conquer them by this spectacle of his terrible crueltie."[25] The skeleton of an Englishman almost certainly killed in Opechancanough's 1622 attack on the Virginia settlements has recently been excavated. His badly fractured cranium is heavily scored in a manner strongly suggesting that he was scalped, probably with an English knife.[26]

The list of Europeans who found scalping among the eastern Indians in the earliest stages of contact could be extended almost indefinitely.[27] But the later descriptions only reiterate the themes of the earlier, while reinforcing them with the continuity of custom. The first characteristic these descriptions share is an expression of surprise at the discovery of such a novel practice. The nearly universal highlighting of scalping in the early literature, the search for intelligible comparisons (such as parchment), the detailed anatomical descriptions of the act itself, and the total absence of any suggestion of white precedence or familiarity with the practice all suggest that an eighteenth-century French soldier's remarks were not disingenuous. "It is shameful for the human race to use such barbarous methods," wrote J. C. B., who had fought beside Indian allies in the 1750s. "Yet, to tell the truth, the idea belongs only to the savages, who were using it before they heard of the civilized nations."[28] For if the men of several different, antagonistic nationalities, divided by religion, history, language, and imperial ambition, had introduced scalping to the Indians, they certainly had no need to cloak their deed in secrecy. Only twentieth-century intellectuals and Indian advocates have found scalping particularly symbolic of white "barbarism." By seventeenth-century standards, it was a rather tame form of corporal desecration. On the other hand, if the Europeans—*any* Europeans—did feel guilty about introducing it, then we are confronted with the implausible spectacle of a Caucasian conspiracy of silence and hypocrisy on a universal scale for more than three centuries. For no one before the nineteenth century ever leveled such an accusation at the whites, although many other European transgressions during the conquest of the Americas have repeatedly been advertised since the early sixteenth century.

The second theme of these descriptions is that the actual removal of an enemy's head-skin was firmly embedded among other customs that could hardly have been borrowed from the European traders and fishermen who preceded the earliest European authors. The elaborate preparation of the scalps by drying, stretching on hoops, painting, and decorating; special scalp yells when a scalp was taken and later when it was borne home on raised spears or poles; the scalplock as men's customary hairdress; scalp-taking as an important element in male status advancement; occasionally nude female custodianship of the prizes; scalp dances; scalps as body and clothing decorations; scalps as non-remunerative trophies of war to be publicly displayed on canoes, cabins, and palisades; elaborate ceremonial treatment of scalps integrated into local religious beliefs; and the substitution of a scalp for a living captive to be adopted to replace a deceased member of the family—all these appear too varied, too ritualized, and too consistent with other native cultural traits over long periods of white contact to have been recent and foreign introductions by Europeans. While in most areas of the world enemy body parts of some kind have been taken as battle trophies, these usually consist of easily removable whole appendages, such as the head, fingers, or ears. But the scalp is a very specialized kind of trophy because it involves only a part of the skin of the head and therefore requires some skill to obtain. More-

over, although scalping was widely practiced in pre-Columbian North Amercia (and also, less widely, in South America),
the specific forms of the associated cultural traits varied markedly from tribe to tribe and area to area, as did their patterning within different cultures. This is not the case with other
traits of Indian cultures that are of known European origins.

The final characteristic of the early accounts is an obvious
stretching for adequate words to describe scalping to a European audience. The noun "scalp" (from a Scandinavian root)
existed in English long before the seventeenth century. It had
two meanings of different ages. The older meaning was "the
top or crown of the head; the skull or cranium," and the more
recent one was the skin covering that upper part of the head,
"usually covered with hair." But in 1601, Holland's edition
of Pliny added a third meaning from a literary acquaintance
with the "Anthropophagi" (Scythians) near the North Pole,
who wore their enemies' "scalpes haire and al, instead of man-
dellions or stomachers before their breasts."[29] Perhaps because few explorers were familiar with the Latin classics, the
new meaning seems to have been ignored by English writers
until 1675, when King Philip's War greatly increased the frequency of scalping. Until then, the best substitutes were com-
pounds such as "hair-scalp" and "head-skin," descriptive
phrases such as "the skin and hair of the scalp of the head,"
or the simple but ambiguous word "head."[30] Likewise, the
only meaning of the verb "to scalp" derived from the Latin
scalpere, "to carve, engrave, scrape, or scratch." Consequently,
English writers were forced to use "skin," "flay," or "exco-
riate" until 1676, when "to scalp" or, colloquially, "to skulp"
became popular.[31]

The French, too, resorted to circumlocutions to convey an
idea of scalping. For the scalp itself they used *tête, peau,
cheveux,* and *chevelure* in various combinations, and *couper,
écorcher,* and *enlever* to indicate the mode of taking it. In
1769 a French account of Colonel Henry Bouquet's expedi-

tion against the Ohio Indians introduced the American words into the language.[32] By the end of the eighteenth century, the Anglo-American words had been borrowed to fill the gaps in the Swedish, German, and Dutch lexicons as well.[33]

The evidence of etymology strengthens the documentary argument for pre-Columbian scalping because the lack of precise and economical words to describe the practice indicates the lack of a concept of scalping, which in turn indicates the absence of the practice itself. European soldiers were guilty of countless barbarities in peace and war, but during the sixteenth and seventeenth centuries they were never known to scalp their victims. Hanging, disemboweling, beheading, and drawing and quartering were commonplace in public executions or in war, but to our knowledge no observer ever described the taking of scalps. In the Elizabethan campaigns against the Irish, for example, where natives were portrayed in terms that mirror the descriptions of American natives a few years later, the English took only heads in an attempt to terrorize their "savage" opponents. Not without reason, the grim, pallid features of human faces lining the path to a commander's tent were chosen as a deterrent rather than impersonal shocks of hair and skin waving from tent poles and pikes.[34] Similarly, when Captain Miles Standish wished to daunt the Massachusett Indians who threatened the nascent Plymouth Colony, he killed Wituwamat, "the chiefest of them," took his head to Plymouth, and set it on the top of the fort with a blood-soaked flag.[35]

On the other hand, the Indian languages of the East contain many specialized expressions referring to the scalp, the act of scalping, and the victim of scalping. Some of these words were recorded quite early by European observers such as Gabriel Sagard.[36] Later vocabularies and dictionaries consistently show well-developed terminology of this topic,[37] implying considerable antiquity for scalping. In the Creek language one word for "scalp" was a compound meaning literally "human head-skin," which could be shortened to simply "head-skin"; both dialects of the related Hitchiti-Mikasuki language had the exact equivalent of "head-skin" as their word for "scalp." But Creek also had another, unanalyzable, and probably older name for the scalp trophy (which by the late nineteenth century had also taken on the meanings "mane of a horse, lock of hair," and—with the addition of a morpheme meaning "woven"—"wig").[38] This unanalyzable form is not known to have been borrowed from another language, so the concept it labeled was probably ancient among the Creeks. The Iroquoian languages, Mohawk, Onondaga, Cayuga, and Seneca, each had for the meaning of "scalp" a simple root (cognate in these languages), not further analyzable, and Oneida had another but partially similar unanalyzable root of the same meaning. These were used in various verbs grammatically identical in each of these languages (all five commonly used a verb referring to "lifting" the scalp, which may be the source, by loan translation, for English "to lift hair" and French *enlever la chevelure*).[39] In the Iroquoian languages, as also in those of the Algonquian family, specialized vocabularies are usually built by compounding ordinary roots and through complex systems of affixes, rather than by the borrowing that is common in European languages. Thus the existence of cognate unanalyzable roots in these languages is especially strong evidence for the antiquity of the associated meaning. The scalping terminology of the Algonquian languages is often extensive and precise, usually involving roots referring to the head or hair but occasionally including incompletely analyzable expressions. Thus, for example, Ojibwa distinguishes between "scalp" and "Sioux scalp"; Eastern Abenaki has a terminological distinction between an enemy scalp that has already been taken and one that is being taken or could be taken; the Fox equivalents for "he scalps him," "he scalps him· (that is, his already-severed head)," and "he scalps it (that is, a severed head)" are not fully transparent in terms of Fox grammar; and the Munsee Delaware word for "scalp" means literally "skin head" not "head skin" (this last supporting Friederici's hypothesis that scalp trophies developed from head trophies).[40]

Words have done the most to fix the image of pre-contact Indian scalping on the American historical record, but contemporary paintings, drawings, and engravings substantially reinforce those images. The single most important picture in this regard is Theodore de Bry's engraving of Le Moyne's drawing of "Treatment of the Enemy Dead by Outina's Forces."[41] Based on Le Moyne's observations in 1564, the 1591 engraving was the first public representation of Indian scalping, one faithful to Le Moyne's verbal description and to subsequent accounts from other regions of eastern America. The details of using sharp reeds to remove the scalp, then drying the green skin over a fire, displaying the trophies on long poles, and later celebrating the victory with established rituals by the native priest lend authenticity to de Bry's rendering and credence to the argument for Indian priority of invention.

Later illustrations are less graphic, but they continue to emphasize the use of scalps as trophies. A fine depiction in a French drawing of 1666 shows two Iroquois warriors conducting an Indian captive, all three wearing scalplocks, one carrying a pole with two circular scalps on one end, of which one with a scalplock is specified as from a male enemy and one without is said to be female.[42] About 1700 a French artist sketched an Iroquois cabin decorated with the scalps (*"testes,"* but clearly drawn as scalps, not heads) of two enemies its owner had killed.[43] In Louisiana between 1732 and 1735 the French artist De Batz painted two Choctaw warriors displaying five scalps (*"chevelures"*), with the stretched skin painted red, hung on long poles.[44] While not all of these depictions were made in the earliest period of contact, they do portray a striking similarity between the scalping customs and uses of

Theodore de Bry's 1591 engraving of Jacques Le Moyne's 1564 drawing of "Treatment of the Enemy Dead by Outina's Forces," the first known representation of Indian scalping. From De Bry's *America*, Pt. II (Frankfurt, 1591).

several different and distant Indian groups, thereby diminishing the likelihood that they were imposed or introduced by white foreigners.

Drawings also reveal another kind of evidence for Indian priority, namely scalplocks. A small braid or lock of hair on the crown, often decorated with paint or jewelry, the scalplock was worn widely in both eastern and western America. Contrary to the notion of scalping as a recent and mercenary introduction, the scalplock possessed ancient religious meaning in most tribes.

In some of the rituals used when the hair was first gathered up and cut from the crown of a boy's head the teaching was set forth that this lock represented the life of the child, now placed wholly in the control of the mysterious and supernatural power that alone could will his death. The braided lock worn thereafter was a sign of this dedication and belief, and represented the man's life. On it he wore the ornaments that marked his achievements and honors, and for anyone to touch lightly this lock was regarded as a grave insult.[45]

If the whites had taught the Indians to scalp one another for money, there is little reason to believe that they were also cozened into making it easier for their enemies by growing partible and portable locks. Something far deeper in native culture and history must account for the practice.

One kind of evidence unavailable to Friederici that alone establishes the existence of scalping in pre-Columbian America is archaeological. If Indian skulls of the requisite age can be found showing unambiguous marks of scalping, then the new wisdom of scalping must be discarded. A wealth of evidence, particularly from prehistoric sites along the Mississippi and Missouri rivers, now seems to indicate just such a conclusion. There are two basic kinds of archaeological evidence of scalping. The first is circular or successive cuts or scratches on the skull vaults of victims who had been previously killed. These cuts are, of course, subject to various interpretations, given the existence of postmortem mutilation in many cultural areas. The trophy skulls found in several Hopewellian burials, for example, frequently exhibit superficial cuts and scratches, apparently made by flint knives in the process of removing the flesh. But there are many examples with cut marks only where they would be caused by customary techniques of scalping.[46]

The second kind of evidence, though not as abundant, is even more conclusive. In a number of prehistoric sites, lesions have been found on the skulls of victims who survived scalping long enough to allow the bone tissue partially to regenerate. Contrary to popular belief, scalping was not necessarily a fatal operation; the historical record is full of survivors.[47] Scalping is the most plausible, if not the only possible, explanation for these lesions that appear exactly where literary and pictorial descriptions indicate the scalp was traditionally cut.[48]

Although the moral fire of the new wisdom of scalping misses the mark, there are several moral issues to be considered in the European adoption of scalping and the use of scalp bounties. These are explored below in Chapters 6 (pp. 142-44) and 8.

From Indian
to European

CHAPTER THREE

The Invasion Within:
The Contest of Cultures
in Colonial North America

IN MY EXPERIENCE, WRITING IS PAINFUL AND PAINSTAKING WORK—
I like to write much less than I like to have written—but research and the conceptual shaping of a book are pure delight.
When I completed my second book early in 1972, the idea for the
next one had been percolating for some time. In retrospect, it
was the logical, almost inevitable, outgrowth of my early work
in the history of education. My first book had dealt with one
man's—John Locke's—influential views on education for the gentle classes of Stuart England. The subject of my second book, *The
School upon a Hill: Education and Society in Colonial New
England*,* was the role of education in one relatively homogeneous culture. Both had been written largely to teach myself
something about the social and cultural history of Anglo-
America and its English progenitor. But both were limited in
scope by youth and inexperience. They ignored the other (North)
American cultures and unduly foreshortened the colonial period
by ignoring the whole sixteenth century.

While searching for sensible limits of study, I had been impressed by Francis Parkman's early and unwavering desire to
write the "history of the American forest," the now-classic story
of the clash of French, English, and Indian cultures. Although I

---

* James Axtell, *The School upon a Hill: Education and Society in Colonial
New England* (New Haven, 1974).

had no desire—or capacity—to bring off a stunning eight-volume
triumph such as his, I felt personally and professionally comfortable with that particular three-culture focus upon a challengingly
spacious but historically integral segment of colonial North
America. Instead of a military approach, I thought a more pacific
tack might breathe some fresh air into Parkman's dusty subject.
My reasons were two. First, a modicum of common sense and
some acquaintance with history told me that war is usually a last
resort in the resolution of conflict. Before that comes learning,
compromise, conversion, and a whole host of other changes that
anthropologists call acculturation. And second, if cultures are
largely normative affairs in which ideas and ideals are primary,
it followed that cultural competition is largely an educational
contest for the hearts and minds of the competitors. Thus the
gradual evolution of the design for *The Invasion Within: The
Contest of Cultures in Colonial North America,* an ethnohistory
of the French, English, and Indian efforts to convert each other.

In the course of doing research, nurturing a family, job hunting, teaching, and writing other books and articles, the outlines
of the book grew like topsy. I came to understand how Harold
Nicolson felt as he sat in his bath in 1949 and decided that he
needed two chapters instead of one to tell the story of King
Edward VII's death. The change of plans was "depressing," he
said, "but right. One simply must be firm with oneself about
getting the architecture of books right." While a similar kind of
literary mitosis was postponing the completion of *The Invasion
Within,* I was invited to delay it still further by Howard Lamar
and Leonard Thompson, former Yale colleagues, who were or-
ganizing an international symposium on comparative frontiers in
North America and South Africa. They asked me to describe the
"Religious Processes" in colonial North America, a request to
which I agreed largely because I was already familiar with the
Catholic and Protestant missions from having written (with
James Ronda) *Indian Missions: A Critical Bibliography* and several papers, articles, and chapters on the subject. The following
essay, which borrows its title from the book of which it is a partial summary, was first read in May 1979 at the symposium and
then revised for publication in the conference proceedings, *The*

*Frontier in History: North American and Southern African Comparisons.** I am grateful to Joseph N. Greene, Jr., the president of the Seven Springs Center where the symposium was held, for permission to reprint it here.

THE INVASION OF NORTH AMERICA BY EUROPEAN MEN, machines, and microbes was primarily an aggressive attempt to subdue the newfound land and its inhabitants, and to turn them to European profit. Because it was not totally unlike that of Europe, the land itself could be brought to terms by the increasingly effective methods of Western technology and capitalist economy. The American natives, however, posed a more serious problem. While they shared certain characteristics with the rest of mankind known to Europe, their cultures were so strange, so numerous, and so diverse that the invaders found it impossible to predict their behavior. If the Europeans hoped to harness, or at least neutralize, the numerically superior natives, they could ill afford to tolerate behavior that was as unpredictable as it was potentially dangerous.

Fortunately, not all natives were inscrutable at all times. European traders quickly discovered that the Indians were no strangers to an economy of barter and exchange. Even without the medium of mutually intelligible languages, Europeans exchanged Indian furs, skins, and food for manufactured goods with the aid of elemental sign languages or trade jargons. Where language was lacking, the familiar behavior of trade communicated the Indians' intentions and terms. Military officers who sought native allies against less receptive natives—or who were sought as allies by native factions—rec-

* James P. Ronda and James Axtell, *Indian Missions: A Critical Bibliography* (Bloomington, 1978). Howard Lamar and Leonard Thompson, eds., *The Frontier in History: North American and Southern African Comparisons* (New Haven, 1981).

ognized with equal ease the normative behavior of military
allies. If their Indian partners seldom conducted war with the
martial discipline of Europe, they at least shared a common
enemy and a common understanding of strategic alliance.

But traders and soldiers were soon greatly outnumbered,
especially in the English colonies, by invaders whose goals
were much less compatible with the life-styles of the eastern
woodland Indians. When European farmers and townsmen
arrived in the New World, they brought no interest in any
aspect of Indian culture or behavior. To these colonists—
who quickly established the distinctive character of the European invasion—the native possessors of the soil stood as living impediments to agricultural "civilization," little different
from stony mountains, unfordable rivers, and implacable
swamps. Since it was highly unlikely that the Indians would
vanish into thin air or exile themselves to some arid corner
of the continent, the best these invaders could hope for was
their pacification and resettlement away from the plowed
paths of prosperity. In any event, they had to be rendered
predictable to make America safe for Europeans.

As if heaven-sent, a small but determined cadre of invaders
offered the ultimate answer to the settlers' prayers. Christian
missionaries, who had come to America in the earliest phases
of invasion, espoused a set of spiritual goals which colored
but ultimately lent themselves to the more material ends of
their countrymen. From the birth of European interest in the
New World, religious men had ensured that the public goals
of exploration and colonization included a prominent place
for the conversion of the natives to Christianity. But the
Christianity envisioned was not a disembodied spiritual con-
struct but a distinct cultural product of Western Europe.
Conversion was tantamount to a complete transformation
of cultural identity. To convert the Indians of America was to
replace their native characters with European personae, to
transmogrify their behavior by substituting predictable Euro-

pean modes of thinking and feeling for unpredictable native modes. By seeking to control the Indians' thoughts and motives, the missionaries sought to control—or at least anticipate—their actions, which could at any time spell life or death for the proliferating but scattered settlements on the farming frontier. Unwittingly or not, they lent powerful support to the European assault upon America by launching their own subversive invasion within.

From its inception, the invasion of North America was launched on waves of pious intent. Nearly all the colonial charters granted by the French and English monarchs in the sixteenth and seventeenth centuries assign the wish to extend the Christian Church and to save savage souls as a principal, if not the principal, motive for colonization.[1] Even patently economic ventures such as the Virginia, Newfoundland, and Susquehannah companies, as one colonist put it, "pretended, and I hope intended" to hold pagan salvation dearer than pounds sterling.[2]

Obviously the mere desire to convert the American natives was insufficient to accomplish the task. The missionaries also had to believe that the Indians were educable. For unless they were potentially convertible, they could never become Christian converts, a thought no missionary could entertain for long and remain in his calling. From their map-strewn studies in London and Oxford the cousins Hakluyt described the Indians as people "though simple and rude in manners, . . . yet of nature gentle and tractable."[3] Richard Eburne, a fellow promoter, agreed. His *Plain Pathway to Plantations* was lined with "exceeding[ly] tractable" natives, who were not only "industrious and ingenious to learn of us and practice with us most arts and sciences" but "very ready to leave their old and blind idolatries and to learn of us the right service and worship of the true God."[4] Since none of these men had ever made the American voyage to take personal measure of the

natives' capacity, they were drawing on the Christian human-
ist's faith in the reforming power of education as well as the
optimism of early explorers for their assessments. In 1609, as
the Virginia Company was outfitting its third fleet for western waters, the Reverend Robert Gray gave classical expression to that belief when he told potential investors, "It is not
the nature of men, but the education of men, which make[s]
them barbarous and uncivill." "Chaunge the education of
men," he predicted, "and you shall see that their nature"—
corrupted at the source by Adam's sin—"will be greatly recti-
fied and corrected."[5] According to Paul Le Jeune, the Jesuit
superior of Quebec, it was optimism such as this that caused
"a great many people in France [to] imagine that all we have
to do is to open our mouths and utter four words, and behold, a Savage is converted."[6]

While the Indians were felt to be ultimately redeemable,
there was one crucial hitch: they were still in a state of "savagery" or "barbarism," which every civilized person knew to
be an "infinite distance from Christianity."[7] They were much
too "degenerate" for religion to flourish or for the Word to
work its magic. The heart of the matter was that they could
not be trusted with the holy church ordinances "whilst they
lived so unfixed, confused, and ungoverned a life."[8] The missionary prospectus was thus drawn for the next century and a
half. All the European missionary societies, Protestant and
Catholic, began and with few exceptions ended their American efforts with the belief that it was necessary to "civilize
Savages before they can be converted to Christianity, & that
in order to make them Christians, they must first be made
Men."[9] The English Protestants never questioned this assumption until a few were forced to in the 1760s by a growing record of crushed hopes and unflattering self-comparisons
with the Canadian Jesuits, most of whom after extensive field
experience had ceased to practice what they had once preached
by the middle decades of the previous century.[10] With scarcely

a dissenting voice in all those years, the missionaries of North America clearly felt it their responsibility to give the Indians "Civilitie for their bodies" before "Christianitie for their soules," for while the second made them *"happy,"* the first made them *"men."*[11]

In implying that the Indians were not yet "men" the Europeans meant one of three things. The first meaning was that the natives were the children of the human race, their passions still largely unrestrained by reason. The second meaning also emphasized their passions, but gave them a much less charitable interpretation. Rather than innocent children, the Indians in this view were little better than animals, incapable of reason and enslaved by the most brutal passions. The third and by far most prevalent meaning, however, was simply that the Indians had not mastered the "Arts of civil Life & Humanity."[12] While civilized Europeans, even the lower classes, could be assumed to have acquired at least the rudiments of these arts through education or social osmosis, the Indians were thought to lack them totally. Consequently, the missionaries' perceived duty was to *"root out* their vicious habits" and "national vices," and to replace them with a "civil, orderly & Christian way of living."[13] As the Recollect friars proposed upon coming to Canada in 1615, the Indians were to be "regulated by French laws and modes of living" in order to render them capable of understanding the "profound mysteries" of Christianity, "for all that concerns human and civil life is a mystery for our Indians in their present state, and it will require more expense and toil to render them men than it has required to make whole nations Christian."[14]

Whenever plans were drawn for "humanizing" the American natives, the English missionaries chose a peculiar phrase that speaks volumes about their religious attitudes and cultural preconceptions. Time and again, from the sixteenth century to the American Revolution, it was said that the first goal of the English was to *"reduce"* the Indians from savagery to "civility."[15] The phrase is puzzling because we would expect a people with a superior self-image to attempt to *raise* their inferiors, rather than *reduce* them, to their level. To my knowledge, only two missionaries during the whole colonial period ever expressed their goal as one of elevation—both only once and both well into the eighteenth century—and even their aberrance was wholly out of character.[16] Why did they speak as if Indian culture needed a kind of *de*grading before measuring *down* to English civility?

The answer lies in the nature of the wholesale changes in Indian culture required by the English—and the French Recollects, Sulpicians, and early Jesuits as well—to render the natives worthy of religious conversion. From the European perspective, the Indians were deficient in three essential qualities: Order, Industry, and Manners. This meant in essence that they were non-Europeans, the polar opposite of what they should be and should want to be. So with characteristic confidence the missionaries proceeded in the heady decades after settlement to prescribe a veritable pharmacopoeia of remedies for their savage condition. Their diagnosis of the natives' deficiencies helps to explain why cultural health could be restored only by *"reducing* them to civility."

The immediate concern of the Europeans was to remove the Indians from their "disordred riotous rowtes and companies, to a wel governed common wealth," from what they took to be civil anarchy to the rule of European law. For of all "humane Artes," the missionaries knew, "Political government is the chiefest."[17] To men accustomed to kings and queens, administrative bureaucracies, standing armies, police, courts, and all the punitive technology of justice known to "civilized" states, the Indians seemed to suffer from unbenign neglect. If they were acknowledged to have any government at all, it was usually the capricious tyranny of an absolute theocrat, such as Powhatan in Virginia or Uncas in Connecticut. More prevalent was the view that the "common

rules of order in the administration of justice"—the rules followed in Parliament or the Estates General—were not observed in Indian society. Indeed, so subtle and covert were
the workings of Indian justice that the colonists were "aston-
ished to find that such societies can remain united" at all.[18]
Cast in such a light, these "wild people" obviously needed
the Europeans to "bring them to Political life, both in Ecclesiastical society and in Civil, for which," the missionaries
assured themselves, "they earnestly long and enquire."[19]

Another disturbing symptom of native disorder was their
"scattered and wild course of life."[20] "Towns they have none,"
wrote an English visitor with England in mind, "being alwayes
removing from one place to another for conveniency of
food."[21] The predominantly hunting tribes of Canada and
Maine were the least fixed because survival depended on following the non-herding big game animals in small family
groups and living off the stingy land. Even their more sedentary southern neighbors spent only five or six months congre-
gated around their corn fields in villages ranging in size from a
few families to a thousand inhabitants. And then they too
broke up and moved more than once in search of fish, shellfish, berries, nuts, game, maple sap, "warme and thicke woodie
bottomes" to escape the winter winds, more wood for their
fires, or simply relief from the fearless fleas of summer.[22]

It was obviously disconcerting to Europeans accustomed to
finding towns in the same place year after year to discover a
village of a hundred wigwams gone "within a day or two" for
parts and reasons unknown.[23] Not only were such a people
physically uncontrollable but, perhaps worse, they were unpredictable, and surprise was the last thing the invaders
wanted in the New World. Equally upsetting was the discovery that the natives, in all their basest "savagery," dared
to break God-graven class lines by usurping the privileges
of the European aristocracy. Forever tweaking the nose of
authority, Thomas Morton of Merrymount all but visibly

rubbed his hands over his observation that when the Indians "are minded to remoove," they "remoove for their pleasures . . . after the manner of the gentry of Civilized nations."[24] The same impish glee cannot describe the pious Edward Johnson of Massachusetts, who nonetheless volunteered that the Indians' wigwams bore an uncanny resemblance to gentlemen's "Summer-houses in England."[25] To have viewed the Indians as America's noblemen, commuting conspicuously between winter "castle" and summer cottage-by-the-sea, would clearly not have served. Better that their movements be seen as the vagrant shiftings of dissolute barbarians. For then, in the name of European civility and the Christian religion, such flagrant "disorder" and "chaos" could be "reduced" and the Indians brought under control.

The natives were considered deficient not only in civil order but in industry as well. In one of his first meetings with the Massachusetts John Eliot told them that they and the English were already "all one save in two things," the first being that the English were Christians and they were not. The second difference was somewhat less obvious but to English minds nearly as important: "we labour and work in building, planting, clothing our selves, &c. and they doe not."[26] The key word in Eliot's comparison was "labour." To the idealistic missionaries, many of whom had pursued the life of learning because their constitutions were "unsuited to labour," it did not mean simply to "work" (as Eliot's additional use of that word implies), for even the Indians could be said to "work" by expending energy and thought upon various tasks. Rather it meant to work *laboriously* in the sense of severe, painful, or compulsory *toil,* the kind that a plowman knows as he walks behind a pair of huge oxen in the late-spring heat.[27] In that sense, of course, the Indians had never known work, a deficiency exacerbated by what all Europeans diagnosed as a congenital "national vice"—idleness.

In the midst of their back-breaking efforts to hew villages

and farms from the American forests, the first settlers were struck by the contrast with their native neighbors. "They are not industrious," observed the Reverend Robert Cushman at second hand, "neither have art, science, skill or faculty to use either the land or the commodities of it, but all spoils, rots, and is marred for want of manuring, gathering, ordering"— that word again—"etc."[28] Nearly two centuries later, when the white frontier had shifted into western New York, the Reverend John Thornton Kirkland, a missionary and the son of a missionary, assured the members of the Massachusetts Historical Society that the situation had not changed in all that time. The Oneida, Stockbridge, and Brotherton Indians, he wrote from personal observation in 1795, "have none of the spirit, industry, and perseverance necessary in those who subdue a wilderness. . . . They seem to have an insurmountable aversion to labour; and though they discover some energy in the chace, wholly want it in husbandry and the arts of life."[29] So tempting was the native way of life that many Indian converts apostatized because, as the English admitted, "they can live with less labour, and more pleasure and plenty, as Indians, than they can with us."[30] In fact, one of the reasons given by colonists who either ran away to the Indians or refused to return from captivity was that amongst the Indians they enjoyed the "most perfect freedom, the ease of living, [and] the absence of those cares and corroding solicitudes which so often prevail with us."[31]

When the colonists found idleness endemic to Indian culture, the cultural norm by which they judged applied to only half the native population—the male half. For upon closer examination it appeared to European observers, almost all of whom were male, that, while Indian men were indeed epitomes of slothful indulgence, the work done by Indian women came respectably, even pitiably, close to the missionaries' ideal of "labour." Since such behavior ran counter to their civilized expectations, there was double cause for raised eyebrows.

According to the Reverend Francis Higginson, one of the "discommodities" of *New-Englands Plantation* was that Indian "Men for the most part live idlely, they doe nothing but hunt and fish" while "Their wives set theire corne and doe all their other worke."[32] The reason for this unequal division of labor was, as most colonists saw it, the refusal of the chauvinistic Indian men "to be seene in any woman like exercise" for fear it "would compromise their dignity too much."[33] "Such [was] the pride of these lazy lords of the wilderness" that European settlers who did not treat their women similarly were blamed "for their folly in spoyling good working creatures."[34]

Bred like all people to an ethnocentric world-view, the European invaders saw what they expected to see in Indian life. Initially jarred by the half-correct observation that native men were not responsible for the agricultural livelihood of their society, the colonists never recovered their visual focus enough to notice that what was normal behavior in Europe did not always obtain in America, that Indian men played a role in their economy every bit as important as European farmers did in theirs, and that Indian women did not view their social position in the light cast by the male observers from another culture.

On their face the European criticisms of Indian "industry" were serious enough, but a number of less overt grievances reveal even more about the cultural preconceptions of the colonists and therefore about the remedial prescriptions that could be expected from the missionaries. The first group of objections, assailing the nature of Indian farming, were stated typically in the form of deficiencies. Not only was native farming done largely by women but it did not employ the deep-cutting plow harnessed to animal power, fences to enclose the fields, or—particularly symbolic—fertilizer in the form of tame animal manure.

Thomas Hariot, one of the Roanoke colonists in 1585, observed that the natives "never enrich the soil with refuse, dung, or any other thing, nor do they plough or dig it as we do in England." Nevertheless, their corn reached prodigious heights and "the yield is so great that little labor is needed in comparison with what is necessary in England."[35] Happily for the Massachusetts Bay Company, John Winthrop decided that the New England natives "inclose noe Land, neither have any setled habytation, nor any tame Cattle to improve the Land by," and so were devoid of any legal claim to their territory.[36] Although the Indians could watch a European plow "teare up more ground in a day, than their Clamme shels [hoes] could scape up in a month," they preferred their own methods throughout the colonial period.[37] To those colonists who swore by the work ethic today recognized as having been shared by Protestants and Catholics alike, there was nothing more galling than to discover that wild "savages" reaped the proverbial fruits of the earth without working up a European-style sweat.

Another criticism of Indian farming was implied by the fact that no more equipment was required than a crude hoe and a few handmade baskets. This meant that the natives' technology was as portable as their housing, which rendered them still more difficult to bring to "order." Without horses, barns, carts, harrows, plows, halters, collars, and harnesses—in other words, without a substantial material investment in the capitalist way of life—the Indians could not be securely anchored to one plot of ground where they could always be found (and disciplined if they got out of line).[38] In addition, without an involvement in the encircling web of credit that husbandry entailed, the Indians could at any time pull up stakes and head for the hinterland, out of the reach of Scriptural and European law.

Trying to persuade the Indians, even the most Christian, to invest in the heavy technology of farming was a task of no little difficulty because it raised their deeply engrained suspicions of anything that threatened their independence and offended their sense of utility. The English, keen entrepreneurs that they were, understood that the civilized citizen was "attached to his country by property, by artificial wants which render that property necessary to his comfortable subsistence."[39] So one of the first tasks of those who would attach the Indians to the English political interest was to "multipl[y] their Wants, and put them upon desiring a thousand things, they never dreamt of before."[40] Thus "their wants will be encreased," reasoned "The Planter" in an eighteenth-century Philadelphia newspaper, "while on us they must in a manner wholly depend to have them supplied."[41] For a society of men uniquely responsive to the marketplace, it was a strategy with promise. But it failed to reckon with the alien psychology of the native Americans, for whom wealth was communal and sharing a sovereign duty. Moreover, "they care for little, because they want but little," William Penn tried to explain to his English partners. "In this they are sufficiently revenged on us. . . . We sweat and toil to live; their pleasure feeds them, I mean, their Hunting, Fishing and Fowling."[42]

Penn's characterization of Indian hunting as "pleasure" introduces a second group of English objections to the Indian division of labor. It was bad enough that women should manage the Indian fields without the aid of either their menfolk or the labor-inducing technology of the English, but almost worse was that those truant warriors misspent their days sporting in the woods or the water. Like the founder of Pennsylvania, colonists up and down the eastern seaboard felt that Indian hunting and fishing were more pleasant pastimes than real work. While they could sometimes appreciate that the native men took "extreame paines" in those pursuits, they could not forgive them for expending their energies in places other than plowed fields or fragrant cow-barns.[43]

A southern gentleman put his finger on the true cause of English concern when he noted, after an extensive survey of the Indian country between Virginia and North Carolina, that native men "are quite idle, or at most employ'd only in the *Gentlemanly* Diversions of Hunting and Fishing."[44] By this William Byrd II, the English-bred scion of one of the wealthiest families in Virginia, indicated that the Indians' greatest offense was the usurpation of aristocratic privilege, the disorderly jumping of class lines. For in England the only people who hunted were members of the upper classes, who did not kill to eat, or poachers who did and risked their ears—or necks—in the attempt. Forests were not public property but belonged to the nobility who regarded them as private game preserves. Guns were expensive and their ownership was generally forbidden by law.

These were the assumptions that the colonists carried to America, where the forests seemed to belong to no man, where guns became a household fixture, where hunting was often a necessity, and where English class lines failed to replicate themselves. In spite of all the social and environmental changes that should have engendered a different outlook toward hunting (and in some instances did toward their own), the colonists who did not rely on Indian hunters for marketable furs and skins continued to view the economic activities of Indian men with Old World eyes. Regarded as the social inferiors of all Englishmen, the Indians were harshly judged by semi-feudal standards that simply made no sense in the New World, much less in an alien culture.

The English had other, seldom articulated, misgivings about Indian hunting that lay just beneath the surface of their vocal disdain. These revolved around the fearful fact that in native society hunting and warfare were but two aspects of the same activity. Not only was warfare conducted according to hunting patterns, but hunting was a sort of ritualized warfare, carried on under strong religious sanctions. The education for one was the training for both. The English—and French—knew only too well that the practice of stealing through the woods to get near the game unnoticed served the warrior equally well in laying ambush upon unsuspecting enemies. Whether intended or not, the English reduction of Indian hunting to a harmless "diversion" served to disarm—at least mentally—a disturbing and dangerous alternative.

Disorder and idleness were structural weaknesses inherent in native society as a whole, but on a personal level, where most Europeans and Indians met, the natives were also seen as woefully deficient. As surely as their government and economy needed reform, their manners cried out for civilizing treatment. Nothing less than total assimilation to European ways would fulfill the uncompromising criteria of "civility," nothing less than renunciation of the last vestige of their former life. For a "Christian" and a "savage" were incompatible characters in the invaders' cosmology, and only a willing departure from all he had known, all he had been, could prepare an Indian for a life of Christ. In European eyes, no native characteristic was too small to reform, no habit too harmless to reduce.

One of the first objects of reform was the Indians' names. To European ears, inured to the peculiar accents of home and the sea, the Algonquian and Iroquoian languages of the eastern woodlands struck a discordant note. Words, including names, were often long and seemingly undifferentiated, full of throaty glottals and short of defining labials. Understandably, the colonists wished to abbreviate, translate, or Europeanize the names of those natives with whom they had any commerce, especially those selected for conversion. Perhaps the easiest way to bestow intelligible European names was to intercept the native child at birth before an Indian name could be given. In "praying towns" and villages with a resident missionary, this was done most readily at the baptism of the child. On such religious occasions Biblical names naturally found favor with the ministers, though just as often

Indian parents preferred common French or English names.

Baptisms were not the only occasions for conferring European names, nor were children the only recipients. The eastern tribes shared a custom of renaming in which an individual could give himself or be given a new name whenever changed circumstances, personal fortune, or mere whim warranted.[45] One of the occasions that might call for a new name was the realization that the friendship of the colonists could be an advantage in trade, politics, or religion. If assuming a short European name would make it easier to deal with the increasingly dominant invaders, many natives were willing to make the change, especially if around their own fires they were still known by their Indian names.

European persistence and Indian preference soon led to a pandoran variety of native names in the areas touched by settlement. Some were quaintly medieval (William of Sudbury), others reminiscent of black slaves who lost their family surnames for a racial tag (Joseph Indian, Miriam Negro, Charles Slave or Panis). Many were either legitimate translations of Indian names (Cornplanter, Blacksnake) or fabricated "Indian" names given by the colonists (Pipe, White-Eyes). Most were simply compromises between utility and history, a union of European given names and native surnames (Pierre Chihwatenha) or translations of surnames (Mercy Fish, Merry Porridge). All, however, forced the natives to compromise their personal identity for the convenience and ideology of the white invaders.

If the intimacy of a personal name could be violated, it is small wonder that the missionaries did not hesitate to pass harsh judgment upon native sexual mores. The most visible cause for concern was the Indians' state of undress, especially in the summer when visits from the colonists were most frequent. Children went completely naked until puberty, men sported only skimpy breechclouts, and women, as one colonial admirer testified, "commonly go naked as far as the Navel downward, and upward to the middle of the Thigh, by which means they have the advantage of discovering their fine Limbs and compleat Shape."[46] In European eyes a direct relation existed between such tempting nudity and the Indians' libidinous behavior. Young people took to sexual exploration early in their teens, and found nothing shameful about their bodies or their amorous potential; they were certainly strangers to the invaders' concept of "fornication." Although adultery was widely prohibited by tribal law, their parents appeared more universally guilty because the Christians did not recognize the validity of Indian divorce, which easily ensued upon the transfer of one spouse's affections and belongings to the lodge of another. By the same token, native polygamy seemed to be rampant when in fact very few tribesmen took more than one wife and they were usually visible sachems or men of importance whose obligations of hospitality required more female hands than two.

The intrusive lengths to which the Europeans would go to "civilize" the American natives has perhaps no better measure than the English missionaries' attempts to proscribe "the old Ceremony of the Maide walking alone and living apart so many dayes."[47] This referred to the widespread native belief that a menstruating woman possessed malevolent powers, capable of poisoning food with her touch, scaring game with her scent, or injuring a man's health with her glance. In nearly all hunting and most horticultural tribes, women "in their courses" withdrew to a small hut in the woods (*wetuomémese* in Narragansett) for the duration, where they lived alone, cooked their own meals with special utensils, and lowered their eyes when a tribesman came near. At the end of a woman's period "she washeth herself, and all that she hath touched or used, and is again received to her husband's bed or family."[48] Despite the intriguing similarity of menstrual seclusion to ancient Jewish custom, the missionaries wanted not only to move the Indians away from a hunting economy, where the menstrual taboo was strongest, but to undercut the whole belief system upon which it was founded. But before they could re-educate the natives in personal hygiene, physiology, and metaphysics, they simply ruled that the Indian woman's time-honored way of dealing with her natural processes was taboo and subject to the scrutiny of foreign men. What the modern woman's movement has called "vaginal politics" was clearly not unknown to the Anglo-Protestants who led the invasion within.

However exemplary the Indians' daily—or nocturnal—behavior, one look told the colonists that the natives needed to be clothed in more than modesty. In the eyes of the invaders, native dress was a phantasmagoria of animal pelts, bird feathers, and reptile skins, of colors and textures as wild as the people themselves. Beautifully tanned leathers were thrown together with bird-wing headdresses, mantles of animal heads, feet, and tails, snakeskin belts, smoky fur robes, and swan's-down ear decorations. Any exposed skin might be covered with totemic tattoos, shell jewelry, bear grease, or lurid paintings. In all seasons frail-looking, soft-soled moccasins were worn without stockings—if at all—while men donned buttock-revealing leather leggings as pants against the cold and underbrush. Clearly such uncouth garb would have to be replaced by fashions à la mode in Boston and Quebec. For if an Indian could be persuaded to change his whole life-style, so that he looked as well as lived and acted like a European, the chances were considered good that he would eventually think European thoughts and believe Christian truths. He would, in effect, cease to be an Indian, the conversion process would be complete, and the colonial "Indian problem" would be solved. The trick, however, was to get the half-naked forest dwellers to look like European colonists. In some respects this proved to be the easiest task of all, but in the end the Europeans enjoyed only partial success. For in the seemingly indifferent matter of personal appearance they encountered the paramount symbol of Indian identity and the rock upon which most white efforts to "reduce" it were broken.

Several obstacles stood in the way of an abrupt change of habit by the Indians. The largest was that the great majority of woodland Indians had small use for fitted clothes designed for brierless farms and open fields. As many colonists discovered to their loss, woven cloth garments were quickly shredded by the rough life of the woods. Moreover, European clothes, if they were to present a civilized appearance, had to be washed, ironed, bought in multiples to reduce wear, stored, and frequently replaced, none of which the Indians were willing or able to do. "Therefore they had rather goe naked," a New Englishman noted, "than be lousie, and bring their bodies out of their old tune, making them more tender by a new acquired habit."[49] Fitted trousers were particularly abhorrent, especially in the South where native men squatted to urinate.[50] The most clothing that the majority of Indians could be induced to buy was a stroud breechclout, a shirt, which they proceeded to wear unwashed until it distintegrated, and a large woolen blanket, which served at once as overcoat, raincoat, blanket, and nightshirt. The heavy European serges, baize, and fustians, cut into fitted garments that restricted movement and ventilation, found little favor in the native markets of North America—until the missionaries gave their proselytes new reason to buy them.

That reason was the European belief that a European appearance visibly segregated Indian converts from their recalcitrant "pagan" brothers, and provided a sign in times of frontier unrest by which "friend Indians" could be readily distinguished from enemies. For the first few decades of settlement this reasoning made some sense. But as the native resistance to foreign cloth weakened, more tribesmen adopted various articles of European dress for their decorative value or because the loss of game made traditional garb impossible.

When the woods became such a sartorial hodgepodge, native intentions and allegiances were much more difficult to discern. But even then, the infallible mark of a Protestant "praying Indian" was his English appearance: short hair, cobbled shoes, and working-class suit. So important was European clothing as a badge of "civility" that an Indian's degree of acculturation could almost be read in his appearance. The more he wished to emulate the invaders and to become one with them, the more Europeanized his dress became and the more pains he took to put aside his native costume. In the eastern woodlands you could often tell a convert by his cover.

But in New England, dress alone was not an infallible guide to the Indian's political allegiance, much less to his religious convictions, unless it was accompanied by an equally decisive *uncovering*—short hair. For nothing symbolized the Indian's identity—his independence, his sense of superiority, his pride—more effectively than his long hair. A willingness to cut his long black hair signaled his desire to kill the Indian in himself and to assume a new persona modeled upon the meek, submissive Christ of the white man's Black Book. Since this was the missionaries' ultimate goal, they wasted no time in persuading their native proselytes to submit to the barber's shears.

When the ministers succeeded, the loss was dramatic. Eastern native hairstyles were infinite and various, many of which would "torture the wits of a curious Barber to imitate."[51] Whether they chose roaches, pigtails, tonsures, scalplocks, baldness, or ingenious combinations thereof, most native men affected some form of long hair and a studied fancy that to many English observers betrayed "the sparkes of natural pride," a vanity that did not seem present in their clothing, houses, or material possessions.[52] As such, their hair drew unexpectedly cutting remarks from the missionaries.

The Puritan abhorrence of long hair was rooted, like many of their values, in Scripture, but it took on political shading

during the English civil wars when the long hair and pow-
dered wigs of "Cavaliers" seemed to run riot in pulpit, court,
and quadrangle. The English battle was soon refought in
New England, where the "roundheads" were led by missionary John Eliot, the vocal minister of the Roxbury congregation. With zeal surprising in a matter of acknowledged "in-
differency," he and his short-haired colleagues proceeded to
prod their congregations, university, and governments into
outlawing "proud fashions" and "the wearing of long haire
after the manner of Ruffians," "wild-Irish," and, not least,
"barbarous Indians."[53]

Whether the wearer was English or Indian, the principal
sin of long hair was pride. And seventeenth-century Englishmen did not need reminding that pride was the original sin
of their spiritual parents, Adam and Eve. In the innumerable
laws, proclamations, and warnings that resulted from the colonial establishment's dismay over long hair, overweening
pride was the "badge" of those who refused to cover themselves with Christian "humility, sobriety, modesty, [and]
shamefastness."[54]

If the Indians had inadvertently or casually worn their hair
long, they would still have offended the Protestants' fine sensitivity to personal pride and vanity, but not as grievously as
they obviously did. For long hair aptly symbolized the Indians' deeper affront to Anglo-Christianity, which was their
characteristic pride and independence. Whenever the European invaders took measure of the native Americans, these
two qualities found the page with great frequency. Secular
men on the frontier might appreciate and even emulate the
Indians, but good Christians, especially ministers, could only
be chagrined that some of God's creatures were not duly
"mortified and humbled" before their creator. As God's servants on earth, the missionaries felt a strong obligation to ensure that the Indians, "the dregs and refuse of Adams lost

posterity," were drawn from their "sinful liberty" into "Subjection to Jehovah."[55]

Setting the pace for those who followed, Eliot's goals were "to convince, bridle, restrain, and civilize" the Indians "and also to humble them." In describing their religious goals, the missionaries most commonly used the metaphor of placing such "heady Creatures" in the "yoke of Christ" and teaching them to "bridle" their savage instincts.[56] In other words, becoming a Christian was comparable to assuming the posture and character of tame cattle—docile, obedient, submissive. Or, in another popular metaphor, their goal was to "reduce" the Indians' proud independence and godless self-reliance to the total dependence of a "weaned child."[57] Since it was total, this dependence was at once political, social, and religious. In short, the Indians would become "civilized." The "savage" would give way to the "civil man" by repressing his native instincts, habits, and desires and quietly taking the political bit in his teeth and the religious yoke upon his neck.

Thus, the meaning of the puzzling phrase, "to reduce them to civility," becomes clear. As long hair symbolized pride for the English, so too did the long-haired Indian. In the Christian cosmology, the proud Indian—wandering, lawless, and unpredictable—occupied the higher place: he was puffed up with self-importance, inflated with a false sense of superiority, and unrestrained by law, labor, or religion, not unlike the Devil whom he was thought to worship. It was therefore an affront to God—and, of course, his Christian soldiers—that the Indians remained in such an unnatural and undesirable state.

What should also be clear is the sincerity of the religious goals of European colonization. If we interpret "conversion" as the invaders did, not as modern theologians do, there can be no doubt that the conversion of the natives was indeed a primary goal—logically and chronologically primary. For given the almost unanimous belief that "savages" had to be "civi-

lized" before they could be "Christianized," the initial problem all the European colonies faced—the natives' dangerous
unpredictability—was soluble by "reducing them to civility."
If in the process the conquerors were served as much as
Christ, who could gainsay their fortune? Certainly not the
missionaries, who were keenly aware that "until Christians
are the absolute masters of the Indians, missionaries will have
scant success without a very special grace of God, a miracle
which He does not perform for every people."[58]

The broad consensus about the goals of the Christian missions in North America, emerging from a common Western
European experience and ideology, entailed a limited range
of conversion methods upon the French and English invaders.
Since the "civilizing" and religious conversion of the Indians
was essentially an educational task, a process of re-education
in effect, the colonists turned naturally to the major social
and educational institutions of their cultures for models and
methods. The institution that promised to work the greatest
number of changes in native culture was the town, the European symbol of "civility" (from the Latin *civis,* citizen) and
locus of law and order. The town was expected to fix, restrain,
and order Indian life, to direct its licentious energies into
productive and predictable channels. *"Reserves"* in New
France and "praying towns" in New England and elsewhere
gave the missionaries some hope of segregating their neophytes and converts from the corrupting example of imperfect colonists and the seductive "paganism" of their native
neighbors. Moreover, they were calculated to severely cramp
the Indians' mobile style by encouraging them to substitute
agriculture for hunting, to build heavy, European-style houses,
to surround themselves with the cumbersome trappings of
European technology, and to remake their civil polity in the
European image. Not the least of their attractions for the
colonists was that congregations of natives would greatly re-

duce the manpower and therefore economic needs of the missions and provide non-European frontier buffers against enemy war parties.

It took only small experience in America for the missionaries to conclude that "if some one could stop the wanderings of the Indians, and give authority to one of them to rule the others, we would see them converted and civilized in a short time."[59] The need, of course, was to give them an economy overnight that would make their seasonal moves unnecessary, for only then could they stay among their fellow converts the year round to receive instruction from a resident priest or pastor and to nurture their new faith. Father Le Jeune was not wrong to observe that "it is the same thing in an Indian to wish to become sedentary, and to wish to believe in God."[60] But his successor as superior of the Canadian missions, Barthelemy Vimont, had a point too when he regretted that the Jesuits had "greater trouble in keeping our Christians than in acquiring them. . . . The land that we clear, the houses that we build for them, and the other aid, spiritual and material, that we endeavor to give them, keep them stationary for a while, but not permanently."[61] If the new townsmen could be fed until they became agriculturally self-sufficient, the praying town had a good chance of fostering substantial changes in the native life-style, the most important of which was the imposition of new forms of government, discipline, and morality.

The fundamental weakness of Indian life, the missionaries felt, was the natives' belief that they ought "by right of birth, to enjoy the liberty of Wild ass colts, rendering no homage to any one whomsoever, except when they like."[62] Since "they are born, live, and die in a liberty without restraint, they do not know what is meant by bridle or bit."[63] Consequently, no aspect of their "reduction to civility" was more essential than persuading or forcing them to place their necks in "the yoke of the law of God," which, translated, meant European-style autocracy, law, and compulsion. When the Jesuit *reserve* of Sillery was settled after 1637, its Algonquin and Montagnais inhabitants felt the need for a civilized form of government to regulate their civil and religious affairs. For the first time in their experience, the men elected by majority vote rather than consensus three magistrates, two moral overseers, and a "Captain of prayers" to assist the hereditary sachem. Four of the winners were "Christians," as was their leader. To prove that the traditional rule of suasion was being replaced by coercion, the new officers borrowed the use of Quebec's dungeon until they could build their own prison to punish (mostly female) breakers of their new adamantine code of morality. "Pagans" who dared to resist their authority were imprisoned, chained, whipped, and starved until they learned to obey "a peremptory command" and to submit humbly to "any act of severity or justice." Even the death penalty was seriously considered as a "perpetual" deterrent to moral turpitude.[64]

For most neophytes, French or English, the "yoke of Christ" must have felt anything but "mild and easy," as the missionaries hoped it would.[65] It was virtually impossible not to run afoul of the law when the law proscribed every aspect of traditional life, great and small. In the twenty-four years after 1650, John Eliot gathered some 1100 Massachusett and Nipmuc Indians into fourteen praying towns. Plymouth's missionaries sponsored eight more towns for 500 persons, and the Mayhews on Martha's Vineyard established still others. Most of the New England towns strongly resembled the seven major Jesuit *reserves* in their puritanical leadership and strict prescription of European ways. Faithful converts who were elected or appointed by the missionaries to office promptly drafted long legal codes to govern the towns, which usually consisted at first of unstable mixtures of zealous converts and resistant traditionalists. Concord's rules passed in 1647 were typical. Fines up to twenty shillings or whippings were meted out for infractions ranging from fighting, "powwowing" (resorting to traditional medicine men), gaming, "fornication," and lice-biting to sporting long hair (male) or bare breasts (female), body-greasing, polygamy, mourning with "a great noyse by howling," and menstrual seclusion. (Adultery, witchcraft, and worshipping any deity but the Christian God were punishable by death under colony law, to which the Indians were already subject.) Predictably, the townsmen were expected not only to give up their former habits but to replace them with English ways. Three laws enjoined them to "observe the Lords-Day," to "fall upon some better course to improve their time than formerly," and, most significant, to "labour after humility, and not be proud."[66]

By compelling the natives to avoid idleness, the praying town laws sought to edge them into a European economy, to transform them from "lazy savages" into *"bons habitants"* and "laborious" husbandmen. Skilled trades for the Indians were seldom considered and, when they were, were quickly shunted aside for fear of providing unnecessary competition for colonial workers. Farming and a variety of marginal home industries, such as the manufacture of brooms, pails, and baskets, berrying, and hunting and fishing for hire, were as far as the praying Indians climbed up the ladder of economic success. But by anchoring their converts to the soil, the missionaries accomplished two important ends, one for themselves and one for the colonists. As Eliot explained, "a fixed condition of life" enabled the natives to be more trusted with the church ordinances because "if any should through temptations, fall under [church] Censure, he could easily run away (as some have done) and would be tempted so to do, unless he were fixed in an Habitation, and had some means of livelihood to lose, and leave behind him."[67] And, as a colonial English soldier happily observed, the colonists had it "more in our power to Distress them" if they shook off the civilized bridle or yoke "as we can revenge ourselves on their fixed habitations, & growing corn."[68] Once again, the missionaries served Christ and conquest without qualm or contradiction.

Being the scholastic products of book learning themselves, the ministers and officials who designed the American missions inevitably turned to formal institutions of education for help in "reducing" the Indians to "civility," hoping thereby to reform their mental as well as physical habits as early as possible. Throughout the colonial period, the missionaries tried to reach Indian children and adults at the same time, to trap native culture, as it were, in a squeeze between generations. Both the Recollects and Jesuits established French-style "seminaries" for Indian children during the first years of their missions, but within five years each had folded for lack of funds, students, and success.[69] They then turned their energies toward native *reserves* near the major centers of French population along the St. Lawrence and to religious missions to remote Indian villages all over New France. The English, by contrast, were initially frustrated in their attempts to convert native adults, so their emphasis shifted perceptibly toward the young. This was a logical emphasis because from the beginning the English hoped to train native preachers, teachers, and interpreters to assume the task of converting their brethren to "civilized" Christianity. The only feasible way to train this cadre of native agents was to catch Indian children early in their development, before the hereditary stain of "savagism" became indelible, and "bring them up English."

The instruments the missionaries chose for this task were traditional English schools and colleges, adapted not one whit to the special needs of Indian students fresh from the forest. Until the eighteenth century, most of them were boarding schools located in English territory, far from the contagion of traditional habits, indulgent parents, and distracting friends. The missionaries agreed with the Jesuits that "the consciousness of being three hundred leagues distant from their own country makes these young men more tractable."[70] Under the nervous eyes and guns of the colonists, the students might have taken an extra stab at docility had they known that their teachers viewed them as "hostages" for the safety of the English in their country and along their borders; chiefs' sons were especially welcome as students for this reason.[71] When they arrived at school, they were effectively quarantined from all contaminating female contact for the duration of their studies, as if they were undergoing a special, long-term puberty rite. In the male world of the missionaries, boys were considered the prime candidates for conversion because it was assumed that they would return to their tribes, assume office by (newly acquired) merit, and lead their "pagan" brethren to "civility." (Girls, when they were noticed at all, were educated separately in the two Rs, religion, and "housewifery" to make them suitable partners for French colonists or Christian Indians.)

The master of such a male school was, of course, a patriarchal figure—serious, pedantic, and strict. Although—or because—Indian parents were "too fond" to "tolerate the chastisement of their children" at home, the missionaries in their colonial strongholds proceeded to institute a birchen government calculated to "humble them, and reform their manners." Schoolmasters such as the Reverend Eleazar Wheelock felt free to administer punishment as they pleased, confident that "Evils so obstinate as those we may reasonably expect to find common in the Children of Savages, will require that which is severe."[72]

As in most classrooms, the medium of instruction and discipline was probably louder and clearer than the message of the curriculum, which was unfailingly traditional: religious catechism, English grammar, arithmetic, Latin, and Greek. When the frustration or boredom of their inactive lives erupted in highjinks, the birch rod covered their skin with welts they had never seen at home. By the eighteenth century the contrast between English schooling and Jesuit proselyting was blatantly obvious, especially to the Indians. In 1772 the Onondaga council rejected Wheelock's offer to educate their children with a sharp reproof. "Brother," they said, "you must learn of the French ministers if you would understand, & know how to treat Indians. They don't speak roughly; nor do they for every little mistake take up a club & flog them."[73]

By the fall of Canada in 1760, the English missions had seldom ventured beyond the safety of well-populated and well-fortified colonial settlements. Their praying towns were surrounded by the proliferating towns and farms of southern New England, as were the great majority of their Indian schools. Only a handful of missionaries had ever ventured into Indian country as far as Maine, New York, or the Ohio country, and then with conspicuous lack of success. This timidity was due to three considerations: their ideological insistence on "reducing the Indians to civility" before trying to convert them to Christianity, the belief of many land-hungry farmers and speculators that "the way of conquering them is much more easie than of civilizing them by faire meanes," and a major ecclesiastical deficiency.[74] Until the opening years of the eighteenth century, the English Protestant churches— with the exception of the Church of England, which showed little interest in Indians at the time—were hampered in their missionary endeavors by an ecclesiastical polity that restricted the ministry to those specifically called by an individual congregation of the elect. A minister without a congregation, no matter how holy or how learned he was, was simply a man without the ministry. He could not administer the sacraments of baptism or communion—the only two recognized— or gather a formal church. Furthermore, despite evangelical assertions to the contrary, the minister was effectively prevented from winning new souls to Christ by being tied to the needs and wishes of his small flock. Unless the unregenerate happened to wander into his congregation on the Sabbath—

and understood English—the minister was not likely to encounter many potential converts. "By [Puritan] principles,"
an Anglican visitor criticized, "no Nation can or could ever
be converted."[75]

By contrast, the Jesuits were organized hierarchically in an
international order, freed from parish work to attack heresy
and paganism wherever it flourished. From the middle of the
seventeenth century, when they gave up the idea of Frenchify-
ing the Indians, the Jesuits took their missions into the remote corners of New France, west to Lake Superior, north to
Hudson's Bay, south to Louisiana. In these places they attempted to insinuate Christianity into the natives' lives with
methods learned less in the scholastic classrooms of France
than in the inhabited forests of America.

The priest's first step was to gain admission to the target
village. An ideal way was to talk a leading man or sachem
into adopting him, which gave him an extensive set of ready-
made relatives, food, shelter, and some measure of physical
protection. Then, by his exemplary behavior, the priest made
every effort to show the villagers that he was no threat to their
continued existence. Without an apparent interest in guns,
women, beaver skins, or land, he sought to convince them
that he had left his refined and comfortable life in Europe
solely to help them reach God and eternal happiness. He especially sought the favor of the children, who had great power
over their parents' affections, not least because he could easily
learn the language from them while teaching them their first
words of French.

While ingratiating himself by learning their language, the
Jesuit began to practice his order's worldwide technique of
acculturating themselves to the natives' way of life to win
their trust for the task ahead. Unlike the Dominicans and
Franciscans within their own church and the Puritans and
Anglicans without, the Jesuits articulated and practiced a
brand of cultural relativism, without, however, succumbing

to ethical neutrality. While they, like all missionaries, sought
to replace the Indians' cosmology and religion with their
own, they were more willing than their Christian counterparts to adopt the external life-style of the Indians until their
goal could be realized. Rather than immediately condemn
and destroy what they found, they carefully studied native
beliefs and practices and tried to reshape and reorient them
in order to establish a common ground on which to begin
conversion.[76] As Father Vimont put it in 1642, "to make a
Christian out of a Barbarian is not the work of a day. . . . A
great step is gained when one has learned to know those with
whom he has to deal; has penetrated their thoughts; has
adapted himself to their language, their customs, and their
manner of living; and, when necessary, has been a Barbarian
with them, in order to win them over to Jesus Christ."[77] In
large measure, whatever success the Jesuits enjoyed was gained
not by expecting less of their converts, as the English accused,
but by accepting more.

   As the priest learned to adjust his ways to those of the Indians, he also began to promulgate his Christian message by
appealing to all their senses. In native hands he put attractive
silver and brass medals, rings, crucifixes, and rosaries as mne-
monic devices to recall his oral message, not unlike their own
wampum belts, medicine sticks, and condolence canes. To
their noses he introduced the mysterious fragrances of incense.
To their lips he lifted holy wafers. To their eyes he offered
huge wooden crosses, candle-lit altars rich with silk and silver,
long brocaded chasubles, and pictorial images of the major
acts in the drama of Christianity. And into their ears he
poured sonorous hymns and chants, tinkling bells, and an
endless stream of Indian words, haltingly, even laughably,
pronounced at first, but soon fluent and cadenced in native
measures. Here his long training in logic, rhetoric, and dispu-
tation stood him in good stead, once he grasped the novel
motivations, interests, and fears of his listeners. Believing that

"in order to convert these peoples, one must begin by touching their hearts, before he can convince their minds," the
priest sought to manage their dispositions by an adroit use of
flattery, bribery, ridicule, insult, "mildness and force, threats
and prayers, labors and tears."[78]

If the priest was at all effective, he would soon succeed in
fomenting a serious factional split between "Christians" and
"Pagans" at all levels of village society, a division he would
quietly work to widen in hopes of placing his converts in all
the positions of civil leadership. By administering the sacraments, especially baptism, only to the deserving after considerable instruction and lasting personal reform, he protected
the hard-won reputation of his flock and the holy ordinances
from familiar contempt.

But his most important goal was to supplant the village
shaman, his chief opposition for the minds of the people. By
his possession of printed truths (which initially impressed the
members of that oral culture), a scientific understanding of
nature (whereby a magnet or compass could be used to attract
a following away from a divination rite), and an unrelenting
questioning of the habitual (which no cultural practice can
long survive), the missionary sought to erode the shaman's
prestige and to establish his own in its place. If the fortuitous
administration of a cordial, the lancet, or baptismal water
happened to rescue a native from the grave, his stock as a
functional replacement for the medico-religious shaman would
rise dramatically. When the priest saw his converts at the
head of village government and himself accepted as the resident shaman, he could consider his mission at least a partial
success. While he had not "civilized" his hosts, he had Christianized them without destroying their usefulness to the
French as hunters, trappers, and military allies. His only re-
maining task, as Father Vimont warned, was to keep his
Christians in the Faith, a task that a village church would
greatly lighten.

While the Jesuits enjoyed several advantages over their English rivals, by no means did they enjoy universal or permanent success in converting the Indians even to Christianity. At the end of two centuries of effort, both the French and the English were forced to admit that they had largely failed to convert the native Americans to European religion and culture.[79] The reasons are not difficult to find. In fact, they are so plentiful and so overwhelming that we should rather wonder how they achieved as much success as they did. The usual explanations, those most commonly given by contemporaries in a spirit of half-hearted expiation, pointed to the regrettable but inevitable results of contact with European cultures: disease (to which the Indians had no immunities), war (fomented by European trade competition and exacerbated by European firearms), alcohol (for whose use the natives had no cultural sanctions), and the immoral example of false Christians (who, instead of raising the Indians' sights, "reduced them to civility"). Cotton Mather spoke for many when he confessed that the Europeans had "very much *Injured* the *Indians* . . . by *Teaching* of them, *Our Vice*. We that should have learn'd them to *Pray,* have learn'd them to *Sin*."[80]

While no one would deny that these external forces did much to undermine the conversion process, the traits within Indian culture that resisted change should be emphasized, as should the defects of the missions themselves. The first and most serious obstacle was native religion.[81] Several of the first explorers and some of their less perceptive colonial followers thought that the Indians had no religion, just as they appeared to have no laws or government (*"ni foi, ni loi, ni roi"*). Shortly, however, a closer look enabled settlers and missionaries to grant the natives a modicum of religious beliefs and observances, but these were seen only as "superstitions" because of their non-Christian character. But one man's superstition is another man's religion, and Indian religion, for all its novelty, was at once bona fide and culturally pervasive, capable of explaining, predicting, and controlling the world in emotionally and intellectually satisfying ways. Like all peoples known to Ethnology, the various native groups of the Northeast each possessed a religion in that they performed "a set of rituals, rationalized by myth, which mobilize[d] supernatural powers for the purpose of achieving or preventing transformations of state in man or nature."[82] Despite their linguistic and cultural differences, they shared enough beliefs and practices to allow generalization, and, to some extent, comparison with Christianity. For the Indians were not as far from the Christian invaders in religious belief as they seemed to be in practice (or ritual), which partially explains the successes of the missions as well as their failures.

Behind all native religion lay a cosmology, a hierarchy of states of being and a science of the principles of their interaction. The most populous tier consisted of supernatural beings known as "spirits" or "souls," who were continuous "selves" capable of changing form. Though they were invisible, they were audible to men, with whom they could interact directly (such as by shaking a tent) and by whom they were manipulable in the right circumstances. Possessing will and consciousness, they knew the future as well as the past because of their continuity. Human souls, for instance, could separate temporarily from the corporeal body in sleep, travel to other realms of experience, and return to inform or instruct the person in dreams. Consequently, dreams were regarded by many missionaries as the heart of native religion, for the Indians believed that the supernatural guidance of their lives came from these "secret desires of the soul," which had to be fulfilled if they were to enjoy health, happiness, and success.[83] In death the soul left the body permanently to travel to an afterlife, which was probably vaguely conceived before the Christians began to preach of Heaven and Hell, but which seemed to be an ethereal version of the happiest life they had known on earth, replete with good hunting, abundant fruits, and fine weather. For the long journey to this spirit village in the Southwest, the soul, which had assumed a visible, anthropomorphic ghostly shape, needed food and proper equipment. So the deceased was buried with small pots of food and the tools of his or her calling, the souls of which items would separate from the physical artifacts and accompany the traveler's soul. Although the missionaries managed to alter some small aspects of Indian burial, they seldom persuaded even their converts to deprive the dead of their grave goods.[84]

Just as angels differed in power and character from the Christian God, so Indian spirits and souls differed from the more powerful "guardian spirits," who enjoyed the ultimate power of metamorphosis, and the "Master Spirit." According to native belief, every plant and animal species had a "boss" or "owner" spirit whose experience encompassed all the individuals of the species. Many Indian myths were narratives of the "self" adventures of these spirits. More importantly, a young man—less commonly a young woman—who sought a supernatural talisman of success underwent a vision quest alone in the woods in hopes of receiving instruction from a guardian spirit. If he was successful, the being he saw became his personal helpmate for the rest of his life, during the course of which it would give additional counsel, usually when ritually called upon in time of need. So important was the possession of a guardian spirit or "manitou," wrote a Moravian missionary late in the eighteenth century, that an Indian without one "considers himself forsaken, has nothing upon which he may lean, has no hope of any assistance and is small in his own eyes. On the other hand those who have been thus favored possess a high and proud spirit."[85] The missionary's task was to humble the favored Indian's pride by giving him the meek spirit of Jesus Christ as a new guardian.

The ultimate being in the Indian pantheon, just as in the Christian, was an all-powerful, all-knowing "Master Spirit" or "Creator," who was the source of all good but was seldom or never seen. More frequently encountered, especially after the advent of the Hell-bearing Europeans, was an evil god, a "matchemanitou," who purveyed devilry and death if not appeased. Much to the chagrin of the missionaries, most of the Indians' religious worship seemed to center on attempts to deflect the maleficences of this deity instead of praising the benefactions of the Creator.

The Indians mobilized the supernatural in their world by a number of religious observances and rituals. Just as in the Christian churches, some of these rituals, such as personal prayer, could be performed by any individual, but many were efficacious only when administered in a communal context by a specially qualified priest or shaman, known to the Europeans as a "powwow," "juggler," or "sorcerer." The native priest was almost always a male religious specialist who through apprenticeship and visions had acquired extraordinary spiritual power. Unlike his Christian counterparts, however, he possessed *personal* supernatural power that allowed him to manipulate the spiritual cosmology on his tribesmen's behalf; he was not a mere intermediary whose only strength lay in explanation and supplication. But because all spiritual power in the native universe was double-edged, capable of both good and evil, the shaman was as feared as he was revered. For while he could induce trances that made him impervious to pain, influence the weather, predict the future, and interpret dreams for the villagers, he could also cause as well as cure witchcraft, the magical intrusion of a small item into the body or the capture of a soul in dream by any person with spiritual "power," which caused illness and eventually death. Bewitchment was the most feared calamity in Indian life because the assailant and the cause were unknown unless discovered by a shaman whose personal power was greater than that of the witch. Because persons exhibiting strange behavior were usually suspected of malicious intentions, the Catholic missionaries who lived with no women, read the hieroglyphical pages of a black book, dipped water on the foreheads of native people, fondled crosses and beads, and mumbled incomprehensible incantations always stood the chance of being branded as witches and shunned if not killed.

By the same token, the Indian shaman was the missionaries' number one enemy because he seemed to hold their potential converts in the devil's thraldom through errant superstition, hocus-pocus, and fear. If he happened to be a sachem as well, as occurred from time to time in New England, the missionary faced a formidable task. For such a man controlled the political and social as well as the expressive and emotional resources of the community. If he could be discredited and supplanted, the missionary might have relatively smooth sailing. But while his opposition persisted, large-scale conversion to a Christian alternative stood little chance of success. So adamant was the resistance of these spiritual leaders that more than one missionary must have entertained the sentiment of an early Virginia minister, who insisted that "till their Priests and Ancients have their throats cut, there is no hope to bring them to conversion."[86]

The second obstacle to the success of the missions was the Indian languages. Although the colonial French and English encountered only four of the major language groups of North America, each tribe—sometimes each village—spoke a distinct dialect that might be largely unintelligible to their neighbors. Unlike the traders and trappers who also pursued their callings in Indian country, the missionaries were denied the company of those female "sleeping dictionaries" who so quickly formed the strangers' tongues to native vocabularies, syntax, and accents. For the clerics, said one of their best linguists, "practice is the only master that is able to teach us."[87] To European ears, the languages themselves were mixtures of great richness and disconcerting poverty. They were rich in proper nouns for concrete objects, in metaphorical expressions of "real beauty," and in a variety of ways to signify the same object or action in various states or relations. But they were poor in abstract words, universals, and of course words from another world. It thus appeared to the Jesuits that "neither the Gospel nor holy Scripture has been composed for them." Even mundane parables to symbolize the Christian mysteries were nearly untranslatable for lack of vocabulary: the natives simply had no words for salt, sin, gold, prison, candle, king, shepherd, or flock. "Their ignorance of the things of the earth," lamented the worldly priests, "seem to close for them the way to heaven."[88] This was an obstacle that neither culture completely overcame.

Another serious obstacle, especially to the French missions, was native marriage. The Catholic priests, of course, regarded monogamous marriage as one of the seven sacraments and divorce as anathema. The Indians, on the other hand, had always exercised, as Father Vimont put it, "a complete brutal liberty, changing wives when they pleased—taking only one or several, according to their inclination." Understandably, "conjugal continence and the indissolubility of marriage, seemed to them the most serious obstacles in the progress of the Gospel."[89] When the Indians understood the marital implications of baptism, many pulled up short of the "yoke of single marriage" that the French wished to impose. As late as 1644 Father Vimont was still complaining that "of all the Christian laws which we propound to them, there is not one that seems so hard to them as that which forbids polygamy, and does not allow them to break the bonds of lawful marriage. . . . It is this that prevents most of the infidels from accepting the Faith, and has caused some to lose it who had already embraced it."[90]

The Christian way of life offered many other stumbling blocks for the Indians. Lenten fasting at the end of winter scarcity (even though the Sorbonne declared the beaver to be a fish for religious purposes); discriminating between people

after death when in life they had been equals; pretending
that Christians professed the one true faith when missionaries
from many denominations hawked their spiritual wares; confining people in the "yoke of God" on the Sabbath when the
struggle for life required a full week; being obsessed by death
and the afterlife, especially by the palpable threat of eternal
torture by fire; asserting that baptism conferred everlasting
life when it was often followed by death—all these practices
and more seemed unreasonable to a people who had been
raised in a religious tradition that was better adapted to the
natural and social world in which they lived.[91]

When the missionaries overstepped the native bounds of
courtesy and pressed them to change their thinking, the Indians made two characteristic responses, both of which constituted serious obstacles to their conversion. If during a theological debate with the missionary a native leader was not
convinced of the wisdom of the Christian position, he would
close it with a subtle plea for toleration. "All your arguments," warned Pierre Biard from experience with the Mic-
macs, "and you can bring on a thousand of them if you wish,
are annihilated by this single shaft which they always have at
hand, *Aoti Chabaya* (they say), 'That is the Indian way of
doing it. You can have your way and we will have ours; every
one values his own wares.' "[92] "If we reply that what they say
is not true, they answer that they have not disputed what we
have told them and that it is rude to interrupt a man when
he is speaking and tell him he is lying."[93] Sometimes the re-
jection could be quite pointed. The Iroquois at Shamokin
minced no words in spurning the offer of the Reverend David Brainerd in 1745 to settle among them for two years,
build a church, and call them together every Sunday "as the
whites do." "We are Indians," they announced, "and don't
wish to be transformed into white men. The English are our
Brethren, but we never promised to become what they are.
As little as we desire the preacher to become Indian, so little

ought he to desire the Indians to become preachers."[94] The preacher left the next day.

The Indians could have raised many objections to Christianity—and often did when pushed far enough—but usually only sachems, speakers, or shamans chose to lock minds with the Europeans on their own dialectical turf. Most simply deployed the ultimate Indian weapon against aggressive Europeans, a weapon that has frustrated the best-laid plans of white men for four centuries. Louis Hennepin, a Recollect priest who worked the Great Lakes and Illinois country, explained why "a savage must not be regarded as convinced as soon as he seems to approve the statements made him."

> Complete indifference to everything is a form of politeness with these Indians; they would consider a man ill bred if he did not agree to everything or if he contradicted arguments in council. Even though the most absurd and stupid things are said, they will always answer "*Niaova*—that is excellent, my brother; you are right." They believe, however, only what they privately choose to believe.[95]

On the receiving end of such treatment, not every missionary agreed that it sprang from "mere Civility." Claude Allouez chalked it up to "dissimulation," "a certain spirit of acquiescence," and "stubbornness and obstinacy."[96] After researching the history of the Canadian missions, Pierre de Charlevoix said it stemmed "sometimes from mere complacency, sometimes from some interested motive, more frequently from indolence and sloth."[97] Whatever its origins—and Hennepin was closer to the truth than his Jesuit counterparts—more European missionaries than one must have asked in frustration, "What can one do with those who in word give agreement and assent to everything, but in reality give none?"[98]

While the Indians deployed their secret weapon in the heat of cultural combat, they were seldom if ever the aggressors. For the path of least resistance was an extension of the

basic Indian toleration of other religions and the correspondent wish to pursue their own. "The *French* in general take
us for Beasts," Adario, the semi-fictional Huron sachem, told
his friend Lahontan, "the Jesuits brand us for impious, foolish, and ignorant Vagabonds. And to be even with you, we
have the same thoughts of you; but with this difference, that
we pity you without offering invectives."[99] Nor did the contrast end there, as Joseph Le Caron saw as early as 1624. "No
one must come here in hopes of suffering martyrdom . . . ,"
he counseled his Recollect brethren, "for we are not in a
country where savages put Christians to death on account of
their religion. They leave every one in his own belief."[100] It
was true, as every missionary knew. But being Christians they
persisted in their attempts to change the Indians.

Yet the missionaries' mediocre showing was due not only
to Indian resistance—which took many forms, including the
show of arms—but to the missions themselves. The poorest
record belonged to the few tardy missionaries who attempted
to preach the English gospel deep in Indian country, where
the long arm of English law did not reach even in the eighteenth century. Unlike their Jesuit competitors who came
early, stayed long, and strove to understand native ways before altering them, they persuaded none and alienated many
with their ethnocentric ineptitude.[101] Only their brothers who
worked among the remnant groups of New England enjoyed
anything like success.

The English missionaries' performance was closely rivaled
by that of the Indian schools, which were also few in number
and short-lived. If consumption or smallpox did not carry the
native students off prematurely, the racism of their English
fellows and masters, the sedentary life of study, corporal punishment, homesickness, and an irrelevant curriculum soon
drove them off. Perhaps those who graduated suffered the
cruelest irony when they discovered that their polite education earned them no place in English society, where merit

faced a color bar, and alienated them from their own. As an Iroquois council observed in rejecting an offer to send more of their sons to William and Mary, "after they returned to their Friends, they were absolutely good for nothing, being neither acquainted with the true methods of killing deer, catching Beaver or surprizing an enemy."[102] The major difficulty for Indian students was that they came to school too late and left too early, and received no social integration, racial tolerance, or love from the English. The passage from Indian to English culture was simply too long and too hard, and the English did little to make it any easier. The contrast with the Indian way of turning white captives into bona fide Indians could not have been starker.[103]

And yet during the colonial period many Indians did become Christians, both genuine and nominal, and adopted in some degree European ways. In New England alone, 91 praying towns were established before the Revolution, and 133 natives had qualified as teachers, catechists, or preachers to Indian congregations.[104] Many Algonquian and Iroquoian people were also persuaded that the Catholic, Anglican, Moravian, or Congregational faiths spoke more to their spiritual and cultural condition than did traditional religions.[105] How do we explain the existence and variety of these conversions while at the same time accounting for those Indian groups who remained stubbornly traditional?

Any explanation must begin with the continuous, long-term changes in native religion that occurred before the arrival of Columbus and his successors. As archaeology, folklore, and historical linguistics prove without question, no aspect of pre-Columbian Indian culture was static. Therefore we should resist the temptation to judge post-contact changes as either happy or tragic deviations from a noble norm of savage innocence. Purposeful change and adjustment was the only norm.

The first discernible changes occurred very early in the

pre-contact period when native groups borrowed particular beliefs, myths, culture heroes, religious artifacts, ceremonies, and even whole cults from other groups, some at considerable distances via long-established trade routes. Through this continuous process of borrowing and transfer, tribes in contiguous culture areas, such as the northeastern woodlands, came to share a large number of religious traits.

The next round of changes took place in response to the bruited arrival of the Europeans in the period of proto- or indirect contact. Before they actually met any Europeans, many tribes encountered often fabulous stories of white "gods" or "spirits," some of the products of their awesome technology, and their selectively lethal diseases. When the invaders finally appeared in Indian villages, thereby inaugurating the period of direct contact, the crisis of intellect precipitated by rampant sickness and death, novel forms of magic, and the unknown was only exacerbated by the need to account for the existence of strange bearded men with white skins and barbarous tongues who were obviously not, like themselves, "original people."[106]

The Indians responded to this general crisis in a variety of ways, depending largely on their geographical and political distance from colonial authority, their economic independence, the health of their population and the succession of leadership, their strength relative to neighbors who may have become allied with the invaders, and their intellectual and emotional flexibility and morale, which was the product of their recent past experience.

Tribes who still enjoyed relatively healthy populations, stable social structures, and political and economic independence could choose to deal with the Christian missionary in at least four ways. They could, as many groups in New England did, direct a steady stream of searching questions at him about the consistency of his theology.[107] Or they could question its applicability to their culture by unleashing their polite but frustrating "secret weapon" of outer agreement and inner disagreement. On the other hand, if the proselytizer annoyed them enough, they could simply ignore him until he despaired and went home, or if he persisted, they could chase him away with arms or kill him as a troublemaker and witch. Whatever course of action they chose, the result was the persistence of traditional religion and the unimpaired authority of the native priest.

Sooner or later, all the eastern tribes began to lose their aboriginal sovereignty and strength. As colonial settlements drew closer, disease tore at the native social fabric, leaving gaps in the web of kinship, political succession, technological expertise, and corporate memory. Trade goods from the shops and factories of Europe became desirable luxuries, then necessities. Entangling alliances forced the tribes into the periodic embrace of the colonial governments when they could no longer play them off against each other. And missionaries were emboldened to plunge into native cantons in search of converts. In these dangerous though not yet fatal circumstances, the native community split into factions as different individuals and interest groups variously perceived the nature of the problems facing them and the best solutions. A dissident minority always had the option of voting with its feet, as was common in pre-Columbian times, by moving to either a more traditional village or a Christian praying town or *reserve*. More frequently, a faction stayed to fight for the political and social control of the community resources and its future religious and cultural direction.

Those who saw an urgent need to adjust to post-European conditions without surrendering their ethnic and cultural identity could exercise two options—if both existed. The first was to join a revitalization movement led by a native prophet or charismatic figure who warned the Indians to reaffirm their ancient beliefs and resume their ancient ways before the Europeans captured their spirits as well as their furs.

Many of these leaders, such as the eighteenth-century Delaware Prophet and Handsome Lake in the early nineteenth century, incorporated Christian elements in their religions while clearly rejecting Christianity itself. Many others, however, were intolerant of any foreign intrusions, seeking to restore their culture to an imagined pre-contact purity.[108]

A second option was also to revitalize native culture but through the selective use of Christianity rather than nativism. Tribes who escaped the worst maladies of European contact had little need of the full "civilized" cure offered by the Christian doctors. To have taken it would have brought on premature cultural suicide. But the complete prescription did contain some useful ingredients, such as political and military alliance, guaranteed land, economic aid, and trade advantages. If to obtain them the Indians had to swallow the bitter pill of religious conversion, the sacrifice was small enough, considering that Christianity might truly satisfy some new intellectual or emotional hunger. If there was none to be satisfied, the convert could simply, in time-honored Indian fashion, add the power of the Christian God to that of his own deities and proceed to syncretize the beliefs and practices of the new religion with the deep structures of his traditional faith. By accepting the Christian priest as the functional equivalent of a native shaman and by giving traditional meanings to Christian rites, dogmas, and deities, the Indians ensured the survival of native culture by taking on the protective coloration of the invaders' culture. Obviously, this brand of Christianity often lay very lightly on the surface of their lives, its acceptance largely expedient to ensure their independence and group identity. But many Indians found in Christianity genuine sources of spiritual strength that helped them cope with their rapidly changing world. As John Smith noticed very early, "all things that were able to do them hurt beyond their prevention, they adore with their kinde of divine worship."[109]

Several tribes who responded even more positively to the mission offerings were the coastal Algonquians of southern New England. So seriously were they crippled by a plague in 1616-18 and so thoroughly overrun by the colonial juggernaut in the following two decades that only John Eliot's complete system of moral rearmament, social reconstruction, and religious revitalization was capable of saving them from ethnic annihilation. Lacking any viable options, large numbers of them, led in many cases by traditional leaders of the "blood," converted to Christianity and the English way of life that accompanied it. Even though their conversion entailed wholesale cultural changes, it preserved their ethnic identity as particular Indian groups on familiar pieces of land that carried their inner history. At the cost of a certain amount of material and spiritual continuity with the past, their acceptance of Christianity—however sincere—allowed them not only to survive in the present but gave them a long lease on life when many of their colonial landlords threatened to foreclose all future options. Ironically, the acute English sense of cultural superiority—which was colored by racism before the eighteenth century—helped the Indians to maintain the crucial ethnic core at the heart of their newly acquired Christian personae. In colonial eyes, they were still Indians and always would be, no matter how "civilized" or Christianized they became. Despite the assimilative goal of the missions, the English had serious limitations as agents of social reconstruction. They were far better at "rooting out" than transplanting.

On any frontier, acculturation is normally a two-way process, especially in the early stages of contact. But in colonial North America the direction of religious change—unlike changes in other aspects of culture—was decidedly unilinear, largely because Indian religion was pragmatically incorporative and tolerant of other faiths, and Christianity was aggressively evangelical and exclusive. Indian religious culture was forever on the defensive, trying to minimize the adjustments necessary to group survival and independence; Christianity sought to cajole or strong-arm the natives into spiritual submission. Any changes in colonial religion were minor and self-generated, and not due to native pressure to convert to a False Face or Midéwiwin society. At most, the Indian presence sporadically brought out the evangelical inheritance of some of the colonial denominations and moved them marginally away from their own narrow brand of tribalism.

To be on the defensive, however, does not imply the total loss of initiative. The Indians were incredibly tenacious of their culture and life-style, but their traditionalism was neither blind nor passive. As the history of the missions clearly shows, the native peoples of the Northeast were remarkably resourceful in adjusting to new conditions, especially in using elements of European religious culture for their own purposes. According to the social and political circumstances in which they found themselves after contact, they accepted the missionaries' offerings in just the amounts necessary to maintain their own cultural identity. They may have made individual or short-term miscalculations of self-interest, white strength, and policy direction—no group is capable of a perfect functionalism—but in general they took what they needed for resistance and accepted only as much as would ensure survival. Because of their creative adaptability and the defects of the mission programs, many Indian people were never fully "washed white in the blood of the lamb." Although their outer lives could be partially "reduced to civility," their inner resources were equal to the invasion within. As long as native people continued to think of themselves as "original people," the religious frontiers of North America remained open.

CHAPTER FOUR

Dr. Wheelock's Little Red School

BECAUSE ETHNOHISTORY DEMANDS SO MANY DIFFERENT SPECIALIZED skills from at least two disciplines, complete ethnohistorians are rare. William N. Fenton is one of them. As a student of all phases and facets of Iroquois culture, as an ethnologist with a keen historical sense, as a master of the library, the museum, and the field, and as a model of and spokesman for the ethnohistorical art, he is without peer. When I was invited in 1976 to contribute an essay to a festschrift to honor his forthcoming retirement from the State University of New York at Albany, I was pleased to be able to express my large debt to his friendship and example.

Appropriately, it was at the Iroquois Conference in 1977 that I read the following essay in Bill's honor. As it turned out, my topic could hardly have been more pertinent. When I was asked to contribute to the festschrift I had just spent several months reading the papers of Eleazar Wheelock, the founder of Moor's Charity School for Indians and later of Dartmouth College, Bill's alma mater. One of the first things I had discovered—which was news mostly to me—was that the majority of Indian students at Wheelock's school were Iroquois. What was not generally known, however, was that Wheelock had designs upon a large piece of Iroquois territory, allegedly to support his school, and that he was so unsuccessful in educating Indians, especially the Iroquois, that he diverted school funds to found Dartmouth, not to create an Indian college, as myth would have it, but to get out of the Indian business by preparing white scholars for missions and the ministry. With facts like those to explain, the irony of my title was inevitable. I was happy to see that Bill took my irreverent disclosures in stride, perhaps because we shared a larger loyalty to historical objectivity and a smaller one to Yale, where he had done his graduate work.

Somewhat less equable was the reaction of the Dartmouth College community when I delivered the paper in Hanover the following October. The Native American Studies people who sponsored the lecture were understandably pleased to have more ammunition for their fight against campus indifference and prejudice. Some of the non-Indians may have equally welcomed it as historical justification for de-emphasizing or dismantling the Native American Studies program, but it probably lent little aid to the alumni cause of reinstating the college's Indian symbol. Although my personal sympathies lie with more and better higher education for Indians who want it, I did not write the essay as a contemporary credo. Having carefully read the pertinent primary sources, I made my judgment on the basis of what I saw happen in the past, not what I wanted to see happen in the future. In this instance, my facts and interpretation probably appeal more to the real Dartmouth Indians than to their collegiate namesakes. On another topic, the invention of scalping, for example, Indian activists are likely to derive small comfort from my findings. What this suggests is that personal biases and sympathies will inevitably lead ethnohistorians to choose certain topics and ask certain questions, but the application of their professional training to the sources may very well lead to conclusions that are if not unwanted at least double-edged.

Oh, E-le-a-zar Whee-lock was a ver-y pi-ous man;
He went in-to the wil-der-ness to teach the In-di-an.

Richard Hovey, "Eleazar Wheelock"

To generations of Dartmouth men—and lately women—
who have sung his praises, Eleazar Wheelock was the pious
founder not only of their beautiful alma mater but of a
venerable tradition of educational benevolence. Popular legend and collegial folklore tell us that Dartmouth was hewn
out of the New Hampshire forest as an "Indian college" to
convert the natives to Christianity and civilization. Although
the Indian symbol of the college's origins has come under
unlikely attack in recent years, the legend itself remains
healthy. The stoic warrior who emblazoned Dartmouth sweat-
shirts and beer mugs and braved frosty autumn afternoons
bare-chested to cheer the football team is all but dead, the
victim of a new generation of unstereotypical Indian students. But the college motto designed by Wheelock still features an aboriginal "voice crying in the wilderness" for the
white man's brand of salvation.

Not surprisingly, the man who did the most to link Dartmouth with the Indians in our historical imagination was
Wheelock himself. An indefatigable publicist and politician,
he assured his friends and tried to persuade his enemies that
his college in Hanover was nothing more than a noble continuation of his Indian school in Lebanon, Connecticut. To
disarm the skeptical, he carefully worded the college charter to certify that Dartmouth was intended "for the education & instruction of Youth of the Indian Tribes in this Land
in reading, writing & all parts of Learning which shall appear necessary and expedient for civilizing & christianizing
Children of Pagans as well as in all liberal Arts and Sci-

ences . . . ," to which he added, as if an afterthought, "and also of English Youth and any others."[1] The New Hampshire legislature, at least, was sufficiently convinced of the Doctor's sincerity to incorporate the college in 1769.

Nor has posterity questioned the official version of Dartmouth's founding, if numerous American histories are any index. Dartmouth usually appears in general textbooks in two places. The most frequent reference is to the Dartmouth College Case in 1819 when alumnus Daniel Webster argued successfully before the Supreme Court that the state of New Hampshire had no right to revoke the college charter and place Dartmouth under state jurisdiction. Few textbooks omit this landmark decision because it established judicial precedent for the protection of private corporations from the power of the state. The other place where Dartmouth appears is the section devoted to the "Great Awakening," that revival of puritanical religious feeling associated with Jonathan Edwards and George Whitefield that began in New England during the late 1730s and soon spread to the Middle Atlantic colonies. In this context Dartmouth always appears in the company of Brown and Princeton as a product of the denominational "College Enthusiasm," a "New Light" (as the revivalists were called) challenge to the spiritual torpor of Yale and especially Harvard. Invariably, the new college in Hanover is described as a direct "outgrowth" of Wheelock's Indian school in Connecticut. Even specialized studies of the Great Awakening perpetuate the legend of the "Indian School at Lebanon [which] was later moved to New Hampshire where it became Dartmouth College."[2]

The "Indian college" tradition has survived largely because it fails to distinguish between Wheelock's (actually Moor's) Indian Charity School and Dartmouth College. The Doctor *did* found and maintain a well-known school for Indians in Connecticut for some fifteen years. He *did* found a college in New Hampshire in 1769 that claimed to have Indian education as its primary focus. And he *did* move the Indian school to Hanover in 1770 to prepare boys for admission to Dartmouth. But the college and the school were always distinct, though Wheelock did little to discourage, and sometimes more than a little to foster, their identification. Only by untangling the histories of these two institutions can we establish Wheelock's true motives in founding Dartmouth and the aptness of the Indian as the college symbol.

According to his own recollection, Eleazar Wheelock was no Johnny-come-lately to Indian affairs. He told an Iroquois council in 1765 that he had had the Indians upon his heart "ever since I was a boy"—he had been born in Windham, Connecticut, in 1711—and that he had prayed daily for their temporal and spiritual salvation for the past thirty years.[3] But not until the Great Awakening did providence bring him his first native student.

After earning a bachelor's degree at Yale, Wheelock had been licensed to preach in 1734 and the following year was called to the pulpit of the Second Congregational Church in Lebanon. When the Great Awakening of religious fervor broke over New England in 1740, Wheelock was its warmest supporter in Connecticut. He traveled extensively, preached persuasively, and served as the chief intelligencer of revival news. But the religious establishment of the colony, the so-called "Old Lights," did not appreciate his itinerancy, the neglect of his own parish, or his promulgation of "a meer *passionate* Religion." So in 1743 he was deprived of his church salary (though not his office) by the General Assembly act "for regulating abuses and correcting disorders in ecclesiastical affairs."[4]

Although Wheelock owned considerable farmland, the loss of his salary prompted him to take a few English boys into his house for college preparation. They were soon joined by Samson Occom, a young Mohegan Indian from New London,

Connecticut, who came to Wheelock with the hope of improving his self-taught literacy in three or four weeks of tuition. As a leading "New Light," Wheelock saw an opportunity to extend the divine hand to New England's non-white pagans, and invited the twenty-year-old Indian to join his small group of students. Occom stayed nearly five years, in which time he became a devoted Christian, an affecting public speaker, and a partial convert to the English way of life. Despite his unusual accomplishments, however, there was no place for a man of his color in English society. He returned to a wigwam and spent the next twelve years in poverty, teaching and preaching to the Montauk Indians on Long Island, binding books, and carving spoons, pails, and gunstocks for his white neighbors, most of whom were his spiritual and intellectual inferiors.[5]

If Occom's postgraduate career did not speak well for the conceptual clarity of Wheelock's later design, the Doctor was unaware of it. In late 1754 he took two Delaware Indian boys under his wing, which prompted a charitable neighbor, Colonel Joshua More, to endow the fledgling school with several buildings and two acres of land. By the summer of 1761 "Moor's Charity School" had accepted ten Indian students from the "remnant" tribes of the northeastern seaboard. But with the fall of Canada a wide door was opened to the relatively uncontaminated "back nations" of America, and Wheelock entered it with a driving vision of tawny souls blanched by the Bible.

General James Wolfe's victory on the Plains of Abraham was well timed, for Wheelock was becoming increasingly disenchanted with the "little Tribes" of New England. Schools set among them, he felt, had always failed because the natives placed no value on the white man's "Learning," led an unsettled, impoverished existence, lacked any social or familial authority, and resented the English masters who tried to impose a "good and necessary Government" over their children.[6]

Samson Occom (1723-1792), the first Indian pupil of the Reverend
Eleazar Wheelock, founder of Moor's Indian Charity School in Lebanon,
Connecticut, and later of Dartmouth College. From a 1768 mezzotint in
the Dartmouth College Archives.

Most damning of all in Wheelock's eyes was their stubborn ingratitude for the inestimable benefits offered by Protestant saints such as himself. It was simply foolish to waste God's time and the public's money on ingrates while there were "such Vast Numbers intirely without Means of Knowledge and"—he was assured by friends—"continually suing and pleading for Missionaries and Schoolmasters to be sent among them."[7] Turning his back on too-familiar local tribes, Wheelock was quickly captured by the unknown challenge of the Six Nations.

He did not have long to wait before confronting the challenge he had so blindly and blithely accepted. On August 1, 1761, three Mohawk boys sent by Sir William Johnson, the British superintendent of Indian Affairs, arrived in Lebanon with "great Caution and Fear." Each brought a horse, "prepared to return in haste, if there should be occasion."[8] One, Joseph Brant, understood a little English and, being the son of a "Family of Distinction," was "considerably cloathed."[9] But his teen-aged companions, Negyes and Center, were nearly naked and "very lousey."[10] Neither could "speak a Word of English."[11] Center was visibly ill, his "blood spoiled" according to the local physician, so he was sent home to die. But not before swallowing the bitter pill of white prejudice. "I was very sorry," Wheelock wrote Johnson, "for the Jealousies which the [English] Schollars conceived concerning the Nature of Center's Disorder while I was gone to Boston, and that there was that said or done which gave him a Disgust."[12] Negyes, too, was soon lost to the cause, for when he accompanied Center home he was "captivated by a young Female and married."[13]

Less than four months later two Mohawk boys arrived to take their places, "direct from the wigwams." One had learned "4 or 5 letters in the Alphabet, the other knew not one, nor could either of them Speak a Word of English." Excepting "two old Blankets & Indian Stockins," their clothing "was not worth Sixpence." And as Wheelock had come to expect of such "poor little Naked Creatures," "they were very lousey, which occasioned considerable Trouble." Yet they were hardly typical schoolboys. Johannes had "carried a Gun" in the army that captured Montreal the previous year—at the age of twelve.[14]

A scant two weeks after their arrival, Wheelock penned a *cri de coeur* that might well stand as the motto of Moor's Charity School: "Few conceive aright of the Difficulty of Educating an Indian and turning him into an Englishman but those who undertake the Trial of it."[15] To the Reverend George Whitefield, who had the good sense not to try, he explained his predicament:

> They would soon kill themselves with Eating and Sloth, if constant care were not exercised for them at least the first year. They are used to set upon the Ground, and it is as natural for them as a seat to our Children. They are not wont to have any Cloaths but what they wear, nor will without much Pains be brought to take care of any. They are used to a Sordid Manner of Dress, and love it as well as our Children to be clean. They are not used to any Regular Government, the sad consequences of which you may a little guess at. They are used to live from Hand to Mouth (as we speak) and have no care for Futurity. They have never been used to the Furniture of an English House, and dont know but that a Wine-glass is as strong as an Hand Iron. Our Language when they seem to have got it is not their Mother Tongue and they cannot receive nor communicate in that as in their own . . . And they are as unpolished and uncultivated within as without.[16]

Predictably, time and experience brought little relief, and Wheelock's list of headaches only grew. Before he moved the school to Hanover in 1770, he tried to turn some 67 native children—49 boys and 18 girls—into English men and women.[17] Many came from the New England tribes with a helpful modicum of English language, dress, and religion, but the largest number—thirty—were Iroquois, tough adolescents like Johannes and Negyes with an ingrained suspicion of the English and their schemes for "reducing" them to "civility." In his *Narrative* of the school to 1771, Wheelock boasted that he had produced forty "good readers, and writers," all sufficiently masters of English grammar and arithmetic and some advanced in Latin and Greek, who had behaved well in school and left with "fair and unblemished characters." But he also admitted that "I don't hear of more than half who have preserved their characters unstain'd either by a course of intemperance or uncleanness, or both; and some who on account of their parts, and learning, bid the fairest for usefulness, are sunk down into as low, savage, and brutish a manner of living as they were in before any endeavours were used with them to raise them up."[18] Six of the best were already dead.

If these twenty apostates are added to the twenty-seven matriculants who dropped out prematurely (most of whom were Iroquois), Moor's Charity School—on its own accounting—enjoyed a success rate in the *short* run of something less than thirty percent. Perhaps this figure fell within the range of Wheelock's expectations after his introduction to the Iroquois. In 1763 he told his public benefactors that "if one half of the Indian boys thus educated shall prove good and useful men, there will be no reason to regret our toil and expence for the whole . . . and if but one in ten does so, we shall have no cause to think much of the expence."[19] In all likelihood the public had somewhat higher hopes for their benefactions, as well they might at an annual cost of £16 to 20 per boy, the equivalent, some critics said, of that for an English boy at Harvard College.[20]

A satisfactory explanation for this inauspicious record is hard to find. Colonial critics suggested that the native students came too late and left too early, that the curriculum was inappropriate, and that the goal of civilizing the Indians before Christianizing them was unnecessary if not impossible in the first place. Wheelock's characteristic response was to lament the heartbreaking "Behavior of some I have taken unwearied pains for" and to turn his energies toward a less frustrating project.[21] Rather than redefine his objectives, he merely sought more malleable subjects. But of all people, the Indians—his students and their parents—had the best insights into the cause of Wheelock's failure, a failure magnified by the boundless ambition and unblinking certitude of his goals.

Like those of his Puritan predecessors, Wheelock's missionary goals were essentially two: to save the Indians from themselves and to save the English from the Indians. The best way to accomplish both was, as he stated so facilely, to turn the Indians into Englishmen. In religious terms one of the primary goals of nearly all the American colonies was the "enlargement of Christian Religion" and the "propagating of the gospel" (Protestant version) to the western hemisphere.[22] In Massachusetts, where Wheelock's great-grandfather landed in 1637, the settlers were enjoined in the royal charter to live such exemplary lives that their "orderlie conversation maie wynn and incite the natives of the country to the knowledg and obedience of the onlie true God and Savior of mankinde, and the Christian fayth."[23] The key word was obedience, as it was to be in all the English dealings with the natives. Unlike the king's patent, most of the colonial plans for Indian missions spoke of *re*ducing rather than *se*ducing Indians to "Civil Societie and Christian Religion."[24] The reason was simple—if you subscribed to the English cosmology. In English eyes the Indians were "savages," beings closer to "brutes" than to true "men," whose unbridled impulses needed to be tamed by God's chosen people.[25]

From such premises it was obvious to "the most sensible Writers" of Wheelock's day that "it is necessary to civilize Savages before they can be converted to Christianity."[26] With fitting medical metaphor, the Doctor said that his educational goal was to "cure the Natives . . . of their Savage Temper" and to "purge all the Indian out" of his students.[27] Even a casual acquaintance with eighteenth-century medical practices will convey the full rigor of the treatment implied. Yet the medicine, however caustic, was administered in the patients' best interests. Without a strong purgative to rid the Indians of their "savage" disorders, their body politic would not absorb the "civilized" antidote to the white man's contaminants—alcohol and land greed. Only a settled agricultural life like that of the English colonists could guarantee the Indians' subsistence "when their Resources from the Wilderness fail, (as they certainly must do, when, and so fast, as the English extend their Settlements among them)."[28] And time was running out, especially for the obstinate Iroquois. "They evidently appear to be in, and very far gone already by, a quick consumption," wrote Wheelock in 1771, "they are wasting like a morning dew . . . before the rising sun."[29]

If the "savages" could be saved from themselves, the English would also be saved from the "savages"—and could turn a pretty penny in the bargain. For Anglicized Indians would no longer threaten the English frontiers, which could then be greatly extended westward. Wheelock and his colleagues were convinced that missions and schools for the Indians were far more effective and far less expensive instruments of colonial policy than guns, armies, and gifts. If the missions had worked as well in practice as they did on paper, they would have been right. "Nothing can be more Agreeable to our Christian Character than to send the Gospel to the benighted Pagans," a like-minded friend wrote Wheelock, "Nothing more Conducive to our Civil Interests than to bring them to a Subjection to the Religion of Jesus."[30] "Civilizing the Indians" was tantamount to "reducing them to Peace and good Order," according to the mission litany, and only by "being civilized, and taught the Knowledge of the only true GOD and SAVIOR" could they be made "good Members of Society, and peaceable and quiet Neighbours."[31] But either way the English stood to gain. "For if [the Indians] receive the gospel," admitted Wheelock, "they will soon betake themselves to agriculture for their support, and so will need but a very small part, comparatively, of the lands which they now claim . . . ; and if they will not receive the gospel, they will, as they have done, waste away before it . . . ."[32]

Wheelock's way of winning the Indians to Christian civility was to induce native children, usually aged eleven to fourteen, to come to his school in Connecticut, far removed from the "pernicious Influence of their Parents Example."[33] There he proceeded to inure them to "Decency and Cleanliness" in the form of soap and water, English clothes, and, of course, the critical difference between handirons and wineglasses.[34] In an atmosphere of beetle-browed piety, they were initiated into the arcana of the Westminster Assembly's *Shorter Catechism,* the English alphabet and grammar, arithmetic, and, in still more abstruse languages, the pastoral classics of ancient Greece and Rome. Since they were designed to return to their own villages as preachers, teachers, and interpreters of the English way, they were encouraged to retain their native languages and to teach them as well to their fellow students—Indians from other tribes and English boys preparing for Indian missions. Their spare time was "improved" by learning a trade, such as blacksmithing, from a local master or "husbandry" from the hands on Wheelock's farm. Native girls were apprenticed to local women to learn "the Female Part, as House-wives, School-mistresses, [and] Tayloresses" whereby they, as the helpmates of the native missionaries, would prevent "their turning savage in their Manner of Living, for want of those who may do those Offices for them."[35] Over all, Wheelock sought to spread a benevolent but firm patriarchalism, to treat them as "My [own] Children" and to make them feel at home as "in a Father's House."[36] What the

Indians, especially the Iroquois, soon discovered, however, was that English children were treated much differently from children in the longhouse.

One of the reasons, perhaps the main reason, Wheelock preferred to locate his school among the English was that he knew the Indians' "great Fondness for their Children" was incompatible with the birchen "Government" necessary to "humble them, and reform their Manners."[37] "Here, he admitted, "I can correct, & punish them as I please, . . . but there, it will not be born."[38] When in 1772 the Onondaga council rejected for the last time Wheelock's offer to educate their children, they condemned ten years of hard usage of Iroquois children at the hands of his self-fulfilling prophecy. Grabbing Wheelock's high-handed son Ralph by the shoulder and shaking him, the council speaker replied with unaccustomed anger: "Brother, do you think we are altogether ignorant of your methods of instruction? . . . We understand not only your speech, but your *manner* of teaching Indian[s]. . . . Brother, take care," he warned, "you were too hasty, & strong in your manner of speaking, before the children & boys have any knowledge of your language." And then in a verbal slap that must have stung the Wheelocks' Protestant souls to the quick, he concluded: "Brother, you must learn of the French ministers if you would understand, & know how to treat Indians. They don't speak roughly, nor do they for every little mistake take up a club & flog them."[39]

The sting of the rod was perhaps the sharpest indignity the Indians suffered, but it was not the only one nor the worst. The school's work program, aimed at teaching the boys in play time to farm, seemed to the boys little more than an elaborate ruse for getting the master's chores done at no expense. Wheelock hoped that part-time farm work would "effectually remove the deep prejudices, so universally in the minds of the Indians, against their men's cultivating lands."[40] Instead, it seemed to confirm them and to create new ones against the Doctor for taking advantage of his students. Long was Wheelock's list of Indian students who were "reluctant to exercise [themselves] in, or learn any thing about Husbandry."[41] Only slightly shorter was the roster of complaining students and parents. John Daniel, a Narragansett parent, told Wheelock that "I always tho't Your School was free to the Natives; not to learn them how to Farm it, but to advance in Christian Knowledge, which wear the Chief motive that caus'd me to send my Son Charles to you; not that I'm anything against his Labouring some for You, when Business lies heavy on you," he allowed, "but to work two Years to learn to Farm it, is what I don't consent to . . . ."[42] The Onondaga council simply made it clear that they expected their children to be treated "as *children* at your house, & not *servants!*"[43] But the last word came from Daniel Simon, a Narragansett and later Dartmouth's first Indian graduate (1777): "if we poor Indians Shall work as much as to pay for our learning," he told Wheelock, "we Can go some other place as good as here for learning."[44]

When Hezekiah Calvin, a Delaware and one of Wheelock's former schoolmasters to the Iroquois, opted out of the Doctor's "Design" in 1768, he let it be known around New England that the inmates of Moor's School were not one big happy family. A Rhode Island correspondent told Wheelock that Calvin had "given the School a bad Charracter," complaining (among other things) that "you use the Indians very hard in keeping of them to work, & not allowing them a proper Privelidge in the School, that you . . . Diot & Cloath them with that that's mean, . . . That Mary [Secutor, a Narragansett] ask'd for a small peice of Cloth to make a p[ai]r of Slippers, which you would not allow her, [saying] twas to[o] good for Indians &c . . . [and] That you wont give no more of the Indians more learning than to Read, & Write—[alleging] 'twill make them Impudent; for which they are all about to leave you."[45]

Regardless of the accuracy of these criticisms, many of the Indians and their tribesmen *felt* them to be true. What was not in doubt, however, was that the Indian students were surrounded on every side by overt prejudice that often exceeded cultural arrogance and fell clearly into the category of racism. Wheelock instinctively knew that native students could never be mixed with English (except those special few who were preparing for Indian missions), "for it hath been found by some few Instances of *Indians* educated elsewhere, that the *English* Students have been apt to look upon them with an Air of *disdain,* which these Sons of *ranging* Liberty cannot so well brook."[46] For this reason even Yale, his alma mater, was inappropriate for his Indian graduates; too many sons of Eli would "disdain in their Hearts to be Associates and Companions with an Indian. And what the Consequences of such Contempt of them will be is not hard to guess."[47]

The problem could also be found closer to home. Wheelock had great difficulty in apprenticing his Indian boys because "their fellow Prentices viz. English Boys will dispise them & treat them as Slaves."[48] In 1765 David Fowler, an older Montauk student, received such an "injury" and "provocations" from the Lebanon townies in a sleighing incident that his mentor was somewhat surprised that his new "Christian forebearance" overcame his native spirit of revenge.[49] Even a young minister turned down Wheelock's offer of an Indian mission because, he said, "[I] should be prodigiously apt to batter some of their Noses, or else Skulk and run for it."[50]

The pestilence of racism, however, infected all of New England, especially during the Seven Years' War and the Indian "rebellion" that concluded it. Wheelock could not raise funds for the school because his potential donors in the colonial legislatures and churches "breath[ed] forth nothing towards [the Indians] but Slaughter & destruction."[51] A collection plate passed in Windsor, Connecticut, in 1763 returned empty save for "a Bullet & Flynt," symbolizing an attitude that survived in Wheelock's own colony long after the frontier hostilities had ceased.[52] Four years later the table conversation of several gentlemen in Middletown was reported to Wheelock, and it could not have pleased—or much surprised—him. They spoke frankly of the hopelessness of converting Indians by anything but "Powder & Ball." On the basis of a wide acquaintance with "human nature," at least as he knew it in New England, one of them declared the Doctor's scheme "absurd & fruitlis" because of "the ireconsilable avertion, that white people must ever have to black. . . . So long as the Indians are dispised by the English we may never expect success in Christianizing of them." For their own parts, the gentlemen confessed that "they could never respect an Indian, Christian or no Christian, so as to put him on a level with white people on any account, especially to eat at the same Table, no—not with Mr [Samson] Ocham himself, be he ever so much a Christian or ever so Learned."[53] As the cultural competition of the seventeenth century gave way to the racial antipathies of the eighteenth, popular support in America for "Grand Designs" such as Wheelock's evaporated.

There was a slim chance that the Indian students could have withstood the corrosive currents of popular prejudice that swirled about them if Wheelock had shown some sensitivity to their cultural dilemma and sustained his originally high sense of their purpose. Unfortunately he did not, for his cultural and theological assumptions were as ethnocentric and racist as those of his neighbors, and the Indians were quickly reduced to a secondary role in their own salvation. If he was not before, the Great Awakening turned Wheelock into a seventeenth-century religious Puritan. For the misnamed "New Lights" of the revival, the religious premises of the old covenant theology acquired renewed relevance. Basic to that theology was a dim view of human nature, which had been corrupted at the source by Adam's fall, and a belief that the original sin, pride, must be constantly crushed in man to allow God's omnipotent will full sway. That in Wheelock's eyes the Indians were the proudest people on earth did nothing to make their life in Moor's School an easy one.

Of all the sins committed by his Indian students, none so angered Wheelock as "Insufferable pride," which he felt to be the foundation of their "Contempt of all Authority," particularly his own.[54] When Jacob Woolley, a twenty-year-old Delaware, got drunk, threw a clench-fisted tantrum, cursed God, and tried to throw his bed out the window, Wheelock judged him not culturally disoriented or personally frustrated but simply guilty of "Pride of Heart," and administered several stripes to "humble & tame him."[55] When he ran away to the Mohegans five months later, Wheelock presented him with an "Indian Blanket" because he had renounced his "polite education" and "herded with Indians (little better than Savages)." A clerical correspondent agreed that this was a "mortification" more "humbling" than blows or stripes, and added his hope to Wheelock's that "God will yet humble him."[56] In such an atmosphere it was inevitable that Wheelock's need to dominate absolutely would collide with the sons of the Mohawks, who were, he complained, "proud and high in their own Esteem above any other Tribe, having long been reckon[e]d at the head of the Nations."[57] In 1767 he rusticated two Mohawk youths, though, understandably, not without some misgivings. "Great William," the natural son of Sir William Johnson by an Indian woman, had been "too proud, & litigious to consist with the Health & well being" of the school. His traveling companion, who had been at the school only a few months, was "so lifted up with his having been in the Wars, and sent to Hell one or two of the poor Savages with his own hand, that [Wheelock's] House was scarcely good enough for him to live in, or any of the School honourable enough to speak to him. . . . There is," the Doctor told Sir William, "& shall be Government in this School."[58]

At the root of Wheelock's unhappy relations with his Indian students was a racial attitude that placed Indians on a level with blacks—on the lowest shelf of humanity. Like many of his contemporaries, Wheelock frequently referred to his "Black" children, especially his "black son" Samson Occom, and to the "Black Tribes" on the frontier who needed his help, a verbal preference that was not lost on his students.[59] Just the way they wrote to him, even as adults, betrays how they must have been treated and taught to think of themselves in his presence. Joseph Johnson must have been taught well. On one occasion he referred to himself as "a Despicable Lump of polluted Clay, as is inclosed in this tawny skin of mine," on another as "your Ignorant Pupil, and good for nothing Black Indian." "If I was an Englishman, & was thus Respected by you," he wrote, "I should be very thankful, but much more doth it now become me, being an Indian, to be humble & very thankfull in very deed." Though Johnson was a Mohegan, he sought temporary relief from his educated self-abasement among the Oneidas in 1768 when "he turn'd pagan for about a week—painted, sung, danc'd, drank & whor'd it, with some of the savage Indians he could find."[60] Hezekiah Calvin, the Delaware drop-out, may have chosen an even apter symbol of protest: he is last seen in prison for "forging a pass for a Negro."[61] As an owner of black slaves for much of his life, Wheelock was perfectly capable of distinguishing the two races; that he did not suggests an unconscious reduction of the people he was consciously trying to elevate and a deep ambivalence about his "Grand Design."

Wheelock's innate distrust of the Indians worked to the surface during the course of the 1760s. Originally he felt that Indian missionaries were superior to Englishmen and gave a dozen reasons in his first *Narrative* (1763). Yet as early as 1760 he was planning to take "poor & promising [English] Youth" into the school "in case of a failure of Indians."[62] By the time the first Iroquois arrived he was no longer talking privately of Indians as schoolmasters, interpreters, *and* missionaries—only of the first two. He was obviously lowering his sights. In 1762 he had his revised plans confirmed by the Boston Board of the Scottish Society that funded much of his work. "If the Design is to Educate only a few that shall be qualified, to be Missionaries, Schoolmasters &c," they wrote, "We Apprehend Indians will not be so proper for these Purposes, as Persons Selected from Among the English."[63] After several frustrating years with his Iroquois students, the Doctor needed only an excuse to complete his institutional shift to white missionaries.

In the winter of 1769 the Oneidas provided one by abruptly withdrawing their six children. They gave Wheelock an innocuous reason, but he suspected two others: that "an ugly fellow" had spread "Slanders" that "their Children were not well treated" at school, and that, having heard a rumor of an impending Indian war with the colonies, they were "not willing their children should be with the English [as hostages] at such a time."[64] Whatever their reasons, Wheelock considered their action providential; he sent the other Iroquois students home and prepared to move to Hanover to found a college for English missionaries. God, he told his English benefactors, had convinced him that "Indians may not have the lead in the Affair, 'till they are made new Creatures." Their "Sloth," "want of Stability," and "doleful Apostacy" disqualified them.[65]

In the future, after the Indian school was transplanted in less fertile New Hampshire soil, Wheelock would prefer native students from the "praying towns" or Indian *reserves* of Canada—St. Francis, Lorette, Caughnawaga—who were descended from adopted English captives, even though most had been raised as Catholics. "Though they were born among the *Indians*," he wrote, "and have been exposed to partake of their national Vices . . . ; yet they appear to be as sprightly, active, enterprising, benevolent towards all, and sensible of Kindnesses done them, as English Children commonly are."[66]

His racial preference was unmistakable, as was his characteristic feeling that the "other" Indians, just over the horizon, were always more susceptible to his designs. These Anglo-Indians, he vowed, were "by far the most promising set of Youths, I have ever yet had from the Indian Country."[67] How quickly he had forgotten his words to Sir William Johnson only a few years before: "The Boys I have from your parts behave very well, better than any I have had from any other Quarter, and it seems to me they are really a much better Breed."[68] Apparently the Doctor wished to begin his experiment in cultural transmogrification with subjects who resembled as nearly as possible his desired results. With the unpromising methods and attitudes he employed, that was perhaps the only way to ensure success.

Wheelock's self-confessed failure to produce a cadre of native missionaries made in his own image met with a timely remedy in 1767 upon the return of Samson Occom and the Reverend Nathaniel Whitaker from a fund-raising tour of England and Scotland. Sent by Wheelock to procure donations for his Indian school, the pair raised more than £12,000 during their two-year sojourn.[69] This enormous windfall enabled Wheelock to sever all ties with the missionary societies upon which he had long depended and to begin a serious search for a way to subordinate his involvement in the unrewarding "Indian business" to a project that gave more scope to his energy, political acumen, and need to dominate. He found such an outlet in Dartmouth, a liberal arts *college* intended primarily for English missionaries that borrowed the name of the *school's* ranking English benefactor, the Earl of Dartmouth.

But the idea of founding such a college was not new to Wheelock; the British donations only made it possible for the first time. As early as 1761 Wheelock had begun to cast his eye around the Northeast for a college site. His heart was initially set on the rich farmlands of Iroquois country, "near

the Bowells of the Pagan Settlements," where he thought fifteen to twenty square miles would suffice to plant a model
Christian community, including a school for Indians and a
college for English missionaries.[70] When it became clear that
the Iroquois and their Anglican protector, Sir William Johnson, would never countenance an invasion of grasping, grim-
lipped New England Congregationalists, Wheelock considered other sites in Ohio, New York, Pennsylvania, and most
of the New England colonies before accepting Hanover's offer
of land and capital. In that day as in ours, colleges were economic boons to their towns, and Dartmouth simply went to
the highest bidder. Wheelock now had the makings of an institution equal to his ambitions and the opportunity to dele-
gate his waning interest in the schooling of Indians. Moor's
Charity School continued to admit Indians after the move to
New Hampshire, but with increasing admixtures of English
students. The dilution of its original purpose and the length-
ening shadow of the college finally closed its doors in 1829.

The subordination of the Indians in Wheelock's new design for Dartmouth College was symbolized nowhere better
than in his first draft of its charter. Dartmouth was being
founded, Wheelock wrote, to educate "Youths of *the English*
and also of the Indian Tribes in this Land in reading, writing & all . . . liberal Arts and Sciences." Then he remembered that several thousand British benefactors had given
thousands of pounds to a charity school primarily for Indians,
not white colonists, and he scratched out the reference to English youth and added it at the end of the passage as if to indicate their subordinate position in his design.[71] In its revised
form the charter became New Hampshire law, and Doctor—
now President—Wheelock proceeded to exhaust his ample
treasury—over the protests of his English trustees—on a liberal
arts college that graduated only three Indians in the eighteenth century and eight in the nineteenth.[72]

But not everyone was fooled by the Doctor's legerdemain,

least of all his "black Son," Samson Occom. With the frank shrewdness he had shown all his troubled life in his dealings with the English, Occom told his mentor, "your having so many White Scholars and so few or no Indian Scholars, gives me great Discouragement. . . . I am very jealous that instead of your Semenary Becoming alma Mater, she will be too alba mater [white mother] to Suckle the Tawnees, for She is already adorned up too much like the Popish Virgin Mary." In short, he accused, "your present Plan is not calculated to benefit the poor Indians."[73]

President Wheelock did not have to be told.

CHAPTER FIVE

Last Rights: The Acculturation of Native Funerals in Colonial North America

AFTER HEARING MY HISTORICAL TESTIMONY ON BEHALF OF THE Mashpee tribe in October 1977, a Boston reporter quipped that much of it had "the flavor of a college seminar," which I chose to take as a compliment. But during my days in court I felt as often like a student as a teacher. One of the most vivid lessons I took away from the trial, a lesson that strongly reinforced what I knew largely from books, was that, while Indian societies made many surface changes to accommodate their white adversaries, they retained over long periods durable substrata of values and beliefs which sustained their distinctive Indian identities. The lesson gained from reconstructing 350 years of Mashpee history and meeting the undeniably Indian heirs and guardians of that legacy was fresh in my mind as I wrote the following essay for delivery at the Iroquois Conference a year later.

Every student of European missionary efforts in North America must be struck by the fact that no aspect of native life was immune from attack. Armed with the belief that pagans must be "civilized" before they can be Christianized, the missionaries sought to recast the whole of native culture in a Western European mold. In order to convey the palpable reality of that goal, I have focused on some of the seemingly trivial aspects of Indian life that carried extra symbolic weight for the Christian reformers, such as hairstyles, menstrual practices, and burial customs.

I was drawn to the history of burial changes for two reasons. The first was that the missionaries' pursuit of their native adversaries to the very grave seemed to me altogether characteristic of the lengths to which they would go to extinguish the Indians' last rights. But, secondly, I was equally fascinated by the dual quality of mortuary customs that allowed the natives to preserve the spirit if not the form of those rites. Unlike most other expressions of cultural life, burials have a subterranean as well as a terrestrial aspect which archaeology is capable of uncovering. But written documents are necessary to interpret the meaning of the archaeological record for the simple reason that the living place the dead in the ground in culturally prescribed ways. Their beliefs about the afterlife and the proper ways to reach it, which often find expression in historical documents, help to explain the grave contents and patterns—and vice versa.

Since the cultural life of the past was as complex and interrelated as our own, we cannot afford to ignore evidence from any quarter, above ground or below, physical or spiritual. One of the principal values of ethnohistory is that it encourages us to see life as a seamless web, not as a crude mosaic of jagged pieces.

THE GREATEST PROBLEM FACING THE EUROPEAN INVADERS OF northeastern North America was not their own supply lines, small numbers, or even national competitions but the unpredictability of the continent's native inhabitants. Without an understanding of their strange and numerous languages, cultural habits, and values, the colonists were simply unable to predict the behavior of the Indians toward them, when that behavior frequently, especially in the early years of contact, meant the difference between life and death. In a new physical and psychic environment, this lack of assurance endangered the stability and even survival of the European colonies, and so had to be remedied.

The general course taken by all the colonial powers to restore self-confidence and eliminate the unknown was to reduce the Indians from cultural and political autonomy to effective dependence upon European institutions and authority. Although various means were employed by different colonies and different interest groups at different times, the ultimate solution was, as most contemporaries saw it, "to reduce [the natives] from barbarism to civility," in other words, to turn them into Europeans.[1] For Europeans spoke intelligible languages, thought intelligible thoughts, worshipped one moderately intelligible God, and acted in intelligible—and therefore predictable—ways. If every aspect of Indian habit and culture could be replaced with a European component, the colonists' "Indian problem" would dissolve into a homogenized European identity, at once familiar, predictable, and safe.

Although the complete transmogrification of another people was a splendidly quixotic goal, the colonial officials and missionaries who were its chief architects seriously sought to strip the Indians of the last vestige of their cultural identity before clothing them in European habits and manners. In exchange for European "civility" while they lived and the Kingdom of Heaven ever after, the natives were expected to relinquish all rights to the life they had known, including the last and most personal right—to die as they pleased.

In death as in life, the colonists' reach exceeded their grasp. The great majority of Indian societies in the colonial period never wholly lost their political or cultural autonomy, which enabled them to deflect the colonists' ultimate arrogations. And even those who succumbed to European political domination often managed to preserve sundry secrets of the heart from the intrusive glare and alien grasp of the invaders. Among them were their concepts of the afterlife and the proper avenues to reach it. For the Indians of the northeastern woodlands were remarkably persistent in honoring and burying their dead according to their own cultural standards, most of which predated the arrival of the Christians from Europe.

Aboriginal funeral customs in northeastern North America consisted of local variations on a basic pattern. When death came to a late-prehistoric woodland Indian, male or female, his relatives—perhaps, as among the Iroquois, those of the opposite moiety or of his spouse's clan—prepared him for burial by dressing him in his finest clothing, painting his face to advantage, laying him in a flexed position, knees drawn to the chest, and wrapping him in a great fur robe. Following a public display of mourning and lamentation, led frequently by professional female mourners, feasts were given and orations made to honor the dead and console the living.

Within a certain number of days, prescribed by the lack of embalming techniques as by ritual custom, the corpse was carried a short distance to the village or clan cemetery. There a round or oval pit had been dug and lined with fur, bark, or woven mats.[2] When the flexed figure was lowered into the shallow grave, his relatives sometimes placed near or on him one of his favorite possessions, such as a man's stone pipe or a woman's shellbead necklace. The body was normally placed on its side, the head oriented in no predominant direction.[3] The grave was filled only after the body had been covered with branches and bark to prevent dirt from touching it. Since some graves were quite shallow as a result of the season, soil conditions, and earth-moving technology, heavy logs or stones were often placed on them to deter marauding animals. And finally, in many—perhaps most—tribes, the graves of prominent warriors and leaders, male and female, were specially marked by circular palisades, painted posts depicting the person's lineage and deeds, elaborate fur draperies, or earthen mounds.[4]

Although the dead were gone, their survivors, especially spouses, were expected to mourn for a prescribed period until

A Narragansett Indian man, aged 30, in the flexed position characteristic of pre-contact burials. Fingers in his mouth and knees drawn to
his chest, he was buried with a few items of European manufacture on
Conanicut Island in Narragansett Bay in the first half of the seventeenth
century. From William Scranton Simmons, *Cautantowwit's House: An
Indian Burial Ground on the Island of Conanicut in Narragansett Bay*
(Providence, R.I.: Brown University Press, 1970).

released by the decedent's kinfolk. Widows cut their hair,
blackened their faces, wore rags, and shunned all company
for as much as a year; widowers also mourned but not as long
or as conspicuously.[5] Out of respect for the dead, cemeteries
were revered and refurbished. If the burial took place in a
house, which was not uncommon, the bark was removed from
the frame and the occupants moved to new quarters.[6] In many
tribes, particularly the Great Lakes Iroquoians and the tribes

of the Delmarva Peninsula, periodic reburials of the cleansed bones of many individual interments in communal ossuaries served to bind the living through the dead.[7] But at no time could the dead be mentioned by name. To do so was considered a serious affront to their relatives, who were painfully reminded of their loss, and even a cause for war between tribes.[8] As Father Joseph Lafitau observed, "no idea is more marked among the Indians in general than respect for the dead and for the memory of their ancestors."[9]

Upon this pattern of custom and respect intruded the Europeans with their ethnocentric preferences and Christian prejudices. Yet the first historic change in native funerals resulted not from the willful impositions of the invaders themselves but indirectly from the seductions of their material goods. At least three-quarters of a century—and probably a full century—before Europeans began to settle the Atlantic coasts, fishermen and other sea-going traders had released a small but steady stream of trade goods into the interior. Glass beads, ship fittings, brass earrings, iron axes and knives were passed along native trading paths from the St. Lawrence and Chesapeake Bay until they reached the Senecas, Susquehannocks, and Hurons.[10] Placing high value on these scarce objects from a novel source, the Indians began to bury them with their dead, perhaps especially with those of social stature and children.[11] As a consequence or coincidentally, the natives also inaugurated a steady increase in grave offerings of their own manufacture. Bows, arrowpoints, pipes, flint knives, medicine pouches, and shell rattles accompanied men to the grave, while women took the pottery, tumplines, combs, necklaces, and mortars they would need in the afterlife. Both were often given small clay pots containing food for the soul on its long journey.[12] By the time the Europeans began to settle the coastal regions, the Indian societies they met had established a custom of multiple grave offerings so firm that it appeared to be of great antiquity. In one sense, of course, it was an ancient custom because many of the Indians' distant ancestors in the Archaic and Early Woodland periods had also buried their dead with various bone and lithic artifacts. But the practice had died down or out in most eastern groups, so what the Europeans unknowingly witnessed early in the seventeenth century was a cultural renewal prompted in part by their own material introductions.[13]

What the Europeans also did not recognize was that the native renaissance of grave offerings coincided with another growing tendency to align the dead on an east-west axis with the head to the west. Until the last half of the sixteenth century, most native cemeteries showed no marked preference for grave orientation. The main late-prehistoric or protohistoric exceptions were the Shenk's Ferry people of Pennsylvania, the occupants of a large village near Madisonville, Ohio, and some Siouan groups in Virginia, who strongly preferred an eastern heading.[14] By about 1580, however, the Senecas and the Susquehannocks, and perhaps the Munsee Delawares as well, began to lay their dead in greater numbers headed west or southwest, a preference shared by the great majority of northeastern tribes by the time of early contact.[15] The simultaneous popularity of heading the dead toward the "land of souls" and providing food for the soul's journey seems to suggest that at least some of the tribes who were experiencing the indirect but powerful impact of the European presence in North America felt a need for some degree of cultural revitalization. European disease, for example, contributed to a funerary renaissance by killing many more people who had not reached relatively old age and whose loss to the social organism needed to be ceremonially healed.[16] The challenge felt by the sixteenth-century Iroquois to form a political league may have provoked religious responses in several other tribes as well.

Although Europeans at a distance had some effect on native funerals, Europeans in close proximity had a good deal more. One of the first things the newly landed colonists and traders saw when they witnessed Indian funerals was the material wealth being buried with the dead. In European eyes, not only valuable trade goods such as guns, kettles, and axes but quantities of beaver, bear, and deer skins and belts of wampum were rotting in the ground for no good reason. Naturally, in such tempting circumstances, the Christian scruples of some colonists were overcome.

As early as 1610 a military party of Virginians combined revenge and robbery when, for the killing of an English messenger, they "Ransacked [the Powhatans'] Temples, Tooke downe the Corp[s]es of their deade kings from . . . their [scaffold] Toambes, And caryed away their pearles, Copper, and braceletts, wherew[i]th they doe decor[at]e their kings funeralles."[17] Ten years later the less belligerent Pilgrims robbed Indian graves on Cape Cod in the spirit of true ethnography. The first grave they excavated contained only a decaying bow and arrows, so they backfilled it and left the rest untouched, thinking "it would be odious unto [the natives] to ransack their sepulchres." But curiosity soon got the better of their good sense when they spied another mound "much bigger and longer than any [they] had yet seen," which they promptly dismantled. Up came finely woven mats, bowls, trays, bows, red ochre, some canvas and iron sailor's gear, a knife, white beads, and the bones of an adult man and a child. Not unlike their professional descendants, these anthropological pilgrims proceeded to speculate about the identity of the adult with the "fine yellow hair." "Some thought it was an Indian lord and king. Others said the Indians have all black hair, and never any was seen with brown or yellow hair. Some thought it was a Christian of some special note, which had died amongst them, and they thus buried him to honor him. Others thought they had killed him, and did it in triumph over him." Unable to agree on his identity, they did agree he was worth robbing and "brought sundry of the prettiest things away" with them. To their credit, when they discovered a large palisaded cemetery shortly after, they "digged none of [the graves] up," even though they were "more sumptuous" than those they had already excavated.[18]

A year later, however, the Pilgrims again desecrated an Indian grave, but for a new reason. Like most groups, the Indians of southern New England were socially differentiated in death as in life. One distinguishing mark of the graves of "noble" figures was a large fur "hearse cloath" propped over the grave or hung from a nearby tree. Accordingly, Pasonayessit, the Massachusett sachem's mother, was covered by "two great Beares skinnes sowed together at full length"—that is, until the Plymouth planters purloined them to eradicate a sign of pagan "superstition." Only luck and matchlocks saved them from the vengeful wrath of the sachem's warriors, who considered it "impious, and inhumane, to deface the monuments of the dead."[19]

The motives of most colonial grave robbers, however, were not as mixed. Simple avarice prompted "the robbing of Pesiccush his sisters grave, & mangling of her flesh" in 1654 by an infamous Rhode Island quartet in search of royal "bootie," as it did the opening of Canadian graves "in order to strip the dead of their robes of beaver skins."[20] Understandably, the Indians were doubly "scandalized," not only that anyone would commit so barbarous a crime against their nations, risking death, the loss of trade, and all-out war, but that the newcomers would stoop so low for a few dirty grave goods when they seemed to possess material riches that far surpassed anything the Indians enjoyed in life or in death. But when prominent Indian men—most likely in the great "Feast of the Dead"—took as much as a ton of "Moose, Otter, and Beaver" robes to the grave with them, we can appreciate the consuming "envy" if not the Christian "pity" aroused in European breasts.[21] Certainly after the fur trade put a premium on the possession of wampum and furs, the Indians, too, could understand the colonists' feelings sufficiently to commit on occasion a serious breach in their own funeral etiquette. As Lafitau and several of our archaeological colleagues have noticed, the Indians' sometimes desperate need for European goods drove "some unscrupulous people to rummage in their ancestors' ashes" for still-usable trade items and wampum with which to purchase others.[22] The emotional effect of native and European grave robbing on the Indians' sense of sanctity of the dead must have been appalling.[23]

Two changes in native mortuary practices may have occurred as a result of grave robbing, one in New England and one over a larger area. I have found no proof for the first, yet it seems likely that once the New England Indians measured the probability of having their leaders' graves internally defiled and externally denuded of their furry monuments by a sanctimoniously "theevish people," they began to disguise them by omitting telltale palisades, mounds, posts, and hangings, and perhaps to dig them not in common cemeteries but in wooded places "where people seldom go."[24] The shift in burial location—if such occurred—may not have significantly altered the Indians' attitudes toward death. But certainly the democratization of grave exteriors—whether the result of furtive traditionalism or Christian conversion—would have upset the social assumptions of most woodland tribes. For like most societies, they accorded their dead treatment commensurate with their social roles and statuses in life. Their burials, therefore, reflected "a great difference betweene persons of noble, and of ignoble, or obscure, or inferior discent."[25] So marked was this social consciousness, wrote Thomas Morton, that the New England Indians "marvell to see no monuments over our dead, and therefore thinke no great Sachem is yet come into those parts [Massachusetts]: or not as yet deade, because they see the graves all alike."[26] To be reduced in

death to an unmarked or a uniformly crossed grave was the
final step in the loss of one's identity, the goal so eagerly
sought by the European missionaries.

Theft-related changes could obviously not alter native practices and attitudes or subject the Indians to colonial authority
fast enough to suit European tastes, so the colonial missionaries—religious and lay, English and French—sought to speed
the process. The first major target, as the Pilgrim episode indicated, was the widespread offering of grave goods to souls
bound for a pagan "heaven." Different national and interest
groups advocated different methods for dealing with the practice. The English missionaries in seventeenth-century New
England and the Moravians in eighteenth-century Pennsylvania and Ohio advocated the complete abolition of grave
offerings and every other mortuary custom that smacked of
"paganism"—which, of course, condemned nearly everything
the Indians did to honor their dead.[27] When the missionaries
were able to establish their authority over the Indians in
segregated praying towns, they were able to curb the inter-
ment of grave goods with some success. But the number of
Indians living in Protestant praying towns was minuscule
compared to that of those who maintained their tribal independence and continued to bury their dead in traditional
ways. Even the rare itinerant missionary could do nothing to
change those ways, especially when the Indians were aided
and abetted by English traders who profited from their rapid
and non-recyclable consumption of trade goods. As a long-
time trader among the Cherokees confessed, "all that is of
royal descent buries a good quantity of goods with him. Likewise all the other common people has vast quantities of all
sorts of goods buried with them which is a great advantage to
the merchants of South Carolina and especially to the Indian
traders that uses [trades] amongst them."[28]

By contrast, in the eastern parts of New France, where
trade goods were less abundant and more costly, many na-

tives reduced or omitted grave offerings less because of Jesuit pressure than the efforts of French traders, the example of French *habitants,* and the need for French goods that had become "indispensable necessities."[29] Indeed, the Jesuits condoned the use of grave offerings as a vital sign of respect for the dead and "convincing proof of [the natives'] belief that souls survive the decay of the tomb."[30] In matters of death as of life, the Jesuit missionaries concentrated their energies on the essentials of religion and allowed their neophytes a wide latitude in the rest of their lives. As the missionary at Lorette explained in 1675, "after removing from them all the superstitions which they had learned in paganism, we have left them the remainder, which serves but to maintain the mutual union which exists between them, and even to inspire devotion in those who witness the ceremonies."[31] The most the Jesuits did to alter the practice of grave offerings was to promote the substitution of religious items—rings, crosses, and rosaries—for native goods or the donation of potential grave goods to the poor who would in return offer prayers for the dead. Only the burial of pet dogs was condemned outright.[32]

More effective in abolishing the practice was self-interest. The French, including traders such as Nicolas Denys, worked hard to persuade the Indians of the "uselessness of this display" and the economic "harm done by it," even to the extent of opening a grave to show them that the offerings had not gone west with the soul of the deceased. But the law of supply and demand was more persuasive. "Since they cannot now obtain the things which come from us with such ease as they had in obtaining robes of Marten, of Otter, or of Beaver, [or] bows and arrows," wrote Denys, "and since they have realised that guns and other things were not found in their woods or in their rivers, they have become less devout" in the observance of their mortuary customs.[33]

It would be easy to conclude from the written record that grave offerings shrivelled in quantity and cultural importance

with the advent of widespread European settlement and mis-
sionization. But we would be misled, for the archaeological
record documents the remarkable persistence of traditional
customs even in spheres of the heaviest Christian influence.
The first grave in the specially designated "Sachem's Cemetery" in Charlestown, Rhode Island, was that of Weunquesh,
the sister of the second sachem named Ninigret. She was laid
to rest about 1686 in an extended, supine position in a hollow log, split, hinged, and chained (to deter grave robbers?)
to resemble an English coffin. Her dress, too, was English—a
green silk robe and matching bonnet—save for a pair of dainty
moccasins, soled in copper. Yet this person of "royal blood"
was accompanied by a rich profusion of grave goods—kettles,
pottery, beads, broaches, coins, spoons, and porringers around
the coffin, Dutch metal pipes and spoons, thimbles, a bottle
of brandy, stone pestles, and much wampum within.[34]

Even more telling were many of the seventeenth-century
graves of the praying Indians of Natick, Massachusetts, John
Eliot's first and most successful Christian reservation. As the
objects of Eliot's obdurate brand of Protestant proselytizing,
the Natick Indians might have been expected to quickly and
permanently forgo their "pagan" funeral customs. But when
numerous graves were disturbed or removed by the town's
growth in the late eighteenth century, wampum and glass
beads, spoons, a bottle "nearly half full of some kind of
liquor," and "several other Indian curiosities" were found
mixed among the bones of their "converted" owners.[35]
Equally revealing were the twenty-one graves in the Indian
cemetery of the Jesuit headquarters at Ste. Marie-among-the-
Hurons. While all the burials were made in wooden coffins
and solemnized according to the rites of the Church, only
some of the bodies were extended and nearly all were surrounded by native and European grave goods—pewter and
clay pipes, seeds, wampum, copper and clay pots, and iron
knives as well as rosaries. One grave even contained the jaw-

bone of a dog, this in the teeth of Jesuit opposition to such offerings.[36]

European proximity fostered a number of other changes in Indian funerals, some the result of native emulation of colonial practices, others of Christian pressure for reform. When the technology was available, Indians in the Northeast sometimes resorted to wooden coffins.[37] But coffins required not only sawn planks but forged nails, which were often in short supply in frontier settlements, so the natives bent on colonial-style burials often made do with split-log imitations, like that of Ninigret's sister. Typical were ten Oneidas wearing medals with the likeness of King George I who were buried in the eighteenth century "in logs hollowed out by burning."[38]

Even when no coffins were available, many Indian groups began to emulate their white neighbors by laying their dead out in a supine, extended posture. In 1689, for example, an English minister noted that the native Virginians "commonly lay their dead all along in the ground as we do," a trend subscribed to by tribes in other colonies at various times.[39] Whether in coffins or bark shrouds, extended burials gradually replaced burials in a flexed position, which undoubtedly carried religious significance. For if contemporary and modern scholarly observers are right, the flexed position—sometimes with fingers in the mouth and surrounded by placental red ochre—symbolized fetal birth and by analogy spiritual rebirth in the afterlife.[40] To extend the body on its back, eyes to the Christian heaven, was to turn it away from the soul's traditional destination in the west. This *may* have represented an important symbolic abandonment of native religion, especially if Christian graves were not uniformly aligned on an east-west axis, as they seem not to have been. But it need not have signified an actual abandonment if the Indians continued to bury their dead headed west. Extended burials may have constituted only a superficial accommodation to European preferences, designed to placate the invaders in

The extended burial of a Delaware Indian man at the Pahaquarra site near the Delaware Water Gap in New Jersey. He died between 1720 and 1750 and was buried, with a flintlock musket cradled in his right arm, next to his wife, who was also extended on her back. A century earlier he probably would have been interred with his bow and arrows. From Herbert C. Kraft, ed., *A Delaware Indian Symposium,* Pennsylvania Historical and Manuscript Commission, Anthropological Series, Number 4 (Harrisburg, 1974).

things of little import while preserving the heart of their traditional beliefs intact. The large number of historic-period extended burials that contain grave goods and head toward the setting sun seems to suggest such a strategy.

There is some literary and archaeological evidence that Christian belief also advocated burial on an east-west axis, but with an eastern emphasis. The small cemetery on Champlain's St. Croix Island, for example, has yielded twenty-three graves in which all the dead were buried with their heads to the west and feet to the east, toward which, it was thought, they would rise and walk on the Day of Judgment.[41] If Christian missionaries urged their native converts to die in an acceptable Christian direction—and I have found no evidence that they did—they would not have disturbed traditional "pagan" practice.

Other changes, however, were potentially more disruptive of traditional faith and practice. In the absence of coffins, Christian corpses were covered directly with dirt. Commonly, especially if they were poor, their naked flesh was shielded by no more than a winding sheet. Indian traditionalists abhorred both conditions and took a great deal of persuasion to suffer them at burial. In the end, however, only resident missionaries who controlled every facet of their neophytes' lives in praying towns—such as the Moravians and a few Jesuits—succeeded in getting them to dress their dead in mean rather than splendid clothing and "to fill up the grave with earth."[42]

In those same centers of Christian influence, mourning customs were severely curtailed, as in New England, or subtly re-channeled, as in Canada. One of the twenty-nine laws governing the praying Indians of Concord, Massachusetts, in 1647 was the commandment: "They shall not disguise themselves in their mournings, as formerly, nor shall they keep a great noyse by howling."[43] Just what the missionaries meant by "disguise" was clarified three years later when the leading convert on Martha's Vineyard buried his infant son. "Here," wrote the missionary proudly, "were no black faces for [the child] as the manner of the Indians is, nor goods buried with it, nor hellish howlings over the dead."[44] By 1675, it was said, "the civilized and christian Indians" of New England had left these customs in their pagan past.[45] In New France, by contrast, the Jesuits transformed native dirges into Latin chants and canticles, but countenanced most other mourning rituals, including death feasts and funeral orations, as tolerable marks of respect for the dead.[46]

Tolerant though they were of some practices, the Jesuits were adamant in segregating the Christian dead from their pagan kinsmen in consecrated cemeteries. They would not even condone the promiscuous mixture of Christian bones in Huron ossuaries but insisted that they be collected and buried separately. A ten-year-old baptized boy who had been buried in the same grave with a close relative was similarly exhumed and placed in consecrated ground.[47] This kind of separation in death and the eternal separation threatened by dual "heavens" worried many traditionalists and hastened not a few conversions. When Christian converts could say to their traditional kinsmen, "little matters it to us what will be done with our bodies after death," a yawning chasm separated the two cultures which only conversion or apostasy could bridge.[48]

The final important change brought about by European contact was the breaking of the nearly universal Indian taboo on referring to the dead by name. Such a keen affront was it to speak to the Delawares of their dead relatives that "they hang their heads and sigh and puff severely."[49] Out of similar respect for the dead, Lafitau observed, "all the [Iroquois] men and women who . . . had similar names have to give them up and take others . . . until, regrets being dissipated and deadened, it pleases the relatives to raise up the tree again and to requicken the dead person." As Lafitau himself discovered, this resuscitation could not occur prematurely. When his fellow missionaries bestowed upon him the Indian name of his predecessor Father Bruyas, who had been dead but four months, the converts at Sault St. Louis reproached him for "raising the tree too soon."[50] Roger Williams noted how among the Narragansetts "if any stranger accidentally name [a dead person], he is checkt, . . . if any wilfully name him he is fined; and amongst States, the naming of their dead *Sachims,* is one ground of their warres."[51] Williams was not exaggerating the gravity of the offense, for in 1665 King Philip took a number of warriors to Nantucket to kill an Indian named John Gibb for mentioning the name of Massasoit, Philip's late father. Only bribery and an English show of force saved the talkative Indian's hide.[52]

The Indians were gradually led to break this important taboo not by the conscious persuasion but by the casual example of the colonists, whose longer, written, and fact-specific brand of history required the frequent recitation of people's names. Lahontan told of how the Indians derided the French when they heard them "recount the Fate of our Parents, our Kings, our Generals, &c."[53] According to Thomas Morton, similar treatment greeted the inquisitive New English. "It was a thing very offensive to them, at our first comming into those parts, to aske of them for any one that had bin dead; but of later times," he wrote in 1632, "it is not so offensively taken, to renew the memory of any deseased person, because by our example (which they are apt to followe) it is made more familiare unto them."[54] Yet even in heavily settled New England change came slowly. As late as 1753 the inhabitants of Mashpee, a Cape Cod praying town, were using the old Algonquian absentative form of nouns to avoid referring to dead persons by name.[55] In the late seventeenth century, Indian land deeds on Nantucket frequently employed in English the circumlocutions of the absentative form to indicate "the old sachem," "the former sachem," "the said sachem," or "he that was sachem."[56]

In no colonial setting was the Indians' choice of how they wanted to die respected, but in very few settings were they denied the choice itself. Outside the praying towns of New England and New France, the Indians changed their funeral customs remarkably little during the colonial period. The majority of changes that were made were freely chosen and of minor importance to the native complex of funeral customs and especially beliefs. Ironically, the essential intolerance of Protestant Christianity and the cultural relativism of Catholicism in New France both worked to ensure the Indians a large measure of freedom in matters mortuary, the Protestants by winning few converts and stiffening the opposition of the rest, the Catholics by allowing syncretic traditionalism. The European colonists impinged even less on that freedom, for their mere example, unaided by fire, fever, or famine, was insufficiently attractive to induce major change. In the end, despite their ultimate designs, the European invaders of North America were unable to deprive the natives of one of their most essential cultural freedoms—their last rites.

From European
to Indian

CHAPTER SIX

The Scholastic Philosophy
of the Wilderness

FOR ALL THE CULTURAL BAGGAGE THEY CARRIED, THE COLONISTS
who came to North America were not self-sufficient. Because the
physical and human geographies of the New World were different—sometimes radically—from those they had left behind, some
of their baggage had to be jettisoned and new ways found of
coping with the necessities of social life. Fortunately, they found
willing guides and instructors in the native peoples, as I learned
in my initial foray into Indian history.

As *The School upon a Hill* was taking shape, it occurred to me
that the New English not only educated their young in the ways
of English Puritan culture but had to have been themselves educated in some of the ways of New England by the Indians. So I
began to read—and in many cases, reread—the primary New England literature on Indian-white contact to see what forms the
Indian education of the English took. Having been led by the
Harvard school of Puritan historians to believe that New England culture was largely an intellectual import, I was surprised
to discover several ways in which the imported culture was
quickly and effectively Native-Americanized. At the same time, I
discovered that I shouldn't have been surprised because anthropologists had long known that "acculturation" always occurs
when two cultures meet. Both "discoveries" soon emerged as the
last chapter of *The School upon a Hill* and as a separate article
in the *William and Mary Quarterly* (July 1972).

Due to an anthropological deficiency in my undergraduate education, I had to acquire a rudimentary understanding of acculturation by serendipitous reading. Having now read systematically much of the literature on acculturation, I realize that the following essay employs a somewhat hit-and-miss concept of acculturation. I can only hope that the lack of conceptual rigor is at least partially mitigated by the novelty and freshness of the answers that emerged from asking a new question of familiar documents, and by Chapters 9 and 10 below. The exciting spaciousness of that question—how and in what ways did the cultures of colonial North America influence each other—continues to intrigue me and is responsible for not only this volume but a proposed three-volume ethnohistory of French, English, and Indian cultural interactions in the greater Northeast, of which *The Invasion Within* is the first.

I n the beginning," John Locke had written, "all the World was *America*." There was no money, no unlimited accumulation of property, and consequently no need for elaborate institutions of government to control human greed. Eminently sociable and peaceloving, men in the state of nature lived "according to reason, without a common Superior on Earth, with Authority to judge between them."[1]

When it appeared in 1690 Locke's picture of the natural condition must have seemed to many Englishmen—whigs at least—a superb blend of historical observation and philosophical acuity. But to three generations of New English colonists it would have appeared overdrawn and dolefully optimistic. For to them primitive New England had not been a natural paradise of "Peace, Good Will, Mutual Assistance, and Preservation," but rather a "State of Enmity, Malice, Violence, and Mutual Destruction," a living hell ignited by its barbarous inhabitants.[2] The Indians threatened to push them into the sea, and nearly succeeded on several occasions, but the threat of physical annihilation was never so alarming to English sensibilities—perhaps because they were blinded to the possibility by their supreme righteousness—as the Indian himself. To the English he stood proudly and defiantly against all that they stood for, all that was good and Christian and civilized. The Indian, in their lights, was immoral, pagan, and barbarous. So, characteristically, they tried to remake him in their own image through the time-honored but formal institutions of English education—the church, the school, and the college. Needless to say, they failed miserably.[3]

But education, if it is any good, is never a one-way process; sensitive teachers will learn as much from their students as their students will from them. Nor is it always a didactic process; the imitation of intangible qualities and behavior patterns is as powerful an educational force as formal instruction, perhaps more so because of the reinforcement provided by the visible embodiment of those qualities in living models. Accordingly, it would be surprising if the English themselves did not learn a great deal from the original inhabitants in the crucible of the New England wilderness.

The shifting frontier between wilderness and "civilization" seems an unlikely place for a school, but the cultures that meet there never fail to educate each other. Although one culture may predominate and tend to teach more than it learns, the educational process is always mutual. Because the New English possessed a clear superiority of technology, government, and population, which eventually tipped the cultural scale against the Indians in a saddeningly total way, it is easy for historians to dwell exclusively on the white efforts to civilize and Christianize the Indians. It is easy but it is also unfortunate, for it neglects the lessons that the English learned from the Indians, lessons which, ironically, helped tip that scale against the Indian's own future.

The Indian served as a teacher to the New English in three guises: as neighbor (their hospitable welcomer and uninhibited visitor), as warrior (their mortal enemy or supportive comrade in arms), and as example (a tempting model of a different way of life). In each of these roles, significantly, he met his white students on the frontier where he was culturally secure and they were exposed, often unsure of what they had left behind and not a little tempted by what they found in the woods. In these remote plantations, where it was rightly feared "many were contented to live without, yea, desirous to shake off all Yoake of Government, both sacred and civil, and so transforming themselves as much as well they could into the Manners of the Indians they lived amongst," he found pupils far more receptive to his teaching than he would ever be to theirs. The best of them were young, like the children of Hannah Swarton, who moved from Massachusetts to Maine for "large accommodations in the world, thereby exposing [them] to be bred ignorantly like Indians," but whatever their age, the English soon learned that, when they were in the woods, however uncomfortable they might be in his presence, the Indian was not only the only teacher available but the best as well.[4]

By a stroke of providence that only a Puritan could fully appreciate, the first two Indians who met the New English spoke their language. Samoset was an Algonquian sagamore from Maine, "where some English ships came to fish . . . amongst whom he had got his language." Having shipped to Cape Cod with one of them, he was on his way down east when he boldly approached the newly arrived Pilgrims at Plymouth and in broken English offered to help. According to their governor William Bradford, "He became profitable to them in acquainting them with many things concerning the state of the country in the east parts where he lived, which was afterwards profitable unto them; as also of the people here, of their names, number and strength, of their situation and distance from this place, and who was chief amongst

them." Even more helpful was Squanto, who had been kidnapped to Spain and escaped to England in 1614 and accordingly spoke better English than Samoset. This "special instrument sent of God" was their pilot, interpreter, and willing
teacher until his death in 1622.[5]

One of the first lessons he taught them, as his brethren
would continue to teach each successive wave of settlers, was
"how to set their corn, where to take fish, and to procure
other commodities." Since the Pilgrims had dropped anchor
in the "weatherbeaten face" of the New England winter, they
had to wait for the spring winds to soften its countenance before they could plant their first crops. But when they did,
"either by the badness of the seed or lateness of the season or
both, or some other defect," all the English wheat and pease
they sowed "came not to good." It was then that Squanto
"stood them in great stead" by extending his agricultural
knowledge to them.[6] He was only the first of many Indians
who were, as the grateful English acknowledged, "our first
instructers for the planting of their *Indian* Corne, by teaching us to cull out the finest seede, to observe the fittest season, to keepe distance for holes, and fit measure for hills, to
worme it, and weede it; to prune it, and dresse it as occasion
shall require."[7] In the early years of settlement the Indians'
liberal tutelage in the natural life of their woods and fields
often provided the English with the slim difference between
survival and starvation.

The Indians' generosity was the more remarkable because
their only previous knowledge of the English was likely to
have been of rapacious seamen and adventurers. As soon as
their initial suspicions were laid to rest by the civil conduct
of settlers who obviously intended to make permanent residence in their land, they extended the English every courtesy, advice, and endeavor to help them. Roger Williams,
who probably knew them better than anyone else, remarked,

> I have acknowledged amongst them an heart sensible of kindnesses, and . . . reaped kindnesse again from many, seaven yeares after, when I my selfe had forgotten. . . . If any stranger come in, they presently give him to eate of what they have; many a time, and at all times of the night (as I have fallen in travell upon their houses) when nothing hath been ready, have themselves and their wives, risen to prepare me some refreshing. . . . In Summer-time I have knowne them lye abroad often themselves, to make roome for strangers, *English,* or others.

Even in the face of possible affront they maintained an affable courtesy by sleeping outdoors "by a fire under a tree, when sometimes some *English* have (for want of familiaritie and language with them) been fearefull to entertaine them." It was a "strange *truth*" indeed to those Englishmen who knew them well that "a man shall generally find more free entertainment and refreshing amongst these *Barbarians,* then amongst thousands that call themselves *Christians.*"[8]

The Indians were also generous with their time and patience, for some of them were "very willing to teach their language to any *English.*"[9] When two cultures intersect, as they frequently did in New English houses and native wigwams, words are not only the most necessary article of commerce but the easiest medium in which to deal. Most Englishmen were not as fortunate as the Pilgrims in having an English-speaking Squanto to help them cope with the American environment and so had to learn something of the Indian's language while teaching him something of theirs. Probably the first words exchanged were the names of natural objects unknown to the other culture. By 1643, for instance, the Indians had incorporated the Englishmen's *chicks, cows, goats, hogs,* and *pigs* into their vocabulary. But the greatest amount of borrowing was understandably done by the English, who were casting virgin eyes on what to them was a new country. At home they had never seen a *moose, skunk,*

raccoon, beaver, caribou, opossum, woodchuck, or *rattlesnake,*
so it was necessary for them to learn their names from the Indians who knew them well. Besides the natural life of New
England the settlers learned to identify many Indian relations—such as *papoose, squaw, powwow, sagamore,* and *sachem*—and cultural artifacts—such as *moccasin, tomahawk,
wigwam, succotash, hominy, toboggan, pemmican,* and *wampum.*[10] Even Indian notions of time were drawn upon. In a
decision of the Plymouth colony court in 1641, for example,
Englishmen were given one or two "moons" to repair or restore the goods they had stolen from an Indian plaintiff.[11]

The names of a few common plants and animals probably
sufficed for most English settlers, but another group of men—
admittedly small—needed to go much farther in their com-
prehension of the Indian language. For it was early recognized that "the way to instruct the *Indians,* must be in their
owne language, not *English.*"[12] These were the Puritan ministers who wanted to bring the Word of the Christian religion
to the unconverted "heathens" around them, in accordance
with the stated goals of the colonization of New England. To
King Charles I, who issued the charter of the Massachusetts
Bay Company in 1628, it was "the principall ende of this
plantation" to "wynn and incite the natives of [the] country
to the knowledg and obedience of the onlie true God and
Savior of mankinde, and the Christian fayth."[13] And so their
task was to find or create in the Indian tongue abstractions or
analogies for the metaphysical presuppositions of the English
religion, a task made doubly difficult by the reticulate complexity of Puritan theology. Although the reception of their
message was disappointing for a variety of reasons, some beyond their control, several ministers were at least able to deliver it in the Indian's own language.

When two cultures meet across a common frontier, there
exists as much potential for conflict as for cooperation, especially when those cultures are at two very different stages of

social development. Even when the chosen leaders of both cultures recognize the futility of war and try to quash the antagonisms and irritations that often feed it, the ardent spirits of the greedy, the proud, and the young can never be thoroughly dampened. In New England the pattern was no different. The initially amicable relations between the English and the Indians soon disintegrated under the pressure of their cultural incompatibility. In 1637, 1675, and almost continually after 1689, Indians made war on the Englishmen who were rapidly spreading their hard heelmarks where soft moccasins had always tread. And from these opponents the English gradually learned to fight "Indian-style," an ability that once again spelled the difference between their destruction and survival in the New World.

Not all tribes were hostile, nor at any one time, which meant that some tribes, those who by proximity or treaty had grown closer to the English way of life, were able, if willing, to fight at the side of the English. Fortunately for the English, some tribes always were willing, for the natives of New England were periodically as divided from each other as their white contemporaries in Europe were.[14] Thus on the unfamiliar wilderness battlefields of America it was as much the friendly Indian as his warring brother who taught the New Englishmen how to fight for their very existence.

The first encounter with Indian warfare, during the Pequot War in Connecticut, was too brief for the English to learn very much and too successful for them to need to. In a conflict that lasted only a few months, the English troops and their Mohegan allies obliterated the Pequots with a final surprise attack and superior firepower. Since the Indians had not yet acquired guns from the Dutch and the French, the English found their fighting methods simply ludicrous. After Mystic Fort, the Pequot stronghold, had been fired and riddled with English bullets, killing most of its five hundred inhabitants, the male survivors charged the English battalia surrounding it with little success, so Capt. John Underhill sent the Mohegans against them "that we might see the nature of the Indian war." By English standards this was so ineffective that "they might fight seven years and not kill seven men. They came not near one another," remarked Underhill, "but shot remote, and not point-blank, as we often do with our bullets, but at rovers, and then they gaze up in the sky to see where the arrow falls, and not until it is fallen do they shoot again. This fight," he concluded, "is more for pastime, than to conquer and subdue enemies."[15]

Its ineffectiveness, however, was not due to lack of European firearms, as Lt. Lion Gardiner, the commander of the English fort at Saybrook, discovered when he went into the nearby fields to retrieve several victims of an Indian raid. Not to his surprise, he found "the body of one man shot through, the arrow going in at the right side, the head sticking fast, half through a rib on the left side, which I took out and cleansed it, and presumed to send to the [Massachusetts] Bay, because they had said that the arrows of the Indians were of no force." When the Indians wanted to kill their opponents, especially the English, they had the means and the skill necessary.[16]

Still the Indians—both friend and foe—were initially impressed with English warfare, which had changed very little from the European style during the seventeen years New England had been colonized. When the Connecticut troops emerged from Fort Saybrook to chase their audacious tormenters, they still "beat up the drum," flew their colors, and marched in serried ranks into the nearest campaign field to "bid them battle." The men were "completely armed, with corselets, muskets, bandoleers, rests, and swords," which, as the Indians themselves related afterward, "did much daunt them." The sight of such martial pageantry must have impressed the Indians' sense of ceremony, but it was the ferocity of the English in battle that truly awed them. After the Mystic Fort massacre, Captain Underhill boasted, "Our Indians came to us, and much rejoiced at our victories, and greatly admired the manner of English-men's fight, but cried Mach it, mach it; that is, It is naught, it is naught, because it is too furious, and slays too many men." The Indians had little to learn about the art of war, it seems, but the English taught them something about its energetic pursuit.[17]

By the same token the English learned at least one technique of wilderness warfare from the natives. When Massachusetts sent one hundred soldiers to Connecticut to quell the Pequots, they were placed under the command of four captains and "other inferior officers," a number unusually large by European standards. So Captain Underhill, one of the officers, felt compelled to explain their deviation from the norm to the English readers of his *Newes from America*. "I would not have the world wonder at the great number of commanders to so few men," he wrote, "but know that the Indians' fight far differs from the *Christian* practice; for they most commonly divide themselves into small bodies, so that we are forced to neglect our usual way, and to subdivide our divisions to answer theirs."[18] Since the Pequot stronghold was ambushed by mass encirclement, a thoroughly European tactic, the American version of "divide and conquer" was not particularly decisive for the English in 1637. However, for more than a century after the outbreak of King Philip's War in 1675, it would prove to be a valuable asset—and even, ironically, on more than one occasion, a liability. But it was only the first of a whole range of military tactics that the English would learn, however tardily, from the New England natives before the Revolution.[19]

In the initial encounters of King Philip's War, which was to be fought largely on terrain very different from Connecticut's rocky forests, the English ensigns still "boldly held up [their] Colours in the Front of [their] Compan[ies]" and the troops still planned to "beat up the Enemies Quarters, or give him Battel, if he durst abide it." But the Indians would have none of this European nonsense, and continued their own successful methods, "seldom or never daring," as a hostile witness put it, "to meet our Soldiers in the open Field, unless when they have very great Advantage as to their Numbers, or Covert of the Woods and Bushes."[20] Some eight months after the start of hostilities an American author had to admit to his English readers that "we have as yet had Nothing like to a Field Battel with the Indians." Nor would they ever. As one warrior told an English captain, "English Fashion is all one Fool; you kill mee, mee kill you! No, better ly somewhere, and Shoot a man, and hee no see! That the best Soldier!"[21]

The "perfidious Subtlety" of their "timerous and barbarous Enemy" thoroughly frustrated the English. One response, typical of uncomprehending students, was to explain away its obvious effectiveness by resort to their own (temporary) inadequacies. The early successes of King Philip's men, wrote the Reverend William Hubbard, the colonies' chief historian of the Indian wars, "must be imputed in a great Measure to our Mens unacquaintedness with the Manner of their fighting, they doing most of their Mischiefs either by Ambushments, sudden Surprizals, or overmatching some of our small Companyes with greater Numbers, having had many Times six or seven to one. [And] possibly also," he admitted, more as an aside than a confession, "many of our Overthrows have proceeded from our too much Confidence in our own Weapons, Courage and Martial Discipline."[22]

Another response, one which would color the whole history of colonial New England, was to adapt as quickly as possible to the uninhibited style of Indian warfare. This had two results, one expected but uncertain and the other unintended but inevitable. As they had hoped, it ultimately enabled the English to defeat their teachers for the hegemony of New England. But two other practices, one a direct loan, the other

an English "improvement," served to lower their own conduct to the "barbarous" levels they so self-consciously deplored. The English "improvement" was the use of dogs, especially mastiffs. When the Reverend Solomon Stoddard of
Northampton recommended to the governor of Massachusetts in 1703 that dogs be used to track Indians and to guard
towns, he was well aware that he was departing from "Christian practice." *"If the Indians were as other people are,"* he
began, "and did manage their warr fairly *after the manner of
other nations,* it might be looked upon as inhumane to pursue them in such a manner." And then, like all apologists of
war, he proceeded to excuse his own "inhumane" suggestion
by dehumanizing the enemy—and in the process a part of
himself. "But they are to be looked upon as thieves and murderers, they doe acts of hostility, without proclaiming war,
they don't appeare openly in the field to bid us battle, they
use those cruelly that fall into their hands." In short, "they
act like wolves and are to be dealt withall as wolves."[23] It was
reasoning such as this, tragically flawed by hubris and lack of
compassion, that allowed an order to be given in nearby Hatfield in 1675 for a female Indian captive "to be torn in pieces
by dogs."[24]

The second practice that diminished the New Englishman's
humanity was scalping, a direct loan from the Indians. On
September 12, 1694, the General Court of Massachusetts
passed an act confining all friendly Indians to a *cordon sani-
taire* and offering bounties "for every [hostile] Indian, great
or small, which they shall kill, or take and bring in prisoner."
Volunteer Indian fighters in "greater or lesser parties"—the
first American bounty hunters—received £50 per head, volunteers under pay, £20, and regular soldiers under pay, £10.
Since the provincial treasurer was not about to trust the word
of every common soldier, the enemy's scalplock had to be produced to receive the bounty, and to prevent fraud a three-
month prison sentence and a fine double the amount of the

bounty were threatened for trying to pass off a false scalp, especially that of a friendly Indian.[25]

As the situation along the eastern frontier worsened, the government steadily increased the scalp bounties until by 1722 individual volunteers were receiving £100 per head, a small fortune to poor soldiers but only a tithe of the actual cost to the country of every Indian taken or killed. But something was obviously gnawing at the New English conscience, for only two months after the initial act of 1704 was passed, the court amended it in the direction of "Christian practice." Instead of rewarding the killing of "every Indian, great or small," a scale graduated by age and sex was established, so that the scalps of "men or youths [twelve years or older] capable of bearing armes" were worth £100 to any company of volunteers, women and boys above the age of ten, only £10, and no reward was given for killing children under ten years. In a gesture of dubious compassion, such children instead were sold as slaves and transported out of the country.[26]

Aware of the moral dangers inherent in fostering such "barbarous" practices, the General Court was careful to limit each enactment to one year. But necessity was strong throughout most of the first half of the eighteenth century, and the bounties were renewed year after year in the hope that more volunteers would turn the tide against the eastern Indians. And so they did. Selected techniques of Indian warfare, placed in the hands of a larger English population already possessed of a more advanced technology, eventually destroyed traditional Indian society in New England, but not before exacting a heavy moral price from the colonists.

It was regrettable that the English resorted to the Indian practice of scalping, but it was probably necessary if they were to survive in the New World. Furthermore, without trying to explain *away* their actions, we should place them in historical perspective. Incredible as it may seem, scalping was a humane improvement upon the standard Indian treatment of their enemies, "it being the custome to cut off their heads, hands, and feete, to beare home to their wives and children, as true tokens of their renowned victorie."[27] In his *Key into the Language of America*, Roger Williams translated the ancient Narragansett word for *"to cut off, or behead,"* observing that "when ever they wound, and their arrow sticks in the body of their enemie, they (if they be valourous, and possibly may) they follow their arrow, and falling upon the person wounded and tearing his head a little aside by his Locke, they in the twinckling of an eye fetch off his head though but with a sorry [dull] knife."[28] Scalping simply seems to have been reserved for enemies slain a considerable distance from home, "in which is their usual Manner, when it is too far to carry the Heads." As soon as the battle was ended, they always made a fire to "carefully preserve the scalps of the head, drying the inside with hot ashes; and so carry them home as trophies of their valour, for which they are rewarded." It was a similar need for proof that prompted the English to encourage the taking of scalps.[29]

But the historical context of scalping included not only the practices of New England but those of old England as well. And even there "barbarism" was not unknown, as Col. Daniel Axtell discovered in 1660. For his part in the beheading of King Charles I, he was "drawne upon a hardle" to the "Tyborne gallow tree," where he was "hanged, cut downe, his body quickly opened and his intrealls burnt; hee was quartred and brought back to Newgate Prison to be boyled and then, as the [nine] others, [his head] to be sett up as his Majesty pleased." In the seventeenth century, the standards of English justice and Indian revenge were never far apart, and the objects of both had little chance of survival. At least the victims of scalping occasionally lived to ripe old age.[30]

Fortunately, the great majority of military techniques learned from the Indians carried much less danger of moral contagion than scalping. Their danger was further reduced by the well-known example of Benjamin Church, who was at once perhaps the best student of Indian fighting and one of the most humane military leaders in colonial New England. His personal account of the not insignificant role he played in King Philip's War and in several eastern campaigns into the eighteenth century, published by his son in 1716, might well have served the New English both as a guide to the conduct of Indian warfare and as a casebook of moral restraint in the face of great temptation.

Much of King Philip's War was waged in the swampy lowlands of the Plymouth colony and Rhode Island, which gave the Indians an added advantage over their inexperienced rivals. "Every Swamp is a Castle to them," lamented Increase Mather, "knowing where to find us, but we know not where to find them, who nevertheless are always at home, and have in a manner nothing but their lives and souls (which they think not of) to loose . . . and they can live comfortably on that which would starve *English-men*."[31] Each of the local swamps was "so full of Bushes and Trees, that a Parcel of Indians may be within the Length of a Pike of a Man, and he cannot discover them; and besides, [each] is so soft Ground, that an Englishman can neither go nor stand thereon, and yet these bloody Savages," marveled a contemporary, "will run along over it, holding their Guns across their Arms (and if Occasion be) discharge in that Posture."[32] The English commanders always ordered their pursuing men out of the swamps at nightfall, "not thinking it Safe to tarry longer in so dangerous a Place, where every One was in as much Danger of his Fellows as of his Foes, being ready to fire upon every Bush they see move (supposing *Indians* were there)." For they had been "taught by late Experience how dangerous it is to fight in such dismal Woods, when their Eyes were muffled with the Leaves, and their Arms pinioned with the thick Boughs of the Trees, as their Feet were continually shackled with the Roots spreading every Way in those boggy

Woods." As far as the English were concerned, it was "ill fighting with a wild Beast in his own Den."[33]

But Church, long a resident of the outreaches of the Plymouth colony and Rhode Island, knew the swamps and their native inhabitants well, which he turned to good advantage when Philip began his assaults on the isolated Plymouth villages in June 1675. Commissioned a captain in the Plymouth militia, he quickly ventured out with raiding parties of colonists and friendly Indians in hopes of catching the "wild Beast in his own Den," having made it clear to the Plymouth Council of War "that if he should take the Command of Men, he should not lye in any Town or Garrison with them, but would lye in the Woods as the Enemy did." In his opinion, forts were "only Nests for Destruction." Once in the woods he put his knowledge of Indian tactics to work while continuing to learn from his Indian comrades.

His manner of Marching thro' the Woods was such, as if he were discovered, they appeared to be more than they were. For he always Marched at a wide distance one from another, partly for their safety: and this was an *Indian* custom, to March thin and scatter. Capt. *Church* inquired of some of the *Indians* that were become his Souldiers, *How they got such advantage often of the English in their Marches thro' the Woods?* They told him, That . . . the *Indians* always took care in their Marches and Fights, not to come too thick together. But the *English* always kept in a heap together, that it was as easy to hit them as to hit an House, [and] that if at any time they discovered a company of *English* Souldiers in the Woods, they knew that there was all, for the *English* never scattered; but the *Indians* always divided and scattered.[34]

Another maneuver which went against European practice was to have his men not all fire at once in volleys "lest the Enemy should take the advantage of such an Opportunity to run upon them with their Hatche[t]s." He avoided ambushes by never "return[ing] the same way that he came" and forbidding his men telltale fires to satisfy their "Epidemical plague of lust after Tobacco." And he could "skulk" with the best of his enemies, always ensuring that he had several Indians in his company because "they exceed most of our *English* in hunting and Sculking in the woods, being always us'd to it; and it must be practised if ever we intend to destroy those *Indian* Enemies." At the final engagement with Philip on Mount Hope in August 1676, Church characteristically advised an officer who was given the honor of approaching first that "his custom in the like cases was to creep with his company on their bellies, until they came as near as they could; and that as soon as the Enemy discovered them they would cry out; and that was the word for his Men to fire and fall on."[35] It was shrewdness like this that leads one to suspect that if several crucial pages were missing from the Indian handbook of war, they were probably taken by Benjamin Church.

Church's knowledge of their ways quickly brought him a large measure of success over the hostile Indians. To an ordinary man this would have presented an overwhelming temptation to visit an understandable rage and thirst for revenge upon his captives. But Church was a man of uncommon mettle. Besides possessing a strong sense of humanity and compassion, he had lived amongst the Indians much of his life and could not erase the instinctive knowledge he had of them as *human beings*. He was simply incapable of the kind of venomous imprecations Cotton Mather would use in 1689 to arouse battlebound New English soldiers to a fighting pitch. *"Vengeance, Dear Country-men! Vengeance upon our Murderers,"* he cried from Boston's North Church. "Let your *Courage,* in the Name of God be daring enough to Execute that *Vengeance* on them . . . *Beat* them small as the *Dust before the Wind,* and *Cast them out,* as the *Dirt in the*

Streets . . . those Ravenous howling *Wolves.*"[36] How different was Church's sense of Christian justice when his Indian
soldiers presented him with Little Eyes, a Sogkonate who had
left the tribe to join Philip upon their making peace with the
English, and threatened to kill Church at the dance celebrating the treaty. The Indians "signified to him that now
he had an opportunity to be revenged on him, but the Captain told them, *It was not English-mans fashion to seek re-*
venge; and, that he should have the same quarter the rest
had."[37]

The same scrupulousness on another occasion earned him
the "loss of the good Will and Respect of some that before
were his good Friends." In July 1675 "a Number of the
Enemy . . . had surrendred themselves Prisoners on terms
promised" by the captain of the English garrison. "And had
their promises to the *Indians* been kept, and the *Indians* farely
treated, 'tis probable that most if not all the *Indians* in those
Parts, had soon followed the Example of those that had now
surrendred themselves; which would have been a good step
toward finishing the War," then only one month old. But in
spite of all that Church and the captain could "say, argue,
plead, or beg, some body else that had more Power in their
hands improv'd it; and without any regard to the promises
made them on their surrendring themselves, they were cary'd
away to *Plymouth,* there sold, and transported out of the
country." It is not difficult to see why this action was "so
hateful" to Church.[38]

Equally disturbing to the captain was the barbarous use of
prisoners by his Indian soldiers which was countenanced by
his superiors. When one of his Mohegans captured a wounded
Indian, "some were for torturing of him to bring him to a
more ample confession, of what he knew concerning his
Country-men. [But] Mr. *Church* verily believing he had been
ingenious in his confession, interceded and prevailed for his
escaping torture." When the army continued its march, the

prisoner's wound "somewhat disinabling him for Travelling, 'twas concluded he should be knock'd on the Head" by his captor before the assembled English troops and their general around a "great fire." "Mr. *Church* taking no delight in the Sport, fram'd an arrant [errand] at some distance among the baggage Horses."[39]

The following year, as the long war was grinding to a climax, Church decimated most of Philip's forces in a swamp fight, taking or killing 173 men. Although the causes for vengeful action had accumulated beyond number after fourteen months of savage fighting, Church ensured that his prisoners were "well treated with Victuals and drink," so well indeed that "they had a merry Night . . . not being so treated a long time before." And thinking they were giving him cause for joy, "some of the *Indians* now said to Capt. *Church, Sir, You have now made* Philip *ready to dye, for you have made him as poor, and miserable as he us'd to make the* English; *for you have now killed or taken all his Relations.*" They concluded by telling him *"that they believed he would now soon have his head."* But instead of bringing delight to a rancorous spirit, wrote his son, *"this [a]bout had almost broke his heart."*[40] In men like Church, the full meaning of Christian charity becomes palpable.

The success with which Benjamin Church selectively adapted the style of Indian fighting to his own uses stands in doleful contrast to the indiscriminate adoptions of other English officers. One of these was Capt. Thomas Lothrop, who was sent on September 18, 1675, with a company of eighty men—"the very Flower of the County of Essex"—to escort a wagon train of corn from Deerfield to beleaguered Hatfield. But on that "most fatal Day, the Saddest that ever befel *New-England,*" according to William Hubbard, his company was ambushed and all but seven or eight men killed, "which great Defeat came to pass by the unadvised Proceeding of the Captain (who was himself slain in the first Assault) although he wanted neither Courage nor Skill, to lead his Souldiers: but having taken up a wrong Notion about the best Way and Manner of fighting with the *Indians* (which he was always wont to argue for) *viz.* that it were best to deal with the *Indians* in their own Way, *sc.* by skulking behind Trees, and taking their Aim at single Persons, which is the usual Manner of the *Indians* fighting one with another; but herein was his great Mistake," Hubbard correctly discerned, "in not considering the great Disadvantage a smaller Company would have in dealing that way with a great Multitude"—the Indians numbered seven to eight hundred that day—"for if five have to deal with one, they may surround him, and every one to take his Aim at him, while he can level at but one of his Enemies at a time. . . . Had he ordered his Men to march in a Body, as some of his Fellow-commanders advised, either backward, or forward, in Reason they had not lost a Quarter of the Number of those that fell that Day by the Edg of the Sword. For the *Indians,* notwithstanding their Subtilty and Cruelty, durst not look an *Englishman* in the Face in the open Field, nor ever yet were known to kill any Man with their Guns, unless when they could lie in wait for him in an Ambush, or behind some Shelter, taking Aim undiscovered."[41] In raw hands the tactics of Indian warfare, like sorcerers' magic, could easily turn upon their apprentices.

Fortunately for the English, not all Indian techniques were double-edged. Two in particular involved only the adoption and use of ordinary native artifacts—the moccasin and the snowshoe. Moccasins, the supreme footwear for fast, quiet forest travel, were made of elk or deerskin, hair side in, "which yet being excellently tann'd by them, is excellent for to travell in wet and snow; for it is so well tempered with oyle," testified Roger Williams, "that the water cleane wrings out; and being hang'd up in their chimney, they presently drie without hurt as my selfe hath often proved."[42] Another advantage was that they were "absolutely necessary for the purpose of ad-

justing their snowshoes," which were made, said one European, "like a large Racket we play at *Tennis* with, lacing
them with *Deers*-guts and the like." "These snowshoes, made
in lozenge shape," said another, "are more than two feet long
and a foot and a half broad . . . by means of which they
easily walk on the snow."[43] In the deep snows of Maine,
where the spring sun comes late in the year, both were necessities, as the colonists realized when the theater of war shifted
to the northern and eastern frontiers after 1689.

The need was not unfelt even earlier, for during the first
winter of King Philip's War "the Foot [soldiers] were unable
to do any Service in the Depth of the Snow, and Sharpness of
the Cold, . . . unless they carried Rackets under their Feet,
wherewith to walk upon the Top of the Snow." But it was
not until June 14, 1704, the same year that the scalp bounty
was raised to £100, that the Massachusetts General Court, in
an act "for the more ready and better pursuit after the Indian
rebels in the winter, upon the snow," ordered that one-half
of the colonial militia "shall, each of them, at his own charge,
be provided with a pair of good serviceable snow-shoes and
mogginsons" before the tenth of November. Officers were to
send to Boston lists of their men who had complied with the
order so that they might be reimbursed three shillings, and
a fine of ten shillings was levied for each neglect. Soon thereafter, to ensure that the militia of each of the four northern
counties received sufficient equipment, the court ordered five
hundred pairs of snowshoes to be made. When the time of
compliance approached, several companies on the frontiers
petitioned the court to raise their reimbursement from three
to five shillings since they found that "a pr of good snow
shoes, Mogesons and bands will cost 10 s money at the least."
The military need for this equipment was so pressing that
the subsidy was raised without a murmur. And not without
reason, for by the following winter, "little or no spoil was
done on any of our frontiers; the enemy being so terrified by

reason of snow-shoes (which most of our men were skillful in) that they never attempted coming at such a season after." Once again, it was the successful adoption of the Indians' own tactics and technology that gave the English the palm and eventually the domination of New England.[44]

People alter their life-styles for both negative and positive reasons. They are always to some degree disappointed or unhappy with their present lives, but perhaps more important, they are also attracted—tempted—by an alternative which seems to answer their dissatisfactions. This alternative life-style is generally personified by familiar living models, people whose mode of living conveys an appearance of harmony, integrity, and contentment. When the settlers of New England became disenchanted with their own lives complicated by the demands of civilization, it was the Indians' more primitive existence that tempted them toward a change of life.

One form of temptation—perhaps among people of different color the most elemental—was sexual. But the attraction seems to have been all on one side; the Indians never cared to lie with white people, even when they enjoyed sovereign power over their bodies in captivity. Only during wartime, when atrocity stories are normally bruited to condition a people's hatred of the enemy, did the English insinuate that the Indians defile "any Woman they take alive, . . . afterwards putting her to Death."[45] Such flagrant propaganda could not stand before the impeccable testimony of the many English women who returned from captivity with their chastity and lives intact. As late as 1724 an English woman could say from a year's experience in captivity that "the Indians are very civil towards their captive women, not offering any incivility by any indecent carriage, (unless they be much over-come in liquor,) which is commendable in them, so far."[46]

One explanation for the Indians' lack of interest in English women emerged during the initial stages of the Pequot

War, when a sixteen-year-old girl captured from Wethersfield reportedly told her English redeemers that the Indians "did solicit her to uncleanness." This may have been mere wishful thinking, for Edward Johnson told a fuller and much different story. "Having taken these two prisoners," he said, "they did not offer to abuse their persons, *as was verily deemed they would,* questioned them with such broken English, as some of them could speak, to know whether they could make Gunpowder. Which when they understood they could not doe, their prize proved nothing so pretious a Pearle in their eyes as before; for seeing they exceeded not their own Squawes in Art, their owne thoughts informed them they would fall abundantly short in industry, and *as for beauty they esteeme black beyond any colour.*" If Johnson was right, English women were not sexually assaulted because they were not attractive to Indian men, who always preferred their own women. "Wherefore," saw Johnson with his English eyes, "their Squawes use that sinfull art of painting their Faces in the hollow of their Eyes and Nose, with a shining black, out of which their tip of their Nose appears very deformed, and their cheeke bone, being of a lighter swart black, on which they have a blew crosse dyed very deepe. This is the beauty esteemed by them." Perhaps it was no coincidence that to these same Indians the Devil appeared "in a bodily shape, sometimes very ugly and terrible, and sometimes like a *white* boy."[47]

The English, on the other hand, suffered from no such cultural inhibitions. Many of them, men and women, could not resist the physical attraction of these magnificent people of "savage hue." The English found many faults with their initially admired hosts over the course of time, but they could never put aside their unreserved admiration for the Indian physique. The sensuality of William Wood's description is at once a good example and an explanation of the Indians' seductive mien.

Of their Stature, most of them being betweene five or six foote high, straight bodied, strongly composed, smooth skinned, merry countenanced, of complexion something more swarthly than *Spaniards*, black hair'd, high foreheaded, blacke ey'd, out-nosed, broad shouldred, brawny arm'd, long and slender handed, out brested, small wasted, lanke bellied, well thighed, flat kneed, handsome growne leggs, and small feete: In a word, take them when the blood briskes in their veines, when the flesh is on their backs, and marrow in their bones, when they frolick in their antique deportments and *Indian* postures; and they are more amiable to behold (though onely in *Adams* livery) than many a compounded phantasticke in the newest fashion.[48]

John Josselyn's evocation of Indian women was no less titil- lating. "The *Indesses* that are young," he wrote, "are some of them very comely, having good features, their faces plump and round, and generally plump of their Bodies . . . and as soft and smooth as a mole-skin, of reasonable good complex- ions, but that they dye themselves tawnie, many prettie Brownetto's and spider finger'd Lasses may be seen amongst them."[49] If the Indians were typically seen as young, wild, passionate, and alluring, but somehow tainted in the blood— as dark beauty is often portrayed in literary convention—the frequency with which the English succumbed to their aroused passions appears in a clearer light.[50]

For succumb they did, as early as 1631. At the September session of the Massachusetts General Court "a young fellow was whipped for soliciting an Indian squaw to incontinency. Her husband and she complained of the wrong, and were present at the execution, and very well satisfied."[51] In the Plymouth colony, where the English lived more closely with their Indian neighbors, the opportunity for cross-cultural unions was greater. During the seventy years of Plymouth's autonomy, several cases of fornication involving colonists and

Indians appeared on the court docket, only one of which ever accused an Indian of attempting English virtue. The conduct of Mary, the wife of Duxbury's Robert Mendame, typified the direction of New England's sexual solicitations. On September 3, 1639, she was sentenced to be "whipped at a cart tayle" through the town and to wear a badge of sin—the scarlet letter—on her left sleeve forever for "useing dallyance divers tymes with Tinsin, an Indian, and after committing the act of uncleanesse with him." Tinsin, who had confessed their crime through an interpreter, was only whipped at the post with a halter about his neck "because it arose through the allurement and inticement of the said Mary, that hee was drawne thereunto." Singularly exceptional was the case of Sam, an Indian, who violated Sarah Freeman "by laying her down upon her backe, and entering her body with his." Ordinarily rape brought the death penalty, but the court, "considering he was but an Indian, and therefore in an incapacity to know the horiblenes of the wickednes of this abominable act," commuted his sentence to a whipping and expulsion from the colony. Since this unique violation of the normal pattern of sexual temptation did not occur until 1682, Sam may well have been sufficiently Anglicized by his familiarity with the English to exchange in a moment of weakness or confusion imported for native standards of beauty and sensuality. If so, it was a costly lapse.[52]

Intercultural dalliance was one thing, and easily handled by English justice and public opinion, but sometimes lust gave way to love, raising the spectre of marriage outside the carefully hedged fold. The problem was raised in a formal way in March 1635 when the Massachusetts General Court entertained and then immediately referred a question concerning the propriety of Indian-white marriages, but it never regained the court's attention. Instead of civil law, public opinion was left to police untoward affections, with what success we can only guess. Only when a mixed couple entered the judicial lists for an offense of a legal nature did the fact of their union come to light.[53]

Probably most couples of necessity lived far from the obdurate center of English society, close to if not actually in the tolerant homes of the Indian partners. If the colonial reaction to Joshua Tift, a "Renegadoe English Man of *Providence*," is an accurate measure, mixed marriages were regarded with an unmerciful eye, especially if the Englishman accepted more than a spouse from the Indians. During the first winter of King Philip's War, English scouts wounded and captured Tift, who "upon some Discontent amongst his Neighbours, had turned *Indian*, married one of the *Indian Squawes*, renounced his Religion, Nation and natural Parents all at once, fighting against them. . . . He had in his Habit conformed himself to them amongst whom he lived. After Examination, he was condemned to die the Death of a Traytor" by hanging and quartering, "which was accordingly done." "As to his Religion he was found as ignorant as an Heathen"—a clear warning to backsliders—"which no doubt caused the fewer Tears to be shed at his Funeral; Standers by being unwilling to lavish Pity upon him that had divested himself of Nature itself, as well as Religion, in a Time when so much Pity was needed elsewhere."[54] It was with such transparent disdain for mixed marriages—those divestments of "Nature itself"—that Connecticut outlawed "renegades" in their 1642 Code of Laws. To discourage "diverse persons [who] departe from amongst us, and take up theire aboade with the Indians, in a prophane course of life," the General Court threatened imprisonment for three years "at least" and a fine or corporal punishment.[55] Perhaps legislation could deter mixed marriages to some degree, but it could never throttle the distinctly "heathenish" mode of life that many Englishmen adopted on the remote borders of colonial society. Of all the dangers posed by the "wast howling wilderness" of America, none was more alarming to the New English than that they and their children could be converted from "civility" to "barbarism" by its seductive freedom and its seducing inhabitants.

When the king's commissioners surveyed the state of New England in 1665, bent on pulling the independent Americans firmly under the royal wing, they found that the people of Maine "for the most part are fishermen, and never had any Government amongst them, and most of them are such as have fled thither from other places to avoyd Justice. Some here are of Opinion," they gloated, "that as many Men may share in a Woman, as they doe in a Boate, and some have done so." If the Maine county court records are any indication, the commissioners had hit upon a hard truth about one notorious New England frontier, but they had only touched the tip of a moral iceburg. Although many men *and* women were indicted for adultery and "living apart from one's spouse," they could not compete numerically with those Down Easters presented at the monthly sessions for slander, drunkenness, profanity, assault, trespass, Sabbath breaking, and, perhaps most telling of all to an orthodox Puritan, neglect of public worship.[56]

The inhabitants of the scattered, lonely farms and fishing villages of Maine represented best those who were, the social critics of the day accused, "contented to live without, yea, desirous to shake off all Yoake of Government, both sacred and civil." And with good reason, for as one plainspoken fisherman informed a Massachusetts minister sent to convert the worshippers of the pine and the cod, "Sir, You are mistaken, you think you are Preaching to the People at the Bay; our main End was to catch Fish." Since their homes had been the brawling seaports of western England, of Cornwall and Devon, not the Puritan villages of East Anglia, no one needed to be told that such men were not highly amenable to the civilized order of the Puritan ideal. In 1639 one struggling official lamented that "every man is a law to him selfe. It is a bad kind of livinge to live in a place where is neather law nor government amonge people." Twenty years later the colony was still so literally lawless that the York County Court ordered fifty copies of the latest Massachusetts statutes for the several towns with the pointed observation that "the well regulateing of Civill Societys depends much In haveing good Laws, which must bee first known before they can bee either executed or obeyed, the necessity whereof being of more then ordinary usse to us in these parts."[57] Harvard's president clearly had his northern neighbors in mind when he observed in 1655 that some "account it their happiness to live in the wast howling wilderness, without any ministry, or schoole, and means of education for their posterity, they have much liberty (they think) by this want, they are not troubled with strict Sabbaths, but they may follow their worldly bussiness at any time, and their children may drudg for them at plough, or hough, or such like servil imployments, that themselves may be eased."[58]

Down Easters may have been the worst, but they were certainly not the only offenders of Puritan sensibilities. The infamous group of Gortonists lived in Rhode Island "without any means for instructing them in the wayes of God, and without any civil Government to keep them in civility or humanity." In her travels through Connecticut in 1704, Sarah Knight of Boston felt that the Indians' polygamous marriages and easy "Stand away" divorces were "too much in Vougue among the English in this Indulgent Colony as their Records plentifully prove, and that on very trivial matters," some "not proper to be Related by a Female pen." But even in the heart of Massachusetts civilized currency had been debased. "There hath been in many professors" of the Puritan faith, scolded the Boston synod in 1679, "an insatiable desire after Land, and worldly Accommodations, yea, so as to forsake Churches and Ordinances, and to live like Heathen, only that so they might have Elbow-room enough in the world." When people moved thus into the shadowed corners of the land, bidding defiance "not only to Religion, but to Civility it self," such places inevitably became "Nurseries of Ignorance, Prophaneness and Atheism," something no good Puritan society could countenance or did.[59]

At the September session of the Massachusetts General Court in 1642, John Winthrop noted, "we were informed of some English to the eastward, who ordinarily traded powder to the Indians, and lived alone under no government." Whereupon a gentleman was dispatched to confiscate their powder and presumably to urge them to more orderly living arrangements. Ten years later the Plymouth Court ordered Joseph Ramsden to move "near unto som naighborhood," having "lived with his family remotely in the woods from naighbours." The unsociable Mr. Ramsden evaded the issue until June 1656 when the court insisted that he move by October or have his house pulled down. He moved. In 1675 the same court ordered three men to "frequent the publicke worship of [some town], and live otherwise orderly" or to leave the colony for "liveing lonely and in a heathenish way from good societie." When the civil authority could no longer stem the flow of land-hungry settlers toward the exposed frontier, the church was beckoned as a last-ditch alternative. If Puritan society could not arrest their movement, Cotton Mather argued, at least the ministry could "Enlighten them; Antidote them; Fortify them with strong *Preservatives*" against the dangers of Indian captivity and Popish delusion.[60]

Mather was not exaggerating the dangers of frontier living; they were real and omnipresent and insidious, especially for the children who were expected to carry the Puritan ideal across the generations. And they were felt very early. Only a year after he had arrived in Massachusetts, John Winthrop, Jr., was warned by an English correspondent "that ye become not a prey to the spoyler, and your children turne heathen." In 1677 the General Assembly of Connecticut, considering the resettlement of wartorn towns, cited the "woeful experiance in the late warr" which showed that "liveing in a single and scattering way, remoate from townships and neighbourhood" weakened the commonwealth and tempted the "posterity of such, most of them are endangered to degenerate into heathenish ignorance and barbarisme."[61]

The New English conception of white "heathenism" was no idle phantom or religious bugbear; its characteristics were increasingly observable as the two cultures of New England mingled and melded across their common frontier. In addition to teaching them *"Our Vice,"* asked Cotton Mather, "have not we also *Followed* the *Indians?* The Indians are Infamous, especially for Three Scandalous Qualities: They are *Lazy Drones,* and love *Idleness* Exceedingly: They are also most impudent *Lyars,* and will invent Reports and Stories at a strange and monstrous rate; and they are out of measure *Indulgent* unto their Children, there is no Family-Government among them.[62] But, O how much do our people Indianize in every one of those Abominable things!" In a perfect phrase, *"Criolian* Degeneracy" inflicted promising New English youth when they were "permitted to run wild in our Woods." Yet the dangers were not only civil, but eternal as well, for in those notoriously "Ungospellized Plantations," where "no *Minister* of God [is] countenanced," "Satan *terribly* makes a *prey* of you, and *Leads you Captive to do his Will."* And all of New England knew the meaning of captivity. As Hampshire County, in Massachusetts's western extremity, expressed it for King George III, "many of our Children . . . were captivated, bred up in popish and pagan Ignorance, and [educational] inlargement never granted; but have become implacable enemies to your own friends."[63]

The history of colonial New England, like that of most societies, has its share of contradictions and anomalies, but perhaps nothing is more inherently intriguing—or more important to our story—than the dramatic difference between the educational power of the Indians and of the English over each other. For beside the doleful failure of English education to "civilize" and Christianize the Indians stands the impressive success with which the Indians converted the English to their "barbarous" way of living. Benjamin Franklin spoke of a decisive century and a half of Ámerican experience when he compared the human results of each process. "When an Indian Child has been brought up among us," he wrote in 1753, "taught our language and habituated to our Customs, yet if he goes to see his relations and make one Indian Ramble with them, there is no perswading him ever to return." But "when white persons of either sex have been taken prisoners young by the Indians, and lived a while among them, tho' ransomed by their Friends, and treated with all imaginable tenderness to prevail with them to stay among the English, yet in a Short time they become disgusted with our manner of life, and the care and pains that are necessary to support it, and take the first good Opportunity of escaping again into the Woods, from whence there is no reclaiming them."[64]

It is too easy, having read only the novelists who have treated this theme, to underestimate the impact of "Indianization" upon the American character by assuming that it was confined to a mere handful of impressionable children and adult misfits. Nothing could be farther from the truth. In 1782 Hector de Crèvecoeur wondered "by what power does it come to pass, that children who have been adopted when young among these people, can never be prevailed on to re-adopt European manners?" But he was not talking of isolated individuals, "for *thousands* of Europeans are Indians," he wrote, "and we have no examples of even *one* of those Aborigines having from choice become Europeans!" And he does not seem to have been exaggerating for literary effect. Firm figures are impossible to come by, as can be imagined, but judging from New England alone, Crèvecoeur's estimate has the ring of truth.[65]

Between 1689 and 1713, the years of the heaviest Indian depredations along the northern and eastern frontiers of New England, about 600 men, women, and children were taken by the Indians and less frequently by the French and marched northward into captivity.[66] Of these, 174 (29 percent) definitely returned to New England, having been ransomed or exchanged for French prisoners. An additional 146 captives (25 percent) exchanged their bondage for French naturalization and baptism by the Catholic Church. This means that if we include those captives who chose to remain with the Indians, anywhere from 25 to 71 percent of English captives may have refused to return to New England. A reasonable estimate, based on the proportion of captives in French and Indian hands in 1705 (5 : 3), would be 40 percent, 25 percent (146) becoming French Canadians, 15 percent (90) becoming full-fledged Indians, and some of them practicing Catholics as well. Indeed this may well be a conservative estimate. For in 1724 during the Three Years' War, the first major outbreak of fighting since the Treaty of Utrecht in 1713, Joseph Stevens wrote the Massachusetts General Court from Canada where he was trying to redeem two of his sons: "Inasmuch as there are upward of Fifty of our People in the hands of the Indians that have been taken in this War, who unless some speedy care be taken to redeem them will probably turn Roman Catholicks and Embrace their Religion, as *above an hundred others (taken Prisoners Before this Warr)* have done, who will by no means be persuaded to Return to their Native Countrey again, but are led on in Superstition and Idolatry."[67] If the Indians were capable of winning the allegiance and affections of 15 percent of all the Americans they captured before 1782, Crèvecoeur's announcement that "thousands of Europeans are Indians" ceases to surprise, but leaves us to search for an explanation.

There were at least three kinds of reasons, each intersecting and reinforcing the others, why so many New Englishmen chose to remain with their Indian captors. Many stayed, in the first place, because they found Indian life morally superior to English civilization and Catholicism more satisfying than Puritanism. According to her Indian husband, Eunice Williams, the celebrated daughter of the Reverend John Williams of Deerfield, "no go" because "her father marry twice times. He no have marry, she go." Sylvanus Johnson, who lived with the Indians from the age of six to ten, "always maintained that the Indians were a far more moral race than the Whites." Another young Deerfield captive, Mary Harris, eventually married an Indian and moved to Ohio, where an English traveler met her in 1751. He wrote in his journal that "she still remembers [after forty-seven years] they used to be very religious in N.E. and wonders how the White men can be so wicked as she has seen them in these woods." About the same time two male captives, recent converts to Catholicism, also condemned New England's fall from religious grace. One said that "he prefers being a slave with the Indians than in his country where there is no religion." (His father was dead and by New England law "whoever has been ransomed, if obliged to borrow the money, is bound to service until he have repaid by his labor the sum he cost.") The other sounded a similar note; he refused redemption because "he hated too strongly the English nation where he was almost a slave to give up his religion and liberty."[68]

Although Puritans resented the Jesuits' perfidious "stratagem[s] to seduce poor children . . . from the simplicity of the gospel to Romish superstition," they could not gainsay the effectiveness of their conversion efforts, especially with younger children who in New England had only begun to catechize and to memorize Scripture. The tenacity of belief possessed by two Deerfield girls, captured at the age of seven and eight respectively, testifies to the Jesuits' success in religious education. Several years after her capture, Mary Field and her Indian husband visited her family in their new Connecticut home. She told her brother Pedajah, who had been born after the Deerfield raid, that someday he would be carried off so that he too could enjoy the Indian life and Catholic religion. Indeed, he thought the attempt was once made in Northfield, but he had escaped in a canoe. After ten years with the Indians, Hannah Hurst married a thirty-two-year-old Indian widower and received baptism in the Catholic Church. The priest wrote in his register that "she has declared many times she does not wish to leave the Savages, with whom she wished to die a Christian." Among Indian captives from New England her stance was not unusual.[69]

The second explanation for the retentive power of Indian culture is the nature of the adoptive process by which captives were thoroughly integrated into the social life and kinship structure of the tribe. When Mrs. James Johnson was adopted by the rich son-in-law of the grand sachem, she later wrote, "I was introduced to the family, and was told [by the interpreter] to call them brothers and sisters, I made a short reply, expressive of gratitude"—a matter of much importance to the Indians[70]—"for being introduced to a house of high rank, and requested their patience while I should learn the customs of the nation. . . . I had a numerous retinue of relations, whom I visited daily . . . [and] my new sisters and brothers treated me with the same attention that they did their natural kindred, but it was," she admitted, "an unnatural situation to me." It would not have been to a younger child who had lost one or both of her own parents, as was the situation of many captives. But even Mrs. Johnson, like so many Englishmen who returned from Indian life, had to defend their singular humanity. Did the colonists "ever adopt an enemy," she asked, "and salute him by the tender name of brother?"[71]

Adoption was the more serious for the Indians because it was often used to replace fallen sons or daughters. And, as Governor Duquesne once told Governor Shirley of Massachusetts, "there is nothing so difficult as to get their slaves [captives] from them, especially when they have distributed them among their Wigwams to make up for their Dead."[72] Twenty-two-year-old Zadock Steele's description of his adoption brings home the mutual benefits that accrued to both captors and captives.

> All the Indians, both male and female, together with the prisoners, assembled and formed a circle, within which one of their chiefs, standing upon a stage erected for the purpose, harrangued the audience in the Indian tongue. Although I could not understand his language, yet I could plainly discover a great share of native eloquence. His speech was of considerable length, and its effect obviously manifested weight of argument, solemnity of thought, and at least human sensibility. I was placed near by his side, and had a fair view of the whole circle. After he had ended his speech an old squaw came and took me by the hand and led me to her wigwam, where she dressed me in a red coat, with a ruffle in my bosom, and ordered me to call her *mother*. She could speak English tollerably well; but was very poor, and therefore unable to furnish me with very sumptuous fare. My food was rather beneath a savage mediocrity; though no doubt my new mother endeavored as far as lay in her power to endear the affections of her newly-adopted yet ill-natured son. . . . As I was blest with an excellent voice for singing, I was the more beloved by, and, on that account, received much better treatment from, my new mother, as well as from other Indians. I was allowed the privilege of visiting any part of the village in the daytime, and was received with marks of fraternal affection and treated with all the civility an Indian is capable to bestow.[73]

As Hector de Crèvecoeur realized, there was "in their social bond something singularly captivating, and far superior to anything to be boasted of among us."[74]

Finally, many New Englishmen became Indians because, as two adult converts acknowledged, they enjoyed "the most perfect freedom, the ease of living, [and] the absence of those cares and corroding solicitudes which so often prevail with us." When the New English had an explanation for the startling desertion of their neighbors from the civilized fold, they refused to impute any responsibility to the educational inadequacies of their own culture and instead blamed the natural condition of man as they knew it. "The human mind is naturally averse to control," said Gen. Benjamin Lincoln, Revolutionary soldier and Indian expert. "All men naturally wish for ease, and to avoid the shackles of restraint." Benjamin Franklin, another Massachusetts man long familiar with the Indians, singled out the "proneness of human Nature to a life of ease, of freedom from care and labour," but he argued with unintended irony, "care and pains . . . are necessary to support . . . our manner of life" with its "infinite Artificial wants." The same perspective obviously appealed to the romantic nature of Hector de Crèvecoeur, who planned to move his family to an Indian village to escape the ravages of the Revolutionary War. "There must be something more congenial to our native dispositions," he wrote with undisguised admiration, "than the fictitious society in which we live; or else why should children, and even grown persons, become in a short time so invincibly attached to it? There must be something very bewitching in their manners, something very indelible and marked by the very hands of nature."[75]

What contemporaries saw as the marking hand of nature was in reality the powerful fist of culture, molding in its image its neophytes from another world. When the Reverend John Williams saw "several poor children, who had been taken from the eastward the summer before, . . . in habit very much like Indians, and in manners very much"—the word is crucial—"*symbolizing* with them," he was witnessing the educational impact of a culture marked by an uncommon integrity, by social cohesion and a unity of thought and action.[76] In short, New English captives stayed with their Indian families because they had become enchanted by

> . . . the scholastic philosophy of the wilderness
> to combat which one must stand outside and laugh
> since to go in is to be lost.[77]

And the arcane complexity of the Puritan philosophy, with its burdens of civility and constraint, could simply not release them from its spell.

CHAPTER SEVEN

The White Indians of Colonial America

IN WRITING THE SCHOOL UPON A HILL AND PARTICULARLY CHAPTER 6 above, I was forcibly struck by the contrast between the educational styles and results of the Indians and the English colonists. Although the colonists were reasonably adept at educating their own kind for the limited number of social and spiritual roles they could expect to play in New (or old) England, they were much less successful at fitting other, ethnically different peoples for those roles or any roles other than the most demeaning. As I tried to show in Chapter 4, the major cause of failure was the unwillingness of the English to take their Indian students into their hearts and homes, the primary agencies of enculturation for their own children. This reluctance was rooted in their overweening sense of cultural and later racial superiority, attitudes that the Indians had no difficulty in perceiving.

At the same time, I learned what a few anthropologists had already known but colonial historians had virtually ignored, namely, that the Indians were not only proficient in educating their own children without resorting to physical compulsion or emotional undercutting, but also in converting enemies—Indian and white, young and old—to their way of life. In "Scholastic Philosophy" I could do no more than sketch the dimensions and seriousness of the Indians' educational threat to the "City upon a Hill," but as soon as the book was completed I returned to the subject of the "white Indians" in order to probe the *process* of conversion that the captives underwent. What emerged after digesting most of the colonial captivity narratives was the following essay, considerably improved by the comments of Robert Berkhofer and Wilcomb Washburn at the 1972 meeting of the Organization of American Historians, and editorial guidance beyond the call of duty from Michael McGiffert, who published it in the January 1975 issue of the *William and Mary Quarterly*.

To judge by the number of times the essay has been reprinted and by the spirited discussions it evokes from my classes, the subject and the irony of "superior" Englishmen becoming bona fide converts to an "inferior" culture must hold intrinsic interest for many students of historical process. Since writing it, I am the more convinced that this novel subject (for both historians and novelists) bristles with inherent drama and cultural and moral implications for colonial and American history, many of which are still uncharted. If my own experience is any guide, its full flavor and meaning can best be savored by reading it in combination with "Dr. Wheelock's Little Red School" and one of Conrad Richter's "ethnohistorical" novels, *The Light in the Forest* (1953), or its sequel, *A Country of Strangers* (1966).

THE ENGLISH, LIKE THEIR FRENCH RIVALS, BEGAN THEIR COLOnizing ventures in North America with a sincere interest in converting the Indians to Christianity and civilization. Nearly all the colonial charters granted by the English monarchs in the seventeenth century assigned the wish to extend the Christian Church and to redeem savage souls as a principal, if not *the* principal, motive for colonization.[1] This desire was grounded in a set of complementary beliefs about "savagism" and "civilization." First, the English held that the Indians, however benighted, were capable of conversion. "It is not the nature of men," they believed, "but the education of men, which make them barbarous and uncivill."[2] Moreover, the English were confident that the Indians would want to be converted once they were exposed to the superior quality of English life. The strength of these beliefs was reflected in Cotton Mather's astonishment as late as 1721 that

> Tho' they saw a People Arrive among them, who were Clothed in *Habits* of much more Comfort and Splendour, than what there was to be seen in the *Rough Skins* with which they hardly covered themselves; and who had *Houses full of Good Things,* vastly out-shining their squalid and dark *Wigwams;* And they saw this People Replenishing their *Fields,* with *Trees* and with *Grains,* and useful *Animals,* which until now they had been wholly Strangers to; yet they did not seem touch'd in the least, with any *Ambition* to come at such Desirable Circumstances, or with any *Curiosity* to enquire after the *Religion* that was attended with them.[3]

The second article of the English faith followed from their fundamental belief in the superiority of civilization, namely, that no civilized person in possession of his faculties or free from undue restraint would choose to become an Indian. "For, easy and unconstrained as the savage life is," wrote the Reverend William Smith of Philadelphia, "certainly it could never be put in competition with the blessings of improved life and the light of religion, by any persons who have had the happiness of enjoying, and the capacity of discerning, them."[4]

And yet, by the close of the colonial period, very few if any Indians had been transformed into civilized Englishmen. Most of the Indians who were educated by the English—some contemporaries thought *all* of them—returned to Indian society at the first opportunity to resume their Indian identities. On the other hand, large numbers of Englishmen had chosen to become Indians—by running away from colonial society to join Indian society, by not trying to escape after being captured, or by electing to remain with their Indian captors when treaties of peace periodically afforded them the opportunity to return home.[5]

Perhaps the first colonist to recognize the disparity between the English dream and the American reality was Cadwallader Colden, surveyor-general and member of the king's council of New York. In his *History of the Five Indian Nations of Canada,* published in London in 1747, Colden described the Albany peace treaty between the French and the Iroquois in 1699, when "few of [the French captives] could be persuaded to return" to Canada. Lest his readers attribute this unusual behavior to "the Hardships they had endured in their own Country, under a tyrannical Government and a barren Soil," he quickly added that "the *English* had as much Difficulty to persuade the People, that had been taken Prisoners by the *French Indians,* to leave the *Indian* Manner of living, though no People enjoy more Liberty, and live in greater Plenty, than the common Inhabitants of *New-York* do." Colden, clearly amazed, elaborated:

> No Arguments, no Intreaties, nor Tears of their Friends and Relations, could persuade many of them to leave their new *Indian* Friends and Acquaintance[s]; several of them that were by the Caressings of their Relations persuaded to come Home, in a little Time grew tired of our Manner of living, and run away again to the *Indians,* and ended their Days with them. On the other Hand, *Indian* Children have been carefully educated among the *English,* cloathed and taught, yet, I think, there is not one Instance, that any of these, after they had Liberty to go among their own People, and were come to Age, would remain with the *English,* but returned to their own Nations, and became as fond of the *Indian* Manner of Life as those that knew nothing of a civilized Manner of living. What I now tell of Christian Prisoners among *Indians* [he concluded his history], relates not only to what happened at the Conclusion of this War, but has been found true on many other Occasions.[6]

Colden was not alone. Six years later Benjamin Franklin wondered how it was that

When an Indian Child has been brought up among us, taught our language and habituated to our Customs, yet if he goes to see his relations and make one Indian Ramble with them, there is no perswading him ever to return. [But] when white persons of either sex have been taken prisoners young by the Indians, and lived a while among them, tho' ransomed by their Friends, and treated with all imaginable tenderness to prevail with them to stay among the English, yet in a Short time they become disgusted with our manner of life, and the care and pains that are necessary to support it, and take the first good Opportunity of escaping again into the Woods, from whence there is no reclaiming them.[7]

In short, "thousands of Europeans are Indians," as Hector de Crèvecoeur put it, "and we have no examples of even one of those Aborigines having from choice become Europeans!"[8]

The English captives who foiled their countrymen's civilized assumptions by becoming Indians differed little from the general colonial population when they were captured. They were ordinary men, women, and children of yeoman stock, Protestants by faith, a variety of nationalities by birth, English by law, different from their countrymen only in their willingness to risk personal insecurity for the economic opportunities of the frontier.[9] There was no discernible characteristic or pattern of characteristics that differentiated them from their captive neighbors who eventually rejected Indian life—with one exception. Most of the colonists captured by the Indians and adopted into Indian families were children of both sexes and young women, often the mothers of the captive children. They were, as one captivity narrative observed, the "weak and defenceless."[10]

The pattern of taking women and children for adoption was consistent throughout the colonial period, but during the first century and one-half of Indian-white conflict, primarily in New England, it coexisted with a larger pattern of captivity that included all white colonists, men as well as women and children. The Canadian Indians who raided New England tended to take captives more for their ransom value than for adoption. When Mrs. James Johnson gave birth to a daughter on the trail to Canada, for example, her captor looked into her makeshift lean-to and "clapped his hands with joy, crying two monies for me, two monies for me." Although the New England legislatures occasionally tried to forbid the use of public moneys for "the Ransoming of Captives," thereby prolonging the Indians' "diabolical kidnapping mode of warfare," ransoms were constantly paid from both public and private funds. These payments became larger as inflation and the Indians' savvy increased. Thus when John and Tamsen Tibbetts redeemed two of their children from the Canadian Indians in 1729, it cost them £105 10s. (1,270 livres). "Being verry Poore," many families in similar situations could ill afford to pay such high premiums even "if they should sell all they have in the world."[11]

When the long peace in the Middle Atlantic colonies collapsed in 1753, the Indians of Pennsylvania, southern New York, and the Ohio country had no Quebec or Montreal in which to sell their human chattels to compassionate French families or anxious English relatives.[12] For this and other reasons they captured English settlers largely to replace members of their own families who had died, often from English musketballs or imported diseases.[13] Consequently, women and children—the "weak and defenceless"—were the prime targets of Indian raids.

According to the pattern of warfare in the Pennsylvania theater, the Indians usually stopped at a French fort with their prisoners before proceeding to their own villages. A young French soldier captured by the English reported that at Fort Duquesne there were "a great number of English Prisoners," the older of whom "they are constantly sending . . . away to Montreal" as prisoners of war, "but that the Indians keep many of the Prisoners amongst them, chiefly young People whom they adopt and bring up in their own way." His intelligence was corroborated by Barbara Leininger and Marie LeRoy, who had been members of a party of two adults and eight children captured in 1755 and taken to Fort Duquesne. There they saw "many other Women and Children, they think an hundred who were carried away from the several provinces of P[ennsylvania] M[aryland] and V[irginia]." When the girls escaped from captivity three years later, they wrote a narrative in German chiefly to acquaint "the inhabitants of this country . . . with the names and circumstances of those prisoners whom we met, at the various places where we were, in the course of our captivity." Of the fifty-two prisoners they had seen, thirty-four were children and fourteen were women, including six mothers with children of their own.[14]

The close of hostilities in Pennsylvania came in 1764 after Col. Henry Bouquet defeated the Indians near Bushy Run and imposed peace. By the articles of agreement reached in October, the Delawares, Shawnees, and Senecas were to deliver up "all the Prisoners in [their] Possession, without any Exception, Englishmen, Frenchmen, Women, and Children, whether adopted in your Tribes, married, or living amongst you, under any Denomination, or Pretence whatever." In the weeks that followed, Bouquet's troops, including "the Relations of [some of] the People [the Indians] have Massacred, or taken Prisoners," encamped on the Muskingum in the heart of the Ohio country to collect the captives. After as many as nine years with the Indians, during which time many children had grown up, 81 "men" and 126 "women and children" were returned. At the same time, a list was prepared of 88 prisoners who still remained in Shawnee towns to the west: 70 were classified as "women and children." Six months later, 44 of these prisoners were delivered up to Fort Pitt. When they were captured, all but 4 had been less than sixteen years old, while 37 had been less than eleven years old.[15]

The Indians obviously chose their captives carefully so as to maximize the chances of acculturating them to Indian life. To judge by the results, their methods were hard to fault. Even when the English held the upper hand militarily, they were often embarrassed by the Indians' educational power. On November 12, 1764, at his camp on the Muskingum, Bouquet lectured the Shawnees who had not delivered all their captives: "As you are now going to Collect all our *Flesh,* and *Blood,* . . . I desire that you will use them with Tenderness, and look upon them as Brothers, and no longer as Captives." The utter gratuitousness of his remark was reflected—no doubt purposely—in the Shawnee speech when the Indians delivered their captives the following spring at Fort Pitt. "Father—Here is your *Flesh,* and *Blood* . . . they have been all tied to us by Adoption, although we now deliver them up to you. We will always look upon them as Relations, whenever the *Great Spirit* is pleased that we may visit them . . . Father—we have taken as much Care of these Prisoners, as if they were [our] own Flesh, and blood; they are become unacquainted with your Customs, and manners, and therefore, Father we request you will use them tender, and kindly, which will be a means of inducing them to live contentedly with you."[16]

The Indians spoke the truth and the English knew it. Three days after his speech to the Shawnees, Bouquet had advised Lt.-Gov. Francis Fauquier of Virginia that the returning captives "ought to be treated by their Relations with Tenderness and Humanity, till Time and Reason make them forget their unnatural Attachments, but unless they are closely watch'd," he admitted, "they will certainly return to the Barbarians."[17] And indeed they would have, for during a half-century of conflict captives had been returned who, like many of the Ohio prisoners, responded only to Indian names, spoke only Indian dialects, felt comfortable only in Indian

clothes, and in general regarded their white saviors as barbarians and their deliverance as captivity. Had they not been
compelled to return to English society by militarily enforced
peace treaties, the ranks of the white Indians would have
been greatly enlarged.

From the moment the Indians surrendered their English
prisoners, the colonists faced a series of difficult problems.
The first was the problem of getting the prisoners to remain
with the English. When Bouquet sent the first group of restored captives to Fort Pitt, he ordered his officers there that
"they are to be closely watched and well Secured" because
"most of them, particularly those who have been a long time
among the Indians, will take the first Opportunity to run
away." The young children especially were "so completely
savage that they were brought to the camp tied hand and
foot." Fourteen-year-old John McCullough, who had lived
with the Indians for "eight years, four months, and sixteen
days" (by his parents' reckoning), had his legs tied "under
the horses belly" and his arms tied behind his back with his
father's garters, but to no avail. He escaped under the cover
of night and returned to his Indian family for a year before
he was finally carried to Fort Pitt under "strong guard."
"Having been accustomed to look upon the Indians as the
only connexions they had, having been tenderly treated by
them, and speaking their language," explained the Reverend
William Smith, the historian of Bouquet's expedition, "it is
no wonder that [the children] considered their new state in
the light of a captivity, and parted from the savages with
tears."[18]

Children were not the only reluctant freedmen. "Several
women eloped in the night, and ran off to join their Indian
friends." Among them undoubtedly were some of the English women who had married Indian men and borne them
children, and then had been forced by the English victory
either to return with their mixed-blood children to a country

of strangers, full of prejudice against Indians, or to risk escaping under English guns to their husbands and adopted culture. For Bouquet had "reduced the Shawanese and Delawares etc. to the most Humiliating Terms of Peace," boasted Gen. Thomas Gage. "He has Obliged them to deliver up even their Own Children born of white women." But even the victorious soldier could understand the dilemma into which these women had been pushed. When Bouquet was informed that the English wife of an Indian chief had eloped in the night with her husband and children, he "requested that no pursuit should be made, as she was happier with her Chief than she would be if restored to her home."[19]

Although most of the returned captives did not try to escape, the emotional torment caused by the separation from their adopted families deeply impressed the colonists. The Indians "delivered up their beloved captives with the utmost reluctance; shed torrents of tears over them, recommending them to the care and protection of the commanding officer." One young woman "cryed and roared when asked to come and begged to Stay a little longer." "Some, who could not make their escape, clung to their savage acquaintance at parting, and continued many days in bitter lamentations, even refusing sustenance." Children "cried as if they should die when they were presented to us." With only small exaggeration an observer on the Muskingum could report that "every captive left the Indians with regret."[20]

Another problem encountered by the English was the difficulty of communicating with the returned captives, a great many of whom had replaced their knowledge of English with an Algonquian or Iroquoian dialect and their baptismal names with Indian or hybrid ones.[21] This immediately raised another problem—that of restoring the captives to their relatives. Sir William Johnson, the superintendent of Indian affairs, "thought it best to advertise them [in the newspapers] immediately, but I believe it will be verry difficult to find the

Freinds of some of them, as they are ignorant of their own Names, or former places of abode, nay cant speak a word of any language but Indian." The only recourse the English had in such instances was to describe them "more particularly . . . as to their features, Complexion etc. That by the Publication of Such descriptions their Relations, parents or friends may hereafter know and Claim them."[22]

But if several colonial observers were right, a description of the captives' physiognomy was of little help after they had been with the Indians for any length of time. Peter Kalm's foreign eye found it difficult to distinguish European captives from their captors, "except by their color, which is somewhat whiter than that of the Indians," but many colonists could see little or no difference. To his Maine neighbors twelve-year-old John Durell "ever after [his two-year captivity] appeared more like an Indian than a white man." So did John Tarbell. After thirty years among the Indians in Canada, he made a visit to his relatives in Groton "in his Indian dress and with his Indian complexion (for by means of grease and paints but little difference could be discerned)." When O. M. Spencer returned after only eight months with the Shawnees, he was greeted with a newspaper allusion "to [his] looks and manners, as slightly resembling the Indians" and by a gaggle of visitors who exclaimed "in an under tone, 'How much he looks like an Indian!' " Such evidence reinforced the environmentalism of the time, which held that white men "who have incorporated themselves with any of [the Indian] tribes" soon acquire "a great resemblance to the savages, not only in their manners, but in their colour and the expression of the countenance."[23]

The final English problem was perhaps the most embarrassing in its manifestations, and certainly was so in its implications. For many Indians who had adopted white captives, the return of their "own Flesh, and Blood" to the English was unendurable. At the earliest opportunity, after bitter memories of the wars had faded on both sides, they journeyed through the English settlements to visit their estranged children, just as the Shawnee speaker had promised Bouquet they would. Jonathan Hoyt's Indian father visited him so often in Deerfield, sometimes bringing his captive sister, that Hoyt had to petition the Massachusetts General Court for reimbursement for their support. In 1760 Sir William Johnson reported that a Canadian Indian "has been since down to Schenectady to visit one Newkirk of that place, who was some years a Prisoner in his House, and sent home about a year ago with this Indians Sister, who came with her Brother now purely to see Said Newkirk whom she calls her Son and is verry fond of."[24]

Obviously the feelings were mutual. Elizabeth Gilbert, adopted at the age of twelve, "always retained an affection toward John Huston, her Indian father (as she called him), for she remembered his kindness to her when in captivity." Even an adult who had spent less than six months with the Indians honored the chief who had adopted him. In 1799, eleven years after Thomas Ridout's release, his friend and father, Kakinathucca, "accompanied by three more Shawanese chiefs, came to pay me a visit at my house in York town (Toronto). He regarded myself and family with peculiar pleasure, and my wife and children contemplated with great satisfaction the noble and good qualities of this worthy Indian." The bond of affection that had grown in the Indian villages was clearly not an attachment that the English could dismiss as "unnatural."[25]

Children who had been raised by Indian parents from infancy could be excused perhaps for their unwillingness to return, but the adults who displayed a similar reluctance, especially the women who had married Indian men and borne them children, drew another reaction. "For the honour of humanity," wrote William Smith, "we would suppose those persons to have been of the lowest rank, either bred up in ig norance and distressing penury, or who had lived so long with the Indians as to forget all their former connections. For, easy and unconstrained as the savage life is, certainly it could never be put in competition with the blessings of improved life and the light of religion, by any persons who have had the happiness of enjoying, and the capacity of discerning, them." If Smith was struck by the contrast between the visible impact of Indian education and his own cultural assumptions, he never said so.[26]

To find a satisfactory explanation for the extraordinary drawing power of Indian culture, we should begin where the colonists themselves first came under its sway—on the trail to Indian country. For although the Indians were known for their patience, they wasted no time in beginning the educational process that would transform their hostile or fearful white captives into affectionate Indian relatives.

Perhaps the first transaction after the Indians had selected their prisoners and hurried them into cover was to replace their hard-heeled shoes with the footwear of the forest—moccasins. These were universally approved by the prisoners, who admitted that they traveled with "abundant more ease" than before. And on more than one occasion the knee-deep snows of northern New England forced the Indians to make snowshoes for their prisoners in order to maintain their pace of twenty-five to thirty miles a day. Such an introduction to the superbly adapted technology of the Indians alone would not convert the English, but it was a beginning.[27]

The lack of substantial food supplies forced the captives to accommodate their stomachs as best they could to Indian trail fare, which ranged from nuts, berries, roots, and parched corn to beaver guts, horseflank, and semi-raw venison and moose, eaten without the customary English accompaniments of bread or salt. When there was nothing to eat, the Indians would "gird up their loins with a string," a technique that at least one captive found "very useful" when applied to himself. Although their food was often "unsavory" and in short supply, the Indians always shared it equally with the captives, who, being hungry, "relished [it] very well."[28]

Sometimes the lessons learned from the Indians were unexpectedly vital. When Stephen Williams, an eleven-year-old captive from Deerfield, found himself separated from his party on the way to Canada, he halloed for his Indian master. When the boy was found, the Indian threatened to kill him because, as Williams remembered five years later, "the Indians will never allow anybody to Hollow in the woods. Their manner is to make a noise like wolves or any other wild creatures, when they call to one another." The reason, of course, was that they did not wish to be discovered by their enemies. To the young neophyte Indian this was a lesson in survival not soon forgotten.[29]

Two other lessons were equally unexpected but instrumental in preparing the captives for even greater surprises when they reached the Indian settlements. Both served to undermine the English horror of the Indians as bloodthirsty fiends who defile "any Woman they take alive" before "putting her to Death." Many redeemed prisoners made a point of insisting that, although they had been completely powerless in captivity, the Indians had never affronted them sexually. Thomas Ridout testified that "during the whole of the time I was with the Indians I never once witnessed an indecent or improper action amongst any of the Indians, whether young or old." Even William Smith admitted that "from every enquiry that has been made, it appears—that no woman thus saved is preserved from base motives, or need fear the violation of her honour." If there had been the least exception, we can be sure that this champion of civilization would have made the most of it.[30]

One reason for the Indians' lack of sexual interest in their female captives was perhaps aesthetic, for the New England

Indians, at least, esteemed black the color of beauty.[31] A more fundamental reason derived from the main purpose of taking captives, which was to secure new members for their families and clans. Under the Indians' strong incest taboos, no warrior would attempt to violate his future sister or cousin. "Were he to indulge himself with a captive taken in war, and much more were he to offer violence in order to gratify his lust, he would incur indelible disgrace." Indeed, the taboo seems to have extended to the whole tribe. As George Croghan testified after long acquaintance with the Indians, "they have No [J]uri[s]diction or Laws butt that of Nature yett I have known more than onest thire Councils, order men to be putt to Death for Committing Rapes, wh[ich] is a Crime they Despise." Since murder was a crime to be revenged by the victim's family in its own way and time, rape was the only capital offense punished by the tribe as a whole.[32]

Equally powerful in prohibiting sexual affronts was a religious ethic of strict warrior continence, the breaking of which was thought to bring misfortune or death. "The Indians will not cohabit with women while they are out at war," noted James Adair, a trader among the southeastern tribes for thirty years, "they religiously abstain from every kind of intercourse even with their own wives, for the space of three days and nights before they go to war, and so after they return home, because they are to sanctify themselves."[33] When William Fleming and his wife were taken from their bed in 1755, the Indians told him "he need not be afraid of their abusing his wife, for they would not do it, for fear of offending their God (pointing their hands toward heaven) for the man that affronts his God will surely be killed when he goes to war." Giving the woman a plundered shift and petticoat, the natives turned their backs while she dressed to emphasize the point.[34]

Captive testimony also chipped away at the stereotype of the Indians' cruelty. When Mrs. Isabella M'Coy was taken from Epsom, New Hampshire, in 1747, her neighbors later remembered that "she did indeed find the journey [to Canada] fatiguing, and her fare scanty and precarious. But in her treatment from the Indians, she experienced a very agreeable disappointment. The kindness she received from them was far greater than she had expected from those who were so often distinguished for their cruelties." More frequent still was recognition of the Indians' kindness to children. Thomas Hutchinson told a common story of how "some of the children who were taken at Deerfield, they drew upon slays; at other times they have been known to carry them in their arms or upon their backs to Canada. This tenderness," he noted, "has occasioned the beginning of an affection, which in a few years has been so rivetted, that the parents of the children, who have gone to Canada to seek them, could by no means prevail upon them to leave the Indians and return home." The affections of a four-year-old Pennsylvania boy, who became Old White Chief among the Iroquois, seem to have taken even less time to become "rivetted." "The last I remember of my mother," he recalled in 1836, "she was running, carrying me in her arms. Suddenly she fell to the ground on her face, and I was taken from her. Overwhelmed with fright, I knew nothing more until I opened my eyes to find myself in the lap of an Indian woman. Looking kindly down into my face she smiled on me, and gave me some dried deer's meat and maple sugar. From that hour I believe she loved me as a mother. I am sure I returned to her the affection of a son."[35]

When the returning war parties approached the first Indian village, the educational process took on a new complexion. As one captive explained, "whenever the warriors return from an excursion against an enemy, their return to the tribe or village must be designated by war-like ceremonial; the captives or spoils, which may happen to crown their valor, must be conducted in a triumphant form, and decorated to every possible advantage." Accordingly, the cheek, chin, and forehead of every captive were painted with traditional dashes of vermilion mixed with bear's grease. Belts of wampum were hung around their necks, Indian clothes were substituted for English, and the men and boys had their hair plucked or shaved in Indian fashion. The physical transformation was so effective, said a twenty-six-year-old soldier, "that I began to think I was an Indian." Younger captives were less aware of the small distance between role-playing and real acceptance of the Indian life-style. When her captor dressed Frances Slocum, not yet five years old, in "beautiful wampum beads," she remembered at the end of a long and happy life as an Indian that he "made me look, as I thought, very fine. I was much pleased with the beautiful wampum."[36]

The prisoners were then introduced to a "new school" of song and dance. "Little did we expect," remarked an English woman, "that the accomplishment of dancing would ever be taught us, by the savages. But the war dance must now be held; and every prisoner that could move must take its awkward steps. The figure consisted of circular motion round the fire; each sang his own music, and the best dancer was the one most violent in motion." To prepare for the event each captive had rehearsed a short Indian song on the trail. Mrs. Johnson recalled many years later that her song was "danna witchee natchepung; my son's was nar wiscumpton." Nehemiah How could not master the Indian pronunciation, so he was allowed to sing in English "I don't know where I go." In view of the Indians' strong sense of ceremonial propriety, it is small wonder that one captive thought that they "Seem[e]d to be Very much a mind I Should git it perfect."[37]

Upon entering the village the Indians let forth with some distinctive music of their own. "When we came near the main Body of the Enemy," wrote Thomas Brown, a captive soldier from Fort William Henry, "the *Indians* made a Live-Shout, as they call it when they bring in a Prisoner alive (different from the Shout they make when they bring in Scalps, which they call a Dead-Shout)." According to another soldier, "their Voices are so sharp, shrill, loud and deep, that when they join together after one has made his Cry, it makes a most dreadful and horrible Noise, that stupifies the very Senses," a noise that naturally frightened many captives until they learned that it was not their death knell.[38]

They had good reason to think that their end was near when the whole village turned out to form a gauntlet from the entrance to the center of the village and their captors ordered them to run through it. With ax handles, tomahawks, hoop poles, clubs, and switches the Indians flogged the racing captives as if to beat the whiteness out of them. In most villages, significantly, "it was only the more elderly People both Male and Female wh[ic]h rece[iv]ed this Useage—the young prisoners of Both Sexes Escaped without it" or were rescued from any serious harm by one or more villagers, perhaps indicating the Indian perception of the captives' various educability. When ten-year-old John Brickell was knocked down by the blows of his Seneca captors, "a very big Indian came up, and threw the company off me, and took me by the arm, and led me along through the lines with such rapidity that I scarcely touched the ground, and was not once struck after he took me."[39]

The purpose of the gauntlet was the subject of some difference of opinion. A French soldier who had spent several years among the northeastern Indians believed that a prisoner "so unfortunate as to fall in the course of the bastonnade must get up quickly and keep on, or he will be beaten to death on the spot." On the other hand, Pierre de Charlevoix, the learned traveler and historian of Canada, wrote that "even when they seem to strike at random, and to be actuated only by fury, they take care never to touch any part where a blow might prove mortal." Both Frenchmen were primarily describing the Indians' treatment of other Indians and white men. Barbara Leininger and Marie LeRoy drew a somewhat different conclusion from their own treatment. Their welcome at the Indian village of Kittanning, they said, "consisted of three blows each, on the back. They were, however, administered with great mercy. Indeed, we concluded that we were beaten merely in order to keep up an ancient usage, and not with the intention of injuring us."[40]

William Walton came closest to revealing the Indians' intentions in his account of the Gilbert family's captivity. The Indians usually beat the captives with "great Severity," he said, "by way of Revenge for their Relations who have been slain." Since the object of taking captives was to satisfy the Indian families who had lost relatives, the gauntlet served as the first of three initiation rites into Indian society, a purgative ceremony by which the bereaved Indians could exorcise their anger and anguish, and the captives could begin their cultural transformation.[41]

If the first rite tried to beat the whiteness out of the captives, the second tried to wash it out. James Smith's experience was typical.

> The old chief, holding me by the hand, made a long speech, very loud, and when he had done he handed me to three squaws, who led me by the hand down the bank into the river until the water was up to our middle. The squaws then made signs to me to plunge myself into the water, but I did not understand them. I thought that the result of the council was that I should be drowned, and that these young ladies were to be the executioners. They all laid violent hold of me, and I for some time opposed them with all my might, which occasioned loud laughter by the multitude that were on the bank of the river. At length one of the squaws made out to speak a little English (for I believe they began to be afraid of me) and said, "No hurt you.' On this I gave myself up to their ladyships, who were as good as their word; for though they plunged me under water and washed and rubbed me severely, yet I could not say they hurt me much.[42]

More than one captive had to receive similar assurance, but their worst fears were being laid to rest.

Symbolically purged of their whiteness by their Indian baptism, the initiates were dressed in new Indian clothes and decorated with feathers, jewelry, and paint. Then, with great solemnity, the village gathered around the council fire, where after a "profound silence" one of the chiefs spoke. Even a hostile captive, Zadock Steele, had to admit that although he could not understand the language spoken, he could "plainly discover a great share of native eloquence." The chief's speech, he said, was "of considerable length, and its effect obviously manifested weight of argument, solemnity of thought, and at least human sensibility." But even this the twenty-two-year-old New Englander could not appreciate on its own terms, for in the next breath he denigrated the ceremony as "an assemblage of barbarism, assuming the appearance of civilization."[43]

A more charitable account was given by James Smith, who through an interpreter was addressed in the following words:

> My son, you are now flesh of our flesh and bone of our bone. By the ceremony that was performed this day, every drop of white blood was washed out of your veins. You are taken into the Caughnewaga [French Mohawk] nation and initiated into a war-like tribe. You are adopted into a great family and now received with great seriousness and solemnity in the room and place of a great man. After what has passed this day you are now one of us by an old strong law and custom. My son, you have now nothing to fear. We are now under the same obligations to love, support and defend you that we are to love and to defend one another. Therefore you are to consider yourself as one of our people.[44]

"At this time," admitted the eighteen-year-old Smith, "I did not believe this fine speech, especially that of the white blood being washed out of me; but since that time I have found that there was much sincerity in said speech; for from that day I never knew them to make any distinction between me and themselves in any respect whatever until I left them . . . we all shared one fate." It is a chord that sounds through nearly every captivity narrative: "They treated me . . . in every way as one of themselves."[45]

When the adoption ceremony had ended, the captive was taken to the wigwam of his new family, who greeted him with a "most dismal howling, crying bitterly, and wringing their hands in all agonies of grief for a deceased relative." "The higher in favour the adopted Prisoners [were] to be placed, the greater Lamentation [was] made over them." After a threnodic memorial to the lost member, which may have "added to the Terror of the Captives," who "imagined it to be no other than a Prelude to inevitable Destruction," the mood suddenly shifted. "I never saw . . . such hug[g]ing and kissing from the women and crying for joy," exclaimed one young recipient. Then an interpreter introduced each member of the new family—in one case "from brother to seventh cousins"—and "they came to me one after another," said another captive, "and shook me by the hand, in token that they considered me to stand in the same relationship to them as the one in whose stead I was placed."[46]

Most young captives assumed the places of Indian sons and daughters, but occasionally the match was not exact. Mary Jemison replaced a brother who had been killed in "Washington's war," while twenty-six-year-old Titus King assumed the unlikely role of a grandfather. Although their sex and age may not always have corresponded, the adopted captives succeeded to all the deceased's rights and obligations—the same dignities, honors, and often the same names. "But the one adopted," reported a French soldier, "must be prudent and wise in his conduct, if he wants to make himself as well liked as the man he is replacing. This seldom fails to occur, because he is continually reminded of the dead man's conduct and good deeds."[47]

So literal could the replacement become at times that no amount of exemplary conduct could alter the captive's reception. Thomas Peart, a twenty-three-year-old Pennsylvanian, was adopted as an uncle in an Iroquois family, but "the old Man, whose Place [he] was to fill, had never been considered by his Family as possessed of any Merit." Accordingly, Peart's dress, although in the Indian style, was "in a meaner Manner, as they did not hold him high in Esteem after his Adoption." Since his heart was not in becoming an Indian anyway, and "observing that they treated him just as they had done the old worthless Indian . . . he therefore concluded he would only fill his Predecessor's Station, and used no Endeavours to please them."[48]

When the prisoners had been introduced to all their new relatives and neighbors, the Indians proceeded to shower them with gifts. Luke Swetland, taken from Pennsylvania during the Revolution, was unusually feted with "three hats, five blankets, near twenty pipes, six razors, six knives, several spoons, gun and ammunition, fireworks, several Indian pockets [pouches], one Indian razor, awls, needles, goose quills, paper and many other things of small value"—enough to make him the complete Indian warrior. Most captives, however, settled for a new shirt or dress, a pair of decorated moccasins, and abundant promises of future kindness, which later prompted the captives to acknowledge once again that the Indians were "a[s] good as their word." "All the family was as kind to me," related Thomas Gist, "as if I had realy been the nearest of relation they had in the world." The two women who adopted Mary Jemison were no less loving. "I was ever considered and treated by them as a real sister," she said near the end of a long life with them, "the same as though I had been born of their mother."[49]

Treatment such as this—and it was almost universal—left an indelible mark on every captive, whether or not they eventually returned to English society. Although captives like

Mrs. Johnson found their adoption an "unnatural situation," they had to defend the humanity of the practice. "Those who have profited by refinement and education," she argued, "ought to abate part of the prejudice, which prompts them to look with an eye of censure on this untutored race. . . . Do they ever adopt an enemy," she asked, "and salute him by the tender name of brother?" It is not difficult to imagine what effect such feelings must have had in younger people less habituated to English culture, especially those who had lost their own parents.[50]

The formalities, purgations, and initiations were now completed. Only one thing remained for the Indians: by their daily example and instruction to "make an Indian of you," as the Delawares told John Brickell. This required a steady union of two things: the willingness and gratitude of the captives, and the consistent love and trust of the Indians. By the extraordinary ceremonies through which they had passed, most captives had had their worst fears allayed. From a state of apprehension or even terror they had suddenly emerged with their persons intact and a solemn invitation to begin a new life, as full of love, challenge, and satisfaction as any they had known. For "when [the Indians] once determine to give life, they give every thing with it, which, in their apprehension, belongs to it." The sudden release from anxiety into a realm of affirmative possibility must have disposed many captives to accept the Indian way of life.[51]

According to the adopted colonists who recounted the stories of their new lives, Indian life was more than capable of claiming their respect and allegiance, even if they eventually returned to English society. The first indication that the Indians were serious in their professions of equality came when the adopted captives were given freedom of movement within and without the Indian villages. Naturally, the degree of freedom and its timing depended on the captive's willingness to enter into the spirit of Indian life.

Despite his adult years, Thomas Ridout had earned his captor's trust by the third night of their march to the Shawnee villages. Having tied his prisoner with a rope to himself the first two nights, the Indian "never afterwards used this precaution, leaving me at perfect liberty, and frequently during the nights that were frosty and cold," Ridout recalled, "I found his hand over me to examine whether or not I was covered." As soon as seventeen-year-old John Leeth, an Indian trader's clerk, reached his new family's village, "my father gave me and his two [Indian] sons our freedom, with a rifle, two pounds of powder, four pounds of lead, a blanket, shirt, match-coat, pair of leggings, etc. to each, as our freedom dues; and told us to shift for ourselves." Eleven-year-old Benjamin Gilbert, "considered as the [Indian] King's Successor," was of course "entirely freed from Restraint, so that he even began to be delighted with his Manner of Life." Even Zadock Steele, a somewhat reluctant Indian at twenty-two, was "allowed the privilege of visiting any part of the village, in the day time, and was received with marks of fraternal affection, and treated with all the civility an Indian is capable to bestow."[52]

The presence of other white prisoners complicated the trust relationship somewhat. Captives who were previously known to each other, especially from the same family, were not always allowed to converse "much together, as [the Indians] imagined they would remember their former Situation, and become less contented with their present Manner of Life." Benjamin Peart, for example, was allowed the frequent company of "Two white Men who had been taken Prisoners, the one from Susquehanna, the other from Minisinks, both in Pennsylvania," even though he was a Pennsylvanian himself. But when he met his captive wife and infant son by chance at Fort Niagara, the Indians "separated them again the same Day, and took [his] Wife about Four Miles Distance."[53]

Captives who were strangers were permitted not only to

visit frequently but occasionally to live together. When Thomas Gist suddenly moved from his adopted aunt's house back to her brother's, she "imajined I was affronted," he wrote, and "came and asked me the reason why I had left her, or what injury she or any of the family had done me that I should leave her without so much as leting her know of it. I told her it was the company of my fellow prisoners that drew me to the town. She said that it was not so far but I mite have walked to see them every two or three days, and ask some of them to come and see me those days that I did not chuse to go abroad, and that all such persons as I thought proper to bring to the house should be as welcom[e] as one of the family, and made many promises how kind she would be if I would return. However," boasted the twenty-four-year-old Gist, "I was obstinate and would not." It is not surprising that captives who enjoyed such autonomy were also trusted under the same roof. John Brickell remarked that three white prisoners, "Patton, Johnston, and Mrs. Baker [of Kentucky] had all lived with me in the same house among the Indians, and we were as intimate as brothers and sisters."[54]

Once the captives had earned the basic trust of their Indian families, nothing in Indian life was denied them. When they reached the appropriate age, the Indians offered to find them suitable marriage partners. Understandably, some of the older captives balked at this, sensing that it was calculated to bind them with marital ties to a culture they were otherwise hesitant to accept. When Joseph Gilbert, a forty-one-year-old father and husband, was adopted into a leading family, his new relatives informed him that "if he would marry amongst them, he should enjoy the Privileges which they enjoyed; but this Proposal he was not disposed to comply with, . . . as he was not over anxious to conceal his Dislike to them." Elizabeth Peart, his twenty-year-old married sister, was equally reluctant. During her adoption ceremony "they obliged her to sit down with a young Man an Indian, and the eldest

Chieftain of the Family repeating a Jargon of Words to her unintelligible, but which she considered as some form amongst them of Marriage," she was visited with "the most violent agitations, as she was determined, at all events, to oppose any step of this Nature." Marie LeRoy's honor was even more dearly bought. When "it was at length determined by the [Indians] that [she] should marry one of the natives, who had been selected for her," she told a fellow captive that "she would sooner be shot than have him for her husband." Whether her revulsion was directed toward the act itself or toward the particular suitor was not said.[55]

The distinction is pertinent because the weight of evidence suggests that marriage was not compulsory for the captives, and common sense tells us that any form of compulsion would have defeated the Indians' purpose in trying to persuade the captives to adopt their way of life. Mary Jemison, at the time a captive for two years, was unusual in implying that she was forced to marry an Indian. "Not long after the Delawares came to live with us, at Wiishto," she recalled, "my sisters told me that I must go and live with one of them, whose name was She-nin-jee. Not daring to cross them, or disobey their commands, with a great degree of reluctance I went; and Sheninjee and I were married according to Indian custom." Considering the tenderness and kindness with which most captives reported they were treated, it is likely that she was less compelled in reality than in her perception and memory of it.[56]

For even hostile witnesses could not bring themselves to charge that force was ever used to promote marriages. The Puritan minister John Williams said only that "great *essays* [were] made to get [captives] married" among the Canadian Indians by whom he was captured. Elizabeth Hanson and her husband "could by no means obtain from their hands" their sixteen-year-old daughter, "for the squaw, to whom she was given, had a son whom she intended my daughter should in time *be prevailed with to marry.*" Mrs. Hanson was probably less concerned that her daughter would be forced to marry an Indian than that she might "in time" want to, for as she acknowledged from her personal experience, "the Indians are very civil towards their captive women, not offering any incivility by any indecent carriage." An observer of the return of the white prisoners to Bouquet spoke for his contemporaries when he reported—with an almost audible sigh of relief—that "there had not been a solitary instance among them of any woman having her delicacy injured by being compelled to marry. They had been left liberty of choice, and those who chose to remain single were not sufferers on that account."[57]

Not only were younger captives and consenting adults under no compulsion, either actual or perceived, to marry, but they enjoyed as wide a latitude of choice as any Indian. When Thomas Gist returned to his Indian aunt's lodge, she was so happy that she "dress'd me as fine as she could, and . . . told me if I wanted a wife she would get a pretty young girl for me." It was in the same spirit of exuberant generosity that Oliver Spencer's adopted mother rewarded his first hunting exploit. "She heard all the particulars of the affair with great satisfaction," he remembered, "and frequently saying, 'Enee, wessah' (this is right, that is good), said I would one day become a great hunter, and placing her forefingers together (by which sign the Indians represent marriage) and then pointing to Sotonegoo" (a thirteen-year-old girl whom Spencer described as "rather homely, but cheerful and good natured, with bright, laughing eyes") "told me that when I should become a man I should have her for a wife." Sotonegoo cannot have been averse to the idea, for when Spencer was redeemed shortly afterward she "sobbed loudly as [he] took her hand, and for the moment deeply affected, bade her farewell."[58]

So free from compulsion were the captives that several

married fellow white prisoners. In 1715 the priest of the
Jesuit mission at Sault-au-Récollet "married Ignace shoe-
tak8anni [Joseph Rising, aged twenty-one] and Elizabeth
T8atog8ach [Abigail Nims, aged fifteen], both English, who
wish to remain with the Christian Indians, not only renounc-
ing their nation, but even wishing to live *en sauvages*." But
from the Indians' standpoint, and perhaps from their own,
captives such as John Leeth and Thomas Armstrong may
have had the best of all possible marriages. After some years
with the Indians, Leeth "was married to a young woman,
seventeen or eighteen years of age; also a prisoner to the Indians; who had been taken by them when about twenty
months old." Armstrong, an adopted Seneca, also married a
"full blooded white woman, who like himself had been a
captive among the Indians, from infancy, but who unlike
him, had not acquired a knowledge of one word of the English language, being essentially Indian in all save blood."[59]
Their commitment to each other deepened their commitment to the Indian culture of which they had become equal
members.

The captives' social equality was also demonstrated by
their being asked to share in the affairs of war and peace,
matters of supreme importance to Indian society. When the
Senecas who had adopted Thomas Peart decided to "make a
War Excursion," they asked him to go with them. But since
he was in no mood—and no physical condition—to play the
Indian, "he determinately refused them, and was therefore
left at Home with the Family." The young Englishman who
became Old White Chief was far more eager to defend his
new culture, but his origins somewhat limited his military
activity. "When I grew to manhood," he recalled, "I went
with them [his Iroquois kinsmen] on the warpath against the
neighboring tribes, but never against the white settlers, lest
by some unlucky accident I might be recognized and claimed
by former friends." Other captives—many of them famous

renegades—were less cautious. Charlevoix noticed in his travels in Canada that adopted captives "frequently enter into the spirit of the nation, of which they are become members, in such a manner, that they make no difficulty of going to war against their own countrymen." It was behavior such as this that prompted Sir William Johnson to praise Bouquet after his expedition to the Ohio for compelling the Indians to give up every white person, even the "Children born of White Women. That mixed Race," he wrote, referring to first-generation captives as well, "forgetting their Ancestry on one side are found to be the most Inveterate of any, and would greatly Augment their numbers."[60]

It is ironic that the most famous renegade of all should have introduced ten-year-old Oliver Spencer to the ultimate opportunity for an adopted captive. When he had been a captive for less than three weeks, Spencer met Simon Girty, "the very picture of a villain," at a Shawnee village below his own. After various boasts and enquiries, wrote Spencer, "he ended by telling me that I would never see home; but if I should 'turn out to be a good hunter and a brave warrior I might one day be a chief.' " Girty's prediction may not have been meant to tease a small boy with impossible delusions of grandeur, for the Indians of the Northeast readily admitted white captives to their highest councils and offices.[61]

Just after Thomas Ridout was captured on the Ohio, he was surprised to meet an English-speaking "white man, about twenty-two years of age, who had been taken prisoner when a lad and had been adopted, and now was a chief among the Shawanese." He need not have been surprised, for there were many more like him. John Tarbell, the man who visited his Groton relatives in Indian dress, was not only "one of the wealthiest" of the Caughnawagas but "the eldest chief and chief speaker of the tribe." Timothy Rice, formerly of Westborough, Massachusetts, was also made one of the clan chiefs at Caughnawaga, partly by inheritance from his Indian father but largely for "his own Super[io]r Talents" and "war-like Spirit for which he was much celebrated."[62]

Perhaps the most telling evidence of the Indians' receptivity to adopted white leadership comes from Old White Chief, an adopted Iroquois.

> I was made a chief at an early age [he recalled in 1836] and as my sons grew to manhood they also were made chiefs. . . . After my youngest son was made chief I could see, as I thought, that some of the Indians were jealous of the distinction I enjoyed and it gave me uneasiness. This was the first time I ever entertained the thought of leaving my Indian friends. I felt sure that it was displeasing to the Indians to have three of my sons, as well as myself, promoted to the office of chief. My wife was well pleased to leave with me, and my sons said, "Father, we will go wherever you will lead us."
>
> I then broke the subject to some of my Indian relatives, who were very much disturbed at my decision. They immediately called the chiefs and warriors together and laid the plan before them. They gravely deliberated upon the subject for some hours, and then a large majority decided that they would not consent to our leaving. They said, "We cannot give up our son and brother" (meaning myself) "nor our nephews" (meaning my children). "They have lived on our game and grown strong and powerful among us. They are good and true men. We cannot do without them. We cannot give them to the pale faces. We shall grow weak if they leave us. We will give them the best we have left. Let them choose where they will live. No one shall disturb them. We need their wisdom and their strength to help us. If they are in high places, let them be there. We know they will honor us."[63]

"We yielded to their importunity," said the old chief, and "I have never had any reason to regret my decision." In public office as in every sphere of Indian life, the English captives found that the color of their skin was unimportant; only their talent and their inclination of heart mattered.

Understandably, neither their skill nor their loyalty was left to chance. From the moment the captives, especially the young ones, came under their charge, the Indians made a concerted effort to inculcate in them Indian habits of mind and body. If the captives could be taught to think, act, and react like Indians, they would effectively cease to be English and would assume an Indian identity.[64] This was the Indians' goal, toward which they bent every effort in the weeks and months that followed their formal adoption of the white captives.

The educational character of Indian society was recognized by even the most inveterately English captives. Titus King, a twenty-six-year-old New England soldier, spent a year with the Canadian Indians at St. Francis trying—unsuccessfully—to undo their education of "Eight or ten young [English] Children." What "an awfull School this [is] for Children," he wrote. "When We See how Quick they will Fall in with the Indians ways, nothing Seems to be more takeing in Six months time they Forsake Father and mother Forgit thir own Land Refuess to Speak there own toungue and Seemin[g]ly be Holley Swollowed up with the Indians." The older the person, of course, the longer it took to become fully Indianized. Mary Jemison, captured at the age of fifteen, took three or four years to forget her natural parents and the home she had once loved. "If I had been taken in infancy," she said, "I should have been contented in my situation." Some captives, commonly those over fifteen or sixteen years old, never made the transition from English to Indian. Twenty-four-year-old Thomas Gist, soldier and son of a famous scout and Indian agent, accommodated himself to his adoption and Indian life for just one year and then made plans to escape. "All curiosity with regard to acting the part of an Indian," he related, "which I could do very well, being th[o]rougherly satisfied, I was determined to be what I really was."[65]

Children, however, took little time to "fall in with the Indians ways." Titus King mentioned six months. The Reverend John Williams witnessed the effects of eight or nine months when he stopped at St. Francis in February 1704. There, he said, "we found several poor children, who had been taken from the eastward [Maine] the summer before; a sight very affecting, they being in habit very much like Indians, and in manners very much symbolizing with them." When young Joseph Noble visited his captive sister in Montreal, "he still belonged to the St. François tribe of Indians, and was dressed remarkably fine, having forty or fifty broaches in his shirt, clasps on his arm, and a great variety of knots and bells about his clothing. He brought his little sister . . . a young fawn, a basket of cranberries, and a lump of sap sugar." Sometime later he was purchased from the Indians by a French gentleman who promptly "dressed him in the French style; but he never appeared so bold and majestic, so spirited and vivacious, as when arrayed in his Indian habit and associating with his Indian friends."[66]

The key to any culture is its language, and the young captives were quick to learn the Indian dialects of their new families. Their retentive memories and flair for imitation made them ready students, while the Indian languages, at once oral, concrete, and mythopoeic, lightened the task. In less than six months ten-year-old Oliver Spencer had "acquired a sufficient knowledge of the Shawnee tongue to understand all ordinary conversation and, indeed, the greater part of all that I heard (accompanied, as their conversation and speeches were, with the most significant gestures)," which enabled him to listen "with much pleasure and sometimes with deep interest" to his Indian mother tell of battles, heroes, and history in the long winter evenings. When Jemima Howe was allowed to visit her four-year-old son at a neighboring Indian village in Canada, he greeted her "in the Indian tongue" with "Mother, are you come?" He too had been a captive for only six months.[67]

The early weeks of captivity could be disquieting if there were no English-speaking Indians or prisoners in the village to lend the comfort of a familiar language while the captives struggled to acquire a strange one. If a captive's family left for their winter hunting camp before he could learn their language, he might find himself, like Thomas Gist, "without any com[p]any that could unders[t]and one word that I spake." "Thus I continued, near five months," he wrote, "sometimes reading, other times singing, never melancholy but when alone. . . . About the first of April (1759) I prevailed on the family to return to town, and by the last of the month all the Indians and prisoners returned, when I once more had the pleasure to talk to people that understood what I said."[68]

Younger captives probably missed the familiarity of English less than the adult Gist. Certainly they never lacked eager teachers. Mary Jemison recalled that her Seneca sisters were "diligent in teaching me their language; and to their great satisfaction I soon learned so that I could understand it readily, and speak it fluently." Even Gist was the recipient of enthusiastic, if informal, instruction from a native speaker. One of his adopted cousins, who was about five or six years old and his "favorite in the family," was always "chattering some thing" with him. "From him," said Gist affectionately, "I learn'd more than from all the rest, and he learn'd English as fast as [I] did Indian."[69]

As in any school, language was only one of many subjects of instruction. Since the Indians generally assumed that whites were physically inferior to themselves, captive boys were often prepared for the hardy life of hunters and warriors by a rigorous program of physical training. John McCullough, aged eight, was put through the traditional Indian course by his adoptive uncle. "In the beginning of winter," McCullough recalled, "he used to raise me by day light every morning, and make me sit down in the creek up to my chin in the cold water, in order to make me hardy as he said, whilst he would sit on the bank smoking his pipe until he thought I had been long enough in the water, he would then bid me to dive. After I came out of the water he would order me not to go near the fire until I would be dry. I was kept at that till the water was frozen over, he would then break the ice for me and send me in as before." As shocking as it may have been to his system, such treatment did nothing to turn him against Indian life. Indeed, he was transparently proud that he had borne up under the strenuous regimen "with the firmness of an Indian." Becoming an Indian was as much a challenge and an adventure for the young colonists as it was a "sore trial," and many of them responded to it with alacrity and zest. Of children their age we should not expect any less.[70]

The captives were taught not only to speak and to endure as Indians but to act as Indians in the daily social and economic life of the community. Naturally, boys were taught the part of men and girls the part of women, and according to most colonial sources—written, it should be noted, predominantly by men—the boys enjoyed the better fate. An Ohio pioneer remembered that the prisoners from his party were "put into different families, the women to hard drudging and the boys to run wild with the young Indians, to amuse themselves with bow and arrow, dabble in the water, or obey any other notion their wild natures might dictate." William Walton, the author of the Gilbert family captivity narrative, also felt that the "Labour and Drudgery" in an Indian family fell to "the Share of the Women." He described fourteen-year-old Abner Gilbert as living a "dronish Indian life, idle and poor, having no other Employ than the gathering of Hickory-Nuts; and although young," Walton insisted, "his Situation was very irksome." Just how irksome the boy found his freedom from colonial farm chores was revealed when the ingenuous Walton related that "Abner, having no useful Employ, amused himself with catching fish in the Lake. . . . Not being of an impatient Disposition," said Walton soberly, "he bore his Captivity without repining."[71]

While most captive boys had "nothing to do, but cut a little wood for the fire," draw water for cooking and drinking, and "shoot Blackbirds that came to eat up the corn," they enjoyed "some leisure" for "hunting and other innocent devertions in the woods." Women and girls, on the other hand, shared the burdens—onerous ones in English eyes—of their Indian counterparts. But Mary Jemison, who had been taught English ways for fifteen years before becoming an Indian, felt that the Indian women's labor "was not severe," their tasks "probably not harder than that [sic] of white women," and their cares "certainly . . . not half as numerous, nor as great." The work of one year was "exactly similar, in almost every respect, to that of the others, without that endless variety that is to be observed in the common labor of the white people . . . In the summer season, we planted, tended and harvested our corn, and generally had all our children with us; but had no master to oversee or drive us, so that we could work as leisurely as we pleased. . . . In the season of hunting, it was our business, in addition to our cooking, to bring home the game that was taken by the [men], dress it, and carefully preserve the eatable meat, and prepare or dress the skins." "Spinning, weaving, sewing, stocking knitting," and like domestic tasks of colonial women were generally unknown. Unless Jemison was correct, it would be virtually impossible to understand why so many women and girls chose to become Indians. A life of unremitting drudgery, as the English saw it, could certainly hold no attraction for civilized women fresh from frontier farms and villages.[72]

The final and most difficult step in the captives' transition from English to Indian was to acquire the ability to think as

Indians, to share unconsciously the values, beliefs, and standards of Indian culture. From an English perspective, this should have been nearly an impossible task for civilized people because they perceived Indian culture as immoral and irreligious and totally antithetical to the civilized life they had known, however briefly. "Certainly," William Smith assumed, "it could never be put in competition with the blessings of improved life and the light of religion."[73] But many captives soon discovered that the English had no monopoly on virtue and that in many ways the Indians were morally superior to the English, more Christian than the Christians.

As early as 1643 Roger Williams had written a book to suggest such a thing, but he could be dismissed as a misguided visionary who let the Narragansetts go to his head. It was more difficult to dismiss someone like John Brickell, who had lived with the Indians for four and one-half years and had no ax to grind with established religion. "The Delawares are the best people to train up children I ever was with," he wrote. "Their leisure hours are, in a great measure, spent in training up their children to observe what they believe to be right. . . . [A]s a nation they may be considered fit examples for many of us Christians to follow. They certainly follow what they are taught to believe right more closely, and I might say more honestly, in general, than we Christians do the divine precepts of our Redeemer. . . . I know I am influenced to good, even at this day," he concluded, "more from what I learned among them, than what I learned among people of my own color." After many decades with them, Mary Jemison insisted that "the moral character of the Indians was . . . uncontaminated. Their fidelity was perfect, and became proverbial; they were strictly honest; they despised deception and falsehood; and chastity was held in high veneration." Even the Tory historian Peter Oliver, who was no friend to the Indians, admitted that "they have a Religion of their own, which, to the eternal Disgrace of many Nations who boast of Politeness, is more influential on their Conduct than that of those who hold them in so great Contempt." To the acute discomfort of the colonists, more than one captive maintained that the Indians were a "far more moral race than the whites."[74]

In the principled school of Indian life the captives experienced a decisive shift in their cultural and personal identities, a shift that often fostered a considerable degree of what might be called "conversion zeal." A French officer reported that "those Prisoners whom the Indians keep with them . . . are often more brutish, boisterous in their Behaviour and loose in their Manners than the Indians," and thought that "they affect that kind of Behaviour thro' Fear of and to recommend themselves to the Indians." Matthew Bunn, a nineteen-year-old soldier, was the object of such behavior when he was enslaved—not adopted—by the Maumee in 1791. "After I had eaten," he related, "they brought me a little prisoner boy, that had been taken about two years before, on the river called Monongahela, though he delighted more in the ways of the savages than in the ways of Christians; he used me worse than any of the Indians, for he would tell me to do this, that, and the other, and if I did not do it, or made any resistance, the Indians would threaten to kill me, and he would kick and cuff me about in such a manner, that I hardly dared to say my soul was my own." What Bunn experienced was the attempt of the new converts to pattern their behavior after their young Indian counterparts, who, a Puritan minister observed, "are as much to be dreaded by captives as those of maturer years, and in many cases much more so; for, unlike cultivated people, they have no restraints upon their mischievous and savage propensities, which they indulge in cruelties."[75]

Although fear undoubtedly accounted for some of the converts' initial behavior, desire to win the approval of their new relatives also played a part. "I had lived in my new habitation about a week," recalled Oliver Spencer, "and having given up all hope of escaping . . . began to regard it as my future home. . . . I strove to be cheerful, and by my ready obedience to ingratiate myself with Cooh-coo-cheeh [his Indian mistress], for whose kindness I felt grateful." A year after James Smith had been adopted, a number of prisoners were brought in by his new kinsmen and a gauntlet formed to welcome them. Smith "went and told them how they were to act" and then "fell into one of the ranks with the Indians, shouting and yelling like them." One middle-aged man's turn came, and "as they were not very severe on him," confessed the new Indian, "as he passed me I hit him with a piece of pumpkin—which pleased the Indians much." If their zeal to emulate the Indians sometimes exceeded their mercy, the captives had nonetheless fulfilled their new families' expectations: they had begun to act as Indians in spirit as well as body. Only time would be necessary to transform their conscious efforts into unconscious habits and complete their cultural conversion.[76]

"By what power does it come to pass," asked Crèvecoeur, "that children who have been adopted when young among these people, . . . and even grown persons . . . can never be prevailed on to re-adopt European manners?"[77] Given the malleability of youth, we should not be surprised that children underwent a rather sudden and permanent transition from English to Indian—although we might be pressed to explain why so few Indian children made the transition in the opposite direction. But the adult colonists who became Indians cannot be explained as easily, for the simple reason that they, unlike many of the children, were fully conscious of their cultural identities while they were being subjected to the Indians' assiduous attempts to convert them. Consequently, their cultural metamorphosis involved a large degree of personal choice.

The great majority of white Indians left no explanations for their choice. Forgetting their original language and their past, they simply disappeared into their adopted society. But those captives who returned to write narratives of their experiences left several clues to the motives of those who chose to stay behind. They stayed because they found Indian life to possess a strong sense of community, abundant love, and uncommon integrity—values that the English colonists also honored, if less successfully. But Indian life was attractive for other values—for social equality, mobility, adventure, and, as two adult converts acknowledged, "the most perfect freedom, the ease of living, [and] the absence of those cares and corroding solicitudes which so often prevail with us." As we have learned recently, these were values that were not being realized in the older, increasingly crowded, fragmented, and contentious communities of the Atlantic seaboard, or even in the newer frontier settlements.[78] By contrast, as Crèvecoeur said, there must have been in the Indians' "social bond something singularly captivating."[79] Whatever it was, its power had no better measure than the large number of English colonists who became, contrary to the civilized assumptions of their countrymen, white Indians.

CHAPTER EIGHT

Scalping: The Ethnohistory of a Moral Question

IN 1956 WILCOMB WASHBURN REMINDED ONE OF THE EARLY GATH-erings of ethnohistorians that "when one studies the contact of two cultures, value problems—that is, moral problems—imme-diately spring up to challenge the writer."* His audience needed reminding at the time, and so do most ethnohistorians today.

The past domination of the ethnohistorical enterprise by an-thropologists and the current infatuation of historians in general with the methods and mores of the "hard" social sciences have tended to blind most ethnohistorians, new and old, to two ele-mental facts. First, as Washburn suggested, ethnohistorians must not only attempt to understand each culture in its own terms, but when these cultures clash, they must come to interpretive grips with the conflict without imposing the parochial standards of their own day on the past. Second, ethnohistorians (who tend to worship at the feet of "scientific detachment") cannot avoid making an assessment of what the clash of cultural values meant to contemporaries (and perhaps what it means for us) even if they would like to. The richly normative character of our lan-guage, not just the "colorful" words but all of it, prevents them. In other words, morality is part of the subject matter of history, and historians, perhaps especially ethnohistorians, are perforce moral critics. To recognize and accept these facts, it seems to me,

* Wilcomb E. Washburn, "A Moral History of Indian-White Relations: Needs and Opportunities for Study," *Ethnohistory*, 4 (1957), 47-61 at 56.

is to move ethnohistory from the pretensions of pseudo-science toward the possibilities and responsibilities of humane art, which history at its best has always been. The issue is not facile and frequent moralizing for the sake of the present, but cultural and human sensitivity to the moral nuances and dilemmas of the past.

In the following essay, written especially for this volume, I have tried to sort out some of the moral meanings and tensions inherent in the English use of scalping and scalp bounties, and in the process to practice what I have preached. According to those strictures, I have tried to be scrupulously fair to all parties and to allow only contemporaries to set the issues and pass judgment. If I have not wholly succeeded, the fault may be as much corporate as personal, for by profession and usually by choice, historians are, like Donne, "involved in mankind," past and present, and their choice of words, tone, and stance cannot fail to register that involvement. We can only hope that our engagement with the past does nothing to obscure and something to illuminate a few of the myriad facets of what it meant to be human in colonial America.

THE SPECTER OF SCALPING HAUNTED THE COLONISTS OF NORTH America, and it continues to bedevil the thinking of America's historians and their readers. The bloody possibility of having one's scalp ripped off to a heart-rending cry of exaltation by a hideously painted, half-naked warrior was understandably terrifying to the colonists whose brand of warfare had not prepared them for such a fate. Despite the perspective of time, the strange horribleness of scalping still fascinates students of history for whom the possibility is much more remote. But to judge by some of their moral and historical observations, it also confounds them. Not only have they contributed importantly to the new myth that European colonists taught the Indians how to scalp by offering them bounties for enemy hair, but they have generally assumed moral postures toward the issue that add little or nothing to our understanding of scalping's impact on early American culture. This essay is an attempt to probe a small but significant feature of the process that helped to Americanize the English colonists by exploring some of the moral, psychological, and social meanings that scalping and scalp bounties held for them.

The myth of the European invention of scalping is only one indication that modern Americans feel guilty about many aspects of Indian-white relations in America, especially during the colonial period. But no more so than did many colonists for numerous offenses, such as making a god of land, dispossessing the Indians of theirs through force, fraud, or unfair exchange, killing rather than converting the natives by giving them the vices, not the virtues, of English society, losing the battle of souls to the Catholic missionaries of New France, and admiring, even preferring, the freedom of Indian society to the civilized constraints of their own. Guilt led to the fabrication of myths to disguise the reality of their deeds and feelings and to the projection of negative traits dimly or fearfully perceived in themselves onto their Indian adversaries.

As the recent accusations of their historical heirs suggest, many colonists also felt guilty about their adoption of certain "barbarous" methods of warfare, especially scalping of the dead. But rather than admitting that by adopting them they had been "reduced to savagery" or had deviated seriously from "civilized" Christian standards, they projected their guilt onto the Indians by insisting that the (mythically) "unprovoked" assaults of savages demanded a savage response. Since guerrilla warfare tends to force the enemy to retaliate in kind, the practice of scalping and the use of scalp bounties by the English may have been only a necessary adaptation of Indian means to English ends, of "savage" tactics to "civilized" (and therefore ultimately "redeeming") strategies, the most important of which was the elimination of the "Indian menace" on the ever-elastic English frontiers. But we should also consider the possibility that for at least some colonists scalping and the attitudes it engendered toward alien people left an ugly scar on their individual psyches and to that extent on the collective mentality of their society.

Obviously, the act of scalping, whether by Indians or Europeans, was morally loaded for contemporaries and carries considerable moral freight in modern discussions of Indian-white relations. How can we, as ethnohistorians, approach moral questions in the past without succumbing to either fruitless outrage or ethnocentric favoritism? Like all historians, we are first obligated to judge each society by its own standards and values, not those of today. We can compare individual choices of action with those made by other people in the same or similar circumstances or with other choices possible for *that* society at *that* time because "we hold people responsible only to the degree that we think them free to choose their course."[1] Second, we must strive to be scrupulously fair to all parties, which is possible only after immersing ourselves so deeply in the historical sources of each society that we are as much or more at home in their time and place than in our own.

When two or more societies and value systems collide, however, ethnohistorians face a problem of judgment that most historians who deal with one society seldom face. Sheer success or results are inappropriate standards because pragmatic "winners" are sometimes moral "losers" on any but the grossest scale. While the normative character of our everyday language will inevitably force us to make value judgments about the actions we describe, we can reduce the dangers of moral absolutism and presentism by letting the conflicting societies judge each other.[2] This technique will not only stress the relativity of cultural values but maintain a strict impartiality toward the conflicts of the past. If the sources for one society are slim, a sensitive application of imagination and empathy to a mastery of the available sources can often establish a culturally valid standard of judgment by which to redress the balance. To the same end, a light use of irony or gentle iconoclasm can effectively prick the pretensions and self-promotions of a dominant society blessed with an advantage of records. If more comment or moral criticism is called for by the complexity, abnormality, or enormity of the conflict situation, the ethnohistorian can use the standards of other contemporary societies, preferably neighbors who found themselves in similar circumstances. Beyond this kind of concrete, contextual treatment, most ethnohistorians will not need or want to go. Personal preference will dictate whether they proceed to apply "quasi-universal" moral standards in a "new cultural context, . . . free from the interpretations and assumptions under which [the original actions were] performed or observed by the participants."[3]

The moral attitudes struck by modern historians over scalping in the colonial period stand in marked contrast to an ethnohistorical approach. One surprising response has been to deny the existence of any moral problem at all, for the colonists or for us. In a section coyly entitled "On the Gentle Art of Scalping," a biographer of Sir William Johnson, the British superintendent of Indian affairs for the northern colonies, claimed that "scalping was then so common that no practical man, like Johnson, would have dreamed of eliminating it from the code of his red allies. . . . A scalp was just a scalp, no more—simply proof that the scalper had done his duty. . . ."[4] In a similar vein, an authority on Pennsylvania's scalp bounties asserted that "colonial Americans were not sensitive about the trade in scalps" and by the 1750s had "grimly accepted the ethics of scalp buying."[5] Even more nonchalant was an historian of the Revolution who held that the scalping done by American riflemen on the frontier was "a natural act," a simple matter "of course and of reprisal."[6]

The more typical response of historians has been to recognize the moral implications of scalping but to interpret the colonists' involvement in two different ways. The more equable interpretation, while admitting that scalp bounties fostered "inhumanity," "callous[ness]," and an "upsurge of brutality," carefully pinned the blame on the "intense heat" and "brutalizing influence of wilderness warfare," not on "sadist savages" or their bloody-minded French instigators, as an older history had done.[7] The other interpretation sought (often unconsciously) to elevate the Indians by degrading the colonists. In a history of the fall of Canada, the great-grandson of a Mohawk woman cited a few random, largely spurious, colonial scalp bounties before commenting, "Christian races, not savage ones, were the inspirations behind these horrible deeds in that bloody dawn of our history when the United States was about to be born."[8] Two historians of New England, though they differed strenuously on most issues, made common cause unwittingly when trying to explain scalping. One, normally a defender of the Puritans, was at pains to show that Indian scalp-taking had English analogues in drawing and quartering and "the displaying of heads on London Bridge and other prominent landmarks." "The seventeenth century," he insisted, "had its share of barbarity on both sides of the Atlantic."[9] The other historian, no friend of the Puritans, thought that scalping in native New England was adopted "as a convenient way to collect provincial bounties for heads without having to lug about the awkward impedimenta attached to the scalps." "If savagery was ferocity," he charged, "Europeans were at least as savage as Indians . . . Indians never achieved the advanced stage of civilization represented by the rack or the Iron Maiden."[10]

If we wish to capture the meaning of scalping for the competing societies of colonial America, we will have to move beyond attempts to rank them on a pejorative scale of "savagery." The "Americanization" of colonial warfare denotes a value-free process of acculturation, the logical starting point of which is the native uses of and attitudes toward scalping. Although the advent of the Europeans and their scalp bounties introduced some changes in Indian scalping, native customs were surprisingly durable throughout the colonial period. In fact, when seeking Indian allies for scalping raids against French or Indian enemies, the English were forced to adapt themselves to native ways, not vice versa. As in many other areas of warfare, native pipers continued to call their own tunes, no matter who paid them.

The eastern woodland Indians took scalps as "visible proofs of their valour," without which "they are afraid that their relations of the combat and the account they give of their individual prowess might be doubted or disbelieved."[11] In those oral societies, a man's word was the touchstone of his integrity and worth as a reliable member of his face-to-face community. But since the honors of war were so eagerly sought and so highly valued, the temptations to exaggerate or even fabricate one's martial achievements were considerable. Having to produce the scalp of the enemy helped to reduce those temptations, as did two other customs. Only the individual scalplock from an enemy's crown was to be lifted, and the scalps were to be publicly displayed on cabin, post, or palisade "until every body has examined and declared them not to have been taken unwarrantably from their Friends; but bravely from their Enemies."[12] A Moravian missionary once asked a Delaware warrior why, if he believed that scalplocks were generous invitations to "take off each other's scalps in war with greater facility," the Indians did not grow hair on the whole head. The Indian patiently replied, "My friend! a human being has but one head, and one scalp from that head is sufficient to shew that it has been in my power. Were we to preserve a whole head of hair as the white people do, *several* scalps might be made out of it, which would be *unfair*. Besides, the coward might thus without danger share in the trophies of the brave warrior, and dispute with him the honour of victory."[13]

Scalps were not mere trophies or booty of war, however. The whorl of hair on the crown and especially male scalp-locks, braided and decorated with jewelry, paint, and feathers, represented the person's "soul" or living spirit. To lose that hair to an enemy was to lose control over one's life, to become socially and spiritually "dead," whether biological death resulted or not. The crucial distinction was the transference of power and identity into the victor's hands. "When the Indians relate their victories," observed John Heckewelder, "they don't say that they have taken so many 'scalps,' but so many 'heads,' in which they include as well those whom they have scalped, but left alive (which is sometimes the case), and their prisoners, as those whom they have killed."[14] Accordingly, when the Iroquois painted pictographs of their exploits on trees or marked the handles of their tomahawks, human figures signified prisoners, bodies without heads, scalps.[15]

Once a warrior possessed his enemy's scalp, he did with it as he wished. Sometimes he wore or displayed it with pride, perhaps on a thong at his side. Rarely, he sacrificed it to a war god in thanksgiving for his success or offered it to another tribe as an inducement to join him on the warpath. But most commonly he adopted it in the room of a living captive to replace a clan member who had died or gave it to another family or allied tribe for the same purpose, perhaps to satisfy a request for such a replacement. Whatever its fate, the scalp was regarded as a living "spirit" not to be trifled with. When the southeastern tribes exposed their enemies' scalps in the squares before their townhouses, "no Woman, Girl, or Boy" could be prevailed upon to go near them at night for "they say, among the Scalps wander the Spirits of the killed."[16]

When the English began to offer their Indian allies bounties for enemy Indian and later French hair, native traditions of scalping underwent a number of adjustments, most of them relatively minor. Iroquois war parties hired by Massachusetts in 1723 to bring the Maine Indian "rebels" into line had their autonomy (and pay) somewhat abridged by the English need for cost accounting. To prevent any garrison from mistaking the Iroquois for hostiles and "for avoiding any doubt or disputes that may arise about the Scalps that may be brought in by any of their parties," two Englishmen were ordered to join each party of ten Indians. Upon their return, the whites were to "certify upon Oath that a Scalp for which a Premium is Demanded is the Scalp of an Enemy Indian with their Age and Sex Slain in Fight and also to receive an Equal Proportion of the Scalp money with them." When the premiums stood at £100 for the scalp of every male over the age of twelve and £50 for that of any other "Killed in fight," fiscal responsibility demanded the exercise of due caution, particularly when a pagan• warrior's oath was considered worthless.[17] In the military heat of the Seven Years' War, several colonies were willing to substitute "sufficient satisfaction" for an Indian's oath that he had produced a legitimate scalp for reward.[18]

Another alteration may have stemmed from sporadic English attempts to humanize frontier warfare, ultimately to their own advantage. In early-eighteenth-century Carolina, the Indians' cruelty to Spanish prisoners knew no bounds "if the *English* [were] not near to prevent it." To revenge Spanish murders and enslavement, explained John Lawson, the natives scalped their prisoners alive, "Notwithstanding the *English* have us'd all their Endeavours" to prevent it, and the Spanish governor of Florida banned scalping and scalp dances among his own Indian tributaries in 1701.[19] Perhaps British regulars, unacquainted with American morality, impinged most heavily on the Indians' customs, but even this came late in the colonial period. When "Gentleman Johnny"

Burgoyne treated with the Iroquois in 1777 to enlist them against the colonial rebels, he told them that he and his officers took it upon themselves

> to regulate your passions when they overbear, [and] to point out when it is nobler to spare than to revenge. . . . Aged men, women, children and prisoners, must be held sacred from the knife or hatchet, even in the time of actual conflict. You shall receive compensation for the prisoners you take [he warned them] but you shall be called to account for scalps. In conformity and indulgence of your customs . . . you shall be allowed to take the scalps of the dead, when killed by your fire and in fair opposition; but on no account, or pretence, or subtilty, or prevarication, are they to be taken from the wounded, or even dying; and still less pardonable, if possible, will it be held, to kill men in that condition, on purpose. . . .[20]

Just how successful Burgoyne was likely to have been in deflecting the Iroquois from their ancient customs can be gauged from the previous actions of others much wiser in the ways of the forest than he. William Johnson, an adopted Iroquois, knew his brethren and the limiting conditions of their warfare well enough to allow them to produce for reward scalps of all ages and sexes. The members of the New York Assembly also knew their native neighbors. When the governor's Council sought to exclude rewards for "Scalping or taking poor women or Children Prisiners" from the scalp act of 1747, the Assembly assured Governor Clinton (who assured Johnson) that "the Money shall be paid when it so happens, If ye Indians insist upon it."[21] Some of the Iroquois's Canadian kinsmen were among the Indians who would not join the French in attacking Quebec in February 1760 "until they were assured that they should be rewarded with the scalps of all the killed and wounded."[22]

Johnson's deep knowledge of Iroquois culture allowed him to enlist his native kinsmen in yet another way without seriously affecting their scalping traditions. As an adopted kinsman married to Molly Brant, an influential Mohawk clan matron, and as the king's superintendent of Indian affairs, Johnson was able to assume the traditional authority of a clan matron in requesting kinsmen to capture an enemy prisoner or scalp to replace a deceased "relative," English or Iroquois. In the summer of 1756, Warraghiyagey (as Johnson was known to the Iroquois) requested a party of Onondagas to bring him a prisoner or scalp to replace his and their friend Tyanogo, Capt. Benjamin Stoddert, who had been killed at Lake George. The following year, Johnson "gave a War Belt to a Mohock named Zacharius in order to go to War & get a Scalp or Prisoner to give in the Room of Anias a Jenundadie who died of the small Pox in the Mohock Castle [village]."[23] While it did little to change the essential operations of Iroquois scalping, Johnson's subtle usurpation of the clan matron's role in instigating wars of revenge was another attempt on his part to reduce their political authority in what he thought should be exclusively councils of men. Beyond the Iroquois, however, Johnson's unusual influence did not extend and most tribes remained free from direct English control.

Yet the white man's bounties also worked upon the native scalping ethic indirectly—and perhaps more powerfully because, strictly speaking, the changes came from within native society. The first change was the transition from a military adventure wholly dominated by the search for personal prestige, tribal honor, and familial revenge to one partially subordinated to the commercial constraints and military needs of white foreigners. Once the Indians had been drawn into the English web of trade, the purchasing power to be gained by killing Indians hostile to the economic and political interests of English suppliers could not be rejected lightly. The more dependent on English clothing, food, and guns the Indians became, the more susceptible their traditional warfare became to commercialization. Indeed, when an Indian leader asked to receive scalp bounties for his military assistance, as did King Hendrick of the Mohawks in 1747 and Teedyuscung of the Delawares ten years later, he effectively certified his dependence on the colonial economy, though not necessarily the surrender of his political autonomy.[24] It comes as no surprise that in the eighteenth century Indian scalp-takers preferred payment in goods rather than currency, and that William Johnson spent ten times more feasting his Iroquois scalping parties and supporting their families during their absence than he did redeeming the scalps they brought him.[25]

Johnson was a major anomaly among colonial officials in adjusting English military needs to the traditions of Indian warfare, but even he contributed to an alteration of the natives' use of enemy scalps. Although he distributed redeemed scalps in acceptably Indian ways, he nonetheless, early in his career as an agent of the colony of New York, *purchased* scalps from their native owners and disposed of them as he, not they, saw fit. The colonial legislatures placed even higher demands on Indian warriors who traditionally displayed their trophies in public. Under the English bounty system, a warrior could not be paid for his services until he had surrendered his enemy's scalp to a colonial official, who then in the honest company of a legislative or judicial committee burned the hairy token or buried it in a secret spot; the last thing the impecunious legislatures wanted was to be duped into paying two large bounties for one small scalp.[26] Only the behavior of the Salem, Massachusetts, selectmen would have made much sense to the Indians. Until 1785, when the town courthouse was torn down, scalps redeemed from local scalp-hunters were hung along its walls for all to see.[27]

The magnitude of the changes entailed upon native warriors by involvement in the English brand of commercial warfare can be glimpsed in two contrasting incidents, one showing the tenacity of native custom, the other the potentially disruptive effects of change. The first took place in an Iroquois encampment in the early years of the American Revolution. Thomas Anburey, a lieutenant in Burgoyne's army, saw several hooped scalps hanging upon poles before the Indians' wigwams, one of which had "remarkably fine long hair." A fellow officer in search of a distinctive American souvenir offered to purchase it, but its Indian owner "seemed highly offended, nor would he part with this barbarous trophy, although he was offered so strong a temptation as a bottle of rum."[28] It is possible that the Indian found the price insultingly low, but more likely he was unwilling to part with a symbol of his prowess and courage at any price, even though Burgoyne was offering no "compensation" for scalps.

The second incident revealed more directly the confusion caused by the impingement of the new commercial ethic upon older native traditions. In May 1757 representatives from Gov. Horatio Sharpe of Maryland met with a group of Cherokees under Warhatchie, chief of the southern towns, at Fort Frederick on the colony's western frontier. The colonists had brought a few presents to induce the Cherokees to continue their incursions upon the Delawares and Shawnees who were raiding the colony's exposed flanks, but, the Indians were told, additional presents would not be forthcoming until prisoners and scalps were handed over to the Maryland authorities as directed by the provincial scalp law of 1756. "With some warmth," Warhatchie replied that merely showing the scalps was sufficient because "it was the Indians Custom to preserve as Trophies the Hair of the Enemies that they killed in Battle and to carry them home to their own People, and in short that if they were not to have the Goods that had been talked of unless they would purchase them with their Prisoners or Scalps they would return home naked as they came thence and that they would think no more of going to War if they were not allowed to keep what they set the highest value on as it procured them most Honour among their own People." Captain Pearis, the colony's Cherokee interpreter, tried to persuade them in private to give up some of the scalps to be destroyed according to the provincial law, but Warhatchie remained obstinate. A second chief, however, promised to send Sharpe the scalps as a "present," though he made it clear that he could not see them destroyed "in such a manner as the Act Directs, lest he should be charged by his own People with selling them." With this compromise, the officials sent for an additional £200 worth of presents—the bounty price of four scalps—and divided them among the natives. Even Warhatchie relented and sent a batch of "Hair" to Sharpe as a gift. But handing over their two prisoners was out of the question; they were destined for adoption as Cherokees.[29]

Governor Sharpe was obviously pleased with the results of his use of Indian mercenaries. Not only did the danger to his frontiers abate, but

> when [the Cherokees] received my Present for the Scalps [he told Lord Baltimore], they gave the Soldiers that were with them a Share, & gave no room to complain of their Behaviour unless their Refusing to give up the Prisoners & to suffer their Scalps to be destroyed . . . can be called criminal. For my part I think they should be indulged in their own Customs as much as possible, & as the Evidence of the Officer & Men that will always go out with them is enough to prevent the Frauds that the Assembly were sollicitous to provide against, I shall endeavour to get that part of the Act which forbids the Agents to pay for any Enemy's Scalps till they are actually burnt repealed at the next Session.[30]

But Edmond Atkin, a South Carolina trader-merchant and the newly appointed superintendent of Indian affairs for the southern colonies, had a different view of the situation. Following William Johnson's expert lead, Atkin thought that Indian allies should be rewarded "in proportion to their Services, . . . without Regard to the Number of Scalps" they produced. Part of his reasoning stemmed from his knowledge of Warhatchie's exploits, which smacked, he said, of "Impudence, Selfishness, and avaric[e]." Apparently the Cherokees had not relinquished all their scalps to the Maryland authorities and had carried them to Winchester to collect the Virginia bounty of £10. When Atkin's appearance in Winchester foiled their "scheme," most of Warhatchie's party—without the chief—stole off "privately" to try their luck at Fort Loudon in Pennsylvania. Atkin managed to warn the fort in time, but allowed the Indians part of the Pennsylvania present anyway, which was transported to Winchester for distribution at his hands. Surely this man who grew wealthy in the Carolina Indian trade knew that the English seldom had honored their 1730 treaty with the Cherokees in which the Indians promised to fight the colonists' enemies for being "furnished with all Manner of Goods that they wanted, by the Carolina Traders." If a sense of guilt as well as equity obliged Atkin to feel that the Cherokees "ought undoubtedly to receive a reasonable Reward for their Time and Trouble, while taken from their Hunts to assist us," and to distribute additional gifts, the Indians had good cause to feel that their reward from one colony was *not* reasonable, especially when they were virtually forced to surrender their trophies of war.[31] William Johnson agreed with them. To the Lords of Trade he complained that the government of Virginia—and by implication his southern counterpart, Atkin—treated the Cherokees, a vital link in the English chain of defense against the encircling French, with "an ill-timed frugality which greatly disgusted them."[32]

By the Seven Years' War, troublesome episodes such as this contributed to the feeling among several colonial officials that Indians should not be eligible for the provincial scalp bounties. Not only did native customs clash with the pragmatic requirements of colonial bureaucracy, but once the Indians were inured to the new commercial ethic of warfare they were prone to other, more serious misdemeanors. One form of cheating was the subdivision of scalps. When a French and Indian war party attacked Fort Lydius on the upper Hudson in the summer of 1757, they killed eleven English soldiers and wounded four. "The Indians, however, brought back thirty-two scalps," noted Montcalm's aide-de-camp; "they know how to make two or even three out of one."[33] The Cherokees employed by the English on the Pennsylvania and Virginia frontiers in the same summer were even more adept at multiplying their honors. Edmond Atkin knew that among the many scalps "hanging exposed in publick" at the army camp in Winchester were a friendly Chickasaw's scalp made into two and the scalps of five Frenchmen cut into twenty. He was doubtless right that the provincial scalp bounties "open a Door to great Fraud & Imposition upon the Colonies or the Donors themselves."[34] On the other hand, *caveat emptor* should have occurred to the English when they agreed to buy hair without telltale scalplocks and attracted needy native sellers to their military markets.

As Atkin's notice of the Chickasaw's murder suggests, opposition to scalp bounties for Indians had another source: "it is encouraging to the utmost *private Scalping,* whereby the most innocent & helpless Persons, even Women & Children, are properly murdered. . . . They are so many Temptations to some Indians to kill others that are our Friends," which might easily engulf the colonial frontiers in a general Indian war.[35] Even more to the point was the danger to Englishmen. When the Pennsylvania Council asked Conrad Weiser, Johnson's shrewd deputy, for his opinion in September 1757 about Indian eligibility for the rewards offered by the 1756 scalp act, he advised them to "Allow as much for Prisoners as you please, rather more than was intended" but that "no Encouragements should be given to the Indians for Scalps, for fear we must then pay for our own Scalps, and those of our Fellow Subjects, as will certainly be the case."[36] Weiser's fears were well grounded in the absence of a foolproof method for distinguishing a French scalp from an English one. From long experience among the Cherokees, Lt. Henry Timberlake knew that "they were pretty hospitable to all white strangers, till the Europeans encouraged them to scalp; but the great reward offered [by the colonial governments] has led them often since to commit as great barbarities on us, as they formerly only treated their most inveterate enemies with."[37] Self-interest, if not Christian compunction, dictated that scalp bounties be confined to Englishmen, particularly "poor white Men, who have been used to the Woods" and "driven from their own Habitations in the back settlements, by the War."[38]

Although colonial officials eventually developed misgivings about English scalping, scalp bounties enjoyed great popularity, especially among frontiersmen, whenever the colonies felt their backs to the wall from Indian or French attacks. The earliest bounties were offered to encourage native allies to kill Indians hostile to the interests of the European governments, the accepted specie of proof being heads. In 1637 the English in Connecticut paid their Mohegan allies for Pequot heads, and in 1641 the Dutch in New Amsterdam paid ten fathoms of wampum for each Raritan head brought in.[39] When King Philip's War erupted in 1675, the Narragansetts of Rhode Island were offered one "Coat (that is, two Yards of Trucking Cloth, worth five Shillings per Yard here)" for every enemy "Head-Skin."[40] But the New English quickly found that Indian allies were neither numerous nor trustworthy enough to solve their military problem, so it was felt necessary to give colonial soldiers a mercenary incentive to pursue Philip's mobile forces. With the tide of events quickly turning to flood, the governments of Connecticut and Massachusetts offered their own men thirty shillings for every enemy "Head." As Col. Benjamin Church, Philip's final nemesis, remarked, "Methinks it's scanty reward and poor encouragement; though it was better than what had been some time before."[41]

With the outbreak of the intercolonial wars in 1689, the frontier inhabitants of first New England and then most of the other colonies had another guerrilla force to contend with. By the late seventeenth century, scalping was so familiar to all European transplants that the French did not scruple to enlist its terrors against their more numerous Protestant neighbors. While the English took and maintained the lead in promoting the white scalping of Indians, to the French goes the distinction of having first encouraged the Indian scalping of whites. In 1688, even before the official declaration of war in Europe, the governor of Canada offered ten beaver skins to the Indians of northern New England for every enemy scalp, Christian or Indian. Not to be outdone, the English regained the palm in 1696 when the New York Council *"Resolved for the future,* that Six pounds shall be given to each Christian or Indian as a Reward who shall kill a french man or indian Enemy."[42] Thereafter, until the Seven Years' War when different motives prompted each to reassess their practices, the French and English governments periodically fostered the scalping of European and Indian enemies by offering bounties or other economic incentives.

Although the New England colonies resorted to scalp bounties in the first three wars with the French and Indians, the popular enthusiasm and official rationale for them appear no more clearly than in Pennsylvania during the Seven Years' War. Pennsylvania had extensive northern and western frontiers bordering on the territory of still-powerful Indian tribes —Delaware, Shawnee, and Iroquois. Only precipitous mountains, with their inaccessible trails and myriad hiding places, separated the land-hungry English from most of the Indians' fertile lands in the Ohio country and along the upper Susquehanna. With the French also ensconced in the Ohio valley from Fort Duquesne northward, war parties of French and Indians had small difficulty in laying waste the province's frontier settlements and killing, scalping, or capturing their inhabitants, which they began to do in earnest in the spring of 1756 following Gen. Edward Braddock's stunning defeat the previous summer. Within a few months, their lightning strikes had thrown the backcountry of Maryland, Virginia, and Carolina as well into total chaos. "All these provinces are laid waste for forty leagues [*ca.* 125 miles] from the foot of the mountains, in the direction of the sea," Governor Vaudreuil informed the French minister of marine in August. "The number of prisoners in these territories since last April [1756], is estimated at about three thousand—men, women and children, in addition to thirteen hundred horses carried off to the River Oyo [Ohio], or the Beautiful River; the houses and barns that have been burnt, and the oxen and cows which have been killed wherever found, have not been counted."[43] The only way to stop this devastation, the English thought, was to seize the offensive from their enemies and force them into a defensive posture, for which their inferior civil and military populations, fragile economies, and weak fortifications were ill-equipped. And the quickest way to mount such an offensive with woodsmen experienced in guerrilla warfare was the scalp bounty.

The most vocal demand for a bounty came from the ravaged settlements themselves, where vengeful inhabitants sought to drop their reliance on distant forts and defense-minded provincial troops and form their own volunteer war parties, financed largely by the bounties on enemy hair. No sooner had Braddock's survivors dragged themselves home than the western tribes, emboldened by their sudden success on the Monongahela, launched a blitzkrieg on the exposed Pennsylvania settlements. When Conrad Weiser met with the recent victims of Bethel, Tulpenhacon, and Heidelberg townships on November 19, 1755, he heard loud threats to all Indians "without Destinction" and even to himself as an Indian lover. Although an impromptu war council of officers, gentlemen, and freeholders raised a militia company and established pay scales, "the People . . . cried out that so much for an Indian Scalp they would have (be they Friends or Enemies) from the Governor." Impatient of action by the Quaker-dominated eastern establishment, they forced Weiser and some other freeholders to "promise them a Reward of four Pistoles for every Enemy Indian man they should kill" until the legislature could act. As for that, Weiser told Lieutenant (and acting) Governor Robert Hunter Morris, "They want to force us to make a Law, that they should have a Reward for every Indian which they kill; They demanded such a Law of us, with their Guns Cocked, pointing it [sic] towards us."⁴⁴ Perhaps the precedent of Maryland and Virginia, who had passed scalp laws in July and August respectively, added insult to injury. To all appearances, a Paxton prophecy had come true: "We must bid up for Scalps and keep the Woods full of our People hunting them," John Harris had warned less than three weeks before, "or they will ruin our Province."⁴⁵

Though tardily, bid them up the government did. In January the governor guaranteed forty pieces of eight for every Indian scalp lifted by a militia company. By April the legislature had raised £1000 for military operations and appointed a board of commissioners to oversee the distribution of scalp and prisoner bounties; $130 went to the taker of the scalp of any male Indian ten years or older. On April 24, Morris explained his strategy to William Johnson, a strategy substantially shared by Virginia and Maryland. "I have been constrained to yield to the importunate Demands of the enraged People (not being able otherwise to afford them a sufficient Protection for want of Arms, Amunition and an equal and compulsory Militia Law)" to declare war on the Delawares and to offer "large rewards for Prisoners and Scalps," he wrote, "hoping that this woud engage such of our Inhabitants as had any courage left, as well as all others in the Neighbouring Provinces, to hunt, pursue and attack them in their own Country and by these means keep them at home for the

Defence of their own Towns and prevent the total desertion of the back Counties. . . ." Although a scalp bounty was "loudly called for on my Return from New York, in December last, and since importunately and frequently repeated," Morris felt he had to wait on Johnson's and the Iroquois attempts to control the Delawares through diplomacy. "I own," he continued, "had I had the least notion that they coud be stopt in the midst of their furious Career, I woud not have gratified the People but dispairing of this, you will agree with me no other method is so likely as this to bring a force into the Enemys Country and drive them from their lurking places and from their Towns."[46]

The persistent English faith in the offensive potential of scalp bounties, however, was seldom rewarded with lasting military success, especially against the countless small raids characteristic of the early stages of the Seven Years' War. Just as Massachusetts's use of Iroquois mercenaries failed to solve her northern frontier problem in the early eighteenth century—salvation could not come from *Maqua ex machina* (in Richard Johnson's apt phrase)—so were irregular scalping parties incapable of stemming the French and Indian tide along the Middle Atlantic frontiers in mid-century.[47] The real source of trouble were the French forts that supported, supplied, and sent out the predominantly Indian war parties, and only disciplined British troops in impressive numbers, aided by artillery and the European art of siege warfare, could hope to neutralize them. English scalping parties could at best make the Indians think twice before leaving their own villages; at worst they could find themselves outfoxed by superior woodsmen and wind up as hairy hoops in those same villages. Governor Morris predicted accurately that bounties "indeed may induce men to go out in company, but the cutting off one or two small partys will put a stop to that kind of war."[48]

A larger impediment to their success was the ingrained de-

fensiveness of the colonists—despite their initial encroach-
ments on Indian and what the French believed to be French
land—and the need of farmers to stay at home in the very
months when Indian men, freed by their horticultural women,
took to the warpath.[49] "Our people are nothing but a set of
farmers and planters, used only to the axe and hoe," groaned
one colonial strategist. "The most we do is to defend our
selves at Home," lamented a Massachusetts minister in 1750,
"but they are for an offensive War." When sixty enemies were
killed near Fort Massachusetts, only three scalps were taken,
"which shows us that our Men will not venture out after the
Enemy on any Scalping Act whatsoever," not even "if they
should be much greater than ever they have been."[50]

The "Love of Money" that colonial officials hoped would
incite their people to "risque their lives in the service and
defence of the country" was a motivating force clearly inadequate to seize the initiative from offense-minded enemies.[51]
The list of complaints that the bounty acts were "ineffectual"
was long.[52] Perhaps the most eloquent testimony to their military failure came from the actions of the Maryland legislature
in 1765. Nine years after the province set aside £4000—one-
tenth of the total war chest—to encourage "Parties of active
Men not only to go in Quest of [hostile Indians] on our Borders, but even to Attack and Annoy them in their own Settlements," a committee of the lower house set fire to nearly half
of it. Virginia's burgesses did not wait as long to admit that
their scalp law did "not . . . answer the purposes thereby intended."[53] They scuttled it in 1758 when it became obvious
that the character of warfare in America was taking a deci-
sively European turn.

Yet when Indian hostilities erupted in Pontiac's uprising
and in the Revolution, the colonists renewed their tarnished
faith in scalp bounties, "the only effectual Weapon against
the Savages," hoping against hope that their efficacy would
outweigh their "abuses" and "Inconveniences."[54] The colo-

nists' ardent faith in scalping parties must have lain less in their lethal efficiency than in the boost they gave to morale and the outlet to revenge. Since the first Revolutionary scalp bounties followed the last of the Seven Years' War proclamations by no more than twenty years, the American officials who promoted them could not have been unaware of their mixed record as offensive weapons. But their popularity whenever frontier settlements suffered from guerrilla raids, whether French, British, or Indian, strongly suggests that bounties were one of the few ways available to colonial leaders to translate the colonists' hurt and anger into offensive zeal against the proper enemy, thereby deflecting it away from themselves. Whether many enemy scalps were actually produced mattered less than filling the woods with audacious, vengeful gunmen who plied the military trade—however irregularly—at a fraction of the cost of maintaining British or provincial troops. For most of these hunters, perhaps, the dangerous, difficult search for revenge probably served to maintain their general mental health by sublimating or exhausting the initially warping excesses of hatred and frustration that drove them. As many bounty hunters discovered to their peril, it was "ill fighting with a wild Beast in his own Den." And "who," many asked, "can catch a fleeing Indian?"[55]

If scalping did not prove to be the colonists' military salvation, it may have contributed to their moral damnation by encouraging an act that contravened their own cultural norms for the conduct of warfare and generalized Christian standards for the treatment of the dead. Just as the changes in traditional Indian scalping must be assessed in their own cultural terms, so must the moral dimensions of English scalping. Moreover, it is necessary to determine the proportion of colonial society that accepted the new ethic of scalping, implicitly or explicitly, for it is manifestly unfair—and historically inaccurate—to ask the innocent and powerless to share equally the moral burdens of society's movers and shakers, however numerous they were. By definition, aberrant behavior, such as scalping by the English colonists, is seldom the work of a whole society, though the attitudes and emotions that give rise to it may be shared by large segments of the society.

There is good reason to think that scalping was familiar and largely acceptable to a substantial portion of the colonial population. To frontier inhabitants, of course, bounties, scalps, and even survivors of scalping were bitter fixtures of life during the war years and vivid memories, frequently renewed in tale and boast, even in peacetime. To judge by the vociferous demand for bounties from the frontiers whenever the Indians turned hostile, few generations could have avoided their emotional impact. But scalping's legacy reached far beyond the frontier into the safer towns and cities of the colonies, even into the highest niches of polite society and to the mother country. Scalp bounties were widely proclaimed through broadsides, newspapers, and military chains of command. Colonial newspapers in wartime were filled with stories of scalping by and of the English, providing material for an already knowledgeable oral culture of news distribution. Graphic descriptions of the victims of Indian attacks, particularly pregnant women and little children, served to kindle the righteous anger of potential bounty hunters, and accounts of colonial successes enticed them into the field. When three New Jersey children were killed in 1756, for example, it was considered (exceptionally) newsworthy by the Philadelphia and New York papers that "none of them were Scalped," though one child's throat was (predictably) "cut quite across" and all were (poignantly) "found Dead with Flowers in their Hands."[56] Even in the fragile interstices of peace, the provocations for English scalping were never far from the colonial consciousness. In 1755 a Philadelphia newspaper noted the appearance of a Mohawk chief and some warriors "among the Ladies on their Assembly Night, where they danced the Scalping Dance with all its Horrors, and almost terrified the Company out of their Wits."[57] Given the "savage" addiction to "treachery," it mattered little that the Mohawks were allies.

If stories about scalps were a pallid substitute for the objects themselves, they could be seen and admired even in civilized circles far from their rough origins. Any inhabitant of Salem, Massachusetts (and no doubt other towns as well) could wander into the town courthouse to view the dusty hair-pieces tacked to the walls. As today, scalps could also be seen in museums. When Gov. Thomas Penn was given the scalp of a notorious Delaware chief in 1758, he "thought of sending it to the British Museum with a plate engraved giving an account of the action" at Kittanning where it was taken.[58] In 1782 a locally lifted scalp was displayed in Pierre-Eugène du Simitière's "American Museum" in Philadelphia.[59] Like soldiers in many wars, America's warriors, particularly British officers, had a habit of collecting souvenirs of their service in the colonial wilds. Gen. George Townshend, Wolfe's successor at Quebec, almost paid dearly for the collection of "scalps & some Indian arms & utensils" he took back to England. After a fashionable dinner party at Townshend's in January 1760, an Indian boy whom the general had given to Lord George Sackville as an American memento "got to the box & found a scalp which he knew by the hair belong'd to one of his own nation. He grew into a sudden fury (tho' but eleven years old) & catching up one of the scalping-knives made at his master with intention to murther him, who in his surprise hardly knew how to avoid him, & by laying open his breast, making signs, & with a few words of French Jargon, that the boy understood, at last with much difficulty pacified him."[60]

More memorable for the colonists was the sight of fresh scalps paraded through the streets of colonial towns such as Albany, Dover, Boston, and New York by strutting English woodsmen or befeathered native allies. Capt. John Lovewell's "brave company," entering Boston in 1725 "in triumph" with ten hooped trophies on poles (Indian-style), could not have failed to stir the blood and admiration of spectators. Only Lovewell's and a Lieutenant Farwell's wearing of wigs made from enemy Indian scalps, which they did to the Scriptural disapproval—more of the wigs than the scalps—of a single eccentric minister, may have won more plaudits for patriotic daring.[61]

Although scalping was considered a male occupation, women, even refined urban ladies, were not ignorant of or necessarily squeamish about it. The story of Hannah Dustin's capture and escape with ten of her captors' scalps, which gained in the telling, was a forceful reminder that the enemies of colonial men were the enemies of all English settlers.[62] The Mohawk scalp dance at the Philadelphia Assembly served the same purpose, as did the frank correspondence between an army officer and a young demoiselle who may have seen the dance four years earlier.[63] Even more telling was Archibald Kennedy's *Serious Advice to the Inhabitants of the Northern-Colonies* in 1755. After hearing the impassioned laments of a roomful of New York ladies that they could not go to war to revenge Braddock's defeat, Kennedy seriously proposed that the young women of the North "enter into an Association, not to admit any Youth of the Age of Eighteen to the smallest Share of their good Graces, until such Time as they had either laid a *French* Scalp, *bona Fide* taken, at their Feet," certifiably served in one campaign, or "shewed a Wound received in Front, in the Defence of their Country."[64] Apparently, the sight of a bloody French scalp—or an Indian's—at their satined feet would not have sent well-bred colonial girls into a faint or pious outrage. By the mid-eighteenth century, it seems safe to say, scalping was as Anglo-American as shillings and succotash.

But by no means was there a colonial consensus that scalping by Englishmen was either necessary or desirable, and calls for the abolition or strict limitation of scalp bounties were frequent if not loud. English culture had a strong conscience that never stopped protesting the colonists' deviation from "civilized" Christian norms, even when arguments from necessity were deafening. The first Massachusetts act of 1694 to encourage volunteers against the Indians offered bounties "for every [hostile] Indian, great or small, which they shall kill, or take and bring in prisoner." In 1704 the act was renewed, but the General Court amended it in the direction of "Christian practice" by establishing a scale of rewards graduated by age and sex and giving no rewards for the scalps of children under ten years. Subsequently, in Massachusetts as well as most of the other colonies, twelve years was the most common age for distinguishing "adult" enemies from children. On two occasions, however, heavily attacked Pennsylvania reverted to ten years, while relatively secure New Jersey and Connecticut could afford to allow Indian boys to reach the age of fifteen and sixteen respectively before putting a high price on their heads.[65]

While some colonists were concerned about the effects of the bounties on Indian lives, others worried about the effects on their own countrymen. As chairman of a committee on volunteers during the 1712 session of the Massachusetts General Court, Samuel Sewall tried to prevent the bounty hunters from turning their bloody work into a "Trade" at the expense of the government. Forced to give in to frontier pressure for "12s 6d Wages [a week] and Subsistence" for the volunteers in addition to the scalp bounty, he tried to degrade the volunteers' special status by ensuring that "stand[ing] forces, Marching and in Garrison might have the same Encouragement as to Scalp Money," which at that time stood at £100. All the talk of mercenary warfare clearly made the judge uneasy, and he concluded that "if persons would not be spirited by love of their wives, Children, Parents, [and] Religion, twas a bad Omen."[66]

Some years later, in Pennsylvania, the Reverend Thomas Barton was nagged by a similar concern. In 1763 the former military chaplain wrote that "the general cry and wish is for what they call a Scalp Act. . . . Vast numbers of Young Fellows who would not chuse to enlist as Soldiers, would be prompted by Revenge, Duty, Ambition & the Prospect of the Reward, to carry Fire & Sword into the Heart of the Indian Country. And indeed, if this Method could be reconcil'd with *Revelation* and the *Humanity* of the English Nation, it is the only one that appears likely to put a final stop to those Barbarians." As more than one reluctant advocate of scalping argued, "necessity pleads an Excuse for following so inhuman an Example, as the shortest way . . . to put an End to such Barbarities."[67]

The most popular excuse was the need for revenge upon the French and/or their Indian allies. "We should deal exactly with them as they do by us, destroy and scalp as they do," argued a New York official. Even a strong opponent of scalping allowed that "Reprisals of the same Kind" were justified by "the Laws of Nations, and indeed by all Laws divine and human."[68] Following an earlier governor's lead in blaming the "Barbarous . . . Scalping [of] the Dead" on French bounties, the Massachusetts lower house passed a scalp act in 1747 to be "aveng'd and retaliated" on the Canadians for warring in a "Way and Manner abhor'd by christian and civilized Nations, and justifiable from the Principles of Self-Preservation only." In the same spirit Gen. Jeffrey Amherst in June 1759 ordered his troops to preserve enemy women and children from harm, but threatened to "revenge" the murder or scalping of any English woman or child by killing—and presumably scalping—two enemy men "whenever he has occasion." A month later, General Wolfe "strictly forb[ade] the inhuman practice of scalping, except when the enemy are [male] Indians, or Canadians dressed like Indians," revealing thereby the standard limitation on even the most sensitive English conscience.[69] As Christians and white Europeans, the French might receive civilized treatment, even when they did not deserve it, but America's savages remained forever beyond the pale.

A few critics, however, remained adamantly opposed to English scalping under any circumstances. The Reverend Hugh Graham thought that bounties even on Indian scalps were "a Blot on Britain's Escutcheon." In 1779 Congress and General Washington were reluctant to give rewards for British scalps for fear "it may be improved by our Enemies to a national Reproach."[70] Gov. Jonathan Law of Connecticut worried less about the fickle eddies of public opinion than about moral absolutes. "As for the giving Premiums for humane Scalps or any other Creatures not equally mischievous to a Wolf," he told Governor Shirley of Massachusetts in 1747, "I must look upon to be unchristian, inhumane and barbarous with as great an Odium and Abhorrence as the good Marquis [Charles de la Boische de Beauharnois, governor of Canada] or any other Gentleman do[e]s or can doe." But in some ways the silent reproach of the British troops under Colonel Henry Bouquet was the most damning. After their surprising victory over the Indians at Bushy Run in August 1763, Bouquet told his commander, "Our brave men disdained So much to touch the dead body of a Vanquished Enemy that Scarce a Scalp Was taken Except by the [American] Rangers and Pack Horses Drivers," most of whom, "Stupified by Fear," had hidden in the bushes during the battle.[71]

Perhaps such uncompromising stances were possible only for those relatively new and unattached to America, such as Bouquet's troops, or safely distant from the danger of French and Indian war parties, as was Governor Law. Colonists within reach of an enemy scalping knife enjoyed small philosophical distance from the vengeful hatred of war, which helps to explain the proposals of a New Yorker who sought earnestly to abolish scalping, especially of "poor Women and innocent

Children," as barbarous and unchristian. Finding no way out of the vicious American cycle of revenge, he recommended to an Albany council of war that, rather than punishing Indian enemies in kind, the English should sacrifice three Indian "Right-Hands or Thumbs" for every "Mother of Children scalped or murdered, or otherwise abused; for every other Female two; [and] for every old Man, or such as are incapable of bearing Arms, or making any Resistance, two." If Frenchmen accompanied war parties that harmed English innocents, "let their Eyes, or the Eyes of those destined for Reprisals, by a gentle Puncture, pay for it, as well as their Hands, (or why not Castration?) and let them return, as live Monuments, and Examples of Cowardice and Cruelty. This will," he predicted, "strike a greater Terror than Death itself."[72] As the endless parade up Tyburn showed, death familiar lost its sting; mutilation did not.

Colonial Englishmen could not escape the judgment of their own religion and culture when they scalped declared enemies out of revenge and necessity. Still less could they do so when they scalped innocents in peacetime and committed other atrocities of the spirit and the flesh. The contorting animosities of war were not easily forgotten in peace. If a provincial officer was "justly incens[e]d" at Indian raids and "determined to scalp all I lay my Hands on with unrelenting Rage," how much more prone were his less disciplined backcountry troopers, who may have lost friends and family to the scalping knife, to forget the constraints of Europeanized warfare after a brief stint in the local militia and to blur the distinction between war and peace.[73] The uneasy period after the Seven Years' War was particularly rife with opportunities for the tardy exercise of vengeance, especially when former soldiers began to seep illegally into the fertile Ohio valley, and Maryland continued to offer scalp money until the fall of 1765. Well after Pontiac's uprising had been put down in the West and peace restored on the Pennsylvania frontiers,

Colonel Bouquet discovered that "one of the Maryland Volunteers, had killed a Shawnee Indian near Fort Pitt & produced a Scalp for the reward; And that Some of the Frontier People were out in the Woods Endeavoring to fall upon some straggling Indians to get their Scalps." And the killing continued, right up to the Revolution when bounties again made it legal. When a British Indian Department officer met with the head warriors of several western nations at Fort Pitt in 1768, they complained that "the English are certainly determined [to ma]ke War on us, or otherwise they would not Scalp our [peop]le—the Scalping those Indians is worse than murdering [them]," declared the officer.[74]

Some atrocities were caused not by an understandable search for revenge but by simple greed. In 1756 four New Jersey men combined to murder a family of loyal Indians, long-time residents of the area, and to pass their scalps in Philadelphia as having been lifted in Pennsylvania. Armed with "Guns, Cutlasses and an Ax," they attacked the wigwam about midnight on April 12. The husband, George, escaped unharmed, but his wife Kate died when one of the men "cut her Head all to Pieces" with the axe and another fired a "Brace of Balls" into her stomach. An eleven-year-old girl was "much bruised about the Head, stabbed in the Shoulders and her Right-hand almost cut off at the Wrist." Her twelve-month-old twin siblings were "cut and gashed in [a] frightful Manner." In the end, none was scalped because George raised an alarm that led to the bounty hunters' arrest. So strong was the temptation to pervert the bounties in this way that when Pennsylvania offered $150 for the return of any English captive of the Indians, the government needed to spell out that it would pay "nothing for their Scalps."[75]

The frontier's craving for scalp money and revenge gave rise to several practices that would have been regarded by traditional Indians as dishonorable to both the warrior and his enemy. One was double-scalping, not to cheat the provincial paymaster (although some men were not above that) but to secure another remunerative trophy when the first had been lost in flight. In 1725, for example, an eighteen-year-old soldier who had been captured by two Indians and carried into the Maine woods managed at night to knock them both on the head and scalp them. But in fording a river on the way home, he lost one scalp and a gun. He eventually collected the bounties on both scalps, however, because when he returned to his garrison a dozen men accompanied him to the place where he had slain his captor and "skin'd another off his head." The young soldier's victim had been dead only a day when he was scalped a second time; a scouting party from Fort Massachusetts took a full week to find one of their Indian victims and scalp him, this in early July which can be very warm in the Hoosic Valley. In a somewhat related vein, Massachusetts once paid £30 to a Northfield man who had spent fourteen months in a Quebec prison with a scalp he had taken just before his capture. The knowledge of how he managed to conceal an Indian scalp from his Indian captors and his French jailers all that time is, unfortunately, one of history's small casualties.[76]

A rather larger casualty, though no one seems to have noticed it at the time, was the morality of a New Jersey patrol alerted in 1758 by a young boy who had wheeled and shot a pursuing Delaware warrior on the Sussex road. Armed with guns and dogs, the local scout went to the scene of action where the dogs picked up a bloody trail. A short search led them to a "great heap of brush" where the Indian was found buried "close under a Log" with his "two Blankets, Tomahawk, Pipe and Tobacco Pouch by his Side." Since he was clearly not deserving of Christian respect, they "took off his Scalp," purloined the grave goods, and marched off to Perth Amboy to collect the provincial bounty.[77] That the incident was reported by the Pennsylvania and New Jersey newspapers without comment or murmur speaks eloquently to the blinding acceptance of the scalp bounty and its morality in eigh-teenth-century America.

What is not explicable—much less excusable—by any dis-cernible English or American standard is the behavior of Col. George Rogers Clark at the taking of the British Fort Sack-ville at Vincennes in 1779. During a temporary truce, a de-tachment of Clark's men captured fifteen or sixteen Indians and whites returning to the fort and brought them bound to the street opposite the fort. Sitting in a ring on the ground, the Indians were serially tomahawked by the Americans as they sang their death songs. Then one of the French soldiers in the scout, Francis Maisonville, was set in a chair "and by Col'l Clarkes order," testified Col. Henry Hamilton, the British commander who watched from the fort, "a man came with a scalping knife, who hesitating to proceed to this excess of barbarity on a defenceless wretch, Colonel Clarke with an imprecation told him to proceed. . . . When a piece of the scalp had been raised the man stopped his hand, he was again ordered to proceed, and as the executor of Col. Clarke's will, was in the act of raising the skin," a brother of the victim who had joined the American cause prevailed on Clark to desist. Maisonville never recovered from this traumatic encounter with American frontier justice: he lost his reason during a long confinement in Williamsburg and committed suicide. According to Hamilton, who may have exaggerated but cer-tainly did not invent the details of this affair, when Clark came to the fort to talk of its surrender, "yet reeking with the blood of those unhappy victims," he spoke "with rapture of his late achievement, while he washed of[f] the blood from his hands stain'd in this inhuman sacrifice."[78]

During the American Revolution each side spread prop-aganda about the other's use of Indian mercenaries, scalp bounties, and atrocities. While exaggerated for effect, most of these stories were plausible because the English in America had seen nearly every imaginable variation on the act of scalping, committed either by Indians or by colonists. But George Rogers Clark's exploits in the streets of Vincennes added a chilling new chapter to scalping's long and bloody history.

In war as in peace, English colonial society judged itself by two standards, one narrowly religious, the other broadly cultural. Thomas Barton referred to them as *"Revelation* and the *Humanity* of the English Nation."* By the second standard and without too much tergiversation, scalping and the use of scalp bounties could be judged acceptable—or at least not wholly objectionable—because they were necessary to the survival and prosperity of the English way of life in America. Scalping, after all, was a new cultural custom, whose method and much of whose morality derived from indigenous sources. The colonists scalped and encouraged others to scalp primarily because their Indian and later French enemies scalped them, and vengeance, like many other Old Testament traits, was deeply engrained in the Protestant English character. As scalping was resorted to with greater frequency and intensity, it developed an institutional status that could accommodate a number of operational and moral variations on the traditional Indian theme. Englishmen could, for example, legitimately scalp not only Indian and French men but also Indian women and children. The scalps could be taken not only upon felling the enemy but up to several days after, when the corpse had obviously reached a state of semi-putrefaction. Scalps could even be torn from buried enemies without overstepping the bounds of acceptable behavior. Of course, some Englishmen objected unreservedly to both scalping and scalp bounties, but they voiced a minority opinion that was all but drowned out by the advocates of the new ethic.

But "Revelation" was a much less flexible measure of social morality. In pure form, it played no favorites and tolerated no change. Its adamantine strictures applied with hard impartiality to all men and all nations. The rub, however, was that the English, even the ministerial custodians of Scripture, were incapable of living a pure text. Since it was obvious that scalping simply would not pass the test of Christian behavior exemplified by the life of Christ, "Revelation" had to be bent to fit the needs of the day. Not unexpectedly, there were many clerics ready to bend it.

The famous ambush of Capt. John Lovewell's volunteer band at Pigwacket (Fryeburg), Maine, on a Sabbath morning in May 1725 was launched as Jonathan Frye, the expedition's young Harvard-trained chaplain, had finished scalping a lone Indian hunter. In the heat of the day-long fight that ensued, Frye scalped another fallen adversary before he was himself wounded and left to die. The Reverend Thomas Smith of Falmouth (Portland) took no such personal risk. Rather, he was one of a group of gentlemen who hired a squad of hardy parishioners to go on a "Scout or Cruse for the killing and captivating of the Indian enemy." In return for supplying the bounty hunters with "Ammunition and Provision," the investors received "one full third Part of fourteen fifteens of the Province Bounty for every Captive or Scalp, and of every Thing else they shall or may recover or obtain." In his journal for June 18, 1757, the minister recorded, "along with pious thoughts, 'I receive 165 pounds 3-3 . . . my part of scalp money.' "[79]

When ministers not only looked the other way but shared in the profits from Indian deaths, the moral barometer of America dipped dangerously low. At the bottom, however, lay the American Revolution, in which Englishmen scalped Englishmen in the name of liberty. Scalping and other techniques of Indian warfare, placed in the hands of a larger European population, eventually sealed the Indians' fate in North America, but not before wreaking upon the white man a subtle form of moral vengeance.

American
Encounter

CHAPTER NINE

The English Colonial Impact on Indian Culture

My approach to any historical subject, whether English education or Indian acculturation, is essentially eclectic: I borrow unabashedly from whatever disciplines or academic specialties I think will shed light on the subject. So far anthropology has proven most congenial to the kinds of enquiries I have been making, which explains in part how I came to ethnohistory. But being by nature and nurture suspicious of unitary answers to complex questions—and all historical questions of cause and effect, persistence and change, are complex—I tend to borrow not the rigorous methodologies, specific questions, or technical vocabularies of the anthropologists, but only their general perspective and angles of vision. Like most ethno*historians*, I have found that asking the historical sources new *questions*, however derived, generates more insights and productive excitement than do new (or old) anthropological *answers* imposed upon the historical data. While this *modus vivendi* may not endear us to apostles of pure anthropology, it injects enough theory to avoid conceptual flabbiness and allows enough freedom to avoid the quickly dated imbroglios of disciplinary schools and methodological cliques.*

One hypothesis I have derived from anthropology is that the *way* people of one culture use or adapt another culture's artifacts (ideas, material objects, institutions, language) is more diagnostic

* E. P. Thompson, "Anthropology and the Discipline of Historical Context," *Midland History*, 1:3 (1971-72), 41-55.

of cultural change or acculturation than *what* they adopt. When Timothy Breen asked me to handle the Indian part of a conference on "Transfer and Change: The Cultural Development of England's Mainland Colonies," I was ready to put the question to the sources because I had just spent two consecutive fellowship years reading widely in colonial-Indian relations, particularly in the ethnohistorical literature on native acculturation. In abbreviated form, the following essay was delivered at the conference, which was generously sponsored by the Illinois chapter of the Society of Colonial Wars and held at the Newberry Library in May 1978.

Although disciplinary crossbreeding is not invariably productive, the conclusion I came to after looking at the form and meaning of native acculturation to colonial English ways seems to support the general proposition provided by anthropology; only further research in ethnohistorical sources can tell whether it holds for other cultures in other places at other times. This result should also alert American historians of every period to the strong possibility that an Indian who has given up the feathers, buckskins, and wigwams of his ancestors has not surrendered his Indian identity, his instinct for survival, or even his ancient sense of superiority to the invaders. Adaptation is less often a sign of capitulation than of capitalization.

UNTIL THE LAST DECADE OF THE NINETEENTH CENTURY, MUCH of America's history was the history of the ever-shifting frontiers among a variety of culture-bearing ethnic groups. America as we know it began as a frontier literally on the Atlantic coast and gradually moved westward, northward, southward, and (lest we ignore the geography of Maine) even eastward until the continent was covered with foreign laws and the American people were inextricably mixed.[1] But this movement toward national fulfillment was slow and far from inexorable, especially before the Revolution. As of 1750 the English colonies had not yet crossed the Appalachians, and the most powerful Indian groups—the Iroquois, Delawares, Creeks, and Cherokees—had refused to vanish from the eastern landscape. And yet the two cultures, native and English, had been in constant contact with each other, sometimes in war, more often in peace, and indelibly marked by the acculturation that such contact entails. For when two peoples meet, they invariably become part of one another, and their histories are henceforth intertwined.[2]

On any frontier, acculturation is a mutual process that affects each culture somewhat differently. The differences derive essentially from the nature of the cultures that meet and the conditions of contact. Cultures can be relatively open and flexible or closed and rigid, depending on such variables as their capacity for corporate definition, size, social integration, kinship and settlement patterns, and attitudes toward, distance from, and relative power vis-à-vis strangers. They can also be aggressive, intent upon directing or inducing change in the cultures they meet, or largely defensive, willing to tolerate other cultures in return for the freedom to determine their own cultural imperatives and strategies. Whatever their natures, the outcome of contact also depends upon the historical time, demographical space, and geographical place in which the cultures meet. The changes that result from this contact vary from microscopic introductions of cultural materials and traits—new cultural contents—to macroscopic alterations of fundamental structures and patterns—new cultural forms for integrating and assimilating foreign elements. Whether a culture survives or dies depends in large measure upon its capacity for creative adaptation to these changes.[3]

In the late sixteenth and seventeenth century England was a rapidly maturing nation bent on full participation in the worldwide competition for faith, fame, and fortune. After some success in subduing the "wild Irish" and clannish Scots at home, the English turned their attention to the untrammeled people and parts of North America. Hoping to outstretch their French, Dutch, and Spanish rivals in the New World, they sent exploring parties, then trading companies, missionary societies, armies, and permanent colonies to what they convinced themselves was a "virgin land," devoid of cultured people or fields.[4] Understandably, this massive assault upon America produced myriad changes in the lives and cultures of the native Americans, some small and temporary but many large and permanent. For although the Indians usually met the colonists in relatively small numbers, the cultural impact of the English presence rippled far beyond the immediate frontiers of contact.

One of the first and most devastating series of changes in Indian society was wrought not by the Englishmen themselves but by the micro-organisms they transported to America in their ships and lungs. Sometimes even before an Indian tribe had actually met the English, they were attacked by foreign diseases to which they had no immunities, triggering outbreaks which modern scientists call, ironically, "virgin soil epidemics."[5] European diseases such as typhus, yellow fever, diphtheria, influenza, dysentery, and, deadliest of all, smallpox often decimated tribes by as much as 50 to 90 percent in a single visitation. Even childhood diseases now relatively benign, such as measles, mumps, whooping cough, and chicken pox, turned killers in native populations that enjoyed no history of exposure and natural immunization.

It has been estimated that during the first century of colonization an average of 1.5 percent of the New England natives died every year from chronic and epidemic diseases, thereby reducing their population at least 80 percent by the mid-eighteenth century.[6] A shipborne "plague" of 1616-18 began the depopulation there by carrying off the whole Patuxet tribe from its favored site at Plymouth (except Squanto, who was kidnapped by an English slaver, and perhaps a handful who escaped to neighboring tribes) and striking so many other Massachusetts natives that "they died on heapes, as they lay

in their houses."[7] Their unburied remains reminded one early
settler of "a new found Golgotha."[8] Villages of the southern
tribes were similarly littered even earlier as Europeans spread
along the Atlantic coast and up its rivers. At Cofitachequi (in
present-day Georgia) in 1540, De Soto's *entrada* found little
food because the population had recently suffered a terrible
plague, perhaps the residue of disease that had decimated
Ayllon's coastal colony in 1526.[9] An English Carolinian believed that by 1709 there was "not the sixth Savage living
within two hundred Miles of all our Settlements, as there
were fifty Years ago."[10] In 1738 even the remote Cherokees
were reduced almost one-half by smallpox inadvertently
packed over the mountains on horseback from Charleston.
Virtually no tribe was untouched by the deadly hand of
pestilence.[11]

Since they were unacquainted with afflictions brought from
the Old World, the Indians could resort only to traditional
cures. The most pervasive throughout North America was the
sweat lodge, a skin-covered hut filled with steam from water
splashed on heated rocks. Having left his clothes at the door,
the patient sat in the sweltering space long enough to purge
body and soul of their impurities, then dove into the nearest
body of cold water. Unfortunately, this was the worst possible
treatment of smallpox and its "violent Fevers," for the cold
water, contemporaries thought, "shutting up the Pores, hin-
ders a kindly Evacuation of the pestilential Matter, and drives
it back; by which Means Death most commonly ensues."[12] So
harmful was this traditional remedy that it might have completely "extinguished" the Cherokee and Catawba nations in
1759 "had they not left off bathing . . . by their own Notions, or by the Advice of the Europeans" who were trading
or garrisoned among them.[13]

The Indians unwittingly contributed to the alarming rates
of their own mortality in other ways. In many tribes, friends
and relatives crowded into the lodge of the stricken to aid the

powwow in his ministrations. Having no sense of and few means of enforcing quarantine, they found to their sadness that "the distemper, if it seizes one, is quickly communicated to all."[14] The only alternative was flight, not only of persons but of houses and whole towns, as it was in contemporary Europe. With all the able-bodied removed, however, the afflicted nearly always succumbed to starvation, dehydration, the cold, or wild animals. Unattended by even their closest relatives, who quickly learned the telltale signs of infectious disease, they died "like rotten sheep," unburied if not unmourned.[15]

The survivors were left to count the staggering costs of their tribal loss. The first and most immediate toll was personal: the psychological despair of having to watch family and friends cut down by unknown diseases in appallingly high numbers—and perhaps the gnawing guilt of having survived at all. "This great mortality being an unwonted thing, feare[d] them the more," wrote Edward Johnson of Massachusetts, "because naturally the Country is very healthy."[16] "Those that are left," noted a Pilgrim in 1622, "have their courage much abated, and their countenance is dejected, and they seem as a people affrighted."[17]

Disease exacted another heavy toll from many survivors, especially in the South. Rather than endure pockmarked faces the rest of their lives, "a great many" smallpox victims, especially the young and handsome, killed themselves by shooting, stabbing, or throwing themselves into fires, rivers, or over cliffs. "For being naturally proud, they are always peeping into their looking glasses," wrote James Adair, a southern trader who kept them well supplied with such, "by which means, seeing themselves disfigured, without hope of regaining their former beauty," they took their lives "with sullen madness."[18] Other diseases had the same effect on other tribes. When John Tanner lived with the Ojibwa in the late eighteenth century, he and many tribesmen were "seized with a violent sickness" which impaired their hearing and caused bleeding from the nose and mouth. "Of the Indians who survived," Tanner remembered, "some were permanently deaf, others injured in their intellects, and some, in the fury occasioned by the disease, dashed themselves against trees and rocks, breaking their arms or otherwise maiming themselves." Unable to hear the game he stalked before it heard him, Tanner too tried to take his own life, but was prevented by his adopted family.[19]

The alterations made by disease in the native social fabric were equally serious and permanent. The mere capacity of the society to reproduce itself was gravely threatened by epidemics which tended to sweep away "whole Families, but chiefly young Men and Children, the very seeds of increase," as a Puritan patriarch put it, ignoring the women of childbearing age who died in equal numbers.[20] The loss of family members tore gaping holes in the extensive web of clans and kinship that shaped an Indian's identity as much as language and residence. Technological skills,[21] leadership, and the group's corporate memory were lost with key adult members, especially elders who, with infants, possessed the least resistance. Political succession at both the clan and tribal levels was thrown into disarray. Settlement patterns were broken as survivors regrouped in new locations or dispersed as members of new polities. But perhaps most important, the natives' religious beliefs, cosmological assumptions, and social morale were battered by the inexplicable fate that had befallen them, predisposing them to seek the material and spiritual help of the newcomers.

The experience of the Roanoke colonists was perhaps typical of the earliest encounters where the English were still strangers to the Indians and therefore understandable only in native terms. In every town where some "subtile devise" had been used against the English, wrote Thomas Hariot, "the people began to die very fast and many in short space;

in some townes about twentie, in some fourtie, in some sixtie, & in one sixe score, which in trueth was very manie in respect of their numbers. . . . This marvelous accident in all the countrie wrought so strange opinions of us, that some people could not tel whether to thinke us gods or men, and the rather because that all the space of their sicknesse, there was no man of ours knowne to die, or that was specially sicke." Thus exalted in the Indians' eyes, the English were called upon by the stricken werowance, Wingina, and many of his followers "to praie and bee a meanes to our God that it would please him either that [they] might live, or after death dwell with him in blisse." By the same token, the native priests, whose credit had been eroded by their inability to control the deadly diseases, "were brought into great doubts of their owne [religion], and no small admiration of ours, with earnest desire in many to learn more. . . ." From such signs Hariot believed that the Carolinians would "in short time be brought to civilitie, and the imbracing of true religion."[22]

The fate of the "Lost Colony" never allowed his prediction a proper trial. But in southern New England, where two major epidemics preceded the first missions, a sequence of events similar to Roanoke's bore Hariot out in some measure. For the natives of eastern Massachusetts and Plymouth, who had suffered the plague of 1616-18 and a virulent smallpox outbreak in 1633, neither contested the Puritans' arrival nor long resisted their profferings of Protestant religion and English culture. It was no accident that the majority of John Eliot's praying towns consisted of Massachuset Indians, who had been reduced from some 4500 to perhaps 750 souls before the *Mayflower* ever dropped anchor in Plymouth Harbor.[23] Nor is it strange that Squanto, who had seen the power and pesthouses of London, "played his own game, by putting the [Wampanoag] Indians in fear and drawing gifts from them to enrich himself, making them believe," among other things, that his English friends "kept the plague buried in the ground, and could send it amongst whom they would."[24] In short, as the most famous acculturated native had quickly learned, invisible agents softened up the enemy before the main army of invaders launched their frontal assaults on his culture.

Diseases often rode into Indian villages on English kettles, blankets, and beads.[25] If a native society managed to remain unscathed by the strangers' microbes, it could scarcely avoid the consequences of their trade. As soon as the English and Indians met, they exchanged gifts as gestures of courtesy, pledges of peaceful intentions, and tokens of economic alliance. Each group considered its own donations "worthless trifles" or common "baubles" and those it received valuable prizes. From their own perspectives, of course, they were not wrong. Beavers to the Indians were ordinary, rather small furs obtained (at least in the beginning of contact) with no great expenditure of time or effort. That a few furs brought them aesthetic treasures such as mirrors, Venetian glass beads, rings, and vermilion, and labor-saving devices such as hatchets, blankets, and copper kettles was a happy discovery throughout native America. Even stranger in Indian eyes was the Englishmen's implausible preference for the greasy beaver robes they had worn for a year or more in their smoky lodges.[26] Far from the hatters' workshops and high fashions of London, they could not appreciate that prolonged wear removed the long guard hairs from the downy, barbed underfur used in felting. Only the English could savor the delicious irony of how "foule hands (in smoakie houses) [had] the first handling of those Furres which are after worne upon the hands of Queens [as muffs] and heads of Princes."[27]

When the honeymoon of gift-giving settled down to a marriage of mutual dependents, the trade nexus began to affect native society in numerous ways. First, the Indians gradually substituted many English goods and materials for their own because they were perceived as functionally equivalent but technologically or aesthetically superior. The major items of trade throughout the colonial period were metal tools—guns, hoes, axes, and knives—and clothing—broadcloths and wool blanketing on the bolt. Understandably, the most common Indian names for the Europeans with whom they traded meant "iron people" or "cloth makers."[28] Although the Indians developed a dependence on the trade for many necessities and some luxuries, they expressed strong preferences for quality workmanship and certain colors.

In 1685 William Byrd, a prominent Virginia trader, asked his English suppliers to "speake to the gun smith that the dogs of all the gun locks have good hold otherwise the Indians will not buy them." Moreover, he added, "I have received great complaints of my [duffield cloths] the colour is too light, a darker blew pleases better."[29] Like Byrd, most English traders found that their native customers preferred "sad" colors, mostly deep blues and reds, "the darker the color the better."[30] If they could not have them, they took their furs elsewhere or refused to hunt altogether. As a party of angry Mohawks told the Dutch traders at Fort Orange in 1626, "Why should we go Hunting? Half the time you have no cloth."[31] The fierce competition between the French, Dutch, and English, and between rival English firms ensured that unhappy Indian customers could satisfy their demands over other counters. Widespread was the lament from English traders that "the Indians of these parts, having so many markets to go to, are much more delicate and wanton than in any other part of the country." So too were the long lists of "the Indians' dislike of particular goods, [and] their refusal [of them]."[32]

But the shift to English goods was not immediate or inevitable by any means. William Wood noted in 1634 that the southern New England Indians, "if their *fancy* drive them to trade," would not buy fitted clothes but rather chose "a good coarse blanket" or "a piece of broad cloth" for double use as a coat and bedclothes. "They love not to be imprisoned in our English fashion," he explained, but added that since the native women "cannot wash them when they be soiled" and replacement was too expensive, "they had rather go naked than be lousy and bring their bodies out of their old tune."[33] Nine more years of acquaintance with English fashions made the Narragansetts no more fond of them. In 1634 Roger Williams observed that "Our English clothes are so strange unto them, and their bodies inured so to indure the weather, [that] . . . in a showre of raine, I have seen them rather expose their skins to the wet then their cloaths, and therefore pull them off, and keep them drie." Out of their strong sense of natural courtesy, "while they are amongst the *English* they keep on the *English* apparell, but pull of[f] all, as soone as they come againe into their owne Houses, and Company."[34]

Over time and according to circumstance the Indians' dependence upon English trade goods became more complete. As early as 1650-75 some 75 percent of the objects used by the Senecas in western New York and found by archaeologists were of European origin.[35] In 1768 Eleazar Wheelock conducted a frustrating search among the eastern Iroquois nations for a native artifact that was "perfectly Simple, and without the least Mixture of any foreign Merchandise" to send as a gift to the Earl of Dartmouth, the benefactor of his future college. A "small specimen" was all he could find because, he apologized, "our Traders have penetrated so far into their Country." Only "some articles which were defaced by Use" were crafted from the traditional materials he sought.[36] In some parts of the South the Indians' need for the English trade was so pronounced that colonists traveling in Indian country were willing to bet their lives on it. Upon finding signs of a large war party nearby, William Byrd II assured his exploring party in 1733 that the northern Indians were then at peace with Virginia and that the Catawbas were "too fond of our trade to lose it for the pleasure of shedding a little English blood," an argument from the "rules of self-interest" that seemed to calm his companions' jumpy nerves.[37] Certainly by the Revolution most of the eastern tribes had become saturated with foreign products.

But the mere presence of English goods in native society, even on a large scale, did not necessarily denote a significant change in Indian culture. Material objects, no less than people, receive their cultural status only by being assigned meaning and value by the members of a society. The form and the function of an object, therefore, are far more important culturally than the material from which it is made. An artifact may be made of several alternative materials, but if its traditional form and function do not change, neither does its cultural meaning.[38]

Most English trade goods were simple substitutions for traditional items: manufactured cloth for animal skins, metal tools for stone, bone, and wooden tools. Many introductions were used not as the English would have but as the Indians interpreted their uses in a native context. The Delawares who were given iron hoes by Henry Hudson wore them around their necks for a whole year until the sailors returned to show them how to make handles. The completed items they quickly found superior to their own clamshell scrapers and digging sticks.[39] Likewise, the Narragansetts who killed and robbed an Englishman in 1636 were found wearing nearly £50 worth of the victim's gold pieces perforated on wampum necklaces.[40] Shiny new copper and brass kettles were sometimes cut up for arrowheads, beads, pendants, jinglers, gaming pieces, and bracelets, and gun barrels sawn off for love flutes and war whistles, just as in the nineteenth-century West baking-powder cans made excellent rattles and crimson longjohns effective substitutes for ceremonial deerskins.[41] Even the splint basketry introduced by the Swedes was a functional replacement for native birchbark, grass, and wooden containers.[42]

Of course, a few trade items were completely new to Indian society and required adjustment to their foreign uses. Jew's harps had no counterparts in native society, nor did flintlock muskets or bottled rum. The Jew's harp was a musical luxury and made little impact on Indian culture, but the gun and alcohol were considerably more powerful in their effects.

Alcohol was introduced to the Indians as a gift, a companionable toast before trading or politicking began in earnest. But it quickly became a staple of the trade itself when the Europeans saw that many natives—though by no means all—acquired a large thirst for it, despite its initially unpleasant taste and their total lack of experience with fermented beverages. Despite its relative weight, "neither capacity or knowledge of the Indians, or their language [was] necessary for the sale of it" and the profits to be made were "considerable," especially when it had been watered.[43]

While the traders were single-minded in their pursuit of profit, their Indian customers drank for several reasons, most of which had roots in traditional culture. Most drinking Indians imbibed only to become thoroughly drunk. "Social" drinking for taste or mildly pleasant sensations was rare. Inebriation alone was the goal and served at least three different purposes. First, it inflated their self-esteem, "for when they are drunk," a Virginian observed, "they say that they are brave men, they have no fear, and can fight any man."[44] Warriors sang "what f[e]ates they have done, what Men, Women, and Children they have kill'd, and what scalps they have taken," while the young people, "professedly given to bravado," were urged by their intoxicated pride "to seek notoriety whereby they may receive attention for some deed or other."[45]

Second, drunkenness gave the Indians, "by custom, a valid excuse for any evil which they might commit in such a condition."[46] "According to them," wrote a French officer, "it is a state so delicious that . . . one is not responsible for his acts."[47] Rather the liquor or the vendor was blamed. So regarded, inebriation—real or feigned—was an ideal way to insult, beat, or kill one's enemies with impunity, for "drunken-ness excuse[d] everything."[48] Since overt aggression against one's tribesmen was taboo and sober revenge usually entailed a potentially endless cycle of killings upon one's family or clan, drinking endowed the revenge motive with new spirit.[49]

The third major purpose of intoxication was to achieve a dreamlike state of religious possession, one capable of "taking them out of themselves" during a socially sanctioned "time-out."[50] For the Indians of North America, the dream was a means of sacred communication, putting them in touch with the spiritual forces of the universe and revealing the inner-most wishes of their souls. If these wishes were not correctly interpreted and satisfied, the body and soul would fall into serious disharmony and the body would sicken and perhaps die. In youth the dream provided the Indian with a personal guardian spirit—a bird, animal, or person—that brought him good fortune and endowed him with spiritual powers. And throughout his life, dreams renewed those powers at critical junctures and taught him, however cryptically, his sacred duties. Intoxication was simply a painless shortcut to the dream state which involved no fasting, sleeplessness, or other forms of sensory deprivation.[51] Consequently, in many tribes a drunken man was regarded as a "sacred person," possessed by a spirit which spoke through his mouth.[52]

Unhappily, not all the effects of "demon rum" were desired or desirable. Despite clerical warnings that liquor would be the "inextinguishable fire" in which they would burn forever, Indians bent on insobriety sometimes—too often to colonial thinking—turned their villages into the very "image[s] of hell" and literally perished in the flames as predicted.[53] Madness, murder, and mayhem seemed to reign when the trader's rund-lets arrived from the English ports. Drunken "frolics" lasting several days often produced several victims of shootings, stab-bings, brawls, burning, biting, and bawdry.

However, the personal costs of drinking could not match

the losses suffered by native society as a whole, losses which owed more to the feverish search for alcohol than to the beverage itself. The desire for rum impelled Indian hunters to kill more game than was necessary to purchase only dry goods, thus hastening the serious ecological imbalance in their territories.[54] When the pelts were taken to the English trading posts, a cup or two of rum could part a hunter.and his catch before he could purchase the next year's necessities. As the Seneca sachems complained at Albany in 1710, "the Bevers you have got from us for Rum if they were to be laid on one heap would reach the Clouds."[55] Alcohol also loosened the Indian's hold on his land. More than one treaty was signed "under the influence," an abuse that fueled Indian-white conflict throughout the colonial period and beyond.[56]

Native leaders were not long in recognizing the baneful effects of the rum flowing into their villages and implored their colonial counterparts to dam it. The arguments they used were two: their people were dying in excessive numbers from drinking-related murders (and, we know also, from exposure and increased susceptibility to colds, pneumonia, and other diseases), and the temperance issue "produce[d] all Evil and Contention between man and wife, between the Young Indians and the Sachims."[57] Although he was factually wrong, Cadwallader Colden took the true measure of liquor's impact upon Indian society when he said that "Drunkenness . . . has destroyed greater Numbers, than all their Wars and Diseases put together."[58]

The impact of firearms was equally powerful. In one sense, the gun was only a more powerful bow that shot lead instead of wood and flint arrows. As such, many of its uses were traditional ones. But its effects upon Indian society went far beyond changes in hunting and warfare, despite—and in some instances because of—certain technological disadvantages. A gun, powder, and shot could be obtained only from an English trader at considerable expense, which made the Indians "depend entirely upon the English," William Byrd noted, "not only for their Trade, but even for their subsistence";[59] bows and arrows could be fashioned from the native environment with no esoteric skill. If a gun broke—as the cheap trading guns did frequently—the Indian was dependent upon a distant English blacksmith for repair; a bow was more readily replaced. A gun was loud in the loading and louder in the shooting, warning enemies and game alike of the danger; an arrow was silent, tipped with surprise. A gun was slow to fire and unreliable in wet weather; a bow could let fly "Several [arrows] in a Minute" in all kinds of weather.[60] In heavy underbrush the bullet's level trajectory was deflected; an arrow could be arched over the terrain.[61]

Nevertheless, the gun had two major advantages which were sufficient to promote its rapid and large-scale adoption by the Indians: it gave them more killing power than bows, and initially its loud report helped traumatize their enemies, adding panic to the prevailing emotions of war.[62] To obtain guns, the Indians changed many of their hunting practices; armed with guns, they wrought several changes in their conduct of war. And each set of changes reverberated throughout Indian society.

For tribes that had maintained a delicate ecological balance before contact, the advent of guns and metal tools and an increased demand for English trade goods led to mounting pressure on the animal populations in their vicinity. As the credit columns in traders' ledgers mounted, the Indians were forced to collect more skins, primarily deer in the South and beaver in the North. Armed with iron axes and chisels (steel traps were not used until the early eighteenth century), Indian hunters smashed beaver dams and lodges to expose whole populations to their guns and iron spears. Deer, which were frequently able to outrun Indian arrows, fell consistently before their fiery "shooting sticks," often from traumatic wounds made by imperfect shots. Ancient taboos against the killing of certain animals, religious respect for all animals, and a conservation ethic that preserved a minimal breeding population for the next year's hunt were eroded by the consuming desire for trade. Game driven from the deforested areas of English settlement often received no respite in the Indian country before being overhunted and reduced to ecologically dangerous levels, thereby skewing the balance of other animals and plants.[63]

By the 1640s, for example, the beaver could scarcely be found in the valleys of the Iroquois. To satisfy their demand for Dutch and later English trade goods, the Iroquois waylaid the fur brigades of the Hurons, Algonquins, and Ottawas headed for Quebec and Montreal, igniting a half-century of intertribal conflict known as "The Wars of the Iroquois."[64] Fierce competition for the shrinking hunting grounds of the East and for the middleman position with the western hunters sent Iroquois war parties as far as Illinois and Wisconsin. Economic rivalries superimposed on traditional ones spawned new confederacies and alliances, bred multi-tribal settlements at key trading locations, and accelerated the deadly cycle of revenge. The result was that the Illinois were annihilated, the Hurons nearly so, and most of the Great Lakes and Ohio valley tribes pushed west. The Iroquois reigned supreme in the Northeast until the American Revolution, largely, some contemporaries thought, because of their superior supply of firearms.[65]

The possession of guns not only contributed to new causes of warfare but changed the ways the Indians waged it. Before contact, Indian warfare consisted primarily of small-scale raids to avenge a tribesman's death, terrorize an enemy village, or secure prisoners for torture or adoption. Undertaken by a mere handful of volunteers seeking war honors, these raids were considered successful when only two or three scalps had been taken. On the warpath and for several days before, the warriors followed a strict course of purification in order to draw divine favor upon their enterprise. Their weapons were bows and arrows, flint knives, and wooden warclubs, used largely in carefully laid ambushes. The only variation on this pattern was an occasional pitched battle between large groups either surrounded by makeshift barricades of logs and brush or protected by woven-cane armor and shields. In such situations the opposing sides kept their distance and lofted arrows at each other with such a trajectory that only the slowest warrior risked serious injury. Before the gun, therefore, Indian warfare was seasonally sporadic, largely symbolic, and relatively low in mortality.[66]

The introduction of European firearms changed all that. Although an arrow was sufficiently lethal, the gun killed faster and more surely, even in the hands of a novice. Wounds were more serious and often developed fatal complications. Native armor could not stop bullets and was quickly abandoned.[67] In the face of armed Englishmen, large Indian armies wisely dispersed behind trees and adopted the guerrilla tactics for which they are justly famous. "Since the Introduction of Fire Arms [the Iroquois] no longer fight in close bodies," Sir William Johnson observed, "but every Man is his own General. I am inclined to think this circumstance has contributed to lessen the power of a Chief."[68]

Perhaps the most important change in native warfare was the generation of new motives. To the traditional motives of revenge and honor, which remained operative—perhaps dominant—throughout the colonial period, were added the desire to control access to trade centers, to seize hunting land from other tribes, to subjugate contiguous tribes to serve as buffers, to obtain slaves for English markets, and to exterminate tribes who did not lend themselves to the realization of these goals. Obviously, the scale of intertribal warfare was greatly enlarged. Small villages whose openness once tested the daring of their enemies now fused into substantial towns encircled by tall palisades.[69] War parties set out more frequently with

more men and returned with fewer, requiring genuine periods of peace to recoup spent forces and populations. The
torture of captives gradually gave way to their adoption to
fill the places of fallen tribesmen.[70] And although war was a
male business, the status of women may have risen at home
in the men's absence as the producers of the tribe's increasingly agricultural food supply, educators of children, reposi-
tories of communal history, and adopters of captives. In some
tribes, particularly the Iroquois and most of the southeastern
tribes, residence may have become increasingly matrilocal and
inheritance matrilineal. On the other hand, as more Indian
men died on the warpath, upsetting the balance of the sexes,
polygyny may have enjoyed renewed popularity.[71]

As any student of colonial history knows, Indian warfare
was directed not only at other Indians but at Europeans as
well. When the English first landed in America they were immediately courted by native tribes seeking their material gifts
and an alliance with their superior technology against traditional enemies. Although the Plymouth and Roanoke colonists thought they were asserting their God-given hegemony
over the tribesmen of Massasoit and Wingina, they were at
the same time being used by the natives for their own calculated purposes.[72] As the English got a firm toehold on the
Atlantic plain and began to multiply, the balance of power
began to shift. The Indians still pursued the politics of self-
interest with consummate skill, learning to play off European
competitors and even English colonies against each other. But
increasingly their dependence upon English trade and their
dangerous proximity to the English settlements (which they
said spread faster than a beargrease spot on a blanket) threw
them ever more firmly into the political embrace of the English.[73] When the English decided to wage war on the colonies of Spain or France or their Indian allies, therefore, many
Indian tribes could not refuse their services as scouts, soldiers,
and even sailors.[74] Forced to play the distasteful role of mer-

cenaries in the Englishman's wars, the Indians were reduced to dependence upon his supplies, schedules, and motivations.[75] The ultimate commercialization of warfare, however, came with the English inauguration of scalp bounties as early as 1637. Indian allies—who were familiar with scalping long before the Europeans arrived—were sent out for the scalps of Indians inimical to English interests, the production of which earned a reward in money or trade goods.[76]

The Indians owed one additional motive for war to the English presence: the desire to secure their tribal sovereignty from English usurpation, their families from English slavery and peonage, and their lands from English acquisition, whether by judicial confiscation, legal purchase, political annexation, or armed conquest. Whenever a tribe or confederacy decided that to suffer a train of colonial abuses and usurpations was no longer in its best self-interest, it could pursue one of two courses. It could, with the help of a charismatic leader, attempt to revitalize its culture by shunning English goods and associations and thereby recapturing the vital integrity of its imagined or actual past.[77] Or, alternatively, it could launch an undeclared attack on the naked flanks of the offending settlements, much as the Yamasees pounced on South Carolina in 1715.

The Yamasees had been zealous commercial partners and military allies of the Charlestown traders for nearly thirty years when the war erupted. Armed with English guns, they not only traded large quantities of deerskins but equally impressive numbers of Indian slaves captured in raids on Spanish Florida, Georgia, and Alabama. But by 1708 their slaving ventures had been so successful that the Spanish mission Indians had been literally wiped out, removing a major source of income. At the same time, a growing colonial population had turned to extensive cattle-raising and rice cultivation, both of which severely reduced the deer herds of the coastal plains where the Yamasees lived. When the Carolina traders totted up their ledgers in 1711, the 400 Yamasee warriors owed more than 100,000 deerskins for trade goods they had received on credit. Faced with serious financial loss, the traders began to demand payment. Many took drastic measures, such as enslaving the debtors or their wives and children.[78] When colonial officials took a census of the Indian villages in the spring of 1715, the Yamasees interpreted it as the opening move in a plot to enslave all the Indians in South Carolina. To avoid slavery, they chose all-out war with their former trading partners.[79]

Predictably, the Yamasees lost their desperate bid for independence, as did the other tribes in eastern America who decided—too late—that the cultural cost of trade with the English was too great. Long Warrior's address to the Cherokees ten years later recognized the sad inevitability of the natives' dilemma. He told them "That they must now mind and Consider that all their Old men were gone, and that they have been brought up after another Manner then their forefathers and that they must Consider that they could not live without the English." By this he meant "That they have all their goods and Arms to Defend themselves (without wch) they could not go to Warr and that they'll always be ruled by them."[80] As a declaration of Indian dependence, his speech could not have been more succinct.

The stage upon which Indians and Englishmen played out their cultural destinies in colonial America extended beyond the trading post and the skirmish line. They met also in English schools and Christian missions where black-robed invaders declared open war on the heart of the Indians' cultural identity. Some of the most critical changes in native culture were made on the far-reaching frontiers of the mind.

From the time they secured their colonial charters from the Crown to the winning of independence, the English maintained that their "principall ende" in coming to America was "to bringe the Indians to the knowledge of the gospell"

through teaching and personal example.[81] Yet the conversion
the English had in mind was not simply religious, for religion in that day, as in ours, was culture-bound, ringed about
with social habits that passed for eternal truths. In a society
ruled by divine-right monarchs, affairs of the spirit were inseparable from affairs of state. Since the goal of colonization
was to transplant a segment of English society in America,
religion was expected to play a tactical role in coping with its
novel human environment. While it was desirable to save the
Indians from themselves, to rescue them from Satan's clutches
and the darkness of paganism, it was more important to save
the English from the Indians. The best way to accomplish
both goals, it was thought, was to "reduce [the Indians] from
barbarism to civility."[82] For, as one eighteenth-century missionary explained, "Civility will prepare them to admit Religion; and Religion will prevent them from falling back into
barbarism."[83] In other words, the ultimate solution to the
colonists' "Indian problem" was to turn the Indians into Englishmen.

The problem with the Indians, as the English saw it, was
their unpredictability and their "savagery," both of which
stemmed from glaring cultural deficiencies: their lives were
ungoverned by civil and social order; they, especially the men,
were strangers to work; their dress and manners lacked all
modesty and taste; and their religion knew neither God Almighty, Jesus Christ, nor John Calvin. As the peculiar need
for "reduction" (instead of elevation) indicated, their "savage" condition was equated with the "sinful liberty" of post-
lapsarian Adamism in which "overweening pride"—the original sin—marred all their thoughts and actions. As God's
"chosen people," therefore, the English missionaries felt they
could do these "heady Creatures" no greater good than to
"bridle" their lawless impulses and force their pagan necks
into the "yoke of Christ."[84]

The means by which the English attempted to effect these

changes were the time-honored institutions of church, school, and apprenticeship, and a colonial invention, the "praying town" or reservation. Praying towns, which represented the missionaries' highest hopes for cultural change, were popular only in southern New England, where the native population had been rapidly eroded by disease and surrounded by English settlements. The function of the praying towns, as devised by John Eliot and Daniel Gookin, was to isolate the Indian neophytes from their "pagan" brothers and from the "civilized" vices that swirled about them, especially the insatiable greed for land and the liquor trade which could in short time reduce viable Indian communities to pathetic "slums in the wilderness."[85] In townships granted by the colonial legislatures, the Indians were encouraged to reproduce the full range of English institutions—churches, schools, jails, homes, farms, and shops—and to govern themselves by English-style laws. Such an arrangement would effectively supply the vital deficiencies in native culture and render the natives much more predictable. Living in immovable houses in permanent towns under English law, the Indians' whereabouts would always be known. Depending upon heavy agriculture for their livelihood, Indian men would learn the value of sweaty "labour," free their wives for spinning and housekeeping, leave the bloody warpath (because their crops were vulnerable to English reprisals), and require much less land than aboriginal hunters, the surplus of which could be sold or given to their ambitious English neighbors. Surrounded by benevolent example, the Indians would Anglicize to the last detail their dress, hygiene, eating habits, names, sexual and marital mores, and, of greatest symbolic importance, their hairstyles. When Indian men subjected their long, carefully groomed black hair to the barber's shears, the last vestige of their "pagan" pride was submerged in the will of the Englishmen's God.[86]

The most popular English instrument of conversion was

the school—sexually segregated, morally guarded, classically oriented, rigorously disciplined, patriarchally dominated, and, until the middle of the eighteenth century, located in English territory. Not only were the students segregated from the cultural pull of their families and friends, but they served as hostages for the good behavior of their tribesmen.[87] Thus the English preference for chiefs' sons, who, if they were successfully converted, were expected to lead their people along the English way. In an atmosphere of pious gravity, the young scholars, aged ten to fourteen, were introduced to the mysteries of the Protestant religion, the English language, Arabic numbers, and Greek and Roman literature. When the frustration or boredom of their inactive lives erupted in high jinks, the birch rod covered their skin with welts they had never seen at home.[88]

By their nature, the praying town and the school were confined largely to the English settlements and to the preliminary task of "civilizing" the Indians in preparation for religious conversion. But the task of substituting one culture for another was so great that the job of converting the Indians to the English brand of Protestant Christianity was often neglected, postponed, or attacked with inadequate forces. Only twenty-two Indian "churches" of the elect (as opposed to mere congregations) had been gathered in New England by 1776, and only a small handful elsewhere, largely because Protestant church organization had no peripatetic missionaries until the eighteenth century and the standards of church election for Indians were more exacting than those for their English neighbors.[89] The contrast between English hopes and Indian results was sharply drawn by Nathaniel Rogers in his 1764 reissue of William Wood's hopeful account of *New England's Prospect,* first published in 1634. To Wood's passage suggesting that the natives of America were susceptible to true "religion," Rogers appended a gloomy footnote: "The christianizing the Indians scarcely affords a probability of success," he

wrote. "As every attempt to civilize them, since the first settlement of this country, hath proved abortive . . . it will rather
appear a Utopian amusement, than a probable pursuit. . . .
The feroce manner of a native Indian can never be effaced,
nor can the most finished politeness totally eradicate the wild
lines of his education."[90]

Such a negative assessment was largely, though not wholly,
warranted by the history of colonial missions. As we have
seen, neither the few English missionaries nor the Indian
schools they founded enjoyed much success. Nevertheless, a
substantial number of Indians did convert, at least partially,
to Christianity and English "civility" during the colonial period, especially in New England.

Any explanation of these conversions must begin with the
crisis of intellect that the Indians experienced upon contact
and the wide range of their responses to English cultural offerings. The first Indian groups to meet the strange bearded
men from the Old World encountered their awesome technology and their selectively lethal diseases at the same time.
Possessed of compasses, guns, books, clocks, and immunity to
the new diseases, the white men were often seen as gods or as
men favored by the gods with powerful "medicine." The Indians believed that the English God exceeded theirs as much
as English guns did their bows and arrows.[91] As the advent of
the English altered more of the natives' world, whole new
sets of problems and questions were raised to which only the
Englishmen's God could reasonably be expected to provide
solutions and answers. "All things that were able to do them
hurt beyond their prevention," noticed John Smith, "they
adore with their kinde of divine worship."[92]

Although eventually English culture was everywhere a force
to reckon with, it was not able to hurt the various Indian
groups in equal measure. Tribes who escaped the worst maladies of English contact, who still enjoyed relatively healthy
populations, stable social structures, and political indepen-

dence, had little need for the full English cure. They could trade with the colonists or fight at their sides against common enemies, but at the same time withdraw their children from English schools to hunt or refuse to give visiting missionaries their normally polite hearing. Any Christianity they espoused either lay very lightly on the surface of their lives or was deeply syncretized with native elements; in whatever degree, its acceptance was calculated to ensure their tribal independence and ethnic identity.[93]

Less fortunate tribes who found themselves surrounded by the colonial juggernaut, their numbers, lands, and independence severely reduced, accepted more of the colonists' religious and cultural offerings, but with the same instinct for survival. Rather than seeking nativistic revitalization, as larger and healthier tribes could, they used the colonial Marshall Plan—the "Eliot Plan" if you will—to the same end. Even though it entailed wholesale cultural changes, it preserved their ethnic identity as particular *Indian* groups on distinctive pieces of land that carried their inner histories. An acceptance of English ways, however sincere, allowed them to survive in the present and gave them a long lease on the future at the cost of a certain amount of material and spiritual continuity with the past. Ironically, the acute English sense of cultural (and later, racial) superiority helped the Indians maintain the crucial ethnic core at the heart of their newly acquired English personae.[94] In English eyes, they were still Indians and always would be, no matter how "civilized" or "Christianized" they became.[95]

It would be easy—and foolish—to lament all the changes in native life as a tragic loss of innocence. It was indeed a loss, but not necessarily a tragic one. Only if we continue to regard the pre-Columbian Indian as the only "real" Indian, as the "noble savage," can we mourn his loss of innocence. Only if we persist in equating courage with mortal resistance to the forces of change can we condemn the praying Indians as cultural cop-outs or moral cowards. For life is preferable to death, and those who bend to live are also possessed of courage—the courage to change and to endure in the face of overwhelming odds against their survival as well as the contempt of their brothers who died with stiff necks. Certainly the Penobscot, Mashpee, Iroquois, Cherokee, Pamunkey, and other Indian peoples who still live in the former thirteen colonies would not disagree.

CHAPTER TEN

The Indian Impact
on English Colonial Culture

No STUDY OF ACCULTURATION IN COLONIAL AMERICA WOULD BE COM-
plete without giving equal consideration to the question of how
English culture was altered by its contacts with native America.
The Society of Colonial Wars conference did not allow time to
do justice to that topic as well as its obverse, so I waited for an
opportune moment to essay it, which came at the May 1980 colloquium of the Institute of Early American History and Culture.
Deadlines are the elixir of scholarly life, I find, because they
furnish impeccable excuses to stop researching and to begin writing. The essay that follows was written to that deadline.

However, I had another long-standing reason for writing it:
my initial enchantment and then growing disappointment with
A. Irving Hallowell's "The Backwash of the Frontier: The Impact of the Indian on American Culture" (1957). I have the
greatest respect for Hallowell's work—his cultural and psychological sensitivity, his focus on people rather than abstractions,
his surehandedness with historical materials—and I still admire
the ethnological assumptions that informed his look at the trans-
cultural traffic on the other side of one of America's oldest and
longest streets. But his essay and many others like it (including
an earlier paper of my own) are unsatisfying largely because they
fail to assess the _ways_ in which Anglo-American culture used or
adapted the Indian artifacts and traits the authors so lovingly
enumerate. While most of these (predominantly anthropological)

authors, especially Hallowell, would not automatically assume that a contemporary Indian driving a pickup truck was or considered himself no longer an Indian, they fail to exercise the same caution when treating the white frontiersmen who selectively adopted Indian ways and means. It is as if they were trying to soften the hard fact that historically white America has had its foot upon the Indian's neck by celebrating the fact that the oppressive foot was often clad in a moccasin.

The remedy for this kind of romantic astigmatism is a healthy dose of equal treatment. One of the benefits of an ethnohistorical perspective is that it forces us to ask of colonial cultures the same kinds of probing, elemental questions we ask of native cultures. In this essay I have asked the same question asked in the previous chapter: if the way one culture adapts artifacts from another is the best index of acculturation, to what extent did English colonial culture become "Indianized" by contact with the culture of native America? I conclude that colonial culture underwent two kinds of change: *adaptive changes* consisting of the temporary adoption of Indian means to predetermined English ends, and *reactive changes* spurred by the ubiquitous presence of the Indians as military foes and cultural foils. The former effects, to which the previous students of white acculturation have devoted all their attention, gave frontier culture much of its color and texture but in the long run made a shallower imprint upon colonial culture as a whole than did the colonists' negative reactions to the Indian challenge. This result, it seems to me, should only be expected in a society whose dominant thrust was to supplant the Indians on American soil. Where the natives were not regarded as superfluous obstacles, as in French Canada, adaptive changes were much more pervasive and intricately woven into the fabric of colonial culture.

As THE CULTURAL HEIRS OF THE ENGLISH "WINNERS," HIStorians of colonial America have been relatively alert to signs of the European impact upon Indian culture, perhaps as a way of explaining the "inevitable" triumph of a "superior" way of life. But they have been far less ready to recognize the surge of cultural influence in the opposite direction. Even ethnohistorians, who learn early that acculturation is a two-way street, have concentrated so intently upon the native side of the frontier that they have largely ignored the important reciprocal changes wrought upon colonial culture. Thus both groups of historians have been unable to convince their colleagues, students, or the general public that the Indians are anything but an exotic if melancholy footnote to American history.[1]

Where historians have not deigned to tread, others have rushed in. Since the last quarter of the nineteenth century, several articles and chapters have treated "The Contributions of the American Indian to Civilization" or "Americanizing the White Man."[2] But most of them are either derivative, unhistorical, or downright foolish. They all suffer from at least one of four major problems. First, with one antiquated exception, they take as their subject all of American history and culture, with no differentiation of sections, classes, demography, or chronology. Second, "Indian" culture is similarly overgeneralized; no allowance is made for tribal, culture area, or even chronological differences. Third, they focus on isolated *materials* or *traits* rather than on cultural *complexes* (how items were used, valued, and integrated by the Indians) or on cultural *creativity* (how they were used, perceived, and adapted by the colonists). And finally, the conclusions of some and the implications of all lack common sense. To suggest, even indirectly, that "what is distinctive about America is Indian, through and through" or that Americans are simply Europeans with "Indian souls"[3] is blithely to ignore the "wholly other" nature of English colonial society—its aggressive capitalism; exploitative attitudes toward natural resources; social hierarchy; nuclear kinship system; religious intolerance; literacy and print communication; linear sense of time; imperialism based on "directed contact" and conquest; superiority complex based on religion, technology, social evolution, and ultimately race; and desire to replicate the major features of the mother society as completely and quickly as possible.

One way to avoid these pitfalls is to limit our study to the first two centuries of American history when the English and the eastern woodland Indians, both relatively homogeneous cultures, commingled and competed for the continent east of the Appalachians. By paying attention to the nature, timing, and extent of the changes induced in colonial culture by the Indian presence, we should be able to assess with some historical accuracy and realism the "Indianization" of American culture in its formative and perhaps most pliable phase. If the Indian impact was not great in the period of closest and most sustained contact, it is likely to have been even smaller in subsequent periods when the frontier constituted an ever-diminishing proportion of America's human and physical geography.

Although the scholarly study of what came to be known as "transculturation" did not begin until the late nineteenth century, the "Indianization" of English culture was recognized throughout the colonial period. Contemporary descriptions took three basic forms. The most common descriptions—which have unduly dominated the historical literature since—lamented the "barbarism" or "savagery" of the colonists who lived in horrid isolation on the frontiers, far from "civilized" settlements. They spoke to the generalized fear of backsliding that is characteristic of all colonial societies founded in the midst of native peoples. The image of "the Indian" in these descriptions was an entirely negative reflection of English metropolitan ideals, seen largely by their clerical and political custodians.[4]

The Puritan ministers of New England were the most vocal critics of scattered frontier settlements, where many "were contented to live without, yea, desirous to shake off all Yoake of Government, both sacred and civil."[5] "There hath been in many professors" of the Puritan faith, scolded the Boston synod in 1679, "an insatiable desire after Land, and worldly Accommodations, yea, so as to forsake Churches and Ordinances, and to live like Heathen, only that so they might have Elbow-room enough in the world."[6] By moving into the shadowed corners of the land, the settlers bade defiance "not only to Religion, but to Civility itself" and exposed their children to the danger of degenerating into "heathenish ignorance and barbarisme."[7] Particularly lamentable was the decline of family government and the sinful indulgence of masters and parents toward their children and servants. "In this respect," observed Increase Mather, "Christians in this Land, have become too like unto the Indians."[8] The cultural consequences of this *"Criolian* Degeneracy" were predictably ghastly. In the "more Pagan [out-]Skirts of *New-England,"* shuddered his son Cotton, "Satan *terribly* makes a *prey* of you, and *Leads you Captive to do his Will."*[9]

But the New England frontier was not the only hotbed of heathenism in America. In the eyes of an Indian missionary from New England, "the whites on the extensive frontiers of [eighteenth-century] Virginia, are generally white Savages, and subsist by hunting, and live like Indians."[10] When the itinerant Anglican minister, Charles Woodmason, preached his way through the Carolina backcountry in the late 1760s, he was as shocked by the "Indianization" of the settlers as any Puritan would have been. The living and behavior of the settlers, predominantly Scots-Irish, were "as rude or more so than the Savages." Bred of unalloyed "Indolence and Laziness," they lived in log cabins "like Hogs," their dirty children ran "half naked" and their women hardly less so. "The Indians are better Cloathed and Lodged," thought Woodmason. Not surprisingly, "many hundreds live in Concubinage—swopping their Wives as Cattel, and living in a State of Nature, more irregular and unchastely than the Indians."

When Woodmason attempted to reduce them to good order through religion, they were "as rude in their Manners as the Common Savages, . . . firing, hooping, and hallowing like Indians" to interrupt his services. When the county sheriff brought a party of Catawba Indian deputies to quell the disturbances, the natives behaved "more quiet and decent than the lawless Crew" of whites. But there was "no bringing of this Tribe into any Order. They are the lowest Pack of Wretches my Eyes ever saw," swore the minister, "or that I have met with in these Woods—As Wild as the very Deer."[11]

The second group of descriptions of "Indianized" colonists were generally more neutral in tone. These characterized the English traders who spent much or all of the year in Indian villages where, for the sake of ingratiating themselves with their customers, they adopted their dress, technology, language, protocol, and other customs, especially sexual ones. Unlike the representatives of the large trading companies of the late eighteenth and nineteenth century, these traders tended to be individual entrepreneurs who owed any pejorative assessment to their character as traders rather than to their adoption of Indian life. John Long, a company trader of considerable experience in both Canada and the northern English colonies, observed that the companies used to "purchase convicts and hire men of infamous character to carry up their goods among the Indians, many of whom ran away from their masters to join the savages."[12] From his long experience in the South Carolina Indian trade, Edmond Atkin knew the village traders to be "generally the loosest kind of People, . . . whose Behaviour, being for the most part the most worthless of Men, is more easy to be conceived than described."[13] James Adair, a southern trader of liberal education, concurred. "Many of the present traders," he wrote, about 1769, "are abandoned, reprobate, white savages," not because they were "Indianized" but rather because they infected the Indians with the worst kinds of English "obscenity and blasphemy."[14]

Far more common were accounts of the traders' ready acceptance of native mores. Perhaps because the traders were among the few Englishmen to intermarry with the Indians, early observers—often other traders—dwelt in loving detail on these cross-cultural unions. John Lawson, for example, spilt much ink over the "trading girls" among the Carolina Indians, whose special haircuts showed that they were "design'd to get Money by their Natural Parts." The hairstyle, Lawson dryly noted, was intended to "prevent Mistakes," a distinct possibility in villages frequented by the Indian traders. On the other hand, many traders took Indian wives "whereby they soon learn the *Indian* Tongue, keep a Friendship with the Savages; and, besides the Satisfaction of a She-Bed-Fellow, they find these *Indian* Girls very serviceable to them, on Account of dressing their Victuals, and instructing 'em in the Affairs and Customs of the Country. Moreover," Lawson continued, "such a Man gets a great Trade with the Savages; for when a Person that lives amongst them, is reserv'd from the Conversation of their Women, 'tis impossible for him ever to accomplish his Designs amongst that People."[15]

Sometimes the unions did not last, and the trader returned to the English settlements, leaving his offspring "like bulls or boars to be provided for at random by their mothers."[16] Perhaps as often, the traders with native wives "have been so allur'd with that careless sort of Life, as to be constant to their *Indian* Wife, and her Relations, so long as they liv'd, without ever desiring to return again amongst the English, although they had very fair Opportunities of Advantages amongst their Countrymen." John Lawson knew several men of this sort.[17]

In other parts of the country, traders became "Indians" only temporarily in order to prepare themselves for higher careers in commerce. According to Anne Grant, the young boys of eighteenth-century Albany were apt to "contract a love of savage liberty which might, and in some instances did, degenerate into licentious and idle habits" by spending every free hour tramping the woods with gun, fishing pole, and axe. When marriage seemed imminent, the boy received a small stake from his father, a Negro boy, and a dugout canoe, into which he piled his jerked beef and Indian corn staples and his trade goods. He began to smoke, dressed himself in "a habit little differing from that of the aborigines," and launched his career as an Indian trader. From the profits of their first venture, the young Albanians often launched themselves on larger careers in New York or on the Atlantic trade routes.[18]

Far more distressing to colonial observers was the third group of "white Indians" on the colonial frontier. These were the relatively small but significant number of colonists who had chosen quite literally to become Indians by running away from colonial society, by not trying to escape after being captured, or by electing to remain with their Indian captors when treaties of peace periodically afforded them the opportunity to return home. In English eyes, the first group, comprised of army deserters, runaway slaves, outlaws, and more generally "renegades," were nothing more than traitors to king, church, and country. Typical of this breed of reckless men were Joshua Tift and William Baker. In 1637 Roger Williams reported that Baker, formerly a Plymouth trader on the Connecticut River, was being pursued by the English authorities for "uncleanes with an Indian squaw, who is now with child by him," and was living with the Mohegans, amongst whom he had "gotten another squaw." The following year Williams learned that this man who "can speake much Indian . . . is turned Indian in nakednes & cutting of haire, & after many whoredomes, is there maried." Such a "fire brand," the minister warned, had best be extinguished before he and surviving Pequots, both bent on revenge, "fire whole townes."[20]

Joshua Tift was considered an even more incendiary character. When he was captured among the Wampanoags by the English in King Philip's War, he was condemned to die the death of a "Traytor" by hanging and quartering. According to the Reverend William Hubbard, his crimes clearly merited such severity for he had "divested himself of Nature itself, as well as Religion." Tift was a "Renegado English-man of *Providence,* that upon some discontent amongst his neighbours, had turned *Indian,* . . . conformed himself [in dress] to them amongst whom he lived . . . , married one of the *Indian Squaws,* [and] renounced his Religion, Nation and natural Parents all at once, fighting against them. . . . As to his Religion he was found as ignorant as an Heathen, which no doubt," Hubbard noted piously, "caused the fewer tears to be shed at his Funeral."[21] It was the potential danger of "renegades" like Baker and Tift that prompted the Connecticut legislature in 1642 to threaten with fines, corporal punishment, and three years imprisonment those "diverse persons [who] departe from amongst us, and take up their aboade with the Indians, in a prophane course of life."[22]

Far more numerous were the colonists—men, women, and children—who had been captured by Indians in wartime and adopted into their families as permanent replacements for lost relatives. In a widely popular literature of captivity narratives, written for public consumption or only family record, the "Indianization" of hundreds, perhaps "thousands," of Englishmen was described in ways that must have set contemporary teeth on edge while planting the troublesome question of how it was accomplished without force, coercion, or bribery. The results were plain to see: captives who had replaced their own language with an Algonquian or Iroquoian dialect; who dressed, moved, and even looked like their new relatives; who had married Indians and had children by them; who became chiefs and respected leaders in their adopted societies; who presumably thought much like Indians; and who strenuously resisted their forced return to white society. It was this conspicuous group of converts to "savagery" who most demanded explanation.[23]

Unfortunately, contemporaries gave explanations much less frequently than they tried to explain *away* the fact that for many Englishmen Indian life held conscious and legitimate attractions. One escape was to resort to the uniquely American adage, "It is very easy to make an Indian out of a white man, but you cannot make a white man out of an Indian."[24] Another was to cast aspersions on the character or sanity of the converts. "For the honour of humanity," wrote the Reverend William Smith in 1765, "we would suppose those persons to have been of the lowest rank, either bred up in ignorance and distressing penury, or who had lived so long with the Indians as to forget all their former connections."[25]

When the colonists did try to explain the conversion of their own, they generally resorted to some form of environmentalism. The earliest and least convincing expression of this theory attributed the strange behavioral changes in the colonists to the influence of the American climate. In 1724 Cotton Mather sent two illustrations of this theory to a team of English physicians interested in climatic power.

> One very observable quality of our Indians has always been this, that they have no family government among them; . . . Their children are the most humored, cockered, indulged things in the world. . . . Now 'tis observable that tho' the first English planters of this country had usually a government and a discipline in their families that had a sufficient severity in it, yet, as if the climate had taught us to Indianize, the relaxation of it is now such that it seems almost wholly laid aside, and a foolish indulgence to children is become an epidemical miscarriage of the country. . . .

By the same token, Mather regretted the growing Indian-like laziness of the colonists, who seemed to be powerless in the grip of the American climate.[26]

Later in the eighteenth century, however, a more sophisticated version of environmentalism dominated attempts to account for the "Indianization" of the colonists. According to this explanation, mankind was divided into three great classes: "The savage lives by fishing and hunting, the barbarian by pasturage, and the civilized man by agriculture." Each class is formed not by one influence, such as climate, but by many, such as "government, . . . mode of husbandry, customs, and peculiarity of circumstances." Thus "the arts of civilization may be expected, in a considerable degree, to correct the effects of the climate."[27]

While it might bear a faint resemblance to a later concept of culture, the early national view of the "stages of society" was hardly value-free. Particularly when asked to explain the transition of men from one stage to another, contemporaries fell back on characterizations that smacked of the perdurable contrast between "savagism" and "civilization." To explain why "civilized" Englishmen frequently chose the life of "savage" Indians, Samuel Stanhope Smith postulated that man was placed on earth at the creation in a civilized state, and that "savage life seems to have arisen only from idle, or restless spirits, who, shunning the fatigues of labor, or spurning the restraints and subordinations of civil society, sought, at once, liberty, and the pleasures of the chace, in wild, uncultivated regions remote from their original habitations." As everyone knew, "once hunters, farewell to the plough." "Men who have once abandoned themselves to the restless and adventurous life of the hunter," Alexis de Tocqueville noted, "feel an insurmountable disgust for the constant and regular labor that tillage requires." "Such is the charm of [the Indians'] wandering and independent state," Smith told his sedentary students at Princeton, "the pleasure of alternately pursuing their game, and reposing in indolence, that many of the citizens of the United States are found voluntarily to renounce all the conveniences of civilization to mingle with the savages in the wilderness, giving the preference to their idle and vagrant habits of life." When contemporaries wished to account for the totally "Indianized" colonists who had chosen native life, this was the kind of argument they summoned. It was simply a law of nature that " all men naturally wish for ease, and to avoid the shackles of restraint."[28]

Those who made a full transition to "savagery" were at least explicable by the prevailing theory. But those who got stuck somewhere between stages, such as frontiersmen, had to run a gauntlet of abuse. Hector de Crèvecoeur described the colonists who chose to live out of the reach of the law and the church as "off-casts," the "impure part" of society, a "mongrel breed," and "the most vicious of our people." "Our bad people are those who are half cultivators and half hunters," he observed, "and the worst of them are those who have degenerated altogether into the hunting state. As old ploughmen and new men of the woods, as Europeans and new made Indians, they contract the vices of both," without, apparently, any of their virtues. Like that of the Indian, the hunter's time was divided between "the toil of the chase, the idleness of repose, or the indulgence of inebriation." Consequently, their characters were cast in the same mold: "ferocious," "gloomy," "unsociable," "profligate," "indolent," "licentious," "erratic," "irreligious," "lawless," and "wild."[29]

Thus, for contemporaries, the "Indianized" colonists played no role in the formation of English colonial culture because their transformation—their degeneration—placed them outside the pale of "civilized" society, outside history itself. Regarded as social deviants who lived on the dark margins of the English frontier or as mental or moral misfits who reverted to "savagery," they were simply not counted as bona fide members of English society, and so their cultural impact could not be weighed. But we are better able to distinguish between climatic mutation and acculturation, to see that English frontiersmen were forced to borrow from their native neighbors and rivals if they wished to master their new environment, and to realize that the Indian impact on colonial culture extended far beyond the frontier into the thoughts, values, and feelings of virtually every Englishman in America. While the colonists who chose to become Indians did remove themselves from English culture, and our focus, their less fully "Indianized" brethren who remained on the English side of the frontier require some attention to establish the exact nature of their cultural adaptations, the reasons for them, and the ways they were used and regarded.

It is significant that all the colonists who were regarded by contemporaries as "white Indians" lived on the wooded frontiers of English settlement, often closer to the villages of their Indian neighbors than to the larger towns and cities of the Atlantic seaboard. With few exceptions, frontier farms encroached upon Indian hunting territories, as did those restless souls who abhorred a plow as much as did any warrior and made their living by the gun. Frontiersmen were primarily woodsmen to whom survival was of greater moment than economic security or prosperity. Limited in their life choices, they chose to live off the uncultivated bounty of the American forests rather than to lose their independence as tenants, servants, or apprentices.

But especially in the early stages of settlement, much of their forest environment was new, strange, and even dangerous—except to the natives who had learned to live with it over centuries. It was therefore as natural as it was necessary for the colonists to borrow some of the Indians' time-tested skills, techniques, and technology for coping with the frontier environment, which included the Indians themselves. Contrary to metropolitan colonial opinion, this cultural exchange did not turn the frontiersmen into Indians, just as

Indians who selectively adopted English habits and articles did not turn into Englishmen. Indian *means* were simply borrowed and adapted to English *ends*. The frontiersmen did not regard themselves as Indians nor did they appreciably alter their basic attitudes toward the native means they employed. If those means were regarded favorably, or at least no longer negatively, it was not because they were Indian but because they *worked* to effect the English conquest of the American environment. Moreover, they were not borrowed in cultural context, as parts of larger, integrated complexes. They were taken piecemeal, while the native values, functions, and structures that surrounded them were ignored. The English goal was mastery of the New World, and to men in a hurry, the end often justifies the means, however alien those means might at first sight seem.

In the beginning the American frontier was on the Atlantic coast and along the banks of the rivers that sliced into the interior. For explorers and settlers newly arrived from England, one of the first orders of business was to familiarize themselves with the new land and its plants, animals, and birds. Some were well known from European experience or from a growing travel literature about other parts of the rapidly expanding world. But many were indigenous only to North America and so had to be named, classified, and related to the known. In such circumstances, it was natural for the English to rely upon the substantial knowledge of the coastal Algonquians for their identification and instruction in their uses.

Equally pressing was the need to communicate with the natives in order to understand their values, motives, and behavior, to be able to predict how they might react in various circumstances to the English presence. On the frontier, where the Indians were equal if not superior in force and numbers, traders needed to understand their economic institutions and motivations, military officers their alliances and modes of warfare, missionaries their religions, political leaders their governments, laws, and protocol, and ordinary farmers and town-founders their systems of land tenure and concepts of property. Again, the likeliest and best teachers were the Indians themselves, provided some means of communication could be found.

Three possibilities existed, all of which were tried at various times. Before sustained contact, explorers and traders managed to converse in hand signs, pidgin trade jargons consisting of word elements from both languages or a third (such as French), and the often burlesque antics of pantomime.[30] These, however, soon proved inadequate for both partners. An alternative, the one most popular with the English, was to have the Indians learn to speak English. Communication in a "civilized" tongue would, it was thought, reduce the potential for misunderstanding and at the same time help to reduce the "savage" mind to "civilized" modes of thought, which was the ultimate solution to the natives' unpredictability. Because of the practical advantages to be gained from a working knowledge of the invaders' tongue, a number of Indians did learn to speak it, only the most famous of whom were Squanto and Samoset. But a third possibility was more popular with the natives, and that was to have the strangers learn to converse in an Algonquian dialect. Despite a good deal of ethnocentric resistance to such a course, the English frontiersmen were often forced to it by demographic and political realities.

The colonists made some effort to encourage professional interpreters to learn the nuances of the major Indian languages, initially (in Virginia) by sending young boys to live with the Indians, later (in New England) by placing apt students in schools with Indian children, who were expected to teach them their native dialects in return for an English education.[31] But most of the frontiersmen who acquired any linguistic skills gained them from living in or near Indian villages and from frequent conversations with native speakers. In this way Edward Winslow, Plymouth's emissary to Massasoit, and Capt. John Smith, Powhatan's nemesis, became capable speakers and Roger Williams, John Eliot, and Thomas Mayhew, missionaries to the New England tribes, gained fluency. Those who followed them and required less than full command of the languages could resort to a number of word lists, phrase books, dictionaries, and grammars, such as Williams's *A Key into the Language of America* (London, 1643).[32]

What Williams systematized and analyzed, other colonists picked up in verbal fragments, sometimes from unsystematic word and phrase lists appended to historical or ethnographic descriptions, such as John Smith's *A Map of Virginia* (Oxford, 1612), which was sent to the colony by the Virginia Company the year following the disastrous Powhatan uprising of 1622.[33] Undoubtedly it was a copy of Smith that John Powell, a young servant in Virginia's Northern Neck, was reading in 1638 "in the field . . . to learne to speake the Indyan tongue" when another servant "desired to buy it of him and would have given him pipes for it," perhaps because he was planning to run off to "the Dutch plantation" to "live like gentlemen" and had to pass through Indian territory to reach it.[34] It was certainly Smith's writings that helped Colonel Norwood win the aid of a Maryland tribe when his party was shipwrecked near the Eastern Shore in 1649. After several frustrating attempts to register their distress and destination to a passing group of natives by signs, Norwood remembered from a distant reading of Smith's travels that the word *werowance*, which one of the Indians kept repeating, meant "king." "That word, spoken by me, with strong emphasis," explained the castaway colonel, "together with the motions of my body, speaking my desire of going to [their chief]," effected the rescue of the group. "This one word was all the Indian I could speak," he admitted, "which (like a little armour well plac'd) contributed to the saving of our lives."

The rescue party, however, also contributed to the peaceful denouement by "discover[ing] their faces with the most chearful smiles, without any kind of arms, or appearance of evil design, . . . shaking hands with every one they met," and repeating *"Ny Top"* (*netop*), which was "soon interpreted to signify my friend."[35]

Both Algonquian words entered the mainstream of Anglo-American speech, as did scores of others. Long after the Indian frontier was pushed beyond the majority of colonial settlements and most settlers had little if any personal contact with the natives, Indian names of places, wildlife, and native artifacts, social relations, and institutions lingered on English tongues to enrich and acculturate the imported language. When the colonists met in the woods the *moose, raccoon, opossum, musquash* (muskrat), *skunk, chipmunk,* and *moonack* (woodchuck), they recognized them by their pure or Anglicized Algonquian names, just as they did numerous species of American fish—*scuppaug, pauhagen,* or *menhaden* (sea herring), *chogset* (blue perch), *cisco* (lake herring), *muskelunge* (pike), and *quasky* (blue-back trout). As they slogged through marshy *muskeg, pocosin* (Virginia), and *pokeloken* (Maine), pestered by *musketoes,* they spotted stands of *tamarack, hickory, chincapin* (chestnut), and *pecan.* Along the seashore they found *mananosay* (Chesapeake soft-shelled clams), *pooquaw* or *quahog* (Long Island Sound hard-shelled clams), and other shellfish used by the Indians to make *wampum* (New England), *sewan* (New York), and *roanoke* (Virginia). Having been initiated by the natives into American foodways, they grew *maize, squantersquash* (New England), *cashaw* and *maycock* (Virginia pumpkin and squash) and learned to extract the tuberous *neshannock* (Pennsylvania white potato) and *tuckahoe* (a southern fungus root). From the corn, parched and ground, they made a variety of Indian dishes such as *hominy, pone, nocake, sagamite,* and *succotash.* In North Carolina they drank a grape beverage called *scuppernong.*

Farther north they smoked *kinnikinnick,* tobacco mixed with sumac and willow leaves, or *sagakomi,* a bear-berry substitute for tobacco, perhaps around Indian fires in *wigwams* with *sanops* (ordinary men), *squaws, papooses, powwows* (shamans), *sachems, werowances, cockarouses* (Virginia elders or chiefs), *sagamores* (northern New England chiefs), and other important *mugwumps* (leaders or great men). Because the Indians were such good hosts, the colonists called their own picnics, outings, and dances after the native *squantums, tuckernucks,* and *canticos.* In Connecticut's Mohegan country, anything so "delightful or pleasant" was remembered as *wauregan.*[36]

Although the colonists used a substantial number of Indian words on and beyond the frontier, they used them in distinctive ways which minimized their normative impact on colonial culture. First, they borrowed Indian words only when English words did not exist, as they did words from Dutch, Spanish, or French. New England's 5000 place-names and the numerous names of wildlife indigenous to North America are typical loans of this kind.[37] But to ears inured to the peculiar accents and cadences of English shires and towns, the Algonquian dialects were simply jarring and confusing. As Edward Eggleston put it with inimitable verbosity in 1900, "the general repulsion to the use of aboriginal words was no doubt increased by the polysyllabic prolixity of the agglutinated vocables that gave stateliness to the intervals of utterance with which a savage broke the monotony of his native taciturnity."[38] Therefore, the words borrowed were often tailored to fit English mouths. Southern New England's *askutasquash* was shortened to its suffix, for example, as was the Virginia dish *rockahominy.* Few colonists were comfortable with *pawscohicora,* so the tree quickly became known as *hickory. Wampumpeak* was unnecessarily long to English thinking; *wampum* gained currency in some parts of the Northeast, *peak* in others. The Jamestown colonists could not pronounce *cawcawwassough* correctly (much less spell it), so they Anglicized it to *cockarouse*.[39]

As is only too apparent from those already given, many Indian words were used only for a season, as long as the objects and concepts to which they referred survived and remained relevant to the colonial experience or until the colonists could supplant them with newly coined English words. Few of us still trip the light fantastic at *canticos,* roast *chincapins* on an open fire, or on February 2 consult the furtive *moonack* about the end of winter. Finally and most important, the colonists looked to the Indians only for individual words, not syntax, grammar, or special patterns of thought and meaning. The loan words were simply incorporated into English modes of ideation and speech, with little or no alteration of the basic contour of English values. Even phrases like "happy hunting ground," "go on the warpath," and "bury the hatchet" were usually poor translations interpreted in pejorative English ways, carrying little cultural freight from their native contexts. As with so many other aspects of native culture, Indian words were tools used to subdue the continent, no more and no less.

From the time the first colonists rowed ashore, they began to borrow items of native material culture, as often by imitation, perhaps, as from verbal instruction. One of their first requirements in the New World was shelter, for "they had now no friends to welcome them nor inns to entertain or refresh their weatherbeaten bodies; no houses or much less towns to repair to, to seek for succour."[40] Some colonists accepted the hospitality of the natives and took temporary refuge in their wigwams, those snug flexed-bough domes covered with bark or reed mats.[41] Others simply built their own wigwams, substituting on occasion a daub-and-wattle chimney at one end for the central smoke-hole of the American houses. The materials were cheap and plentiful, and the design simplicity itself, as many New England adventurers happily discovered.

When Christopher Levett landed upon the Maine coast in 1623 to reconnoiter the Council of New England's domain, he built a "Wigwam, or house, in one houres space." "It had no frame" of sawn timbers, he told his English readers, who would not easily understand, "but was without forme or fashion, only a few poles set up together, and covered with our boates sailes which kept forth but a little winde, and less raigne and snow."[42] Settlers of the nascent Massachusetts Bay towns of Watertown, Boston, Salem, Woburn, and Marblehead seem to have had similar problems because they, too, could not duplicate the natives' watertight construction. Some covered their wigwams with thatch, as they would have at home, which kept off "the short showers from their Lodgings, but the long raines penetrate[d] through, to their great disturbance in the night season."[43] A more serious problem was fire. Wooden chimneys and thatched roofs were a volatile combination, which prompted the Massachusetts authorities to outlaw them in 1631. But the wigwam design itself lived on wherever English immigrants needed time and perhaps money to build more substantial frame houses.[44]

And yet the wigwam had no lasting effect on colonial culture. Not only was its use confined largely to New England, but it was considered only a stopgap measure, primarily by the poor who could not employ others to build permanent housing for them with some expedition or in advance of their arrival. The average settler built a conventional English frame house of clapboard and shingles as fast as possible in an effort to replicate the familiar surroundings of home. Playing Indián in a crude, cramped wigwam held no romance for him, especially with a cold rain dripping down his neck. He was only too thankful that well before 1652 "the Lord hath been pleased to turn all the wigwams, huts, and hovels the English dwelt in at their first coming, into orderly, fair, and well-built houses."[45]

If the Indians did little to put a roof over the colonist's

head, they did a great deal more to fill his belly. Since America was 3000 sea miles from the metropolitan sources of supply, the settlers needed to become economically self-sufficient as soon as possible. This need was all the more pressing when the ships that brought the colonists left them with insufficient supplies to stretch to the first harvest, or sold them at usurious rates. The gap was filled, as every American schoolchild knows, by the coastal Algonquians who readily shared their own food and showed the ignorant newcomers how to grow, catch, and gather the distinctive foods of their new environment.

In 1609 two Powhatan prisoners, Kemps and Tassore, taught the Jamestown colonists "how to order and plant" their first 30 or 40 acres of corn, that "Salvage trash" that many idlers "so scornfully repine[d] at" until Captain Smith billeted them among the neighboring Indians. There, necessity taught them "how to gather and use their fruits as well as themselves," a palatable lesson that soon soured relations with the Powhatans.[46] When the factionalized white militants, still riven by idleness and disease, decided that even Indian food was preferable to starvation, they forced the natives, often at gunpoint, to contribute their precious supplies of corn. It mattered little to them that the tribesmen themselves might starve, have insufficient seed for the next planting, or be unable to render unto Powhatan their customary tribute-in-kind. Abuses such as this prompted the Powhatans to rise up in 1622 in an attempt to expel the invaders, but too late. While still numerically inferior, the acquisitive colonists had become firmly wedded to a profitable economy based on tobacco—another Indian crop—and looked to the outbreak of war with singular relish. As one leader wrote after the attack which killed some 350 colonists, the English,

who hitherto have had possession of no more ground then their waste and our purchase . . . may now by right of

Warre, and law of Nations, invade the Country . . . whereby wee shall enjoy their cultivated places, turning the laborious Mattocke into the victorious Sword (wherein there is more both ease, benefit, and glory) and possessing the fruits of others labours. Now their cleared grounds in all their villages (which are situate in the fruitfullest places of the land) shall be inhabited by us, whereas heretofore the grubbing of woods was the greatest labour.[47]

The first colonists in New England had no need to resort to such tactics because the deadly plague of 1616-18 had swept most of the native planters off their cleared fields around Plymouth and Massachusetts Bay, leaving the land free for the settlers' taking. But, as elsewhere along the Atlantic coast, Indian know-how was needed to bring them to fruition. Landing on Cape Cod in the dead of winter, the urbanized Pilgrims knew enough about farming to recognize that the caches of multi-colored Indian corn they disinterred constituted their best hope for spring planting. So they took it with the intention of repaying the natives when their crops should prosper. Fortunately, twenty acres of Indian corn did prosper because the six acres sown in English barley and pease "came not to good." The Indian who stood between the colonists and starvation was, of course, Squanto, who showed them "both the manner how to set [the Indian corn], and after how to dress and tend it."[48] Equipped only with hoes, the farmers were taught to plant four or five seeds in hills about five or six feet apart rather than to broadcast seed carelessly over a fully plowed field, as they would have done at home. When the stalks of corn began to mature, beans were planted in the same hills. The nitrogen-fixing beans slowed the depletion of the soil while the cornstalks supported the bean tendrils during growth. Still later, Indian squashes and pumpkins were planted between the hills, further maximizing the use of the land.

Another valuable lesson Squanto taught them was to set

two or three herring or alewives in each hill as fertilizer because, he said, the former Indian fields being used at Plymouth were "old." (He might well have added that New
England soils were not rich even in pristine condition.)
Naturally, the Pilgrims assumed that, since an Indian had
showed them this trick, the use of fish fertilizer was an Indian
practice, an assumption that subsequent generations have
also made.[49] In truth, the coastal Algonquians—who were the
only natives near an annual supply of alewives—did not use
fish to fertilize their own fields: they used nothing. The use
of well-spaced hills and the chemistry of bean-and-corn agriculture depleted the soil less rapidly than European practices,
and when it was nearly exhausted, it was easier to clear new
fields by girdling trees and firing the underbrush than it was
to carry numerous loads of fish from distant streams and
shores to merely postpone the inevitable. Besides, fields left
fallow for a time could always be reclaimed with minimal
clearing. Ironically, Squanto did not teach the Pilgrims an
old Indian custom but rather a European technique he had
seen used in England, Newfoundland, or other northern colonies in North America while serving the Newfoundland
Company after his rescue from slavery in Spain.[50]

Succeeding generations of New England farmers were less
concerned about the provenience of fish fertilizer and other
techniques of Indian agriculture than they were about its
labor-saving, economic, and culinary potential. That corn
breads, puddings, and other dishes—most of them prepared
according to native recipes—were nutritious and edible was
quickly discovered. But so too was the fact that traditional
Indian farming required a good deal of back-breaking hoeing.
Since English men had somewhat taller backs to break and
smaller reservoirs of time and patience than the Indian
women who did the farming in Algonquian societies, the
colonists quickly adapted native agriculture to their own familiar uses. Tree girdling and burning to clear the fields were

popular enough with the newcomers as were the use of hills, fish fertilizer, and interstitial planting of squash and such. But to avoid laborious hoeing, the English formed hills by cross-plowing the fields at six-feet intervals and reduced the frequency of weeding by plowing between the original furrows once in mid-summer.[51] Moreover, as soon as necessity allowed, the settlers began to supplant corn with traditional English grains, reserving the American food largely for the "baser sort" among themselves, cattle fodder (stalks and ears), export to the West Indies and other colonies, and trade with northern tribes for more profitable furs. After the first few decades of settlement, most colonial farms devoted no more than half their fields to Indian corn, and even these were increasingly plowed and manured in conventional English fashion.[52]

Corn, beans, and squash were not the only American products to succor the stomachs and pocketbooks of English frontiersmen. Early voyages to the New World were financed by the sale of sassafras in London, while later colonists were enriched by the marketing of ginseng. Maple sugar sweetened many a colonial dish when the expense or unavailability of refined cane sugar required. Potatoes and wild rice were added easily to English diets, as were clams, lobsters, and other exotic foods from the sea. But perhaps the most common additions to the frontier menu were fish and game predominantly taken and prepared by Indian methods. In the absence of lines, seines, and hooks, the colonists imitated the Indians by fishing with sapling weirs, spears, arrows, scoop-nets, and jacklights. (Few Englishmen tried to rope and ride the giant sturgeon to exhaustion as some of the southern Indians did.)[53] When caught, the fish were commonly split and baked on planks, Indian-style, before an open fire or smoked over it.

In the ways of the forest, of course, the Indians were past masters, and any colonist who wished to survive, much less prosper, there apprenticed himself to them with alacrity.

Frontier boys at an early age learned, like their native counterparts, to imitate bird and animal calls, to shoot the bow
and arrow, to stalk, to set snare and dead-fall traps, and to
scent beaver traps with castoreum. With age and experience,
the best frontiersmen became adept at setting life-like decoys,
ferreting out hibernating bears, tracking, skinning, jerking
thinly sliced meat over a slow fire, chasing down molting wild-
fowl with a club, tanning skins with the fat and brains of the
animal, and preserving fresh game by packing it inside and
out with snow.[54] In pursuit of game, the colonists quickly
adopted the springy snowshoe which allowed winter travel at
speeds, one expert thought, greater than those possible on
dry land; the toboggan for transporting supplies out and
game back; and the bark or dugout canoe—light and maneu-
verable on shallow or rapid waters. But occasionally more
than technology was borrowed; Indian values, too, sometimes
played a small role in helping the English adapt to their new
environment. The forest laws of Connecticut's Indians "were
esteemed so just, and their equity appeared in such a glaring
light," noted a minister in 1729, "that our English hunters
have governed themselves by them in their fishery and hunting, and determined controversies by these old customs."[55]

As many English tenderfeet discovered to their great sor-
row, life in the American wilderness could be hazardous to
one's health if proper care was not taken. Again, the Indians
had much to offer the colonists by way of prevention and
cure. Because lying on the damp ground bred colds and rheu-
matism in woodsmen of all races, the English learned to emulate the healthy natives by lying with their feet to the fire
when "abroad in the woods" and even "at home." If a person
failed to hear the rattlesnake's warning and was bitten, the
Indians could usually prevent death by applying a variety of
"snake roots" to the wound. Similarly, they could heal arrow
wounds with herbal or bark poultices. So many frontier teas,
poultices, and decoctions were made to native prescription

that "Indian doctors" did a brisk business in many settlements, loath to anger their gods by revealing to the white
men the ancient secrets imparted to them alone. Most of the
cures were bona fide. At least 170 indigenous drugs listed in
the official *Pharmacopeia of the United States* were discovered and used by the Indians north of Mexico, the great majority in the eastern woodlands.[56] Among them were aborti-
facients and drugs to promote temporary sterility and to ease
childbirth, which may have been of some interest to colonists
unstereotypically concerned not to have large families. In
1769 a Connecticut physician requested a missionary among
the Oneidas to "make Enquiry, what Medicines the Indian
Parturient Women take antecedent to Delivery which occasions so easy a Travail—they have given some of our [English]
Captives Medicines which have had very Extraordinary Effects to Ease their Travail Pains."[57] Given the characteristic
Indian jealousy of their trade secrets, it is unlikely that he
ever received an answer.

Frontier life was as hard on clothes as it was on bodies, so
many Englishmen wisely adopted elements of native garb,
partly of necessity, partly to reduce wear and tear, and partly
to blend less obtrusively into the landscape they shared with
the Indians and the animals they hunted. The first to go were
the bright colors seen in most English clothes, even those of
the much maligned Puritans. Colonial woodsmen quickly
found that for stalking wild game or enemies—or being
stalked—red coats, blue trousers, and yellow waistcoats were
signal failures. Far better were the forest's natural dull shades
of brown and green. Another early change was the substitution of moccasins for hard-heeled cobbled shoes. Indian war
parties headed for white settlements always carried extra pairs
of moccasins for their captives to wear on the long journey
home, a change of footwear the captives usually welcomed, as
did the "white Indians" who remained on the English side of
the frontier. Moccasins were superior in the woods because

they were cheap to make, easy to repair, quickly winterized by stuffing them with deer's hair, dry leaves, or grass, and as silent as the deer from whose skin they were made. Their chief drawback was that, despite natural oils, they were not waterproof. "In wet weather," one frontiersman noted, "it was usually said that wearing them was 'A decent way of going barefooted.' "[58] But they could be wrung out and dried more quickly than heavier leather shoes, as the frontier minister Roger Williams "often proved."[59]

Somewhat less popular than moccasins were *mitasses,* or long, fitted deerskin leggings, and breechclouts, which in most parts of colonial America were not widely worn on the frontiers until the eighteenth-century wars with the French and Indians. In Indian encampments or isolated hunting camps, such dress on an Englishman would not have seemed out of place. But in more "civilized" settlements even in the back-country, it must have raised many a female's consciousness. Like their native counterparts, strapping young colonists in leggings and breechclouts exposed "the upper part of the thighs and part of the hips." "Instead of being abashed by this nudity," lamented a frontier minister, the English warriors were actually "proud" to appear in public in their Indian outfits. When they sauntered into his church services, he quipped, their appearance "did not add much to the [religious] devotion of the young ladies."[60]

The final item of frontier clothing borrowed at least in part from the Indians was the hunting shirt, which gained great symbolic importance for Virginians in the early stages of the Revolution. The shirt was initially made of buckskin in imitation of native prototypes, but the colonists learned as quickly as the Indians had that wet buckskin "sticks to the skin, and is very uncomfortable, requires time to dry, with caution to keep it to its shape."[61] By the eighteenth century at the latest, therefore, linsey-woolsey, coarse linen, or canvas had become the dominant material for the shirt, which was simply "a kind of loose frock, reaching half way down the thighs, with large sleeves, open before, and so wide as to lap over a foot or more when belted." Often attached was a large cape or hood, "sometimes handsomely fringed with a ravelled piece of cloth of a different colour," and invariably the belt held a tomahawk on the right and on the left a scalping knife in a leather sheath.[62] Clad in moccasins, leggings, and hunting shirt, the English warrior was virtually indistinguishable from his American archetype. Which was precisely the symbolic identification the rifle companies from Virginia's backcounties wanted to make when they turned out in such dress in the spring of 1775 to oppose the king's redcoats.[63] Throughout the colonial period, whenever the colonists asserted their social or cultural distinction from the mother country, they commonly identified themselves as "Indians" to suggest their lack of sophistication and untutored virtue.[64] When the perpetrators of the Boston Tea Party donned "Mohawk" disguises and the Virginia "shirtmen" arrayed themselves *au sauvage,* however, more than literary metaphor was intended. These native Americans also sought to announce their fierce determination to defend their natural rights to a king whose memory of the obduracy of "savage" warfare needed only a slight jogging.

The "Indianized" Virginians and other colonial militiamen who emerged during the Revolution were not novelties in colonial America, for English warfare had been forced to acculturate from the earliest encounters with the Indians in the seventeenth century. Until the Seven Years' War, when France finally realized that the English meant not merely to contain French expansion but to obliterate totally the French presence in North America, warfare in America consisted largely of frontier skirmishes, raids, and ambushes conducted on Indian principles. With the exception of a few European naval attacks upon coastal towns, the military assaults thrown at the English colonies invariably came from the Indian side of the frontier, spearheaded largely by Indian warriors even when led or accompanied by Frenchmen. As the English pushed the Indian frontiers steadily back in the older colonies and created them in new colonies, the natives seldom had long to wait for sufficient provocation to seek revenge. In having to respond frequently to Indian attack, the English colonists readily adopted several aspects of native warfare that they hoped would help them beat the enemy at his own deadly game.

Some of the most permanent adoptions were technological, especially in the northeastern colonies where sustained encounters with the Indians occurred during King Philip's War in 1675-76 and the four intercolonial wars after 1689. Since Indian warfare consisted primarily of cat-and-mouse raids of stealth and surprise, the only way the English could effectively retaliate was to learn to play the cat: to overtake the raiders in the woods, to lay their own ambushes on likely warpaths leading to the English settlements, or to catch Indian villages unawares with their own "commandoes." The one indispensable piece of equipment for these tasks was the moccasin. English scouts would not think of setting off without several pairs, nor would rangers and light infantry trained in the eighteenth century by one of the American-experienced British officers, such as Lord George Howe, John Forbes, or Henry Bouquet. Without "Indian shoes," the officers warned the colonial legislatures, "they can't perform their duty."[65] Moccasins were also the accepted footwear for Indian-style snowshoes, which enabled the militia of the northern colonies to forestall enemy raids and to carry fire into the heart of enemy territory in the winter, which before contact the conventions of both Indian and continental warfare had accounted a time of informal truce. Thanks largely to snowshoes, a season "which before was dreaded as most hazardous" frequently became the time of "greatest safety," even along the exposed frontiers of New England.[66]

Whatever good fortune the colonists enjoyed—and it seldom lasted long—was due also to a number of other adaptations to the necessities of Indian warfare. In the American forests, war conducted with long or even half pikes, heavy matchlocks with rests, carriage cannon, brightly colored uniforms, ponderous supply trains, and female camp followers was quickly reduced to "a meer Farce" by the French and Indians who, "being lightly cloathed and armed," lamented one colonial reformer, "are sometimes in our Front, sometimes in our Rear, and often on all Sides of us, Hussar Fashion, taking the Advantage of every Tree and Bush."[67] Although regular British troops did not adapt their equipment or tactics to the Indian enemy appreciably until the Seven Years' War, their officers were prepared to do so by considerable experience with guerrilla warfare in Austria, Flanders, and the Scottish Highlands during the 1740s and 1750s.[68] Many colonial militia, especially rangers on frontier patrol, responded with greater alacrity to the need for light, camouflaged clothing (including deerskin breeches and hunting shirts or light jackets), short muskets with browned barrels to prevent telltale glints in the sun, small packs to carry personal blankets and field provisions (sometimes Indian *nocake* or parched corn meal), tomahawks, and scalping knives—a reduction of perhaps 25 to 35 pounds from the standard issue of the British soldier.[69]

Because European military discipline was considered by many "of little use" in the American woods, colonial soldiers altered their tactics as well as their uniforms.[70] When the English fought their first battles with the Indians, they beat up the drum, flew the colors, and marched in massed ranks into the nearest open field to engage the enemy—who, of course, thought the whole display sheer madness and remained concealed in the woods. Prolonged exposure to this frustratingly "uncivilized" enemy and frequent lessons from native allies in King Philip's and subsequent wars forced numbers of colonial commanders to the realization that "in this country," as General John Forbes admitted in 1758, "wee must comply and learn the Art of Warr, from Ennemy Indians or anything else who have seen the Country and Warr carried on in itt."[71] After Braddock's defeat in 1755, even regular army officers had to concede that massed fire was ineffective against scattered, concealed targets unless it was combined with disciplined movement: bayonet charges, flanking actions, and tactical retreats. Large deployments of regular troops eventually carried the day in North America, but not until the troops learned to reach their destination without serious damage.[72] In Indian country, travel was extremely hazardous, so the colonists took a page from the native manual of war and marched out in thin "Indian file," separated by several paces and covered on all sides by scouts, flankers, and perhaps dogs. Superfluous noise and smoking were prohibited. To avoid ambush, return was never made on the same trail, and river banks were well secured before crossing. When attacked, the commander cried "Tree all!" and the men scattered for cover, from which they would not all fire at once to avoid an assault during reloading. Finally, maneuvers appropriate to American conditions would be executed to draw the covert enemy into error or a more open engagement, where disciplined English fire could take its toll.[73]

In war as in peace, English frontiersmen "Indianized" themselves only as much as was necessary to give them the upper hand in their struggle with America and its native peoples. Their goal was not to become Indian, nor did their selective and piecemeal adaptations of native techniques and technology make them so. While it may be true in a physiological sense that "you are what you eat," in no sense could it be said that the colonists' consumption of Indian corn rendered them cultural Indians. While superficially "clothes makes the man," the adoption of Indian moccasins and forest garb did not necessarily turn the English frontiersmen into

Indians, any more than a modern Boy Scout Indian dance team qualifies for an arts grant from the Bureau of Indian Affairs. And while the brutal imperatives of Indian warfare often forced English soldiers to fight guerrilla-style, they did not become Indian in their goals or values.

To have become truly Indian, the colonists would have had to think like Indians, to value the same things that the Indians valued, and, most important, to identify themselves as Indians and their future with native society. A significant number of Englishmen did make this complete transition from one culture to another; these were the "white Indians" who melted into historical anonymity behind the Indian frontier. But those colonists who remained on the frontiers of English society chose to remain Englishmen and to pursue English goals by largely English means. Their adaptation of selected facets of native material culture did little or nothing to alter their self-identities as "civilized" Englishmen nor their goal of mastering the American environment and its denizens, no matter how fallen from cultural grace their colonial superiors found them. If there were any doubts about their ultimate allegiance to the English way of life, their sacrifice of lives and martial vengeance whenever the Indians made war on the frontier settlements should have proven them groundless. If the intensity of their commitment to king, church, and cashbox was less than that of their seaboard brethren, they still regarded themselves as white Christian Englishmen, an identity that distinguished them sharply from their Indian friends and enemies.

While the colonists borrowed consciously and directly from Indian culture only on the frontier, English colonial culture as a whole received a substantial but indirect impress from the Indians by being forced to confront the novel "otherness" of native culture and to cope with its unpredictability, pride, and retaliatory violence. Having the Indians as sometime adversaries and full-time contraries helped not only to reinforce the continuity of vital English traits and institutions but to Americanize all levels of colonial society more fully than the material adaptations of the frontiersmen. These *reactive changes* were, in large measure, responsible for transforming colonial Englishmen into native Americans in feeling, allegiance, and identity, a change without which, John Adams reminded us, the American Revolution would have been impossible.[74] While the growing political opposition to the British ministry during the 1760s and 1770s eventually led the colonies to coordinated armed resistance and a united declaration of independence, the whole colonial experience of trying to solve a related series of "Indian problems" had much to do with giving the colonists an identity indissolubly linked to America and their apprenticeship in political and military cooperation.

One of the earliest changes induced by the realities of Anglo-Indian relations was the reordering of colonial priorities. According to the early English promotional literature and the royal charters of the majority of colonies, the primary goal in settling the New World was the conversion of the natives to Christian "civility," followed by the enhancement of overseas trade with the natives and the extension of the English empire at the expense of her European rivals.[75] However, the early English encounters with the Indians of Roanoke, Virginia, Connecticut, Cape Cod, and Maine made it obvious that the order of these goals was the product of armchair explorers and missionaries who had never met the Indians on their own ground. Not only were the natives far from eager to receive the blessings of Christ, as some wishful thinkers had promised they would be, but they maintained a tenacious sense of superiority to English cultural values, even as they admired and adapted some of their material culture. Moreover, in asserting this unexpected superiority, the natives often resisted the intruders with armed force, rendering

the exposed English beachheads and settlements highly unsafe in wartime and potentially unsafe at all times.

Due largely to these depressing and often deadly develop-
ments, the operative English goals rather quickly shifted to
give paramount importance to the pacification of the natives,
sometimes by Bible and blanket, more often by statute and
sword. More than any other factor, this change forced to the
forefront the major thrust behind English colonization in
North America—the establishment of an Anglo-Protestant empire as a bulwark against the imperial designs of Catholic
Spain and France. Conversion remained an important goal,
but it was reduced to instrumental status in the hierarchy of
colonial objectives. Reducing the "savages" to "civility" con-
sumed more time and therefore assumed more importance
than simply converting them to Christianity. As the Catholi-
cized Indians of Canada demonstrated after 1689, mere conversion was no guarantee of English safety, for it did little to
dampen the natives' ardor for war or to sublimate their ferocious conduct of it. Only a complete change of cultural identity, it was thought, could ensure that an Indian convert
would never slip from praying to preying. As events proved,
the English were not wrong in their thinking, but the reluctance of most Indians to commit cultural suicide elevated
even higher the imperatives of empire while lowering those
of religion.

Although conversion of the natives suffered some demotion
in the operative scheme of colonial values, the idealism of the
original goal retained its power in New England and helped
to evangelize its "tribal" Protestant churches.[76] Even before
the English settlements began to spread beyond the lands de-
populated by the plague of 1616-18, the need to acquire more
land and to forestall any native opposition to its acquisition
called for the establishment of praying towns among the
neighboring Indians. If the Indians could be persuaded to
exchange the life of the hunter and warrior for that of the

farmer, they would require much less land for their livelihood, and their military prowess would be greatly weakened.
At the same time, the churches of Massachusetts were being
reminded of the religious goal of their colonial charter by
Anglican and Parliamentary critics at home and by the noisy
success of the Canadian Jesuits who were teaching their neophytes to bear crosses against the Devil but would soon teach
them to bear arms against heretics. Thus goaded into action
(as well as by tensions inherent in Puritan theology), New
England Congregationalism slowly discarded its defensive, genealogical shell and began to evangelize the black, white, and
particularly tawny peoples of the region who were not fortunate enough to have been born to "elect" parents.[77] The missionary thrust of John Eliot and the Mayhews, the New England Company, the Commissioners of the United Colonies,
and later the Mathers, Judge Samuel Sewall, and many others
forcibly reminded the English that God was no longer the exclusive deity of a small white clan but in his majesty and
grace was capable and desirous of serving many tribes. To accommodate this renewed vision of the evangelical church, the
Protestant churches of New England and the Middle Atlantic
colonies created in the early decades of the eighteenth century
an ecclesiastical niche for roving missionaries who did not
have to be called by a congregation to exercise their sacra-
mental office. This change, in turn, gave a healthy push to
the aggressive denominationalism that altered the religious
landscape of eighteenth-century America. The denominational competition for white souls after 1740 coincided with
and in some instances followed a similar competition for key
Indian missions.[78]

Despite the efforts of many zealous individuals and charitable societies, the great majority of eastern woodland Indians
were "reduced" not to civility by religion but in numbers
and morale by disease, alcohol, warfare, unfair trading practices, loss of land, and prejudice. As countless Englishmen ac-

knowledged throughout the colonial period, the sad fact was that English missionary efforts were sporadic, often half-hearted, and powerless to counteract the negative example of nominal christians who failed to practice what they preached. "They met with Enemies when we came amongst them," lamented a North Carolinian in 1709, "for they are no nearer Christianity now, than they were at the first Discovery, to all Appearance."[79] "We that should have learn'd them to *Pray*, have learn'd them to *Sin*," admitted a New England minister, while a Pennsylvania missionary of long experience was confident that "our vices have destroyed them more than our swords."[80] Honest laments such as these exacerbated the feelings of declension and failure that gnawed at the souls of second- and third-generation Christians and cast the self-proclaimed righteousness of the English colonists in doubt as they strove to claim God's special grace in their successive battles with the Indians, the French, and the king. Judged by the purity of their earliest religious goal, the English record in Indian relations made it impossible for men of conscience to deny that either the colonies were basely born or they grew up in bastardly fashion.

The stubborn persistence of Indian culture also provided a deeply disturbing counterpoint to the English missionary efforts and was therefore instrumental in shaping colonial culture in two additional ways. First, the generalized European fear of barbarism that worried colonial planners and leaders was given specific shape and meaning by the Indian embodiment of the "heathenism" that seemed so contagious to English frontiersmen and by the greater danger of Englishmen converting to an Indian way of life in captivity or, worse still, voluntarily as "apostates" and "renegades." When Cotton Mather warned New England that in "Ungospellized Plantations" on the frontier "Satan *terribly* makes a *prey* of you, and *Leads you Captive to do his Will*," his audience knew that Satan wore moccasins, breechclout, and warpaint.[81]

Second, and more generally, the Indians contributed crucially to the English definition of themselves in America by symbolizing the "savage" baseness that would dominate human nature if man did not—paradoxically—"reduce" it to "civility" through government, religion, and the capitalistic work ethic. "The Indian became important for the English mind, not for what he was in and of himself," Roy Harvey Pearce reminded us long ago, "but rather for what he showed civilized men they were not and must not be."[82] Because the early settlers were "especially inclined to discover attributes in savages which they found first but could not speak of in themselves," they defined themselves "less by the vitality of their affirmations than by the violence of their abjurations."[83] Even the faithful descriptions of native culture by keen observers such as Roger Williams and Daniel Gookin were prefaced by self-reflexive editorials. Wrote Gookin of the New England Algonquians in 1674, "Here we may see, as in a mirror, or looking glass, the woful, miserable, and deplorable estate, that sin hath reduced mankind unto naturally, and especially such as live without means of cultivating and civilizing, as these poor, brutish barbarians have done for many ages."[84] While all peoples to some extent define themselves by contrast with other peoples, the English colonists forged their particular American identity more on an Indian anvil than upon other European colonists or Africans. If that identity was ambivalent and paradoxical, the colonists' persistent (though declining) faith in the salvation of savages and the obdurate character of Indian culture were in no small part responsible.[85]

For the whole spectrum of colonial society, urban and rural, the Indians as ungrateful objects of religious charity and as cultural contraries were not as frustrating, alarming, or influential as the Indian enemy. As masters of an unconventional warfare of terror, they seared the collective memories, imaginations, and even subconscious of the colonists, leaving a

deep but blurred intaglio of fear and envy, hatred and respect. Having the American natives as frequent and deadly
adversaries—and even as allies—did more not to "Indianize"
but to "Americanize" the English colonists than any other
human factor and had two contradictory results. When native
warfare frustrated and humbled the English military ma-
chine, its successes cast into serious doubt the colonists'
vaunted sense of superiority as God's chosen people, especially when the only recourse seemed to be the hiring of
equally "savage" mercenaries.[86] At the same time, victorious
Indians seemed so insufferably insolent—a projection of the
Christians' original sin—that the colonists redoubled their efforts to claim divine grace and achieve spiritual and social regeneration through violence.[87] One of the pathetic ironies of
early America is that in attempting to exterminate the wound-
ing pride of their Indian enemies, the colonists inflated their
own pride to sinful proportions.

The Indians' brand of unannounced, "skulking," bush-
whacking warfare, involving the "indiscriminate slaughter of
all ranks, ages and sexes," atrocious mutilation, and captivity
for torture or permanent adoption, gave rise to several colonial reactions.[88] The first reaction to the offensive war of the
Indians (which was in reality retaliation for previous wrongs,
real or perceived) was a well-founded increase in fear and
paranoia. Since the Indians might attack at any time of day
and in any season, "one is never sure either that they are
there or that they are not[,] hence we have to beware of them
all the time."[89] Few colonial frontiersmen and farmers did
not know personally a victim of a silent arrow, a concealed
musket, or the scalping knife, knowledge that could not help
but raise a morbid curiosity about one's own or loved ones'
chances for survival. And the fear cut deep. When the Reverend Ebenezer Parkman of Westborough, Massachusetts, left
an Indian couple to hoe his cornfields in 1726, his wife, who
was recovering from childbirth complications, became "very

much affrighted with the Indians, and full of fear of what they might do." Though the Indians could not have shown greater peace and good temper, explained the minister, "the Weakness of her Body brought strange apprehensions in the mind."[90] Similar apprehensions overwhelmed young Mercy Short in 1692 when she was assaulted by a devil "not of a Negro, but of a Tawney, or an Indian colour." Her "Captivity to Spectres" closely resembled the actual captivity she had suffered two years earlier because her tormentor was always accompanied by "some French canadians, and some Indian Sagamores," a party that a Salem witch confessed had accompanied her to sabbats "to concert the methods of ruining New England."[91] Even from the comparative safety of Princeton, New Jersey, in 1755 a young mother told a friend in Boston, "You cant conceive . . . what a tender Mother under goes for her children at such a day as this, to think of bring[ing] up Children to be *dashed against the Stones by our barbarous enemies*—or which is worse, to be inslaved by them, & obliged to turn *Papist*."[92] When the Indians were on the warpath—and even when they were not—they were never far from the colonists' thoughts.

The second reaction to the Indian offensive was the development of a defensive "fortress mentality," which in turn reinforced the colonists' sense of being a chosen if momentarily abandoned people. As the Israelites had suffered oppression and attack in another wilderness, the English felt themselves beseiged by Satan's minions in the form of pagan Indians and papistical Frenchmen. A common response to this predicament, made largely though by no means exclusively by the New English, was to search their communal soul for private and public sins that might have driven God to withdraw his special protection and to allow the forces of anti-Christ to scourge them. "O our *Sins,* our *Sins,*" cried the daughter of Jonathan Edwards at the news of Braddock's defeat, "they are grown to the very heavens, & call aloud for Vengence, the

Vengence that the Lord has sent."[93] Significantly, the Lord's whip in the English jeremiads most frequently assumed the form of an Indian attack, not the aggression of other Europeans, slave rebellion, pestilence, or drought. The prescribed remedy for spiritual backsliding was to eschew anything that smacked of Indianization—"*Criolian* Degeneracy" as Cotton Mather called it—and to drive the Devil out of the land, even if the land happened to be his in the first place. By killing satanic Indians, the colonists sought to regain God's favor and to fulfill his providential promise in America. Although they did not feel that they had fully done so until the reduction of Canada in 1760 removed both enemies at once, the nature of the military effort expended in that holy quest further distinguished colonial culture from that of its English progenitor.

Most of the American colonists had never seen battle in Europe, but even professional soldiers were sickened by the atrocities committed by the Indians on their victims, alive and dead, young and old, male and female. European warriors were as resourceful as the Indians in killing their enemies, but most could not match—or understand—the natives' postmortem desecration of the human body. Even an enemy in embryo was considered potentially dangerous and "torn from [the murdered mother's] pregnant womb and elevated on a stick or pole, as a trophy of victory and an object of hor[r]or, to the survivors of the slain."[94] Of the niceties of torture most Englishmen were also ignorant until they watched the Indians at work or discovered the charred remains of one of their victims.

Being thus forced to confront such a heinous enemy, the colonists were frequently torn from their "civilized" moorings and swept into the kind of "savage" conduct they deplored in their enemies, motivated conspicuously by cold-blooded vengeance. In their mounting fury, especially in the eighteenth century, they fell to the slaughter and torture (except by fire) of Indian prisoners, even women and children, encouraged in part by government bounties that paid only a fraction more for living prisoners than for their scalps.[95] During King Philip's War, the colonial militia looked largely to surrogates to sate their appetite for revenge. A wounded Indian prisoner narrowly escaped torture only to be "knock'd on the Head" by native allies before an assembly of English troops and their general. In another theater of the war, a female prisoner was ordered "to be torn in pieces by dogs." Two years later, in the fishing village of Marblehead, a group of women emerging from church set upon two Indian prisoners from Maine and with their bare hands literally tore them apart. An eyewitness reported that "we found [the Indians] with their heads off and gone, and their flesh in a manner pulled from their bones."[96]

But with the expansion and prolongation of Indian warfare during the four wars for empire, the soldiers themselves set to work with savage determination, often inspired by the invocations of their ministers. "Our holy Religion teaches us to bear *personal* Injuries without *private* Revenge," Samuel Davies lectured a Virginia company in 1755, "But *national* Insults, and Indignities ought to excite the *public* Resentment."[97] At the beginning of the first "French and Indian" war, Cotton Mather had been less ambiguous. The Indians of Maine, he reminded an audience of soldiers, "have horribly Murdered some scores of your dear Country-men, whose Blood cries in your Ears, while you are going to fight, *Vengeance, Dear Country-men! Vengeance upon our Murderers.*"[98] But many colonists, particularly the swelling ranks of those who had lost friends and relatives in Indian raids, needed no sermons to act, even in peacetime. Throughout the eighteenth century, some of their worst atrocities upon Indian victims departed sufficiently from acceptable conduct to be noticed by the colonial establishment, but most of them were unobjectionable according to the standards of the day. A visitor from England might record in his diary in 1760 that

"Some People have an Indian's Skin for a Tobacco Pouch," but an officer in Sullivan's campaign against the Iroquois in 1779 could note matter-of-factly that he was given a pair of boot tops made from the freshly skinned legs of two enemies.[99]

Although the colonists were never able to realize their ambitions, they did from time to time desire to commit the worst atrocity of all—genocide. This urge was the product not only of the frustrating encounter with Indian warfare but of the extreme ethnocentrism and racism of a people laboring under the illusion that they were chosen by God to wash America "white in the blood of the Lamb." Perhaps the first secular expression of genocidal intent was recorded in Virginia after the Powhatan uprising of 1622, but predictably New England gave the expression a Scriptural twist. In 1640 the governments of New Haven and Connecticut "declared their dislike of such as would have the Indians rooted out, as being of the cursed race of Ham," indicating that those who had called for—and nearly gotten—the total extirpation of the Pequots three years earlier were still not satisfied.[100] As the soldier-poet Roger Wolcott saw it from the security of the eighteenth century, the Mystic Fort fight with the Pequots was Armageddon, different even from the capture of French Louisbourg in 1745 at which he was second in command:[101]

> Fate has determined that this very day
> Shall try the title of America:
> . . .
> If this day's work by us be once well done,
> America is for the English won:
> But if we faint or fail in this design,
> The numerous nations will as one combine
> . . .
> and with violence
> Destroy the English and their settlements.

Although the sentiment if not the phrase "The only good Indian is a dead one" flourished longest on the colonial frontiers, seaboard adherents to its philosophy were not in short supply. In 1711, for example, the Virginia House of Burgesses cast aside the governor's inexpensive proposal to calm the Indian frontier by a regulated trade and educational missions and voted with a "violent disposition" a £20,000 war bill "for exterpating all Indians without distinction of Friends or Enemys."[102] When General Jeffrey Amherst allowed smallpox blankets to be sent among his native adversaries during Pontiac's uprising, the British high command had become infected with the deadliest strain of colonial hatred which had been gestating for over a century and a half.[103]

For all their best—and worst—efforts, the English colonists could not make the Indians disappear either by converting them or by burying them. The costs, both moral and financial, were simply too great. But in trying to overcome the stubborn resistance of the Indians, the political and social history of the colonies was altered in significant ways. Since the Indians would not hold still for conventional English warfare, the cost of fighting them was very high. Untrained militiamen were simply not equal to the task, so frontier defenses of rangers and cavalry patrolling between chains of forts had to be mounted.[104] These new expenses were borne largely by the colonial legislatures, which in general gained parity with, if not superiority to, the royal governors during the eighteenth century. The legislatures themselves were frequently riven by the factionalism of seaboard representatives who did not accede to frontier demands for more protection, economic relief, and equal representation. The Quakers lost their political grip on Pennsylvania, for instance, primarily because their pacifism and legislative economies failed to protect the westerners from the Indian raids of the Seven Years' War.

It soon became obvious that the colonies could not cope with their Indian problems alone. Powhatan's uprising gave the Virginia Company the *coup de grâce* and King Charles I tucked the colony under his wing. Later in the century Massachusetts's inability to defend her northern borders from French and Indian incursions led to her and New Hampshire's incorporation in the imperial system as royal colonies. In the final showdown with the French in the Seven Years' War, of course, the colonies were heavily dependent on British troops whose support contributed to a soaring national debt at home. When English taxpayers refused to underwrite American defense costs alone after the war and Parliament tried to assess the colonial beneficiaries, these levies and the manner in which they were obtained formed the backbone of the colonial grievances against the mother country that led to open rebellion in 1776.

It is both fitting and ironic that the symbol chosen by Revolutionary cartoonists to represent the American colonies was the Indian, whose love of liberty and fierce independence had done so much to Americanize the shape and content of English colonial culture.[105] It is fitting because the Indians by their long and determined opposition helped to meld thirteen disparate colonies into one (albeit fragile) nation, different from England largely by virtue of having shared that common history of conflict on and over Indian soil. It is ironic because after nearly two centuries of trying to take the Indians' lives and lands, the colonists appropriated not only the native identity but the very characteristics that thwarted the colonists' ultimate arrogations.

Notes

CHAPTER ONE

1. Robert C. Euler, "Ethnohistory in the United States," *Ethnohistory,* 19 (1972), 202; Harold Hickerson, *The Chippewa and Their Neighbors: A Study in Ethnohistory* (New York, 1970), 7.
2. Richard M. Dorson, "Ethnohistory and Ethnic Folklore"; Wilcomb E. Washburn, "Ethnohistory: History 'In the Round'"; David A. Baerreis, "The Ethnohistoric Approach and Archaeology"; and Nancy Oestreich Lurie, "Ethnohistory: An Ethnological Point of View" appeared in *Ethnohistory,* 8 (1961), 12-92, as did the comments of Eleanor Leacock, John C. Ewers, and Charles A. Valentine (pp. 256-80).
3. William N. Fenton, "The Training of Historical Ethnologists in America," *American Anthropologist,* n.s. 54 (1952), 328-39; Fenton, "Ethnohistory and Its Problems," *Ethnohistory,* 9 (1962), 1-23; Fenton, "Field Work, Museum Studies, and Ethnohistorical Research," *ibid.,* 13 (1966), 71-85; Charles Hudson, "Folk History and Ethnohistory," *ibid.,* 52-70; William C. Sturtevant, "Anthropology, History, and Ethnohistory," *ibid.,* 1-51; Bernard S. Cohn, "Ethnohistory," in David L. Sills, ed., *International Encyclopedia of the Social Sciences,* 17 vols. (New York, 1968), 6:440-48; Bernard L. Fontana, "American Indian Oral History: An Anthropologist's Note," *History and Theory,* 8 (1969), 366-70; Deward E. Walker, Jr., "Ethnology and History," *Idaho Yesterdays,* 14 (Spring 1970), 24-29; Robert M. Carmack, "Ethnohistory: A Review of Its Development,

Definition, Methods, and Aims," *Annual Review of Anthropology*, 1 (1972), 227-46; Gordon M. Day, "Oral Tradition as Complement," *Ethnohistory*, 19 (1972), 99-108; Euler, "Ethnohistory in the United States," 201-7; Raymond D. Fogelson, "On the Varieties of Indian History: Sequoyah and Traveller Bird," *Journal of Ethnic Studies*, 2 (1974), 105-12. See also Michael D. Olien, *Ethnohistory: A Bibliography* (Athens: University of Georgia, Department of Anthropology, March 1969).

4. A. L. Kroeber and Clyde Kluckhohn, *Culture: A Critical Review of Concepts and Definitions*, Papers of the Peabody Museum of American Archaeology and Ethnology, 47 (Cambridge, Mass., 1952); David Bidney, *Theoretical Anthropology* (New York, 1953), chs. 2-5, 9, 14; Clyde Kluckhohn, "Parts and Wholes in Cultural Analysis," in Daniel Lerner, ed., *Parts and Wholes* (New York, 1963), 111-33; Milton Singer, "The Concept of Culture," in Sills, ed., *International Encyclopedia of the Social Sciences*, 3:527-43; Robert F. Berkhofer, Jr., *A Behavioral Approach to Historical Analysis* (New York, 1969), chs. 5-7; Clifford Geertz, *The Interpretation of Cultures* (New York, 1973), ch. 1; Louis Schneider and Charles M. Bonjean, eds., *The Idea of Culture in the Social Sciences* (Cambridge, 1973); Roger M. Keesing, "Theories of Culture," *Annual Review of Anthropology*, 3 (1974), 73-97; David M. Schneider, "Notes Toward a Theory of Culture," in Keith H. Basso and Henry A. Selby, eds., *Meaning in Anthropology* (Albuquerque, 1976), 197-220.

5. See, for example, William Christie Macleod, *The American Indian Frontier* (New York, 1928); Allen W. Trelease, *Indian Affairs in Colonial New York: The Seventeenth Century* (Ithaca, 1960); Barbara Graymont, *The Iroquois in the American Revolution* (Syracuse, 1972); Gary B. Nash, *Red, White, and Black: The Peoples of Early America* (Englewood Cliffs, N.J., 1974); Edmund S. Morgan, *American Slavery–American Freedom: The Ordeal of Colonial Virginia* (New York, 1975); and Francis Jennings, *The Invasion of America: Indians, Colonialism, and the Cant of Conquest* (Chapel Hill, 1975). I have reviewed these books (except the first) in "The Ethnohistory of Early America: A Review Essay," *William and Mary Quarterly*, 3d ser. 35 (1978), 110-44. See also Jack D. Forbes, "Frontiers in American History and the Role of Frontier Historians," *Ethnohistory*, 15 (1968), 203-35.

6. Bernard W. Sheehan, "Indian-White Relations in Early America," *WMQ*, 3d ser. 26 (1969), 269, 272, 283-85.

7. Julian H. Steward, "The Direct Historical Approach to Archaeol-

ogy, *American Antiquity*, 7 (1942), 337-43; William Duncan Strong, "Historical Approach in Anthropology," in A. L. Kroeber, ed., *Anthropology Today: An Encyclopedic Inventory* (Chicago, 1953), 386-97; J. V. Wright, "The Application of the Direct Historical Approach to the Iroquois and the Ojibwa," *Ethnohistory*, 15 (1968), 96-111. I am grateful to Nancy Lurie for a long letter describing some of the heuristic uses of the "ethnographic present."

8. Hickerson, *Chippewa and Their Neighbors*, 7; Ernest Gellner, "Time and Theory in Social Anthropology," *Mind*, 67 (1958), 182-202; E. E. Evans-Pritchard, *Anthropology and History* (Manchester, Eng., 1961), 1-2, 10-11; Margaret T. Hodgen, *Anthropology, History, and Cultural Change*, Viking Fund Publications in Anthropology, 52 (Tucson, 1974); Robert A. Nisbet, *Social Change and History: Aspects of the Western Theory of Development* (New York, 1969); Nancy O. Lurie, "Culture Change," in James A. Clifton, ed., *Introduction to Cultural Anthropology: Essays in the Scope and Methods of the Science of Man* (Boston, 1968), 275-303.

9. Fenton, "Training of Historical Ethnologists," 335-36. See also Fenton, "Cultural Stability and Cultural Change in American Indian Societies," *Journal of the Royal Anthropological Institute*, 80 (1953), 169-74; Nisbet, *Social Change and History*, chs. 7-8; and Verne F. Ray, ed., *Cultural Stability and Cultural Change: Proceedings of the 1957 Spring Meeting of the American Ethnological Society* (Seattle, 1957).

10. Fenton, "Field Work," 75.

11. Lurie, "Ethnohistory: An Ethnological Point of View," 83. See also Sturtevant, "Anthropology, History, and Ethnohistory," 13-17; Euler, "Ethnohistory in the United States," 202; Cohn, "Ethnohistory," in Sills, ed., *International Encyclopedia of the Social Sciences*, 6:443-44.

12. Leacock's comment, *Ethnohistory*, 8 (1961), 258-59.

13. Fenton, "Ethnohistory and Its Problems," 11.

14. William N. Fenton, *American Indian and White Relations to 1830: Needs and Opportunities for Study* (Chapel Hill, 1957), 21-22, and "Field Work," 75.

15. Evans-Pritchard, *Anthropology and History*, 5. See also Sturtevant, "Anthropology, History, and Ethnohistory," 18.

16. Sturtevant, comment on two papers on new approaches in Indian history, Organization of American Historians, St. Louis, Apr. 9, 1976.

17. Anthony F. C. Wallace, *The Death and Rebirth of the Seneca* (New

York, 1970); Bruce G. Trigger, *The Children of Aataentsic: A History of the Huron People to 1660,* 2 vols. (Montreal and London, 1976); and James A. Clifton, *The Prairie People: Continuity and Change in Potawatomi Indian Culture 1665-1965* (Lawrence, Kan., 1977).

18. Peter Gay, *Style in History* (New York, 1974), 212.

19. Wilcomb E. Washburn, "A Moral History of Indian-White Relations: Needs and Opportunities for Study," *Ethnohistory,* 4 (1957), 47-61; Washburn, "Relations Between Europeans and Amerindians During the Seventeenth and Eighteenth Centuries: The Epistemological Problem," paper delivered at the International Colloquium on Colonial History, University of Ottawa, Nov. 1969; John Higham, "Beyond Consensus: The Historian as Moral Critic," *American Historical Review,* 67 (1962), 609-25; Roy Harvey Pearce, "From the History of Ideas to Ethnohistory," *Journal of Ethnic Studies,* 2 (1974), 86-92; Gordon Wright, "History as a Moral Science," *AHR,* 81 (1976), 1-11.

20. Jennings, *Invasion of America,* ix-x.

21. Lord Acton, *Essays on Freedom and Power,* ed. Gertrude Himmelfarb (Boston, 1948), 52, quoting Burke.

22. Higham, "Beyond Consensus," 625.

23. Robert Redfield, *The Primitive World and Its Transformations* (Ithaca, 1953), 159; Washburn, "Ethnohistory: History 'In the Round,' " 36.

24. Bruce G. Trigger, "Brecht and Ethnohistory," *Ethnohistory,* 22 (1975), 55.

25. H. Stuart Hughes, *History as Art and as Science: Twin Vistas on the Past* (New York, 1964), 22-41; Fenton, "Training of Historical Ethnologists," 328-39.

CHAPTER TWO

1. "Cornplanter's talk," Draper Collection, 16 F 277, State Historical Society of Wisconsin, Madison. We are grateful to Anthony F. C. Wallace for this reference. See his *The Death and Rebirth of the Seneca* (New York, 1970), 327-28. Chronologically next, although rarely if ever cited, are the 1864 comments of the orientalist and early anthropologist Richard F. Burton. He cited Herodotus on Scythian scalping and mentioned several references "to prove that the Anglo-Saxons and the French still scalped about A.D. 879," con-

cluding from this, in the Eurocentric diffusionist fashion of his time, that "the modern American practice is traceable to Europe and Asia," even though he also clearly believed it to be pre-Columbian in America (since he said that although the modern scalp knife is iron, "formerly it was of flint, obsidian, or other hard stone") ("Notes on Scalping," *Anthropological Review*, 2 [1864], 48-52). Georg Friederici reported that his extensive search for Burton's references—other than Herodotus—was fruitless (*Skalpieren und ähnliche Kriegsgebräuche in Amerika* [Braunschweig, 1906], 134).

2. Dorothy Clarke Wilson, *Bright Eyes: The Story of Susette La Flesche, an Omaha Indian* (New York, 1974), 221.

3. Leslie A. Fiedler, *The Return of the Vanishing American* (New York, 1968), 42; Peter Farb, *Man's Rise to Civilization as Shown by the Indians of North America from Primeval Times to the Coming of the Industrial State* (New York, 1968), 123-24; Edgar S. Cahn, ed., *Our Brother's Keeper: The Indian in White America* (Washington, D.C., 1969), 176, italicized in original.

4. "Hec Ramsey," NBC-TV, Dec. 18, 1972; *The New Yorker*, Nov. 27, 1971, 104.

5. We are grateful to Mr. Josephy for a transcript of his testimony pertaining to scalping (personal communication, May 24, 1979). In 1970 he wrote that the "origin [of scalping] has recently come into question. . . . But the practice of scalping, or customs close to it— such as the cutting off of ears—was not unknown to Europeans before the discovery of America. Poachers received such treatment in England, and it is certain that, in some parts of the New World, whites introduced scalping to tribes that had never practiced it themselves" (*The Indian Heritage of America* [New York, 1968], 305). Today he states that he is uncertain about the origins of scalping.

6. Vine Deloria, Jr., *Custer Died for Your Sins: An Indian Manifesto* (New York, 1969), 6-7. For other versions of the new wisdom see Jane Willis, *Geniesh: An Indian Girlhood* (Toronto, 1973), 199: "It *was* white men—the Conquistadors—who originated scalping"; and Robert F. Heizer, ed., *The Destruction of California Indians* (Santa Barbara and Salt Lake City, 1974), 267: "Many anthropologists believe that [scalping] was not an aboriginal custom, but was a practice introduced on the east coast by the French and English, from whence it spread westward." In the film *Soldier Blue* (1971), the Indianized white heroine also attributes scalping to the "white man" without attributing national blame. The widely circulated

Heritage of Canada (n.p., 1978), published by *Reader's Digest,* features an article entitled "Scalping: White Men Taught the Indians How," which states that "scalp-taking was virtually unknown to North American Indians before the arrival of Europeans" (p. 50).

7. *The Flint Journal,* Sept. 8, 1975. We are grateful to Clark Hallas for the relevant issues of this journal. The story received notice in the Indian press as well (*Wassaja,* Oct. 1975).

8. *Flint Journal,* Sept. 10, 1975.

9. In a long interview with the *Washington Post* on July 6, 1976, veteran Indian movie actor Iron Eyes Cody blasted Hollywood for its lack of historical accuracy. Scalping, he pointed out as an example, "began with the Mexicans and the bounty hunters. They show a lot of blood and scalping today, but Indians fought each other for a thousand years and never took scalps. That's a lot of baloney that Fenimore Cooper and all those people wrote." In a similar vein, Art Raymond, an Oglala Sioux educator and legislator, denied that the Indians were morally responsible for scalping in an address to the National Council of Teachers of English at their 1976 annual meeting in Chicago. In a story picked up by the Associated Press, Raymond pointed his finger at Europeans for introducing scalping (*New York Times,* Nov. 28, 1976). "Do you still scalp your enemies?" is commonly asked Indians even today. Eddie Littlelight, a Crow, supplied several Indian responses to this ignorant and rude question, finally delighting his French journalist interlocutor with a tale about a Crow delegation visiting Germany the previous year on a tour organized by the State Department and the many German Indian-hobbyist clubs. At a formal banquet for 300 people the question was asked once again, whereupon Big Elk is said to have pulled from his pocket a bunch of blond and brunette scalps, and cut short the banquet by replying with a broad grin that he had himself lifted these scalps in Normandy from seven German officers, who were not even S.S. officers (Jean Raspail, *Les Peaux-rouges aujourd'hui* [Paris, 1978], 275).

10. Friederici, *Skalpieren.*

11. Georg Friederici, "Scalping in America," Smithsonian Institution, *Annual Report . . . June 30, 1906* (Washington, D.C., 1907), 423-38 (hereafter cited as Friederici, "Scalping in America"). This is an abstract of the original, omitting all of the massive documentation that was typical of Friederici's careful scholarship, and considerably shortening the details on the aboriginal distribution and post-European spread of scalping in North America. Entirely omitted

are sections on head and other body-part trophies, largely in Mexico and South America (pp. 77-101), on methods of removing the scalp, preparing it, and using it (pp. 105-15), on beliefs and customs relating to the head, hair, and scalp (pp. 115-31), and a survey of evidence for scalping outside the Americas (pp. 131-37). Thus most of the book did not appear in English.

12. Frederick Webb Hodge, ed., *Handbook of American Indians North of Mexico*, Smithsonian Institution, Bureau of American Ethnology, Bulletin 30 (Washington, D.C., 1910), s.v. "Scalping," by J[ames] M[ooney], 482-83.

13. *Encyclopaedia Britannica*, 11th ed., s.v. "Scalping"; *ibid.*, 1967 ed., s.v. "Scalping."

14. *Encyclopedia Americana*, 1963 ed., s.v. "Scalping."

15. H. P. Biggar, ed., *The Voyages of Jacques Cartier . . .* , Public Archives of Canada, Publication No. 11 (Ottawa, 1924), 177. We have made our own translations from the French and Spanish throughout this article. Biggar translated "les peaulx de cinq testes" as "five scalps," which is faithful but anachronistic. In 1558 André Thevet noted that if the St. Lawrence Indians "prennêt aucũs de leurs ennemis, . . . ils leur escorchent la teste, & le visage, & l'estendent à un cercle pour la secher" (*Les Singularitez de la France antarctique* [Paris, 1558], fol. 154v).

16. Garcilaso de la Vega, *La Florida del Inca*, ed. Emma Susana Sperati (Mexico City and Buenos Aires, 1956), 181, 182. In Garcilaso de la Vega, *The Florida of the Inca . . .* , trans. and ed. John Grier Varner and Jeannette Johnson Varner (Austin, Tex., 1951), 257, 258-59, the translators justify their use of "scalp" in these two passages.

17. Fray Gregorio de Beteta, "Relacion de la Florida . . ." [1549], in T. Buckingham Smith, *Colección de rarios documentos para la historia de la Florida* (London, 1857), 1:190-202, esp. 196, 200; full translation in David B. Quinn, ed., *New American World: A Documentary History of North America to 1612*, 5 vols. (New York, 1979), 2:190-97

18. Fray Augustin Davila Padilla, *Historia de la fundacion y discurso de la Prouincia de Santiago de Mexico* (Madrid, 1596), 260. A rather too free translation of this section is in John R. Swanton, *Early History of the Creek Indians and Their Neighbors*, Smithsonian Inst., Bur. of Am. Ethnol., Bull. 73 (Washington, D.C., 1922), 231-39, and reprinted in Quinn, ed., *New American World*, 2:240-47 (the relevant passage is on p. 245).

19. Jacques Le Moyne de Morgues, in Theodor de Bry, *Brevis narratio eorum quae in Florida Americae prouīcia Gallis acciderunt* [= his America. pt. II] (Frankfurt, 1591), pls. 15-16, in Paul Hulton, *The Work of Jacques Le Moyne de Morgues, a Huguenot Artist in France, Florida, and England*, 2 vols. (London, 1977). The Latin text and the engravings are reproduced in Hulton, *Work of Jacques Le Moyne*, 2:pls. 107-8, a new English translation (revised in our quotation above), *ibid.*, 1:15-16, with commentary on p. 208. For the date of, and Le Moyne's presence on, the raids see *ibid.*, 1:6, 41. Le Moyne wrote and painted his recollections some twenty years after his experiences in Florida, and both he and Theodor de Bry, who engraved the pictures for publication after the artist's death, are known to have taken artistic liberties with ethnographic details in many pictures. Nevertheless, the verbal and pictorial representations of scalping agree in important details that most subsequent accounts designate as typical of Indian methods of scalping.

20. H. P. Biggar, ed., *The Works of Samuel de Champlain* . . . , Publications of the Champlain Society, 6 vols. (Toronto, 1922-36), 1: 102-3, 108.

21. *Ibid.*, 2:102-3, 106.

22. Marc Lescarbot, *The History of New France*, ed. and trans. W. L. Grant, Publ. of Champlain Soc., 3 vols. (Toronto, 1907-14), 3:271 (English), 449 (French). Grant also writes that Lescarbot's reprint of Cartier's passage about the Toudamans' scalps "proves that the habit of scalping was not, as has been asserted, introduced into North America by Europeans" (*ibid.*, 2:124, n. 2). He then refers the reader to Friederici's study.

23. Father Gabriel Sagard, *The Long Journey to the Country of the Hurons*, ed. George M. Wrong, trans. H. H. Langton, Publ. of the Champlain Soc. (Toronto, 1939), 153 (English), 348 (French).

24. "Narrative of a Journey into the Mohawk and Oneida Country, 1634-1635," in J. Franklin Jameson, ed., *Narratives of New Netherland, 1609-1664*, Original Narratives of Early American History (New York, 1909), 148. Only a few French traders preceded Van den Bogaert to the Iroquois, and they had no reason to teach their customers how to scalp. We are grateful to Charles Gehring of the New York State Library for a transcription of the original Dutch manuscript in the Henry Huntington Library, San Marino, Calif., and for his help in tracking down other Dutch words and phrases for "scalp." He informs us that in the late 1680s the Dutch began to substitute *kruyn* ("crown" of the head, or "pate") for *lock(en)*

(literally "lock[s]" of hair) and that the New York English, who frequently used Dutch interpreters, often mentioned "the crowns" of slain enemy warriors (personal communication, Dec. 22, 1975).

25. John Smith, *A Map of Virginia* . . . [Oxford, 1612], in Philip L. Barbour, ed., *The Jamestown Voyages under the First Charter, 1606-1609* (Hakluyt Society Publications, 2d ser. 136-37 [Cambridge, 1969]), 137:372.

26. Ivor Noël Hume, "First Look at Lost Virginia Settlement," *National Geographic,* 155 (1979), 735-67. With oral information and additional photographs, J. Lawrence Angel, the physical anthropologist who analyzed the skeleton, convinced us on June 1, 1979, of the likelihood of this interpretation.

27. Friederici, *Skalpieren,* 8-37. Useful collections of later as well as early references are in Regina Flannery, *An Analysis of Coastal Algonquian Culture* (Washington, D.C., 1939), 124-25, and Nathaniel Knowles, "The Torture of Captives by the Indians of Eastern North America," *Proceedings of the American Philosophical Society,* 82 (1940), 151-225 (on scalps, pp. 194-217).

28. Sylvester K. Stevens *et al.,* eds., *Travels in New France by J.C.B.* [1751-61] (Harrisburg, Pa., 1941), 68.

29. *Oxford English Dictionary,* s.v. "Scalp"; Caius Plinius Secundus, *The historie of the world,* trans. Philemon Holland, 2d ed., 2 vols. (London, 1614), 1:154.

30. John Josselyn, *An Account of Two Voyages to New-England* . . . [London, 1675] (Boston, 1865), 114; [Nathaniel Saltonstall], *The Present State of New-England with Respect to the Indian War* . . . [London, 1675], in Charles H. Lincoln, ed., *Narratives of the Indian Wars, 1675-1699,* Orig. Narrs. of Early Amer. Hist. (New York, 1913), 30, 34; Daniel Gookin, *Historical Collections of the Indians in New England* [1674] (*Collections of the Massachusetts Historical Society,* 1st ser. 1 [1792]), 162 (hereafter cited as Gookin, *Historical Collections of the Indians*).

31. *OED,* s.v. "Scalp"; [Saltonstall], *Present State of New-England,* in Lincoln, ed., *Narratives of Indian Wars,* 28-29; N[athaniel] S[altonstall], *A New and Further Narrative of the State of New-England* . . . [London, 1676], *ibid.,* 98-99; Josselyn, *Account of Two Voyages,* 114.

32. Paul Robert, *Dictionnaire alphabétique et analogique de la langue française* (Paris, 1953-64), s.v. "Scalper"; Georg Friederici, *Amerikanistisches Wörterbuch* (Hamburg, 1947), s.v. "Scalp"; Karl König, *Überseeische Wörter im Französischen (16.-18. Jahrhundert),* Bei-

hefte zur Zeitschrift für Romanische Philologie, 91 Heft (Halle, 1939), 188-89.

33. *OED*, s.v. "Scalp" (verb); Philp Motley Palmer, *Neuweltwörter in Deutschen*, Germanische Bibliothek, 42 Band (Heidelberg, 1939), 124-25; *Woordenboek der Nederlandsche Taal* ('s Gravenhage and Leiden, 1882-), s.v. "Scalpeeren."

34. See David Beers Quinn, *The Elizabethans and the Irish* (Ithaca, 1966); Nicholas P. Canny, "The Ideology of English Colonization: From Ireland to America," *William and Mary Quarterly*, 3d ser. 30 (1973), 575-98; and James Muldoon, "The Indian as Irishman," *Essex Institute Historical Collections*, 111 (1975), 267-89, for lack of evidence of scalping. Quinn is "almost certain [scalping] was not practised in Europe, and certainly [it] was not in Ireland" (personal communication, Oct. 7, 1975). It hardly seems worth arguing whether European practices were more barbaric than Indian ones, if that is one aspect of the new mythology on scalping. European display of trophy heads lasted far beyond the seventeenth century; for example, Englishmen were photographed posing jauntily with the severed heads of Chinese "pirates" in Kowloon about 1900 (George Woodcock, *The British in the Far East* [New York, 1969], facing 29), and in 1931 the British in Burma displayed the heads of executed participants in Saya San's Peasant Rebellion (Ba Maw, *Breakthrough in Burma: Memoirs of a Revolution* [New Haven, Conn., 1968], xv; John F. Cady, *A History of Modern Burma* [Ithaca, 1958], 316, n. 88). American soldiers in Vietnam within the last decade sometimes took and kept ears as trophies (some were confiscated by army authorities and sent to the Smithsonian for forensic identification by physical anthropologists). These and other recent examples suggest racism as an element in barbarity.

35. Sydney V. James, Jr., ed., *Three Visitors to Early Plymouth: Letters about the Pilgrim Settlement in New England During Its First Seven Years . . .* (Plimoth Plantation, 1963), 31.

36. Gabriel Sagard, *Dictionnaire de la langue huronne* (Paris, 1632), s.v. "Membres & parties du corps humain"; "Narrative of a Journey," in Jameson, ed., *Narratives of New Netherland*, 158; Jacques Bruyas, *Radices verborum Iroquaeorum*, [John Gilmary Shea's] Library of American Linguistics, 10 (New York, 1862).

37. Henry R. Schoolcraft, *Notes on the Iroquois . . .* (Albany, 1847), 393; [David] *Zeisberger's Indian Dictionary*. ed. Eben Norton Horsford (Cambridge, Mass., 1887); Bishop [Friedrich] Baraga, *A Dic-*

tionary of the Otchipwe Language . . . , 2 vols. (Montreal, 1878-80), 1: *English-Otchipwe,* 221, 231, 2: *Otchipwe-English,* 79, 346; Sebastian Rasles [Sébastien Râle], *A Dictionary of the Abnaki Language,* ed. John Pickering, *Memoirs of the American Academy of Arts and Sciences,* n.s. 1 (1833), 412; George Lemoine, *Dictionnaire Français-Algonquin* (Quebec, 1911); Montague Chamberlain, *Maliseet Vocabulary* (Cambridge, Mass., 1899); Rev. Silas Tertius Rand, *Dictionary of the Language of the Micmac Indians* (Halifax, N.S., 1888); Lemoine, *Dictionnaire Français-Montagnais* (Boston, 1901); Cyrus Byington, *A Dictionary of the Choctaw Language,* ed. John R. Swanton and Henry S. Halbert, Smithsonian Inst., Bur. of Am. Ethnol., Bull. 46 (Washington, D.C., 1915). A more thorough search would undoubtedly uncover many more examples.

38. Albert S. Gatschet, *A Migration Legend of the Creek Indians* . . . , 2 vols. (Philadelphia and St. Louis, 1884-88), 1:223, 2:12 (l. 4), 48, 91; Mary R. Haas, "Creek Vocabulary," MS, *ca.* 1940, in Sturtevant's possession; R. M. Loughridge and David M. Hodge, *English and Muskokee Dictionary* . . . [St. Louis, 1890] (Philadelphia, 1914). For Hitchiti, see Gatschet, *Migration Legend,* 2:22 (l. 13); for Mikasuki, Sturtevant, 1950-52, MS field notes.

39. Floyd G. Lounsbury, personal communications, June 3, 7, 1979, citing for Oneida, Cayuga, and Onondaga his own MS field notes; for Onondaga, MS field notes by Alexander Goldenweiser and William N. Fenton; for Seneca, Wallace L. Chafe, *Seneca Morphology and Dictionary,* Smithsonian Contributions to Anthropology, 4 (Washington, D.C., 1967), entry 1218; and for Mohawk, Bruyas, *Radices,* 82.

40. Ives Goddard, personal communication, May 30, 1979, citing for Ojibwa, Baraga, *Dictionary of the Otchipwe;* for Eastern Abenaki, [Râle], *Dictionary of the Abnaki Language,* ed. Pickering; for Fox, William Jones, *Fox Texts* (American Ethnological Society, *Publications,* 1 [Leyden, 1907]), 188 (ll. 22-23), 190 (l. 5), 218 (ll. 16-17), as well as Truman Michelson, "The Traditional Origin of the Fox Society Known as 'The Singing Around Rite,'" *Fortieth Annual Report of the Bureau of American Ethnology* . . . *1918-1919* (Washington, D.C., 1925), 541-615 (p. 602, l. 4), and Michelson, *Contributions to Fox Ethnology,* Smithsonian Inst., Bur. of Am. Ethnol., Bull. 85 (Washington, D.C., 1927), 84 (ll. 11-12); and for Munsee, his own MS field notes.

41. Hulton, *Work of Jacques Le Moyne,* pl. 107.

42. Reproduced in Bruce G. Trigger, ed., *Northeast,* in William C. Sturtevant, ed., *Handbook of North American Indians,* 15 (Washington, D.C., 1978), 299.

43. *Les raretés des Indes. Codex Canadiensis* (Paris, 1930), original in Gilcrease Institute, Tulsa, Okla., attributed, probably wrongly, to Charles Bécard de Granville; reproduced in Alvin M. Josephy, Jr., ed., *The American Heritage Book of Indians* (New York, 1961), 190-91.

44. A. De Batz, watercolor in Bushnell Collection, Peabody Museum, Harvard University, reproduced and described in David I. Bushnell, Jr., *Drawings by A. De Batz in Louisiana, 1732-1735 . . .* (Washington, D.C., 1927), 11-12, pl. 5; similar scalps are carried by a Tunica warrior in the same collection, pl. 2.

45. Hodge, ed., *Handbook of American Indians,* s.v. "Hair dressing" by Alice C. Fletcher, and "Scalping" by M[ooney]; Friederici, *Skalpieren,* 104-6, 127-28; Friederici, "Scalping in America," 425, 437. Several scalplocks may be seen on the Indian scalps displayed at the Museum of the American Indian in New York City, an excellent exhibit that emphasizes their non-mercenary nature as war trophies. It also contains a rare scalp of a black man. In 1906 Friederici had found only two literary references to the scalping of blacks by the eastern Indians (*Skalpieren,* 106; "Scalping in America," 438). One of the scalplocks paid for by Pennsylvania during the Revolution found its way into Pierre-Eugène du Simitière's American Museum" in Philadelphia. His accession list under July 1782 records "a Scalp taken from an Indian killed in September, 1781, in Washington County near the Ohio in this State by *Adam Poe,* who fought with two Indians, and at last kill'd them both, it has an ornament a white wampum bead a finger long with a Silver Knob at the end the rest of the hair plaited and tyed with deer skin. Sent me by the President and the Supreme executive Council of this state with a written account of the affair" (quoted in Henry J. Young, "A Note on Scalp Bounties in Pennsylvania," *Pennsylvania History,* 24 [1957], 217).

46. Charles C. Willoughby, *The Turner Group of Earthworks, Hamilton County, Ohio* (Cambridge, Mass., 1922), 61; George K. Neumann, "Evidence for the Antiquity of Scalping from Central Illinois," *American Antiquity,* 5 (1940), 287-89; Wilda Anderson Obey, "The Arvilla People," *Minnesota Archaeologist,* 33:3, 4 (1974), 1-33; N. S. Ossenberg, "Skeletal Remains from Hungry Hall Mound 2," MS (1964), Royal Ontario Museum, Toronto, Canada, table 1, 21;

Walter Raymond Wood, *Nanza, The Ponca Fort* (Madison, Wis., 1960), 86-87; Donald E. Wray, "The Kingston Lake Sequence," MS (n.d.), Illinois State Museum, Springfield; Lucile E. Hoyme and William M. Bass, *Human Skeletal Remains from the Tollifero (Ha6) and Clarksville (Mc14) Sites, John H. Kerr Reservoir Basin, Virginia,* Smithsonian Inst., Bur. of Am. Ethnol., Bull. 182 (Washington, D.C., 1962), 378-80, pls. 102-4.

47. Friederici, *Skalpieren,* 107-8, collected references to 48 scalping survivors, 33 white and 15 Indian. Among many additional documented instances are the following: Gookin, *Historical Collections of the Indians,* 162; Samuel Penhallow, *The History of the Wars of New-England with the Eastern Indians . . .* (Boston, 1726), 72; [Andrew M. Welch, M.D.], *A Narrative of the Life and Sufferings of Mrs. Jane Johns, who was Barbarously Wounded and Scalped by Seminole Indians, in East Florida* (Baltimore, 1837); J. H. Trumbull and C. J. Hoadly, eds., *The Public Records of the Colony of Connecticut . . . ,* 15 vols. (Hartford, 1850-90), 5:26; S[altonstall], *A New and Further Narrative,* in Lincoln, ed., *Narratives of Indian Wars,* 99; A. W. Putnam, *History of Middle Tennessee or, Life and Times of Gen. James Robertson* (Nashville, 1859), 128, 153-54, 294, 355. The human capacity to survive scalping and primitive medical treatment is exemplified in James Robertson, "Remarks on the Management of the Scalped-Head," *Philadelphia Medical and Physical Journal,* 2:2 (1805-6), 27-30, who advocated boring the exposed skull in numerous places with an awl to allow new flesh to generate. About 1940 Ángel Palerm, a curious young foreign visitor to two small isolated settlements on the northwest Mexican frontier, was shown three elderly people who had survived scalping. Each had a circular area of scar tissue at the apex of the head. Two claimed they had been captured by Apaches about 1900 and one by Yaquis some time between 1900 and 1910. They said that after they had been captured, the Indians removed their scalps to turn in for scalp bounties, and then cured their wounds with native herbal remedies in order to keep them alive for other purposes (Palerm, personal communication, May 17, 1976).

48. Charles Snow, "Possible Evidence of Scalping at Moundville," *Alabama Museum of Natural History,* Paper No. 15, pt. 2 (1941), figs. 9-10; H. Hamperl and W. S. Laughlin, "Osteological Consequences of Scalping," *Human Biology,* 31 (1959), 80-89; Ossenberg, "Skeletal Remains from Hungry Hall Mound 2," MS; and personal communications from William S. Laughlin, Apr. 22, 1975; T. D. Stewart,

Feb. 25, 1975; Ray Baby (telephone), May 2, 1975; and Donald Lenig, Oct. 11, 1975. An excellent study which confirms our conclusions is Douglas W. Owsley and Hugh E. Berryman, "Ethnographic and Archaeological Evidence of Scalping in the Southeastern United States," *Tennessee Archaeologist,* 31 (Spring 1975), 41-58.

CHAPTER THREE

1. See, for example, *Edits, ordonnances royaux, déclarations et arrêts du conseil d'état du roi concernant le Canada,* 3 vols. (Québec, 1854-56), 1:3, 5-6, 3:11; Merrill Jensen, ed., *American Colonial Documents to 1776,* in David C. Douglas, ed., *English Historical Documents,* 12 vols. (New York, 1955), 9:65, 82, 85, 93.

2. Charles Orr, ed., *History of the Pequot War* (Cleveland, 1897), 110-11; Mary Francis Farnham, ed., *The Farnham Papers, 1603-1688, Documentary History of the State of Maine, Collections of the Maine Historical Society,* 2d ser. 7 (1901), 8-9; Peter Force, ed., *Tracts and Other Papers Relating Principally to the Origin, Settlement, and Progress of the Colonies in North America,* 4 vols. (Washington, D. C., 1836-47), vol. 3, no. 1, p. 5; Samuel Purchas, *Hakluytus Posthumus or Purchas His Pilgrimes* [London, 1625], 20 vols. (Glasgow, 1903-5), 19:406-9; Julian P. Boyd and Robert J. Taylor, eds., *The Susquehannah Company Papers,* 11 vols. (Wilkes-Barre, Pa., and Ithaca, 1930-71), 1:255.

3. E. G. R. Taylor, ed., *The Original Writings and Correspondence of the Two Richard Hakluyts,* Hakluyt Society Publications, 2d ser. 76-77 (London, 1935), 76:164-65; see also 77:223, 339.

4. Richard Eburne, *A Plain Pathway to Plantations* [London, 1624], ed. Louis B. Wright (Ithaca, 1962), 55-56.

5. Robert Gray, *A Good Speed to Virginia* (London, 1609), fols. C1v-C2r. See also Reuben Gold Thwaites, ed., *The Jesuit Relations and Allied Documents,* 73 vols. (Cleveland, 1896-1901), 5:33, 6:229-31, 19:39 (hereafter cited as *JR*), and *Father Louis Hennepin's Description of Louisiana* [Paris, 1683], ed. Marion E. Cross (Minneapolis, 1938), 145.

6. *JR,* 9:91.

7. *New Englands First Fruits* [London, 1643], in Samuel Eliot Morison, *The Founding of Harvard College* (Cambridge, Mass., 1935), 421.

8. *Collections of the Massachusetts Historical Society,* 3d ser. 4 (1834), 90. See also Chrétien Le Clercq, *The First Establishment of the Faith in New France* [Paris, 1691], ed. and trans. John Gilmary Shea, 2 vols. (New York, 1881), 1:111, 141-42.

9. James Sullivan *et al.,* eds., *The Papers of Sir William Johnson,* 14 vols. (Albany, 1921-65), 7:506 (hereafter cited as *Johnson Papers*). See, for example, Le Clercq, *First Establishment of the Faith,* 1:110-11, 214, 222; *Colls. Mass. His. Soc.,* 3d ser. 4 (1834), 14-15; William Hubbard, *The Present State of New-England* (London, 1677), 86-87 (2d pag.); *Ecclesiastical Records, State of New York,* 6 vols. (Albany, 1901-5), 1:398; John R. Bartlett, ed., *Records of the Colony of Rhode Island and Providence Plantations, in New England,* 10 vols. (Providence, 1856-65), 1:297-98.

10. Jean Delanglez, *Frontenac and the Jesuits,* Institute of Jesuit History Publications (Chicago, 1939), 35-65.

11. William Crashaw, *A Sermon Preached in London before the right honorable the Lord La Warre . . . Febr. 21. 1609* (London, 1610), fols. D4r, K1v.

12. *Johnson Papers,* 5:511.

13. *A Letter from the Rev^d Mr. Sergeant of Stockbridge, to Dr. Colman of Boston* (Boston, 1743), 3, 5; *Collections of the Rhode Island Historical Society,* 4 (1838), 138; Jonathan Edwards to Joshua Paice, Feb. 24, 1752, Andover-Newton Edwards Collection, folder 1752b (transcript), Yale University Library, New Haven, Conn.

14. Le Clercq, *First Establishment of the Faith,* 1:214.

15. Taylor, *Writings of the Hakluyts,* 2:214; Hubbard, *Present State of New-England,* 86 (2d pag.); Farnham, ed., *Farnham Papers,* 24; Nathaniel B. Shurtleff and David Pulsifer, eds., *Records of the Colony of New Plymouth, in New England,* 12 vols. (Boston, 1855-61), 10:285-86, 368; Gray, *Good Speed to Virginia,* fols. C2v, C4r-v; Clayton Colman Hall, ed., *Narratives of Early Maryland, 1633-1684,* Original Narratives of Early American History (New York, 1910), 20, 84, 90; George Washington to Richard Henry Lee, Feb. 8, 1785, American Philosophical Society, Philadelphia, Pa.

16. *A Letter from the Rev^d Mr. Sergeant,* 3; Eleazar Wheelock, *A Continuation of the Narrative of the Indian Charity-School in Lebanon, in Connecticut, From . . . 1768, to . . . 1771* (Hartford, 1771), 20.

17. [George Peckham], *A True Reporte of the late discoveries . . . of*

the New-found Landes (London, 1583), fol. F3r; Gray, *Good Speed to Virginia,* fol. D2r.

18. Adriaen Van der Donck, *A Description of the New Netherlands* [Amsterdam, 1655], ed. Thomas F. O'Donnell (Syracuse, N.Y., 1968), 100.

19. *New England Historical and Genealogical Register,* 36 (1882), 296; *Colls. Mass. His. Soc.,* 3d ser. 4 (1834), 126, 137.

20. *Ibid.,* 269.

21. John Josselyn, *An Account of Two Voyages to New England Made during the years 1638, 1663* [London, 1674] (Boston, 1865), 99.

22. Roger Williams, *A Key into the Language of America* (London, 1643), 46-48; *Colls. Mass. His. Soc.,* 1st ser. 1 (1792), 132; Van der Donck, *New Netherlands,* 81-82.

23. Josselyn, *Account of Two Voyages,* 99; Williams, *Key into the Language of America,* 47.

24. Thomas Morton, *New English Canaan* [Amsterdam, 1637], in Force, *Tracts,* vol. 2, no. 5, p. 20.

25. [Edward] *Johnson's Wonder-Working Providence, 1628-1651,* ed. J. Franklin Jameson, Orig. Narrs. of Early Amer. Hist. (New York, 1910), 162.

26. *Colls. Mass. His. Soc.,* 3d ser. 4 (1834), 50.

27. *Oxford English Dictionary,* s.v. "labour" and "toil."

28. *A Journal of the Pilgrims at Plymouth: Mourt's Relation* [London, 1622], ed. Dwight B. Heath (New York, 1963), 91-92.

29. *Colls. Mass. His. Soc.,* 1st ser. 4 (1795), 63, 71, 73.

30. Hugh Jones, *The Present State of Virginia* [London, 1724], ed. Richard L. Morton (Chapel Hill, 1956), 62.

31. J. Hector St. John de Crèvecoeur, *Letters from an American Farmer* [London, 1782] (London: Everyman's Library, 1912), 215.

32. Force, *Tracts,* vol. 1, no. 12, p. 13.

33. Lyon Gardiner Tyler, ed., *Narratives of Early Virginia, 1606-1625,* Orig. Narrs. of Early Amer. Hist. (New York, 1907), 101; J. Franklin Jameson, ed. *Narratives of New Netherland, 1609-1664,* Orig. Narrs. of Early Amer. Hist. (New York, 1909), 107.

34. *Diary of David McClure . . . 1748-1820,* ed. Franklin B. Dexter (New York, 1899), 68; William Wood, *New Englands Prospect* (London, 1634), 10.

35. Thomas Harriot, *A briefe and true report of the new found land of Virginia* [1588], in David B. Quinn and Alison M. Quinn, eds., *Virginia Voyages from Hakluyt* (London, 1973), 56.

36. *Winthrop Papers* (Boston: Massachusetts Historical Society, 1929-), 2:120.

37. Wood, *New Englands Prospect,* 87.

38. Gavin Cochrane, Treatise on the Indians of North America Written in the Year 1764, Ayer MS NA 176, ch. 7, Newberry Library, Chicago, Ill.

39. Samuel Stanhope Smith, *An Essay on the Causes of the Variety of Complexion and Figure in the Human Species* [New Brunswick, N.J., 1810], ed. Winthrop D. Jordan (Cambridge, Mass., 1965), 240.

40. Robert Beverley, *The History and Present State of Virginia* [London, 1705], ed. Louis B. Wright (Chapel Hill, 1947), 233.

41. *The American Magazine and Monthly Chronicle for the British Colonies* (Philadelphia: William Bradford), 1:2 (Nov. 1757), 83.

42. Albert C. Myers, ed., *Narratives of Early Pennsylvania, West New Jersey, and Delaware, 1630-1707,* Orig. Narrs. of Early Amer. Hist. (New York, 1912), 233.

43. Tyler, ed., *Narratives of Early Virginia,* 103.

44. *William Byrd's Histories of the Dividing Line betwixt Virginia and North Carolina,* ed. William K. Boyd (New York, 1967), 116 (my emphasis).

45. Rev. John Heckewelder, *History, Manners, and Customs of the Indian Nations Who Once Inhabited Pennsylvania and the Neighbouring States* [Philadelphia, 1818], rev. ed. Rev. William C. Reichel (Philadelphia, 1876), 141; John Lawson, *A New Voyage to Carolina* [London, 1709], ed. Hugh Talmage Lefler (Chapel Hill, 1967), 204; *Colls. Mass. His. Soc.,* 1st ser. 10 (1809), 108.

46. Beverley, *History of Virginia,* 166.

47. *Colls. Mass. His. Soc.,* 3d ser. 4 (1834), 40.

48. Edward Winslow, *Good Newes from New England* [London, 1624], in Alexander Young, ed., *Chronicles of the Pilgrim Fathers of Plymouth from 1602 to 1625* (2d ed., Boston, 1844), 364.

49. Wood, *New Englands Prospect,* 73.

50. George Alsop, *A Character of the Province of Mary-land* (London, 1666), 72; [James] *Adair's History of the American Indians* [London, 1775], ed. Samuel Cole Williams (Kingsport, Tenn., 1930), 8-9; Bernard Romans, *A Concise Natural History of East and West Florida,* 2 vols. (New York, 1775), 1:42.

51. Wood, *New Englands Prospect,* 72.

52. *Ibid.,* 73.

53. James Axtell, *The School upon a Hill: Education and Society in Colonial New England* (New Haven, 1974), 160-65.

54. Robert G. Pope, ed., *The Notebook of the Reverend John Fiske, 1644-1675*, Publications of the Colonial Society of Massachusetts, 47 (1974), 133; *Proceedings of the Massachusetts Historical Society*, 2d ser. 29 (1895), 99.

55. *Colls. Mass. His. Soc.*, 3d ser. 4 (1834), 50, 109, 142, 178, 208.

56. *Ibid.*, 40, 50; John Eliot, *A Brief Narrative of the Progress of the Gospel amongst the Indians in New England* (London, 1671), 8. See also *JR*, 5:177; 12:61.

57. *Winthrop Papers*, 1:158-59; *Pubs. Col. Soc. of Mass.*, 29 (1933), 147-48. See also *Word from New France: The Selected Letters of Marie de L'Incarnation*, ed. and trans. Joyce Marshall (Toronto, 1967), 77, 84.

58. *Hennepin's Description of Louisiana*, 180.

59. *JR*, 12:169. I have translated *"sauvage"* not as "savage," which has a pejorative ring to modern ears, but as "Indian," which more nearly approximates the neutral descriptive quality of the original. See also *JR*, 6:83, 147, 3:143.

60. *JR*, 14:215.

61. *JR*, 25:113.

62. *JR*, 6:243.

63. *JR*, 12:61.

64. *JR*, 18:101-7, 22:83-85; *Word from New France*, 105-6. See James P. Ronda, "The Sillery Experiment: A Jesuit-Indian Village in New France, 1637-1663," *American Indian Culture and Research Journal*, 3:1 (1979), 1-18.

65. *JR*, 12:61.

66. Alden T. Vaughan, *New England Frontier: Puritans and Indians, 1620-1675* (Boston, 1965), 346-47.

67. *Colls. Mass. His. Soc.*, 3d ser. 4 (1834), 227.

68. Cochrane, Treatise on Indians, Ayer MS NA 176, ch. 7.

69. Delanglez, *Frontenac and the Jesuits*, 35-40; Lucien Campeau, *Les commencements du Collège de Québec (1626-1670)*, Cahiers d'Histoire des Jésuites, 1 (Montreal, 1972), 51-76.

70. *JR*, 12:63.

71. *An Essay towards Propagating the Gospel among the Neighbouring Nations of Indians in North America* (New London, Conn., 1756), 16; R. A. Brock, ed., *The Official Letters of Alexander Spotswood, Lieutenant-Governor of the Colony of Virginia, 1710-1722*, Collections of the Virginia Historical Society, n.s. 1-2 (1882-85), 1:121-22, 124, 134, 174; *Word from New France*, 223, 233; *JR*, 6:155.

72. *JR*, 5:197, 221, 35:251; Papers of Eleazar Wheelock, MS 762667.2, Dartmouth College Library, Hanover, N.H.

73. James Dow McCallum, ed., *The Letters of Eleazar Wheelock's Indians* (Hanover, N.H., 1932), 287-88.

74. Susan M. Kingsbury, ed., *Records of the Virginia Company of London*, 4 vols. (Washington, D.C., 1906-35), 3:557.

75. Thomas Lechford, *Plain Dealing: or, Newes from New-England* [London, 1642], in *Colls. Mass. His. Soc.*, 3d ser. 3 (1833), 80.

76. See Peter Duignan, "Early Jesuit Missionaries: A Suggestion for Further Study," *American Anthropologist*, 60 (1958), 726; J. H. Kennedy, *Jesuit and Savage in New France* (New Haven, 1950), 109; René Fülöp-Miller, *The Power and Secret of the Jesuits* (New York, 1930), pt. 5; *JR*, 12:117-25, 33:143-47.

77. *JR*, 23:207-9.

78. *JR*, 53:203-5.

79. See, for example, John Halkett, *Historical Notes Respecting the Indians of North America* (London, 1825), 214, 218-19, 231-32, 256-57, 295; Alexis de Tocqueville, *Democracy in America* [Paris, 1835], trans. Henry Reeve and Francis Bowen, ed. Phillips Bradley, 2 vols. (New York, 1945), 1:336-55; [Jeremy Belknap], "Has the Discovery of America Been Useful or Hurtful to Mankind?," *The Boston Magazine* (May 1784), 281-85, esp. 283.

80. Cotton Mather, *The Way to Prosperity* (Boston, 1690), 27.

81. The following paragraphs are based on a large number of primary sources, such as the *Jesuit Relations* and the Eliot tracts. The following secondary works are also pertinent: Anthony F. C. Wallace, *Religion: An Anthropological View* (New York, 1966); Wallace, *The Death and Rebirth of the Seneca* (New York, 1970); Hartley Burr Alexander, *The World's Rim: Great Mysteries of the North American Indians* (Lincoln, Neb., 1953); Ruth M. Underhill, *Red Man's Religion: Beliefs and Practices of the Indians North of Mexico* (Chicago, 1965); Ruth Benedict, *The Concept of the Guardian Spirit in North America*, Memoirs of the American Anthropological Association, 29 (Menasha, Wis., 1923); M. R. Harrington, *Religion and Ceremonies of the Lenape, Indian Notes and Monographs*, 2d ser. 19 (New York: Museum of the American Indian, 1921); Ake Hultkrantz, *The Religions of the American Indians*, trans. Monica Setterwall (Berkeley, 1979); Cara E. Richards, *Man in Perspective: An Introduction to Cultural Anthropology* (New York, 1972), ch. 7.

82. Wallace, *Religion,* 107.
83. Wallace, *Death and Rebirth of the Seneca,* 59-75.
84. Below, Chapter 5.
85. *David Zeisberger's History of the Northern American Indians,* ed. Archer Butler Hulbert and William Nathaniel Schwarze (Columbus: Ohio State Archaeological and Historical Society, 1910), 132-33.
86. John Smith, *Works, 1608-1631,* ed. Edward Arber (Birmingham, Eng., 1884), 564.
87. *JR,* 67:147.
88. *JR,* 20:71.
89. *JR,* 10:63, 18:125.
90. *JR,* 3:149, 15:125, 18:125, 23:165, 25:247.
91. For some of the obstacles that the French missionaries had to run, see Alfred G. Bailey, *The Conflict of European and Eastern Algonkian Cultures, 1504-1700* (2d ed., Toronto, 1969), ch. 11; Kennedy, *Jesuit and Savage in New France,* chs. 6-9; André Vachon, "L'eau-de-vie dans la société indienne," Canadian Historical Association, *Report* (1960), 22-32.
92. *JR,* 3:123.
93. *Hennepin's Description of Louisiana,* 178.
94. William M. Beauchamp, ed., *Moravian Journals Relating to Central New York, 1745-66* (Syracuse, N.Y.: Onondaga Historical Association, 1916), 7.
95. Pierre de Charlevoix, *History and General Description of New France* [Paris, 1744], ed. and trans. John Gilmary Shea, 6 vols. (New York, 1870), 2:77; *Hennepin's Description of Louisiana,* 26-27.
96. Albert H. Smyth, ed., *The Writings of Benjamin Franklin,* 10 vols. (New York, 1905-7), 10:100; *JR,* 52:203.
97. Charlevoix, *History of New France,* 2:77-78.
98. *JR,* 1:275.
99. Baron de Lahontan, *New Voyages to North-America* [The Hague, 1703], ed. Reuben Gold Thwaites, 2 vols. (Chicago, 1905), 2:570.
100. Le Clercq, *First Establishment of the Faith,* 1:221-22.
101. James Axtell, "The European Failure To Convert the Indians: An Autopsy," *Papers of the Sixth Algonquian Conference, 1974,* ed. William Cowan, National Museum of Man, Mercury Series, Canadian Ethnology Service, Paper No. 23 (Ottawa, 1975), 274-90.
102. Leonard W. Labaree *et al.,* eds., *The Papers of Benjamin Franklin* (New Haven, 1959-   ), 4:482-83.

103. For the striking contrast between the educational methods of the Indians and the English, see below, Chapters 4 and 7.

104. Frederick L. Weis, "The New England Company of 1649 and Its Missionary Enterprises," *Pubs. Col. Soc. Mass.*, 38 (1947-51), 150.

105. See, for example, John Wolfe Lydekker, *The Faithful Mohawks* (New York, 1938); Elma E. Gray and Leslie Robb Gray, *Wilderness Christians: The Moravian Mission to the Delaware Indians* (Ithaca, 1956); Marion J. Mochon, "Stockbridge-Munsee Cultural Adaptations: 'Assimilated Indians,'" *Proceedings of the American Philosophical Society*, 112 (1968), 182-219.

106. Many self-given tribal names simply meant "true" or "original people."

107. James P. Ronda, "'We Are Well As We Are': An Indian Critique of Seventeenth-Century Christian Missions," *William and Mary Quarterly*, 3d ser. 34 (1977), 66-82.

108. Charles E. Hunter, "The Delaware Nativist Revival of the Mid-Eighteenth Century," *Ethnohistory*, 18 (1971), 39-49; Wallace, *Death and Rebirth of the Seneca*, pt. 3.

109. Tyler, ed., *Narratives of Early Virginia*, 108.

CHAPTER FOUR

1. A convenient copy of the charter may be found in Jere R. Daniell, "Eleazar Wheelock and the Dartmouth College Charter," *Historical New Hampshire*, 24:4 (Winter 1969), 3-44, and in Frederick Chase, *A History of Dartmouth College and the Town of Hanover, New Hampshire (to 1815)*, ed. John K. Lord (2d ed., Brattleboro, Vt., 1928), Appendix A.

2. Harry J. Carman, Harold C. Syrett, and Bernard W. Wishy, *A History of the American People*, 2 vols. (3d ed., New York, 1967), 1:104; Richard B. Morris, William Greenleaf, and Robert H. Ferrell, *America: A History of the People* (Chicago, 1971), 90; Charles Sellers and Henry May, *A Synopsis of American History* (Chicago, 1963), 41; David Hawke, *The Colonial Experience* (Indianapolis, 1966), 443; Edwin Scott Gaustad, *The Great Awakening in New England* (New York, 1957), 105, 108; Alan Heimert and Perry Miller, eds., *The Great Awakening* (Indianapolis, 1967), lvi; Richard L. Bushman, ed., *The Great Awakening* (New York, 1970), 20-21.

3. E. B. O'Callaghan, ed., *The Documentary History of the State of New-York*, 4 vols. (quarto ed., Albany, 1849-51), 4:223.

4. Gaustad, *Great Awakening in New England*, 74-75; James Dow McCallum, *Eleazar Wheelock, Founder of Dartmouth College* (Hanover, N.H., 1939), ch. 2.

5. Harold Blodgett, *Samson Occom* (Hanover, N.H., 1935), chs. 1-3.

6. O'Callaghan, ed., *Doc. His. of N.Y.*, 4:202.

7. WP 760628. WP stands for Papers of Eleazar Wheelock [1728-1779], Dartmouth College Library, Hanover, N.H., and is followed by the calendar number as given in *A Guide to the Microfilm Edition of The Papers of Eleazar Wheelock* (Hanover, N.H.: Dartmouth College Library, 1971). The first three digits indicate the year of the manuscript: e.g., 760628 is 1760.

8. Eleazar Wheelock, *A Continuation of the Narrative of the State, &c. of the Indian Charity-School, at Lebanon, in Connecticut; From Nov. 27th, 1762, to Sept. 3d, 1765* (Boston, 1765), 22.

9. Eleazar Wheelock, *A plain and faithful Narrative of the Original Design, Rise, Progress, and Present State of the Indian Charity-School At Lebanon, in Connecticut* (Boston, 1763), 40.

10. WP 762113.

11. WP 761625.1.

12. WP 761602.3.

13. Wheelock, *A plain and faithful Narrative*, 42.

14. WP 761625.1, 762113.

15. WP 761664.3.

16. WP 761404.

17. Eric P. Kelly, "The Dartmouth Indians," *Dartmouth Alumni Magazine* (Dec. 1929), 122-25.

18. Eleazar Wheelock, *A Continuation of the Narrative . . .* (Hartford, 1771), 19-20.

19. Wheelock, *A plain and faithful Narrative*, 28-29.

20. WP 762165.

21. WP 772174.1.

22. Mary Frances Farnham, ed., *The Farnham Papers 1603-1688, Documentary History of the State of Maine, Collections of the Maine Historical Society*, 2d ser. 7 (1901), 21; Edmund S. Morgan, ed., *The Founding of Massachusetts: Historians and the Sources* (Indianapolis, 1964), 453.

23. Morgan, ed., *Founding of Massachusetts*, 320.

24. *Colls. Maine His. Soc.*, 2d ser. 7 (1901), 24; Morgan, ed., *Founding of Massachusetts*, 320.

25. See above, Chapter 3, pp. 44-61.

26. James Sullivan *et al.*, eds., *The Papers of Sir William Johnson*, 14 vols. (Albany, 1921-65), 7:506.

27. WP 762521.1, 764560.1.

28. WP 766504.4.

29. Wheelock, *Continuation of the Narrative* (1771), 22; Eleazar Wheelock, *A Continuation of the Narrative* . . . ([Portsmouth,] N.H., 1773), 13.

30. WP 758618.

31. Eleazar Wheelock, *A Brief Narrative of the Indian Charity-School, in Lebanon in Connecticut, New England* . . . (London, 1766), 9, 21.

32. Wheelock, *Continuation of the Narrative* (1773), 12-13.

33. Wheelock, *A plain and faithful Narrative*, 25.

34. Eleazar Wheelock, *A Continuation of the Narrative* . . . (Hartford, 1775), 11.

35. Wheelock, *A plain and faithful Narrative*, 15.

36. WP 767427.1; Wheelock, *A plain and faithful Narrative*, 40.

37. Wheelock, *A plain and faithful Narrative*, 44; WP 762667.2.

38. WP 762667.2.

39. James Dow McCallum, ed., *The Letters of Eleazar Wheelock's Indians* (Hanover, N.H., 1932), 287-88.

40. Wheelock, *Continuation of the Narrative* (1771), 5.

41. WP 774657.

42. McCallum, ed., *Letters of Wheelock's Indians*, 231.

43. *Ibid.*, 287.

44. *Ibid.*, 221.

45. *Ibid.*, 65.

46. Wheelock, *Brief Narrative*, 6.

47. WP 756615.

48. WP 764268.1.

49. WP 765164.1.

50. WP 770367.

51. WP 758422.

52. WP 763581.

53. WP 767604.1.

54. WP 763666.2.

55. McCallum, ed., *Letters of Wheelock's Indians*, 255; WP 763666.2.

56. WP 763659, 763666.2.

57. WP 767265.2.

58. WP 767163.

59. WP 762516, 761304.1; Eleazar Wheelock, *A Continuation of the Narrative* . . . (London, 1769), 16.

60. McCallum, ed., *Letters of Wheelock's Indians,* 131, 141, 148, 183.

61. WP 769209.2.

62. WP 760566.

63. WP 762412.1.

64. WP 769255; Wheelock, *Continuation of the Narrative* (1771), 16.

65. WP 769255, 769274.2.

66. Wheelock, *Continuation of the Narrative* (1775), 11; Gordon M. Day, "Dartmouth and Saint Francis," *Dartmouth Alumni Magazine* (Nov. 1959), 28-30.

67. Wheelock, *Continuation of the Narrative* (1775), 14.

68. WP 764574.

69. Leon Burr Richardson, ed., *An Indian Preacher in England* (Hanover, N.H., 1933); Blodgett, *Samson Occom,* ch. 6.

70. WP 761129.1, 763204, 763407.2.

71. WP 769663.2. See also Daniell, "Eleazar Wheelock and the Dartmouth College Charter," 29.

72. Kelly, "The Dartmouth Indians," 122-25; Leon B. Richardson, "The Dartmouth Indians, 1800-1893," *Dartmouth Alumni Magazine* (June 1930), 524-27.

73. Blodgett, *Samson Occom,* 122-23, 135.

CHAPTER FIVE

1. See above, Chapter 3.

2. The major exception to the pattern of individual interments was scaffold or tree burials, perhaps a practice required by the frozen ground in winter and early spring; for some tribes, burials in the floors of houses or in storage or refuse pits may have grown from the same necessity. Erminie Wheeler Voegelin, *Mortuary Customs of the Shawnee and Other Eastern Tribes,* Indiana Historical Society, *Prehistory Research Series,* 2:4 (1941-44), 341-42 (table IX); Alanson Skinner, "Archaeology of the New York Coastal Algonkin," American Museum of Natural History, *Anthropological Papers* 3 (1909), 233; Wendell S. Hadlock, "Three Contact Burials from Eastern Massachusetts," Massachusetts Archaeological Society, *Bulletin,* 10:3 (April 1949), 65; Howard A. MacCord, Sr., "The Brown Johnson Site—Bland County, Virginia," Archaeological Society of Virginia, *Quarterly Bulletin,* 25:4 (June 1971), 243; Herbert

C. Kraft, *The Archaeology of the Pahaquarra Site* (*A Preliminary Report*) (South Orange, N.J.: Archaeological Research Center, Seton Hall University, 1976), 56; Walter A. Kenyon, "Geometry of Death: The Neutral Indian Cemetery at Grimsby," *Rotunda: The Magazine of the Royal Ontario Museum,* 12:3 (Fall 1979), 29; Bernhard J. Stern, ed., "The Letters of Asher Wright to Lewis Henry Morgan," *American Anthropologist,* n.s. 35 (1933), 138-39.

3. The only exceptions to the pattern of corpses laid on the side were adults who were rarely placed in a supine position (legs still flexed), infants who were frequently laid in an extended, supine position, and predominantly Hudson River and Delawaran adults who were placed in a sitting position on a stool, block of wood, or stone. Adriaen Van der Donck, *A Description of the New Netherlands* [Amsterdam, 1655], ed. Thomas F. O'Donnell (Syracuse, N.Y., 1968), 87; J. Franklin Jameson, ed., *Narratives of New Netherland, 1609-1664,* Original Narratives of Early American History (New York, 1909), 87, 176; David I. Bushnell, Jr., *Native Cemeteries and Forms of Burial East of the Mississippi,* U.S. Bureau of American Ethnology, *Bulletin,* 71 (1920), 70-71, 87; Peter Lindeström, *Geographia Americae,* trans. Amandus Johnson (Philadelphia, 1925), 250.

4. This profile is based on a large number of archaeological and historical reports for the late-prehistoric, protohistoric, and early-historic periods. Among the most comprehensive are Voegelin, *Mortuary Customs of the Shawnee,* 341-42 (table IX); Bushnell, *Native Cemeteries,* 1-160; Carl F. Miller, *Archaeology of the John H. Kerr Reservoir Basin, Roanoke River, Virginia-North Carolina,* BAE *Bull.,* 182 (1962), 206-17, 239-43, 334-50, 380-92; Joseph L. Benthall, *Archaeological Investigation of the Shannon Site, Montgomery County, Virginia* (Richmond: Virginia State Library, 1969), 43-77; John Witthoft and W. Fred Kinsey III, eds., *Susquehannock Miscellany* (Harrisburg: Pennsylvania Historical and Museum Commission, 1959), 19-60, 99-119, 136-47; William Scranton Simmons, *Cautantowwit's House: An Indian Burial Ground on the Island of Conanicut in Narragansett Bay* (Providence, 1970); Charles F. Wray and Harry L. Schoff, "A Preliminary Report on the Seneca Sequence in Western New York, 1550-1687," *Pennsylvania Archaeologist,* 23:2 (July 1953), 53-63; Marian E. White, "An Early Historic Niagara Frontier Iroquois Cemetery in Erie County, New York," *Researches and Transactions of the New York State Archaeological Association,* 16:1 (1967); W. J. Wintemberg, *Roe-*

buck Prehistoric Village Site, Grenville County, Ontario, National Museum of Canada, *Bulletin,* 83, Anthropological Series, 19 (1936).

5. Voegelin, *Mortuary Customs of the Shawnee,* 341-42 (table IX); Van der Donck, *New Netherlands,* 87; Father Chrestien Le Clercq, *New Relation of Gaspesia,* ed. and trans. William F. Ganong (Toronto: The Champlain Society, 1910), 301-2; [James] *Adair's History of the American Indians* [London, 1775] ed. Samuel Cole Williams (Kingsport, Tenn., 1930), 195-98; *David Zeisberger's History of the Northern American Indians,* ed. Archer Butler Hulbert and William Nathaniel Schwarze (Columbus: Ohio State Archaeological and Historical Society, 1910), 88-90; Pierre de Charlevoix, *Journal of a Voyage to North-America,* 2 vols. (London, 1761), 2: 191-92; Father Joseph François Lafitau, *Customs of the American Indians Compared with the Customs of Primitive Times,* ed. and trans. William N. Fenton and Elizabeth L. Moore, 2 vols. (Toronto: The Champlain Society, 1974-77), 2:241-45.

6. Edward Winslow, *Good Newes from New England* [London, 1624], in Alexander Young, ed., *Chronicles of the Pilgrim Fathers of the Colony of Plymouth from 1602 to 1625* (2d ed., Boston, 1844), 363.

7. Bushnell, *Native Cemeteries,* 73ff.; Karl Schmitt, Jr., "Patawomeke: An Historic Algonkian Site," Arch. Soc. of Va., *Q. Bull.,* 20:1 (Sept. 1965), 1-36; Robert L. Stephenson and Alice L. L. Ferguson, *The Accokeek Creek Site: A Middle Atlantic Seaboard Culture Sequence,* University of Michigan, Museum of Anthropology, Anthropological Papers, 20 (1963), 59-74; D. S. Davidson, "Burial Customs in the Delmarva Peninsula and the Question of Their Chronology," *American Antiquity,* 1 (1935), 84-97; Douglas H. Ubelaker, *Reconstruction of Demographic Profiles from Ossuary Skeletal Samples: A Case Study from the Tidewater Potomac,* Smithsonian Contributions to Anthropology, 18 (1974), 8-14; Kenyon, "Geometry of Death," 27-32; Kenneth E. Kidd, "The Excavation and Identification of a Huron Ossuary," *Amer. Antiq.,* 18 (1953), 359-79.

8. Charlevoix, *Journal of a Voyage,* 2:189, 192; Lafitau, *Customs of the American Indians,* 2:240; Van der Donck, *New Netherlands,* 87; Lindeström, *Geographia Americae,* 250; Simmons, *Cautantowit's House,* 58; Roger Williams, *A Key into the Language of America* (London, 1643), 5, 202; Thomas Morton, *New English Canaan* [London, 1632], in Peter Force, ed., *Tracts and Other Papers Relating Principally to the Origin, Settlement, and Progress*

of the Colonies in North America, 4 vols. (Washington, D.C., 1836-47), vol. 2, no. 5, p. 36.

9. Lafitau, *Customs of the American Indians*, 2:230.

10. John Witthoft, "Archaeology as a Key to the Colonial Fur Trade," *Minnesota History* 40:4 (Winter 1966), 204-5; Bruce G. Trigger, *The Children of Aataentsic: A History of the Huron People to 1660*, 2 vols. (Montreal, 1976), 1:236-45; Henry W. Heisey and J. Paul Witmer, "Of Historic Susquehannock Cemeteries," *Pa. Arch.*, 32:3-4 (Dec. 1962), 104, 129. The Draper site (*ca.* 1500 A.D.) at the Toronto Airport has yielded a few brass fragments (James V. Wright, personal communication, Oct. 26, 1979).

11. Robert P. Carroll and John H. Reeves, Jr., "Conner's Midden, A Halifax County, Virginia, Indian Site," Arch. Soc. of Va., *Q. Bull.*, 10:2 (Dec. 1955), n.p.; Wray and Schoff, "Seneca Sequence," 55; Heisey and Witmer, "Historic Susquehannock Cemeteries," 104; Jacob W. Gruber, "Patterning in Death in a Late Prehistoric Village in Pennsylvania," *Amer. Antiq.* 36 (1971), 64-76; William A. Ritchie, "Dutch Hollow, an Early Historic Period Seneca Site in Livingston County, New York," *Research Records of the Rochester Museum of Arts and Sciences*, 10 (1954), 5.

12. Heisey and Witmer, "Historic Susquehannock Cemeteries," 105; Witthoft and Kinsey, *Susquehannock Miscellany*, 32, 49, 113; Carroll and Reeves, "Conner's Midden," n.p.; Ritchie, "Dutch Hollow," 28; Earnest A. Hooton, "Indian Village Site and Cemetery near Madisonville, Ohio," *Papers of the Peabody Museum of American Archaeology and Ethnology*, 8:1 (1920), 17; *Zeisberger's History of the Northern American Indians*, 90; Simmons, *Cautantowwit's House*, 46. The Iroquois still buried their dead with "soul food" in the 1820s and the 1950s. William N. Fenton, "Answers to Governor Cass's Questions by Jacob Jameson, A Seneca," *Ethnohistory*, 16:2 (Spring 1969), 123; Annemarie Anrod Shimony, *Conservatism Among the Iroquois at the Six Nations Reserve*, Yale University Publications in Anthropology, 65 (1961), 242.

13. Ritchie, "Dutch Hollow," 35, 61; Herbert C. Kraft, "Indian Prehistory of New Jersey," in Kraft, ed., *A Delaware Indian Symposium*, Pa. His. and Mus. Comm., Anthrop. Ser., 4 (Harrisburg, 1974), 28, 38, 44-45; Wray and Schoff, "Seneca Sequence," 55; W. Fred Kinsey III and Jeffrey R. Graybill, "Murry Site and Its Role in Lancaster and Funk Phases of Shenk's Ferry Culture," *Pa. Arch.*, 41:4 (Dec. 1971), 13; Witthoft and Kinsey, eds., *Susque-*

hannock Miscellany, 32; William A. Ritchie and Robert E. Funk, *Aboriginal Settlement Patterns in the Northeast,* New York State Museum and Science Service, Memoir 20 (Albany, 1973), 355-60, 366; Trigger, *Children of Aataentsic,* 1:109, 111, 137-39, 147.

14. Kinsey and Graybill, "Murry Site," 17; Hooton, "Indian Site near Madisonville, Ohio," 15-16; Benthall, *Shannon Site,* 43; Howard A. MacCord, "The Crab Orchard Site," Eastern States Archaeological Federation, *Bulletin,* 31 (1972), 8; MacCord, "The Quicksburg Site, Shenandoah County, Virginia," Arch. Soc. of Va., *Q. Bull.,* 27:3 (March 1973), 121-40; MacCord, "The Elm Hill Site, Mecklenburg County, Virginia," *ibid.,* 23:2 (Dec. 1968), 63-83; Gruber, "Patterning in Death," 64-76.

15. Wray and Schoff, "Seneca Sequence," 56-59; Heisey and Witmer, "Historic Susquehannock Cemeteries," 104-5; Herbert C. Kraft, *The Minisink Site: A reevaluation of a late prehistoric and early contact site in Sussex County, New Jersey* (South Orange, N.J.: Arch. Res. Center, Seton Hall Univ., 1978), 50, 55 (table 12); Maurice Robbins, "Some Indian Burials from Southeastern Massachusetts, Part 1," Massachusetts Archaeological Society, *Bulletin,* 20:2 (Jan. 1959), 17-32; Charles C. Willoughby, "Indian Burial Place at Winthrop, Massachusetts," *Papers of the Peabody Mus. of Amer. Arch. and Ethnol.,* 11:1 (1924), 1-37; Simmons, *Cautantowwit's House,* 52, 55, 60, 68.

16. For archaeological evidence of disease, see Kenyon, "Geometry of Death," 29-30; Wray and Schoff, "Seneca Sequence," 55; Ritchie, "Dutch Hollow," 6, 10, 13; R. P. Gravely, Jr., "The Madison Cemetery [Dan River, N.C.]," East. St. Arch. Fed., *Bull.,* 26-27 (1969), 11-12; Dena F. Dincauze, "An Introduction to Archaeology in the Greater Boston Area," *Archaeology of Eastern North America,* 2:1 (Spring 1974), 57. The social importance of funeral rites in traditional, tightly knit communities is explored in Arnold van Gennep, *The Rites of Passage,* trans. Monika B. Vizedom and Gabrielle L. Caffee (Chicago, 1960), ch. 8; Robert Hertz, *Death & The Right Hand,* trans. Rodney and Claudia Needham (Glencoe, Ill., 1960), 76-86; Robert Blauner, "Death and Social Structure," *Psychiatry,* 29 (1966), 378-94; David E. Stannard, *The Puritan Way of Death: A Study in Religion, Culture, and Social Change* (New York, 1977), 126-34; Keith Thomas, *Religion and the Decline of Magic* (London, 1971), 605-6.

17. George Percy, "A Trewe Relacyon of . . . Virginia," *Tyler's Quarterly Historical and Genealogical Magazine,* 3 (1922), 263.

18. *A Journal of the Pilgrims at Plymouth: Mourt's Relation* [London, 1622], ed. Dwight B. Heath (New York, 1963), 21, 27-28, 34.

19. Williams, *Key into the Language of America*, 203; Morton, *New English Canaan*, in Force, *Tracts*, vol. 2, no. 5, pp. 35-36, 72-73.

20. *Collections of the Massachusetts Historical Society*, 4th ser. 6 (1863), 287; Charlevoix, *Journal of a Voyage*, 2:153.

21. Nicolas Denys, *The Description and Natural History of the Coasts of North America (Acadia)*, ed. and trans. William F. Ganong (Toronto: The Champlain Society, 1908), 439; Father Gabriel Sagard, *The Long Journey to the Country of the Hurons*, ed. George M. Wrong, trans. H. H. Langton (Toronto: The Champlain Society, 1939), 209.

22. Lafitau, *Customs of the American Indians*, 2:239; Wray and Schoff, "Seneca Sequence," 54, 58; Witthoft and Kinsey, eds., *Susquehannock Miscellany*, 105; Witthoft, "Archaeology as a Key," 209.

23. For other examples of European grave robbing and religious desecration, see *Father Louis Hennepin's Description of Louisiana* [Paris, 1683], trans. Marion E. Cross (Minneapolis, 1938), 125; *Lieut. Henry Timberlake's Memoirs, 1756-1765*, ed. Samuel Cole Williams (Johnson City, Tenn., 1927), 90-91; *Proceedings of the Council of Maryland, 1667-1687/8* (Baltimore, 1887), 480; *Records and Files of the Quarterly Courts of Essex County, Massachusetts*, (Salem, 1913), 3 (1662-67), 399-400; Lindeström, *Geographia Americae*, 251.

24. Morton, *New English Canaan*, in Force, *Tracts*, vol. 2, no. 5, p. 73; Charles E. Cleland, ed., *The Lasanen Site: An Historic Burial Locality in Mackinac County, Michigan*, Publications of the Museum, Michigan State University, Anthropological Ser. 1:1 (1971), 94-95.

25. Morton, *New English Canaan*, in Force, *Tracts*, vol. 2, no. 5, p. 36; Winslow, *Good Newes*, in Young, *Chronicles of the Pilgrim Fathers*, 363. On the social differentiation of burials in general, see Lewis R. Binford, "Mortuary Practices: Their Study and Their Potential," in James A. Brown, ed., *Approaches to the Social Dimensions of Mortuary Practices*, Memoirs of the Society for American Archaeology, 25, issued as *Amer. Antiq.*, 36:3, pt. 2 (July 1971), 6-29.

26. Morton, *New English Canaan*, in Force, *Tracts*, vol. 2, no. 5, p. 36.

27. *Colls. Mass. His. Soc.*, 3d ser. 4 (1834), 116, 259; *Zeisberger's History of the Northern American Indians*, 89.

28. Alexander Long, "A Small Postscript of the ways and maners of

the Indians called Charikees" [1725], ed. David H. Corkran, *Southern Indian Studies*, 21 (Oct. 1969), 26.

29. Denys, *Description of the Coasts of North America*, 440.

30. Lafitau, *Customs of the American Indians*, 2:252.

31. Reuben Gold Thwaites, ed., *The Jesuit Relations and Allied Documents*, 73 vols. (Cleveland, 1896-1901), 60:33 (hereafter cited as *JR*).

32. *JR*, 8:267-69 (dogs), 37:49, 62:39, 63:183-85.

33. Denys, *Description of the Coasts of North America*, 440, 442.

34. Howard M. Chapin, "Indian Graves: A Survey of the Indian Graves that have been Discovered in Rhode Island," Rhode Island Historical Society, *Collections*, 20:1 (Jan. 1927), 18-19.

35. William Biglow, *History of the Town of Natick, Massachusetts* (Boston, 1830), 15-16. I am grateful to Kathleen Bragdon for this reference.

36. Wilfred Jury and Elsie McLeod Jury, *Sainte-Marie Among the Hurons* (Toronto, 1954), 92-93.

37. *Colls. Mass. His. Soc.*, 3d ser. 4 (1834), 65; *JR*, 8:269, 32:71; *Zeisberger's History of the Northern American Indians*, 89; Fenton, "Answers to Gov. Cass's Questions," 123; George G. Heye and George H. Pepper, "Explorations of a Munsee Cemetery near Montague, New Jersey," *Contributions from the Museum of the American Indian, Heye Foundation*, 2 (1915-16), 76; Kraft, *Pahàquarra Site*, 57-59; Bushnell, *Native Cemeteries*, 23-24, 88.

38. Bushnell, *Native Cemeteries*, 34, 40, 88; Duane H. King and Danny E. Olinger, "Oconastota," *Amer. Antiq.*, 37:2 (1972), 223, 226.

39. Stanley Pargellis, ed., "The Indians in Virginia . . . 1689," *William and Mary Quarterly*, 3d ser. 16 (1959), 234. See also Wray and Schoff, "Seneca Sequence," 59, 61; Kraft, *Minisink Site*, 49, 52; Hadlock, "Three Contact Burials," 65; Foster H. Saville, "A Montauk Cemetery at Easthampton, Long Island," Mus. of the Amer. Indian, Heye Foundation, *Indian Notes and Monographs*, 2:3 (1920), 75; George H. Abrams, "The Cornplanter Cemetery," *Pa. Arch.*, 35:2 (Aug. 1965), 66-67 (fig. 1). The Shenk's Ferry people of Pennsylvania and the late-prehistoric inhabitants of Madisonville, Ohio, were unusual in burying most of their dead in an extended position well before the contact period. Barry C. Kent, Ira F. Smith, and Catherine McCann, *Foundations of Pennsylvania Prehistory*, Pa. His. and Mus. Comm., Anthrop. Ser. 1 (Harrisburg, 1971), 334; Hooton, "Indian Site near Madisonville, Ohio," 11.

40. Harris Hawthorne Wilder, "Excavation of Indian Graves in Western Massachusetts," *Amer. Anthrop.*, 7 (1905), 299-300; Hadlock,

"Three Contact Burials," 65; Simmons, *Cautantowwit's House*, 60; Binford, "Mortuary Practices," 12.

41. Jacob W. Gruber, "Champlain's Dead: The Cemetery at St. Croix" (unpublished paper). Thanks to Professor Gruber for a copy of his paper. See also Walter Johnson, *Byways in British Archaeology* (Cambridge, Eng., 1912), 243-67.

42. *Zeisberger's History of the Northern American Indians*, 89; *JR*, 8:257-59, 35:95-97, 60:33, 39.

43. *Colls. Mass. His. Soc.*, 3d ser. 4 (1834), 40.

44. *Ibid.*, 116.

45. Daniel Gookin, *Historical Collections of the Indians in New England* [1674], ed. Jeffrey H. Fiske (Towtaid, N.J., 1970), 19.

46. *JR*, 34:100.

47. *JR*, 8:253-55, 10:305-7, 23:31, 26:209-11, 60:31.

48. *JR*, 30:123.

49. Charlevoix, *Journal of a Voyage*, 2:189, Lindeström, *Geographia Americae*, 250-51. Gabriel Sagard testified that only when "it is cast up at [the Hurons] that one of their relations is dead" did he see them lose self-control (*Long Journey*, 202).

50. Lafitau, *Customs of the American Indians*, 2:240-41.

51. Williams, *Key into the Language of America*, 202.

52. Simmons, *Cautantowwit's House*, 58.

53. Baron de Lahontan, *New Voyages to North-America*, ed. Reuben Gold Thwaites, 2 vols. (Chicago, 1905), 2:473.

54. Morton, *New English Canaan*, in Force, *Tracts*, vol. 2, no. 5, p. 36.

55. Kathleen Bragdon and Ives Goddard, personal communications, Oct. 27, 1979.

56. Nantucket Registry of Deeds, Bk. 2, pp. 1 (1678), 5 (1686), Nantucket Historical Association, Nantucket, Mass. Elizabeth Little kindly drew these deeds to my attention.

CHAPTER SIX

1. John Locke, *Two Treatises of Government*, ed. Peter Laslett (Cambridge, Eng., 1960), Bk. II, sec. 49, 319, sec. 19, 298.

2. *Ibid.*, sec. 19, 298.

3. See above, Chapters 3-5.

4. William Hubbard, *The History of the Indian Wars in New England* [1677], ed. Samuel G. Drake, 2 vols. (Roxbury, Mass., 1865),

2:256-57; Emma Lewis Coleman, *New England Captives Carried to Canada* . . . , 2 vols. (Portland, Me., 1925), 1:204-5.

5. William Bradford, *Of Plymouth Plantation 1620-1647*, ed. Samuel Eliot Morison (New York, 1952), 79-81.

6. *Ibid.*, 81, 85.

7. William Wood, *New Englands Prospect* . . . (London, 1634), 70.

8. Roger Williams, *A Key into the Language of America* . . . [1643], in *The Complete Writings of Roger Williams*, 7 vols. (New York, 1963), 1:36, 46-47. Daniel Gookin, perhaps the second best authority, wrote that "they are much given to hospitality in their way. If any strangers come to their houses, they will give him the best lodging and diet they have" (*Historical Collections of the Indians in New England* [1674], *Collections of the Massachusetts Historical Society*, 1st ser. 1 [1792], 153, hereafter cited as *Historical Collections of the Indians*).

9. Thomas Lechford, *Plain Dealing: or, Newes from New-England* [1642], *Colls. Mass. Hist. Soc.*, 3d ser. 3 [1833], 104 (hereafter cited as *Plain Dealing*).

10. Williams, *Complete Writings*, 1:73, 129; H. L. Mencken, *The American Language: An Inquiry into the Development of English in the United States* (New York, 1919), 51-53; John Josselyn, *An Account of Two Voyages to New-England* [1675], *Colls. Mass. Hist. Soc.*, 3d ser. 3 (1833), 251-94 (hereafter cited as *Account of Two Voyages*).

11. Nathaniel B. Shurtleff, ed., *Records of the Colony of New Plymouth in New England*, 12 vols. (Boston, 1855-61), 2:20 (June 17, 1641).

12. Lechford, *Plain Dealing*, 106.

13. Edmund S. Morgan, ed., *The Founding of Massachusetts: Historians and the Sources* (Indianapolis, 1964), 320.

14. Alden T. Vaughan, *New England Frontier: Puritans and Indians, 1620-1675* (Boston, 1965), 37-38, 55.

15. Charles Orr, ed., *History of the Pequot War* (Cleveland, 1897), 82, 84. Roger Williams observed the same kind of fighting among the Narragansetts to the East (*Complete Writings*, 1:204).

16. Orr, ed., *Pequot War*, 130.

17. *Ibid.*, 60-62, 84; Vaughan, *New England Frontier*, 40.

18. Orr, ed., *Pequot War*, 51 (my emphasis).

19. Vaughan, *New England Frontier*, 153-54.

20. Hubbard, *Indian Wars*, 1:70-71, 133-34.

21. Charles H. Lincoln, ed., *Narratives of the Indian Wars 1675-1699*,

Original Narratives of Early American History (New York, 1913), 57, 238.

22. Hubbard, *Indian Wars*, 1:132; 2:259-60.

23. Solomon Stoddard to Joseph Dudley, Oct. 22, 1703, *New-England Historical and Genealogical Register*, 24 (1870), 269-70 (my emphasis).

24. Increase Mather, *The History of King Philip's War*, ed. Samuel G. Drake (Boston, 1862), 101n.

25. *The Acts and Resolves . . . of the Province of the Massachusetts Bay . . . ,* 21 vols. (Boston, 1869-1922), 1:175-76, 594. Just how a bona fide scalp was to be distinguished from a false one was not suggested.

26. *Ibid.,* 1:530, 558, 594, 2:259; Samuel Penhallow, *The History of the War of New-England with the Eastern Indians . . .* [1726] (Cincinnati, 1859), 48, 93.

27. Wood, *New Englands Prospect,* 84.

28. Williams, *Complete Writings,* 1:78.

29. Hubbard, *History of the Indian Wars,* 2:206.

30. William L. Sachse, *The Diurnal of Thomas Rugg, 1659-1661* (London, 1961), 116. For only a few of the scalping victims who survived, see Penhallow, *Wars of New-England,* 76; Hubbard, *Indian Wars,* 1:129; Gookin, *Historical Collections of the Indians,* 162.

31. Mather, *King Philip's War,* 206-7.

32. Lincoln, ed., *Narratives of the Indian Wars,* 31.

33. Hubbard, *Indian Wars,* 1:85, 87.

34. Benjamin Church, *The History of King Philip's War* [1716], ed. Henry Martyn Dexter (Boston, 1865), 67, 122-23; Church, *The History of the Eastern Expeditions against the Indians and French* [1716], ed. Dexter (Boston, 1867), 86.

35. Church, *King Philip's War,* 28, 32-33, 121, 133, 145; Church, *History of Eastern Expeditions,* 133.

36. Cotton Mather, *Souldiers Counselled and Comforted* (Boston, 1689), 28.

37. Church, *King Philip's War,* 110.

38. *Ibid.,* 45-47.

39. *Ibid.,* 66.

40. *Ibid.,* 137-38.

41. Hubbard, *Indian Wars,* 1:112-13, 212.

42. Williams, *Complete Writings,* 1:145.

43. Father Sébastien Râle to Monsieur his Brother, Oct. 12, 1723, in Reuben Gold Thwaites, ed., *The Jesuit Relations and Allied Docu-*

ments, 73 vols. (Cleveland, 1896-1901), 67:135; Josselyn, *Account of Two Voyages,* 297.

44. Hubbard, *Indian Wars,* 1:158, 2:130; *Mass. Acts and Resolves,* 1:547, 8:42, 92, 429; Penhallow, *Wars of New-England,* 41.

45. Lincoln, ed., *Narratives of the Indian Wars,* 30.

46. Samuel G. Drake, ed., *Tragedies of the Wilderness* . . . (Boston, 1846), 125.

47. Orr, ed., *Pequot War,* 71; J. Franklin Jameson, ed., *Johnson's Wonder-Working Providence 1628-1651,* Orig. Narrs. of Early Amer. Hist. (New York, 1910), 149-50, 263 (my emphasis).

48. Wood, *New Englands Prospect,* 62-63.

49. Josselyn, *Account of Two Voyages,* 294.

50. Wilcomb E. Washburn, "A Moral History of Indian-White Relations: Needs and Opportunities for Study," *Ethnohistory,* 4 (1957), 51.

51. James Kendall Hosmer, ed., [John] *Winthrop's Journal "History of New England" 1630-1649,* Orig. Narrs. of Early Amer. Hist., 2 vols. (New York, 1908), 1:67.

52. Shurtleff, ed., *Plymouth Colony Records,* 1:132, 6:98.

53. Nathaniel B. Shurtleff, ed., *Records of the Governor and Company of the Massachusetts Bay in New England,* 6 vols. (Boston, 1853-54), 1:140 (Mar. 4, 1635).

54. Hubbard, *Indian Wars,* 1:162; Lincoln, ed., *Narratives of the Indian Wars,* 67.

55. J. Hammond Trumbull and C. J. Hoadly, eds., *The Public Records of the Colony of Connecticut,* 15 vols. (Hartford, 1850-90), 1:530.

56. William Willis *et al.,* eds., *Documentary History of the State of Maine, Collections of the Maine Historical Society,* 2d ser. 4 (1889), 298 (hereafter cited as *Documentary History of Maine*); Charles Thornton Libby *et al.,* eds. *Province and Court Records of Maine,* Maine Hist. Soc., Publications, 1-5 (Portland, Me., 1928-), hereafter cited as *Maine Records.*

57. Hubbard, *Indian Wars,* 2:256; Cotton Mather, *Magnalia Christi Americana* (London, 1702), Bk. 1, 15; *Documentary History of Maine,* 3:171, July 10, 1639; *Maine Records,* 2:78, July 4, 1659.

58. Charles Chauncy, *Gods Mercy, Shewed to his People* . . . (Cambridge, Mass., 1655), 15-16.

59. Jameson, ed., *Johnson's Wonder-Working Providence,* 223; Sarah Knight, *The Private Journal kept by Madame Knight, On a Journey from Boston to New-York in the Year 1704* (Albany, 1865), 55;

Increase Mather, *The Necessity of Reformation* . . . (Boston, 1679), 7; Joseph Easterbrooks, *Abraham the Passenger* (Boston, 1705), 3.

60. Jameson, ed., *Winthrop's Journal*, 2:80; Shurtleff, ed., *Plymouth Colony Records*, 3:6-7, 5:169; Cotton Mather, *Frontiers Well-Defended* (Boston, 1707), 50.

61. Edward Howes to John Winthrop, Jr., Nov. 9, 1631, *Winthrop Papers* (Boston: Massachusetts Historical Society, 1929-), 3:55; Trumbull and Hoadly, eds., *Connecticut Colony Records*, 2:328.

62. Cotton here followed his father Increase, who contended in 1679 that the chief fault of New England was in family government, in which too many parents and masters were "sinfully indulgent" toward their children. "In this respect, Christians in this Land, have become too like unto the Indians" (*Necessity of Reformation*, 5).

63. Cotton Mather, *The Way to Prosperity* (Boston, 1690), 27, 34; Mather, *A Letter to Ungospellized Plantations* (Boston, 1702), 14; Mather, *The Present State of New England* . . . (Boston, 1690), 32; Henry Lefavour, "The Proposed College in Hampshire County in 1762," *Proceedings of the Massachusetts Historical Society*, 66 (1936-41), 53-79 at 77.

64. Leonard W. Labaree *et al.*, eds., *The Papers of Benjamin Franklin* (New Haven, 1959-), 4:481-82 (May 9, 1755).

65. J. Hector St. John de Crèvecoeur, *Letters from an American Farmer* . . . [1782] (London, 1912), 213-15 (my emphasis). Pierre de Charlevoix tells us that the French "in rather large numbers" were equally captivated by the Indian mode of life and would not return to "civilization" (*Le Journal d'un Voyage* . . . *dans l'Amérique Septentrionnalle* [Paris, 1744], 6:32-33).

66. In 1972, when this essay first appeared, I had roughly calculated from Coleman, *New England Captives*, 1:ch. 4, that about 600 New English had been captured in this period. A recent computer-assisted study by Alden Vaughan and Daniel Richter has established that only 520 persons were captured and that only (an admittedly conservative) 7.1 percent stayed with the Indians. While I gladly accept a *somewhat* lower figure for New England's "white Indians," I do not agree with all their quantitative manipulations or their conclusions about the relative educational success of the Indians and the New English ("Crossing the Cultural Divide: Indians and New Englanders, 1605-1763," *Proceedings of the American Antiquarian Society*, 90, pt. 1 [Oct. 1980], 23-99).

67. Coleman, *New England Captives*, 2:153 (my emphasis).

68. Erwin H. Ackerknecht, "White Indians," *Bulletin of the History of Medicine*, 15 (1944), 35; Coleman, *New England Captives*, 1: 120-21, 2:88, 312.

69. John Williams, *The Redeemed Captive Returning to Zion* . . . [Boston, 1707] (Springfield, Mass., 1908), 52-53, 58, 70; Coleman, *New England Captives*, 2:78, 96.

70. When Stephen Williams showed some eagerness to be bought by a Frenchman, his Indian captors prevented it and threatened him with death for being ungrateful for his preservation and adoption. "It is no wonder," he wrote, "that children that are small will not speak to their friends when they come to see them, but they will scofe and deride them, because the indians have taught them so, will be angry if they do otherwise" (*What Befell Stephen Williams in his Captivity* [Deerfield, Mass., 1889], 9).

71. *A Narrative of the Captivity of Mrs. Johnson* . . . [Walpole, N.H., 1796] (Springfield, Mass., 1907), 67-68, 71, 76-77.

72. Coleman, *New England Captives*, 2:254.

73. *The Indian Captive; or a Narrative of the Captivity and Sufferings of Zadock Steele* [Montpelier, Vt., 1818] (Springfield, Mass., 1908), 70-72.

74. Crèvecoeur, *Letters*, 215.

75. *Ibid.*, 215; Labaree *et al.*, *Franklin Papers*, 4:481-83; Crèvecoeur, *Letters*, 215.

76. Williams, *Redeemed Captive*, 37, emphasis mine.

77. Marianne Moore, "New York," *Observations* (New York, 1924), 65.

CHAPTER SEVEN

1. See, for example, Samuel Purchas, *Hakluytus Posthumus or Purchas His Pilgrimes* [London, 1625], 20 vols. (Glasgow, 1905-6), 19:406-9, and Merrill Jensen, ed., *American Colonial Documents to 1776*, in David C. Douglas, ed., *English Historical Documents*, 12 vols. (New York, 1955), 9:65, 82, 85, 93.

2. Robert Gray, *A Good Speed to Virginia* (London, 1609), sigs. [C1*v*]-C2*r*. See also Michael Wigglesworth, *God's Controversy with New-England* [1662], Massachusetts Historical Society, *Proceedings*, 12 (1873), ll. 57-68, 169; H. H. Brackenridge in Archibald Loudon, ed., *A Selection, of Some of the Most Interesting Narratives, of Outrages, Committed by the Indians, in Their Wars, with the White People*, 2 vols. (Carlisle, Pa., 1808-11), 1:v; and [William

Smith, D.D.], *Historical Account of Colonel Bouquet's Expedition Against the Ohio Indians, in 1764* [Philadelphia, 1765] (Cincinnati, 1868), 77-78 (hereafter cited as *Bouquet's Expedition*).

3. Cotton Mather, *India Christiana* (Boston, 1721), 28-29. See also Solomon Stoddard, *Question, Whether God is not Angry with the Country for doing so little towards the Conversion of the Indians?* (Boston, 1723), 10.

4. *Bouquet's Expedition*, 80-81.

5. I am presently at work on a book entitled *The Invasion Within: The Contest of Cultures in Colonial North America* that will explore both the Europeans who ran away to join Indian societies and the many reasons for the English—and French—failure to convert the Indians to civilization and Christianity. For a preliminary discussion of the latter subject, see above, Chapter 3.

6. Cadwallader Colden, *The History of the Five Indian Nations of Canada* (London, 1747), 203-4 (1st pag.).

7. Benjamin Franklin to Peter Collinson, May 9, 1753, in Leonard W. Labaree *et al.*, eds., *The Papers of Benjamin Franklin* (New Haven, 1959-   ), 4:481-82.

8. J. Hector St. John de Crèvecoeur, *Letters from an American Farmer* [1782] (London, 1912), 215. Other contemporaries who recognized the disparity between Indian and European conversion results were Pierre de Charlevoix, *Journal of a Voyage to North-America*, 2 vols. (London, 1761), 2:108; Joseph Doddridge, *Notes on the Settlement and Indian Wars of the Western Parts of Virginia and Pennsylvania, from 1763 to 1783, Inclusive* [Wellsburgh, Va., 1824], ed. Alfred Williams (Albany, 1876), 218; Adolph B. Benson, ed., *Peter Kalm's Travels in North America: The English Version of 1770*, 2 vols. (New York, 1937), 2:456-57; Johann David Schoepf, *Travels in the Confederation [1783-1784]*, trans. and ed. Alfred J. Morrison (Philadelphia, 1911), 1:283; J. P. Brissot de Warville, *New Travels in the United States of America, 1788*, trans. Mara Soceanu Vamos and Durand Echeverria, ed. Durand Echeverria (Cambridge, Mass., 1964), 420; John F. Meginness, *Biography of Frances Slocum, the Lost Sister of Wyoming* (Williamsport, Pa., 1891), 196; and Felix Renick, "A Trip to the West," *American Pioneer*, 1 (1842), 79.

Later students of the "white Indians" are John R. Swanton, "Notes on the mental assimilation of races," *Journal of the Washington Academy of Sciences*, 16 (1926), 493-502; Erwin H. Ackerknecht, " 'White Indians': Psychological and Physiological Peculiarities of White Children Abducted and Reared by North American Indians," *Bulletin of the History of Medicine,* 15 (1944), 15-36; A. Irving Hallowell, "American Indians, White and Black: The Phenomenon of Transculturalization," *Current Anthropology,* 4 (1963), 519-31; and J. Norman Heard, *White into Red: A Study of the Assimilation of White Persons Captured by Indians* (Metuchen, N.J., 1973). All four draw upon western captives as well as colonial in a search for ethnological generalizations. See also Richard Drinnon's *White Savage: The Case of John Dunn Hunter* (New York, 1972).

9. This generalization is based on a reading of over 100 captivity narratives and accounts.

10. [William Walton], *The Captivity and Sufferings of Benjamin Gilbert and His Family, 1780-83* [Philadelphia, 1784], ed. Frank H. Severance (Cleveland, 1904), 27 (hereafter cited as *Captivity of Benjamin Gilbert*).

11. [Susannah] Johnson, *A Narrative of the Captivity of Mrs. Johnson* [Walpole, N.H., 1796], reprint of 3d rev. ed. [1814] (Springfield, Mass., 1907), 36; Emma Lewis Coleman, *New England Captives Carried to Canada . . . ,* 2 vols. (Portland, Me., 1925), 1:120-21, 132, 2:159-60, 261; Samuel G. Drake, ed., *Tragedies of the Wilderness . . .* (Boston, 1846), 100, 168, 280.

12. This is not to say that no expense was involved for the English in securing the release of captive colonists, but it was in the nature of modest presents rather than exorbitant ransoms. Sylvester K. Stevens and Donald H. Kent, eds., *The Papers of Col. Henry Bouquet,* 19 vols. (Harrisburg, Pa., 1940-43), 17:28, 169, 18:182-84 (hereafter cited as *Bouquet Papers*).

13. In the 1770s Guy Johnson and George Croghan, both authorities on the Indians of the Middle Atlantic colonies, thought that the English prisoners had been "generally adopted" rather than put to death ("The Opinions of George Croghan on the American Indian," *Pennsylvania Magazine of History and Biography,* 71 [1947], 157; "Guy Johnson's Opinions on the American Indians," *ibid.,* 77 [1953], 322). See also Mary Jemison's remarks in James E. Seaver, *A Narrative of the Life of Mrs. Mary Jemison* [Canandaigua, N.Y., 1824], ed. Allen W. Trelease (New York, 1961), 46-47 (hereafter cited as *Life of Mary Jemison*). While older men and women could be ransomed from the Middle Atlantic tribes, most Indians who had adopted English children could not be persuaded to "sell [their] own Flesh and Blood," not even for "one thousand

Dollars," as the Indian father of twelve-year-old Elizabeth Gilbert put it (*Captivity of Benjamin Gilbert*, 103, 107).

14. "Further Examination of Michael La Chauvignerie, Jun'r, 1757," in Samuel Hazard *et al.*, eds., *Pennsylvania Archives*, 3 (1853), 306; "Examination of Barbara Liningaree and Mary Roy, 1759," *ibid.*, 634; "Narrative of Marie Le Roy and Barbara Leininger, for Three Years Captives Among the Indians," *PMHB*, 29 (1905), 417-20.

15. James Sullivan *et al.*, eds., *The Papers of Sir William Johnson*, 14 vols. (Albany, 1921-62), 11:446, 484-91, 720-21 (hereafter cited as *Johnson Papers*); *Bouquet Papers*, 18:253; William S. Ewing, "Indian Captives Released by Colonel Bouquet," *Western Pennsylvania Historical Magazine*, 39 (1956), 187-203. On his two-month journey to a conference with the western Indians in 1760, John Hays saw 23 English prisoners; at least 14 were children. Their average age was 10 years. Two other prisoners were women, one aged 22 and the other "A[l]most A Woman" (*Pennsylvania Archaeologist*, 24 [1954], 63-83).

16. *Johnson Papers*, 11:466, 728.

17. *Bouquet Papers*, 17:51.

18. *Ibid.*, 38; "Provincial Correspondence: 1750 to 1765," in Samuel Hazard *et al.*, eds., *Register of Pennsylvania*, 4 (1829), 390; *A Narrative of the Captivity of John McCullough, Esq.*, in Loudon, ed., *Selection of Some of the Most Interesting Narratives*, 1:326-27; *Bouquet's Expedition*, 80.

19. "Provincial Correspondence," 390-91; *Johnson Papers*, 11:496-98.

20. *Bouquet's Expedition*, 76, 80; *Johnson Papers*, 4:500; "Provincial Correspondence," 390; "Relation by Frederick Post of Conversation with Indians, 1760," *Pa. Archives*, 3 (1853), 742. I have translated Post's phonetic German spelling.

21. "Prisoners Delivered to Gov., by the Six Nations, 1762," *Pa. Archives*, 4 (1853), 100-101; *Johnson Papers*, 11:720-21; Coleman, *New England Captives*, 1:323, 2:58. In a "List of Prisoners deliv[ere]d up by the Shawanese Nations of Indians at *Fort Pit, 10th May 1765*," the following names were among those given for 14 captives who had been with the Indians from 2 to 10 years: Wechquessinah ("cant speak Eng[li]sh. knows not from whence taken"), Joseph or Pechyloothume, Jenny or Ketakatwitch, Wapatenaqua, and Nalupeia, sister to Molly Bird (*Johnson Papers*, 11:720-21). In an earlier list were Sour Mouth, Crooked Legs, Pouter or Wynima, David Bighead, Sore Knee, Sour Plumbs (*Bouquet Papers*, 18:248). It would be important to know if these names were given in deri-

sion to resistant, older captives, or in good humor to accepting, younger ones.

22. *Johnson Papers*, 11:812; *Bouquet Papers*, 17:39-41.

23. Benson, ed., *Peter Kalm's Travels*, 2:457; Coleman, *New England Captives*, 1:296, 2:11; O. M. Spencer, *The Indian Captivity of O. M. Spencer* [New York, 1835], ed. Milo Milton Quaife, reprint of 1917 ed. (New York, 1968), 168-69; Samuel Stanhope Smith, *An Essay on the Causes of the Variety of Complexion and Figure in the Human Species* [Philadelphia, 1787] (2d ed., New Brunswick, N.J., 1810), 70n-71n. See also Bernard W. Sheehan, *Seeds of Extinction: Jeffersonian Philanthropy and the American Indian* (Chapel Hill, 1973), ch. 1, esp. 40-42; and Doddridge, *Notes on the Settlement and Indian Wars*, 91.

24. Coleman, *New England Captives*, 2:91, 117-18; *Johnson Papers*, 10:160, 11:728. O. M. Spencer's Indian father for "several years" paid him an annual visit (*Indian Captivity of O. M. Spencer*, 171).

25. *Captivity of Benjamin Gilbert*, 181; Thomas Ridout, "An Account of My Capture By the Shawanese Indians . . ." [1788], *Blackwood's Magazine*, 223 (1928), 313.

26. *Bouquet's Expedition*, 80-81.

27. Drake, ed., *Tragedies of the Wilderness*, 128; Stephen Williams, *What Befell Stephen Williams in his Captivity* [Greenfield, Mass., 1837], ed. George Sheldon (Deerfield, Mass., 1889), 5; John Williams, *The Redeemed Captive Returning to Zion* [Boston, 1707] (Springfield, Mass., 1908), 14, 30.

28. Captivity narrative of Joseph Bartlett in Joshua Coffin, *A Sketch of the History of Newbury . . .* (Boston, 1845), 332; *An Account of the Remarkable Occurrences in the Life and Travels of Col. James Smith* [1799], in Howard Peckham, ed., *Narratives of Colonial America, 1704-1765* (Chicago, 1971), 82; Samuel Lee to Nehemiah Grew, 1690, *Publications of the Colonial Society of Massachusetts*, 14 (1911-13), 148.

29. *What Befell Stephen Williams*, 6; Drake, ed., *Tragedies of the Wilderness*, 61.

30. Charles H. Lincoln, ed., *Narratives of the Indian Wars, 1675-1699*, Original Narratives of Early American History (New York, 1913), 30; Drake, *Tragedies of the Wilderness*, 125, 145; Ridout, "Account of My Capture," 303; *Bouquet's Expedition*, 78; "Provincial Correspondence," 390-91.

31. J. Franklin Jameson, ed., *Johnson's Wonder-Working Providence, 1628-1651*, Orig. Narrs. of Early Amer. Hist. (New York, 1910), 150,

263; "Morrell's Poem on New England," *Collections of the Massachusetts Historical Society,* 1st ser. 1 (1792), 135.

32. Charles Thomson in Thomas Jefferson, *Notes on the State of Virginia,* ed. William Peden (Chapel Hill, 1955), 200; "Opinions of George Croghan," 157. See also *Life of Mary Jemison,* 73, and Sylvester K. Stevens *et al.,* eds., *Travels in New France by J. C. B.* (Harrisburg, Pa., 1941), 69.

33. [James] *Adair's History of the American Indians* [London, 1775], ed. Samuel Cole Williams (Kingsport, Tenn., 1930), 171.

34. Jeremy Belknap, *The History of New Hampshire,* 3 vols. (2d ed., Boston, 1813), 1:229.

35. Drake, ed., *Tragedies of the Wilderness,* 61, 115-16, 145, 158; Thomas Hutchinson, *The History of the Colony and Province of Massachusetts-Bay,* ed. Lawrence Shaw Mayo, 2 vols. (Cambridge, Mass., 1936), 2:104n; Mrs. Harriet S. Caswell, *Our Life Among the Iroquois* (Boston, 1892), 53. See also *Life of Mary Jemison,* 47, 57, and Timothy Alden, ed., "An Account of the Captivity of Hugh Gibson . . . ," *Colls. Mass. His. Soc.,* 3d ser. 6 (1837), 153. The source of Hutchinson's information was Williams, *Redeemed Captive.* Jacob Lunenburg was bound so tightly on his captor's back that he was somewhat crippled for life (Coleman, *New England Captives,* 2:215).

36. Johnson, *Narrative of the Captivity of Mrs. Johnson,* 62; [Titus King], *Narrative of Titus King* . . . (Hartford, 1938), 10; Meginness, *Biography of Frances Slocum,* 65. See also Peckham, ed., *Narratives of Colonial America,* 89; Howard H. Peckham, ed., "Thomas Gist's Indian Captivity, 1758-1759," *PMHB,* 80 (1956), 297; [Zadock Steele], *The Indian Captive; or a Narrative of the Captivity and Sufferings of Zadock Steele* . . . [Montpelier, Vt., 1818] (Springfield, Mass., 1908), 68; Loudon, ed., *Selection of Some of the Most Interesting Narratives,* 1:303-4.

37. Johnson, *Narrative of the Captivity of Mrs. Johnson,* 57-58; Drake, ed., *Tragedies of the Wilderness,* 129; King, *Narrative of Titus King,* 8.

38. *A Plain Narrative of the Uncommon Sufferings and Remarkable Deliverance of Thomas Brown, of Charlestown, in New-England* (2d ed., Boston, 1760), in *Magazine of History with Notes and Queries,* Extra Number no. 4 (1908), 8, 12; *The History of the Life and Sufferings of Henry Grace, of Basingstoke in the County of Southampton* [Reading, Eng., 1764] (2d ed., London, 1765), 12. See also Peckham, ed., *Narratives of Colonial America,* 81; Peck-

ham, ed., "Thomas Gist's Indian Captivity," 298; Drake, ed., *Tragedies of the Wilderness,* 269, 272; and *Captivity of Benjamin Gilbert,* 56, 121.

39. Beverley W. Bond, Jr., ed., "The Captivity of Charles Stuart, 1755-57," *Mississippi Valley Historical Review,* 13 (1926-27), 66; "Narrative of John Brickell's Captivity Among the Delaware Indians," *American Pioneer,* 1 (1842), 46.

40. Stevens *et al.,* eds., *Travels in New France by J. C. B.,* 68; Charlevoix, *Journal of a Voyage,* 1:369-70; "Narrative of Marie Le Roy and Barbara Leininger," 409.

41. *Captivity of Benjamin Gilbert,* 56.

42. Peckham, ed., *Narratives of Colonial America,* 81. See also Alden, ed., "Captivity of Hugh Gibson," 143; Loudon, ed., *Selection of Some of the Most Interesting Narratives,* 1:306; and *Life of Mary Jemison,* 44.

43. Steele, *Indian Captive,* 70-71; Johnson, *Narrative of the Captivity of Mrs. Johnson,* 66.

44. Peckham, ed., *Narratives of Colonial America,* 91-92.

45. *Ibid.;* "John Brickell's Captivity," 46; Johnson, *Narrative of the Captivity of Mrs. Johnson,* 68.

46. *Life of Mary Jemison,* 44-47; *Captivity of Benjamin Gilbert,* 107, 123; Loudon, ed., *Selection of Some of the Most Interesting Narratives,* 307; Peckham, ed., "Thomas Gist's Indian Captivity," 299; Luke Swetland, *A Very Remarkable Narrative of Luke Swetland . . . Written by Himself* (Hartford, n.d.), 7-8.

47. *Life of Mary Jemison,* 46; King, *Narrative of Titus King,* 14; Stevens *et al., Travels in New France by J. C. B.,* 73. See also *Johnson Papers,* 13:191, and Charlevoix, *Journal of a Voyage,* 1:373.

48. *Captivity of Benjamin Gilbert,* 126-27, 135.

49. Swetland, *Remarkable Narrative,* 5; Peckham, ed., "Thomas Gist's Indian Captivity," 299; *Life of Mary Jemison,* 47.

50. Johnson, *Narrative of the Captivity of Mrs. Johnson,* 67-68, 71, 76-77.

51. "John Brickell's Captivity," 44; *Bouquet's Expedition,* 78. The Canadian captors of Titus King told him that "I Should never go hum [home] that I was an Indian now and must be and Do as they Did" (King, *Narrative of Titus King,* 14).

52. Ridout, "Account of My Capture"; John Leeth, *A Short Biography of John Leeth* [Lancaster, Ohio, 1831], ed. Reuben Gold

Thwaites (Cleveland, 1904), 28; *Captivity of Benjamin Gilbert*, 109; Steele, *Indian Captive*, 72.

53. *Captivity of Benjamin Gilbert*, 81, 83.

54. Peckham, ed., "Thomas Gist's Indian Captivity," 301; "John Brickell's Captivity," 54. Joseph Bartlett also lived with other white captives while a prisoner in Canada (Coffin, *Sketch of the History of Newbury*, 332-33).

55. *Captivity of Benjamin Gilbert*, 74, 87, 124; Alden, ed., "Captivity of Hugh Gibson," 149. Women were not the only captives alarmed by the specter of forced marriage. When Thomas Gist was first brought to the Huron village where he was to be adopted, he was made to stand naked at a post for an hour "while the Indian Ladies was satisfied as to their sight. For my part," he recalled, "I expected they was going to chuse some of the likeliest of us for husbands, by their standing and looking so long at us in this condition" (Peckham, ed., "Thomas Gist's Indian Captivity," 298).

56. *Life of Mary Jemison*, 52-53.

57. Williams, *Redeemed Captive*, 131 (my emphasis); Drake, ed., *Tragedies of the Wilderness*, 125 (my emphasis); "Provincial Correspondence," 390-91.

58. Peckham, ed., "Thomas Gist's Indian Captivity," 301; *Indian Captivity of O. M. Spencer*, 82, 120, 129.

59. Coleman, *New England Captives*, 2:107; *Biography of Leeth*, 39-40; Orlando Allen, "Incidents in the Life of an Indian Captive," *American Historical Record*, 1 (1872), 409. The "8" used by the French in Indian words signifies "w," which did not exist in French.

60. *Captivity of Benjamin Gilbert*, 135; Caswell, *Our Life Among the Iroquois*, 54; Charlevoix, *Journal of a Voyage*, 1:371; *Johnson Papers*, 4:620.

61. *Indian Captivity of O. M. Spencer*, 92-93.

62. Ridout, "Account of My Captivity," 295; Coleman, *New England Captives*, 1:21, 296, 325-26, 2:190-91.

63. Caswell, *Our Life Among the Iroquois*, 54-55.

64. A. Irving Hallowell has coined the unwieldy term "transculturalization" to denote the process whereby individuals, rather than groups, are detached from one society, enter another, and come under the influence of its customs and values ("American Indians, White and Black," 519-31).

65. King, *Narrative of Titus King*, 17; *Life of Mary Jemison*, 57; Peckham, ed., "Thomas Gist's Indian Captivity," 302.

66. Williams, *Redeemed Captive*, 37; Drake, ed., *Tragedies of the Wilderness*, 169-70.

67. *Indian Captivity of O. M. Spencer*, 120-21; Drake, ed., *Tragedies of the Wilderness*, 161.

68. Peckham, ed., "Thomas Gist's Indian Captivity," 300-301.

69. *Life of Mary Jemison*, 48; Peckham, ed., "Thomas Gist's Indian Captivity," 301.

70. Loudon, ed., *Selection of Some of the Most Interesting Narratives*, 1:307; *Indian Captivity of O. M. Spencer*, 65.

71. Renick, "A Trip to the West," 78; *Captivity of Benjamin Gilbert*, 98-100.

72. "Narrative of the Capture of Abel Janney by the Indians in 1782," *Ohio Archaeological and Historical Quarterly*, 8 (1900), 472; *Indian Captivity of O. M. Spencer*, 113, 117-18; Peckham, ed., "Thomas Gist's Indian Captivity," 300; *Life of Mary Jemison*, 55-56. See also James Axtell, ed., *The Indian Peoples of Eastern America: A Documentary History of the Sexes* (New York, 1981), ch. 4.

73. *Bouquet's Expedition*, 81.

74. Roger Williams, *A Key into the Language of America* (London, 1643); "John Brickell's Captivity," 47-49; *Life of Mary Jemison*, 72-73; Douglass Adair and John A. Schutz, ed., *Peter Oliver's Origin & Progress of the American Rebellion: A Tory View* (San Marino, Calif., 1961), 5; Coleman, *New England Captives*, 2:312. In 1758 four pro-English Delaware chiefs accused the English of treaty-breaking and hypocrisy. "We .Love you more than you Love us, for when we take any Prisoners from you we treat them as our own children; we are Poor and we cloath them as well as we can, you see our own children are as naked as the first, by this you may see our hearts are better then your heart" ("Journal of Frederick Post," *Pa. Archives*, 3 [1853], 534).

75. "Further Examination of Michael La Chauvignerie," 306; *Narrative of the Life and Adventures of Matthew Bunn . . .* [Providence, *ca.* 1796] (7th rev. ed., Batavia, N.Y.), 11; Loudon, ed., *Selection of Some of the Most Interesting Narratives*, 1:311; *Captivity of Benjamin Gilbert*, 112.

76. *Indian Captivity of O. M. Spencer*, 86; Peckham, ed., *Narratives of Colonial America*, 108.

77. Crèvecoeur, *Letters*, 214.

78. *Ibid.*, 215; Charles S. Grant, *Democracy in the Connecticut Frontier Town of Kent* (New York, 1961); Richard L. Bushman, *From*

Puritan to Yankee: Character and the Social Order in Connecticut, 1690-1765 (Cambridge, Mass., 1967); Kenneth Lockridge, "Land, Population and the Evolution of New England Society 1630-1790," Past and Present, 39 (1968), 62-80; Gary B. Nash, Quakers and Politics: Pennsylvania, 1681-1726 (Princeton, 1968); Kenneth A. Lockridge, A New England Town, The First Hundred Years: Dedham, Massachusetts, 1636-1736 (New York, 1970); Edward M. Cook, Jr., "Social Behavior and Changing Values in Dedham, Massachusetts, 1700 to 1775," William and Mary Quarterly, 3d ser. 27 (1970), 546-80; Patricia U. Bonomi, A Factious People: Politics and Society in Colonial New York (New York, 1971); James A. Henretta, The Evolution of American Society, 1700-1815: An Interdisciplinary Analysis (Lexington, Mass., 1973); Kenneth Lockridge, "Social Change and the Meaning of the American Revolution," Journal of Social History, 6 (1973), 403-39. Indeed, it may well be that the adults who chose to become Indians did so for some of the reasons that many of their countrymen turned to revolution.

79. Crèvecoeur, Letters, 215.

CHAPTER EIGHT

1. John Higham, "Beyond Consensus: The Historian as Moral Critic," American Historical Review, 67 (1962), 609-25 at 624.

2. For an excellent application of this technique, see W. J. Eccles, Frontenac, The Courtier Governor (Toronto, 1959), 182-83, which treats Denonville's enslavement of Iroquois warriors for the king's galleys.

3. Wilcomb Washburn, "Relations Between Europeans and Amerindians During the Seventeenth and Eighteenth Centuries: The Epistemological Problem," paper delivered at the International Colloquium on Colonial History, University of Ottawa, Ottawa, Ontario, Nov. 1969, pp. 12-13.

4. Arthur Pound, Johnson of the Mohawks (New York, 1930), 243-44.

5. Henry J. Young, "A Note on Scalp Bounties in Pennsylvania," Pennsylvania History, 24 (1957), 207-18 at 207-8.

6. Howard Swiggett, War Out of Niagara: Walter Butler and the Tory Rangers (New York, 1933), 47.

7. Douglas Edward Leach, Arms for Empire: A Military History of

the British Colonies in North America, 1607-1763 (New York, 1973), 107, 132-33; Pound, *Johnson of the Mohawks*, 243-45.

8. James Oliver Curwood, *The Plains of Abraham* (Garden City, N.Y., 1928), 126n.

9. Alden T. Vaughan, *New England Frontier: Puritans and Indians, 1620-1675* (Boston, 1965), 40-41. The passage is unchanged in the 1979 revised edition (New York).

10. Francis Jennings, *The Invasion of America: Indians, Colonialism, and the Cant of Conquest* (Chapel Hill, 1975), 160, 163, 166.

11. Rev. John Heckewelder, *History, Manners, and Customs of the Indian Nations Who Once Inhabited Pennsylvania and the Neighbouring States*, rev. ed. Rev. William C. Reichel (Philadelphia, 1876), 215.

12. [William Gerard], *DeBrahm's Report of the General Survey in the Southern District of North America*, ed. Louis DeVorsey, Jr. (Columbia, S.C., 1971), 109.

13. Heckewelder, *History*, 215-16.

14. *Ibid.*, 216.

15. Sir William Johnson to Arthur Lee, Feb. 28, 1771, E. B. O'Callaghan, ed., *The Documentary History of the State of New-York*, 4 vols. (quarto ed., Albany, 1849-51), 4:273.

16. DeVorsey, ed., *DeBrahm's Report*, 111.

17. James Phinney Baxter, ed., *Documentary History of the State of Maine, Collections of the Maine Historical Society*, 2d ser. 23 (1916), 131-32, 139-40 (hereafter cited as *Doc. His. of Maine*). See below, p. 220 for Maryland soldiers who accompanied a Cherokee war party.

18. William Waller Hening, ed., *The Statutes at Large; Being a Collection of all the Laws of Virginia*, 13 vols. (Richmond, 1819-23), 6:565.

19. John Lawson, *A New Voyage to Carolina* [London, 1709], ed. Hugh Talmage Lefler (Chapel Hill, 1967), 10; James W. Covington, "Apalachee Indians, 1704-1763," *Florida Historical Quarterly*, 50 (1972), 366-84 at 369.

20. Thomas Anburey, *Travels through the Interior Parts of America* [London, 1789], 2 vols. (Boston, 1923), 1:170-72.

21. James Sullivan *et al.*, eds., *The Papers of Sir William Johnson*, 14 vols. (Albany, 1921-65), 1:87, 9:8, 25 (hereafter cited as *Johnson Papers*).

22. Captain John Knox, *An Historical Journal of the Campaigns in North America for the Years 1757, 1758, 1759, and 1760* [London,

1769], ed. Arthur G. Doughty, 3 vols. (Toronto: The Champlain Society, 1914-16), 2:348.

23. *Johnson Papers,* 2:375, 9:586-87, 780; see also *ibid.,* 9:28, 2:375, and E. B. O'Callaghan and Berthold Fernouw, eds., *Documents Relative to the Colonial History of the State of New York,* 15 vols. (Albany, 1856-87), 7:134, 152, 864 (hereafter cited as *N.Y. Col. Docs.*). In 1710 the Senecas condoled with Governor Hunter of New York for the loss of one of his lieutenants with a scalp and four beaver pelts (*The Letters and Papers of Cadwallader Colden,* 9, *Collections of the New-York Historical Society,* 68 [1935], 393).

24. *N.Y. Col. Docs.,* 6:363; *Minutes of the Provincial Council of Pennsylvania,* 10 vols. (Philadelphia and Harrisburg, 1851-52), 7:712, 732.

25. *Johnson Papers,* 9:22-31.

26. Clifford K. Shipton, *Sibley's Harvard Graduates: Biographical Sketches of Those Who Attended Harvard College* (Cambridge, Mass., 1873-), 7:16; *Journals of the House of Representatives of Massachusetts* (Boston: Massachusetts Historical Society, 1919-), 6:210; William Hand Browne et al., eds., *Archives of Maryland,* 52 (1935), 488-89; Samuel Hazard et al., eds., *Pennsylvania Archives,* 1st ser. 2 (1853), 641.

27. A. C. Goodell, Jr., "The Centennial Anniversary of the Meeting of the Provincial Legislature in Salem, October 5, 1774," Essex Institute, *Historical Collections,* 13 (1875), 26-27.

28. Anburey, *Travels,* 1:237. Perhaps the officer was spared the danger that General George Townshend encountered upon returning to England with a scalp collection. See below, p. 231.

29. *Archives of Maryland,* 6 (1888), 558-63. On the New York frontier in 1777, Timothy Edwards wrote to his commander: "The affair of scalping as relating to Indians is delicate but your knowledge of their disposition will conduct you into such measures as will not deprive them of trophies of warlike achievement" (Gates MSS, microfilm, reel 3, p. 210, New-York Historical Society, New York, N.Y.).

30. *Archives of Maryland,* 9 (1890), 6.

31. *Pa. Archives,* 1st ser. 3 (1853), 185-87, 200.

32. *N.Y. Col. Docs.,* 7:277-78.

33. *Adventure in the Wilderness: The American Journals of Louis Antoine de Bougainville, 1756-1760,* ed. and trans. Edward P. Hamilton (Norman, Okla., 1964), 142.

34. *Pa. Archives,* 1st ser. 3 (1853), 200. Harriette Simpson Arnow,

Seedtime on the Cumberland (New York, 1960), 199, mentions nine scalps made from two during Lord Dunmore's War (1775).

35. *Pa. Archives,* 1st ser. 3 (1853), 199.

36. *Mins. of the Prov. Council of Pa.,* 7:735.

37. *Lieut. Henry Timberlake's Memoirs, 1756-1765* [London, 1765], ed. Samuel Cole Williams (Johnson City, Tenn., 1927), 78.

38. *Pa. Archives,* 1st ser. 3 (1853), 199.

39. Charles Orr, ed., *History of the Pequot War* (Cleveland, 1897), 138; E. B. O'Callaghan, comp., *Laws and Ordinances of New Netherland, 1638-1674* (Albany, 1868), 28-29.

40. Charles H. Lincoln, ed., *Narratives of the Indian Wars, 1675-1699,* Original Narratives of Early American History (New York, 1913), 34.

41. William Hubbard, *The Present State of New-England* (London, 1677), 22; Benjamin Church, *Diary of King Philip's War, 1675-76,* ed. Alan and Mary Simpson (Chester, Conn., 1975), 156.

42. *N.Y. Col. Docs.,* 3:562, 4:150n.

43. *Ibid.,* 10:484.

44. Paul A. W. Wallace, *Conrad Weiser, 1696-1760, Friend of Colonist and Mohawk* (Philadelphia, 1945), 414; *Pa. Archives,* 1st ser. 2 (1853), 511.

45. *Archives of Maryland,* 52 (1935), 176-77; Hening, ed., *Statutes,* 6: 550-51; Leonard W. Labaree *et al.,* eds., *The Papers of Benjamin Franklin* (New Haven, 1959–   ), 6:233, n.7.

46. *Pa. Archives,* 1st ser. 2 (1853), 543, 546, 620; *Johnson Papers,* 2: 443-44. See also *Archives of Maryland,* 6 (1888), 435; 52 (1935), 651; Hening, ed., *Statutes,* 7:122; J. Hammond Trumbull and C. J. Hoadly, eds., *The Public Records of the Colony of Connecticut,* 15 vols. (Hartford, 1850-90), 9:228-29; *J. of the Mass. House of Reps.,* 21 (1946), 99; 22 (1947), 71; 32, pt. 1 (1957), 87-88; George Sheldon, *A History of Deerfield, Massachusetts,* 2 vols. (Deerfield, 1895-96), 2:635 (continuous pag.).

47. Richard R. Johnson, "The Search for a Usable Indian: An Aspect of the Defense of Colonial New England," *Journal of American History,* 64 (1977), 623-51 at 643.

48. *Pa. Archives,* 1st ser. 2 (1853), 629.

49. Stanley McCrory Pargellis, *Lord Loudon in North America* (New Haven, 1933), ch. 1; I. K. Steele, *Guerillas and Grenadiers: The Struggle for Canada, 1689-1760* (Toronto, 1969), 69, 123-24. In 1758 a British major under General John Forbes warned a young officer that "the Inhabitants [of Pennsylvania] are very incapable of

giveing advice how to Act upon the offensive, as their views are only turn'd how to defend themselves" (Alfred Procter James, ed., *Writings of General John Forbes* [Menasha, Wis., 1938], 186).

50. [John Mitchell], *The Contest in America Between Great Britain and France* (London, 1757), 137; Rev. Benjamin Doolittle, *A Short Narrative of Mischief done by the French and Indian Enemy, on the Western Frontiers of the Province of Massachusetts-Bay* [1744-48] (Boston, 1750), 20.

51. *Archives of Maryland*, 6 (1888), 435; Hening, ed., *Statutes*, 7:122.

52. *Archives of Maryland*, 52 (1935), 651; *Papers of Benjamin Franklin*, 6:455-56; *J. of the Mass. House of Reps.*, 23 (1948), 389; 24 (1949), 14; Nathaniel Bouton, ed., *Provincial Papers: Documents and Records Relating to the Province of New-Hampshire* (Manchester, N.H., 1868), 2:428.

53. *Archives of Maryland*, 9 (1890), 6; 52 (1935), 651; 59 (1942), 64-65.

54. *Pa. Archives*, 1st ser. 8 (1853), 218; *Mins. of the Prov. Council of Pa.*, 9:191-92; *Minutes of the Supreme Executive Council of Pennsylvania*, 6 vols. (Harrisburg, 1852-53), 2:311-12. See also *Pa. Archives*, 1st ser. 7 (1853), 362; 8 (1853), 167, 176, 189-90, 227, 283, 393.

55. William Hubbard, *The History of the Indian Wars in New England* [1677], ed. Samuel G. Drake, 2 vols. (Roxbury, Mass., 1865), 1:87; Hamilton, ed., *Adventure in the Wilderness*, 141.

56. William A. Whitehead *et al.*, eds., *Documents Relating to the Colonial, Revolutionary, and post-Revolutionary History of the State of New Jersey, Archives of the State of New Jersey*, 1st ser. 20 (1898), 33, 35 (hereafter cited as *N.J. Archives*).

57. *N.J. Archives*, 1st ser. 19 (1897), 488.

58. Carl Van Doren and Julian P. Boyd, eds., *Indian Treaties Printed by Benjamin Franklin, 1736-1762* (Philadelphia, 1938), lxxiin.

59. See above, p. 328 n.45.

60. Hugh Honour, *The New Golden Land* (New York, 1975), 128.

61. Jeremy Belknap, *History of New Hampshire*, 3 vols. (2d ed., Boston, 1813), 2:52; John Farmer and Jacob Bailey Moore, eds., *Collections, historical and miscellaneous*, 3 vols. (Concord, N.H., 1822-24), 3:151; Autobiographical narrative of Hugh Adams, pp. 15, 43, Belknap MSS, Mass. His. Soc., Boston, Mass. See also *Johnson Papers*, 1:53, and *N.Y. Col. Docs.*, 6:620.

62. Kathryn Whitford, "Hannah Dustin: The Judgement of History," Essex Institute, *Historical Collections*, 108 (1972), 304-25.

63. Henry Bouquet to Anne Willing, Sept. 17, 1759, *The Papers of Henry Bouquet* (Harrisburg, Pa., 1951-   ), 4:115-17.

64. Archibald Kennedy, *Serious Advice to the Inhabitants of the Northern Colonies, on the Present State of Affairs* (New York, 1755), 18-19.

65. *The Acts and Resolves, Public and Private, of the Province of the Massachusetts Bay*, 21 vols. (Boston, 1869-1922), 1:530, 558, 594, 2:259; *Pa. Archives*, 1st ser. 2 (1853), 620 (1756); *Mins. of the Prov. Council of Pa.*, 9:191-92 (1764); *Collections of the New Jersey Historical Society*, 4 (1852), 305-6; Trumbull and Hoadly, eds., *Conn. Col. Recs.*, 9:229.

66. M. Halsey Thomas, ed., *The Diary of Samuel Sewall*, 2 vols. (New York, 1973), 2:691 (June 13, 1712).

67. Van Doren and Boyd, eds., *Indian Treaties Printed by Franklin*, lxxii-lxxiii; *Johnson Papers*, 1:772.

68. *Johnson Papers*, 1:772; *Proposals to Prevent Scalping, &c. Humbly offered to the Consideration of a Council of War* (New York, 1755), 3.

69. *Doc. His. of Maine*, 9:259; *J. of the Mass. House of Reps.*, 23 (1948), 295-96; Knox, *Journals*, 1:438, 468.

70. Knox, *Journal*, 1:196, n.3; *Pa. Archives*, 1st ser. 7 (1853), 569-70.

71. *Collections of the Connecticut Historical Society*, 15 (1914), 82-83 (Aug. 26, 1747); Sylvester K. Stevens and Donald H. Kent, eds., *Wilderness Chronicles of Northwestern Pennsylvania* (Harrisburg, 1941), 265-66.

72. *Proposals to Prevent Scalping*, 4-5.

73. *Papers of Benjamin Franklin*, 6:382.

74. *Johnson Papers*, 6:102, 11:540.

75. *N.J. Archives*, 1st ser. 20 (1898), 43-44; *Mins. of the Prov. Council of Pa.*, 7:89.

76. Samuel Penhallow, *The History of the Wars of New England, with the Eastern Indians* [1703-22] (Boston, 1726), facs. ed. Edward Wheelock (Williamstown, Mass., 1973), 111 and Notes, 35; Sheldon, *Deerfield*, 637 (1755); *J. of the Mass. House of Reps.*, 24 (1949), 116, 123 (1747); Emma Lewis Coleman, *New England Captives Carried to Canada*, 2 vols. (Portland, Me., 1925), 2:193-95. The few acculturated Indians who hired out to Braddock in 1755 committed a similar breach of their own scalping etiquette because they could not collect the general's £5 bounty without tangible proof (Charles Hamilton, ed., *Braddock's Defeat* [Norman, Okla., 1959], 25).

77. *N.J. Archives*, 1st ser. 20 (1898), 243-44.

78. "The Haldiman Papers," *Michigan Pioneer and Historical Collections,* 9 (1886), 501-2.

79. *Sibley's Harvard Graduates,* 6:407-8, 7:176-77.

CHAPTER NINE

1. This is not to minimize the importance of the Spanish frontiers in the Southeast and Southwest, but merely to emphasize the westward procession of Anglo-American law and institutions from the eastern seaboard. See Donald J. Lehmer, "The Second Frontier: The Spanish," in Robert G. Ferris, ed., *The American West: An Appraisal* (Santa Fe, N.M., 1963), 141-50.

2. Jack D. Forbes, "Frontiers in American History and the Role of the Frontier Historian," *Ethnohistory,* 15 (1968), 203-35; Robert F. Berkhofer, Jr., "Space, Time, Culture and the New Frontier," *Agricultural History,* 38 (1964), 21-30; Robin F. Wells, "Frontier Systems as a Sociocultural Type," *Papers in Anthropology,* 14 (1973), 6-15; James Axtell, "The Ethnohistory of Early America: A Review Essay," *William and Mary Quarterly,* 3d ser. 35 (1978), 110-44.

3. Melville J. Herskovits, *Acculturation: The Study of Culture Contacts* (New York, 1938); Ralph Linton, ed., *Acculturation in Seven American Indian Tribes* (New York, 1940), chs. 8-10; George Devereux and Edward M. Loeb, "Antagonistic Acculturation," *American Sociological Review,* 8 (1943), 133-47; Homer G. Barnett *et al.,* "Acculturation: An Exploratory Formulation," The Social Science Research Council Summer Seminar on Acculturation, 1953, *American Anthropologist,* n.s. 56 (1954), 973-1002; Edward M. Bruner, "Cultural Transmission and Cultural Change," *Southwestern Journal of Anthropology,* 12 (1956), 191-99; Edward H. Spicer, "Types of Contact and Processes of Change," in Spicer, ed., *Perspectives in American Indian Culture Change* (Chicago, 1961), ch. 8; Nancy O. Lurie, "Culture Change," in James A. Clifton, ed., *Introduction to Cultural Anthropology: Essays in the Scope and Methods of the Science of Man* (Boston, 1968), 275-303.

4. David Beers Quinn, *England and the Discovery of America, 1481-1620* (New York, 1974); Quinn, *The Elizabethans and the Irish* (Ithaca, 1966); Quinn, *North America from Earliest Discovery to First Settlements,* New American Nation Series (New York, 1977); A. L. Rowse, *The Expansion of Elizabethan England* (London,

1955); Francis Jennings, "Virgin Land and Savage People," *American Quarterly*, 23 (1971), 319-41; Jennings, *The Invasion of America: Indians, Colonialism, and the Cant of Conquest* (Chapel Hill, 1975).

5. Alfred W. Crosby, "Virgin Soil Epidemics as a Factor in the Aboriginal Depopulation in America," *WMQ*, 3d ser. 33 (1976), 289-99.

6. Sherburne F. Cook, "The Significance of Disease in the Extinction of the New England Indians," *Human Biology*, 45 (1973), 485-508; Cook, *The Indian Population of New England in the Seventeenth Century*, University of California Publications in Anthropology, 12 (Berkeley, 1976).

7. Thomas Morton, *New English Canaan* (London, 1632), ch. 3.

8. *Ibid.*

9. Charles Hudson, *The Southeastern Indians* (Knoxville, Tenn., 1976), 104-5, 110.

10. John Lawson, *A New Voyage to Carolina* [London, 1709], ed. Hugh Talmage Lefler (Chapel Hill, 1967), 232.

11. [James] *Adair's History of the American Indians* [London, 1775], ed. Samuel Cole Williams (Kingsport, Tenn., 1930), 244. For the history of disease among colonial Indian populations, see Percy M. Ashburn, *The Ranks of Death: A Medical History of the Conquest of America*, ed. Frank D. Ashburn (New York, 1947); Alfred W. Crosby, Jr., *The Columbian Exchange: Biological and Cultural Consequences of 1492* (Westport, Conn., 1972); E. Wagner Stearn and Allen E. Stearn, *The Effect of Smallpox on the Destiny of the Amerindian* (Boston, 1945); John Duffy, "Smallpox and the Indians in the American Colonies," *Bulletin of the History of Medicine*, 25 (1951), 324-41; Duffy, *Epidemics in Colonial America* (Baton Rouge, 1953); Calvin Martin, "Wildlife Diseases as a Factor in the Depopulation of the North American Indians," *Western Historical Quarterly*, 7 (1976), 47-62; William H. McNeill, *Plagues and People* (New York, 1976).

12. Lawson, *New Voyage to Carolina*, 17, 232. For sweat lodges, see Harold E. Driver, *Indians of North America* (2d rev. ed., Chicago, 1969), 132-33; Virgil J. Vogel, *American Indian Medicine* (Norman, Okla., 1970) , 46-47, 254-57.

13. [William Gerard], *DeBrahm's Report of the General Survey in the Southern District of North America*, ed. Louis DeVorsey, Jr. (Columbia, S.C., 1971), 107.

14. M. Le Page Du Pratz, *The History of Louisiana* (London, 1774),

305; Alfred W. Crosby, " 'God . . . Would Destroy Them, and Give Their Country to Another People . . . ,'" *American Heritage*, 29 (Oct.-Nov. 1978), 39-42. When Edward Winslow visited the ailing Massasoit in 1623, "we found the house so full of men as we could scarce get in . . . There were they, in the midst of their charms for him" (Winslow, *Good News from New England* [London, 1624], in Edward Arber, ed., *The Story of the Pilgrim Fathers, 1606-1623, A.D.* [Boston, 1897], 549-50).

15. William Bradford, *Of Plymouth Plantation, 1620-1647*, ed. Samuel Eliot Morison (New York, 1952), 87, 270-71; E. E. Rich, ed., *Cumberland House Journals and Inland Journals, 1775-82*, Hudson Bay Record Society, 15 (London, 1952), 224-26, 231-35, 240, 263-65. Roger Williams wrote of the Narragansetts: "I have often seene a poore House left alone in the wild Woods, all being fled, the living not able to bury the dead: so terrible is the apprehension of an infectious disease, that not only persons, but the Houses and the whole Towne takes flight" (*A Key into the Language of America* [London, 1643], 196).

16. [Edward] *Johnson's Wonder-Working Providence, 1628-1651*, ed. J. Franklin Jameson, Original Narratives of Early American History (New York, 1910), 41.

17. Alexander Young, ed., *Chronicles of the Pilgrim Fathers* (Boston, 1841), 258. See William Walker's remarks from Hudson's Bay in 1781: "The Natives they are of such a kind of people that if they should have the misfortune to lose one of their family, that they have not courage to hunt Provisions for themselves, let alone killing of furrs for that Season" (Rich, ed., *Cumberland House Journals*, 263).

18. *Adair's History of the Indians*, 245. See also Du Pratz, *History of Louisiana*, 306; George Catlin, *Letters and Notes on the Manners, Customs, and Conditions of the North American Indians*, 2 vols. (London, 1844), 2:257; and Bernard DeVoto, ed., *The Journals of Lewis and Clark* (Boston, 1953), 19. Adults were more prone to pitting or pock-marking than children (Duffy, *Epidemics in Colonial America*, 107-8).

19. *A Narrative of the Captivity and Adventures of John Tanner* [New York, 1830], ed. Edwin James (Minneapolis, 1956), 95-98.

20. *Johnson's Wonder-Working Providence*, 41. The most numerous victims of European epidemics at three Susquehannock sites between 1580 and 1650 were young women of child-bearing age (17-19) (Henry W. Heisey and J. Paul Witmer, "Of Historic Susque-

hannock Cemeteries," *Pennsylvania Archaeologist*, 32:3-4 [1962], 104, 120).

21. After the epidemic of 1780-81 the quality of Missouri Valley native pottery declined abruptly due to the loss of expert female potters. The introduction of metal kettles by European traders reduced the quantity (Donald J. Lehmer, *Introduction to Middle Missouri Archeology*, National Park Service, Anthropological Papers, 1 [Washington, D.C., 1971], 172-75).

22. David Beers Quinn, ed., *The Roanoke Voyages, 1584-1590*, Hakluyt Society Publications, 2d ser. 104-5 (London, 1955), 104:372, 375-81.

23. Cook, *Indian Population of New England*, 29-35. Many of Eliot's converts confessed that serious sickness had impelled them to seek the Englishmen's God (John Eliot and Thomas Mayhew, *Tears of Repentance* [London, 1653], in *Collections of the Massachusetts Historical Society*, 3d ser. 4 [1834], 231, 239, 254, 257, 259).

24. Bradford, *Plymouth Plantation*, 99.

25. Heisey and Witmer, "Historic Susquehannock Cemeteries," 104-5.

26. Emma Helen Blair, ed., *The Indian Tribes of the Upper Mississippi Valley and Region of the Great Lakes*, 2 vols. (Cleveland, 1911), 1:307.

27. Williams, *Key into the Language of America*, 166. For a modern appreciation of the irony, see Marianne Moore's poem, "New York," in *Observations* (New York, 1924), 65.

28. The Narragansetts called the Europeans "Coatmen" or "swordmen" (Williams, *Key into the Language of America*, 59). The Mohawks referred to the Dutch as "iron-workers" or "cloth makers," while the Hurons called the French "Iron People" (Bruce G. Trigger, *The Children of Aataentsic: A History of the Huron People to 1660*, 2 vols. [Montreal, 1976], 307, 360, 617-18). The Pocumtucks of northern New England knew the French as "knife men" (Gordon M. Day, *The Mots loups of Father Mathevet*, National Museum of Man, Publications in Ethnology, 9 [Ottawa, 1975], 424n).

29. Marion Tinling, ed., *The Correspondence of the Three William Byrds of Westover, Virginia, 1648-1776*, 2 vols. (Charlottesville, 1977), 1:29-30.

30. Williams, *Key into the Language of America*, 160; A. J. F. van Laer, trans. and ed., *Documents Relating to New Netherland 1624-1626 in the Henry E. Huntington Library* (San Marino, Ca., 1924), 228-31. For the Indians' strong color preferences, see Kenneth E. Kidd, "The Cloth Trade and the Indians of the Northeast

During the Seventeenth and Eighteenth Centuries," Royal Ontario Museum, Division of Art and Archaeology, *Annual for 1961*, 48-56; Thomas Elliot Norton, *The Fur Trade in Colonial New York, 1686-1776* (Madison, Wis., 1974), 31; *Winthrop Papers*, (Boston: Massachusetts Historical Society, 1929–   ), 3:150; and K. G. Davies, ed., *Letters from Hudson Bay, 1703-04*, Hudson Bay Record Society, 25 (London, 1965), 137, 279.

31. Van Laer, ed., *Documents Relating to New Netherland*, 231.

32. Davies, ed., *Letters from Hudson Bay*, 134-37, 278-84, 290.

33. William Wood, *New England's Prospect* [London, 1634], ed. Alden T. Vaughan (Amherst, Mass., 1977), 84 (my emphasis). Rev. John Clayton noted that the Virginia natives "will not buy any more cloaths, than they have present use for, though they might have them never so cheap: they will not provide new ones, till the old be worn out" (Stanley Pargellis, ed., "The Indians in Virginia . . . 1689," *WMQ*, 3d ser. 16 [1959], 230).

34. Williams, *Key into the Language of America*, 121. Edward Winslow noted that even the praying Indians of Massachusetts "carefully keep [their English "Apparell"] till meeting time" (*The Glorious Progress of the Gospel amongst the Indians in New England* [London, 1649], in *Colls. Mass. His. Soc.*, 3d ser. 4 [1834], 87).

35. This figure may be high; metal and glass survive in the ground better than their native equivalents. Charles F. Wray and Harry L. Schoff, "A Preliminary Report on the Seneca Sequence in Western New York, 1550-1687," *Pa. Arch.*, 23 (1953), 53-63; John Witthoft, "Archaeology as a Key to the Colonial Fur Trade," *Minnesota History*, 40 (1966), 203-9.

36. Eleazar Wheelock to the Earl of Dartmouth, Dec. 22, 1768, Wheelock Papers 768672, Dartmouth College Library, Hanover, N.H. See also Theophilus Chamberlain to E. W., Onowadgegh [Iroquois territory], Oct. 4, 1766, Wheelock Papers 766554: "Our Indians are in some measure like those in New England much degenerated, both as to their Customs, their Dress and their Impliments"; and William Bartram's "Observations on the Creek and Cherokee Indians" [1789], *Transactions of the American Ethnological Society*, 3, pt. 1 (1853), 29: "They have neglected their own manufactures for those supplied them cheaply and in abundance from Europe. . . . Therefore, we must seek for their arts and sciences among nations far distant from the settlements of the white people."

37. Louis B. Wright, ed., *The Prose Works of William Byrd of Westover* (Cambridge, Mass., 1966), 393.

38. George I. Quimby and Alexander Spoehr, "Acculturation and Material Culture—I," *Fieldiana-Anthropology*, 36:6 (July 1951), 107-47; H. G. Barnett, "Culture Processes," *American Anthropologist*, n.s. 42 (1940), 21-48; Barnett, "Invention and Culture Change," *American Anthropologist*, n.s. 44 (1942), 14-30.

39. Rev. John Heckewelder, *History, Manners, and Customs of the Indian Nations Who Once Inhabited Pennsylvania and the Neighbouring States* [1819], rev. ed. Rev. William C. Reichel (Philadelphia, 1876), 74.

40. Charles Orr, ed., *History of the Pequot War* (Cleveland, 1897), 139.

41. Quimby and Spoehr, "Acculturation and Material Culture," 107-47; Barnett, "Culture Processes," 37; Davies, ed., *Letters from Hudson Bay*, 134; Wray and Schoff, "Preliminary Report on Seneca Sequence," 57, 60; Witthoft, "Archaeology as a Key," 207; Thomas M. N. Lewis and Madeline Kneberg, *Hiwassee Island: An Archaeological Account of Four Tennessee Indian Peoples* (Knoxville, Tenn., 1946, 1970), 133-34, pls. 85C, 86B, 87B. The Milwaukee Museum's permanent exhibit on culture change has a baking-powder can rattle and several other white items adapted to native use. (My thanks to Nancy Lurie for a guided tour and advice.)

42. Ted J. Brasser, *A Basketful of Indian Culture Change*, National Museum of Man, Canadian Ethnology Service, Paper No. 22 (Ottawa, 1975).

43. Sir William Johnson to the Earl of Hillsborough, Aug. 14, 1770, in E. B. O'Callaghan and Berthold Fernouw, eds., *Documents Relative to the Colonial History of the State of New-York*, 15 vols. (Albany, 1856-87), 8:226 (hereafter cited as *N.Y. Col. Docs.*).

44. Pargellis, "Indians in Virginia," 230. A Swiss traveler in Virginia in 1701-2 observed that the drunken Indians "make wonderful faces and act as if they were angry and wanted to strike their enemy" ("The Journey of Francis Louis Michel," trans. William J. Hinke, *Virginia Magazine of History and Biography*, 24 [1916], 132).

45. "Capt. Wm. Hyde's Observations of the 5 Nations at New Yorke 1698," ed. William N. Fenton, *American Scene Magazine*, 6:2 (1965), n.p.; "[François Vachon de] Belmont's History of Brandy," trans. and ed. Joseph P. Donnelly, *Mid-America*, 34 (1952), 45, 49, 62-63. The French were the most astute analysts of native drinking habits, which were largely similar throughout eastern North America.

46. "Belmont's Brandy," 45.

47. *Adventure in the Wilderness: The American Journals of Louis Antoine de Bougainville, 1756-1760,* trans. and ed. Edward P. Hamilton (Norman, Okla., 1964), 225.

48. "Belmont's Brandy," 63.

49. Craig MacAndrew and Robert B. Edgerton, *Drunken Comportment: A Social Explanation* (Chicago, 1969), 149-55; "Belmont's Brandy," 45; Pierre Boucher, *Canada in the Seventeenth Century* [Paris, 1664], trans. Edward Louis Montizambert (Montreal, 1883), 52-53; A. Irving Hallowell, *Culture and Experience* (Philadelphia, 1955), 141-42.

50. "Belmont's Brandy," 46.

51. Ruth M. Underhill, *Red Man's Religion* (Chicago, 1965), ch. 10; Ruth Benedict, *The Concept of the Guardian Spirit in North America,* Memoirs of the American Anthropological Association, 29 (Menasha, Wis., 1923); Anthony F. C. Wallace, "Dreams and Wishes of the Soul: A Type of Psychoanalytic Theory Among the Seventeenth-Century Iroquois," *American Anthropologist,* n.s. 60 (1958), 234-48; Wallace, *The Death and Rebirth of the Seneca* (New York, 1969), 59-74; Weston La Barre, "The Narcotic Complex of the New World," *Diogenes,* 48 (1964), 125-38.

52. Hamilton, ed., *Adventure in the Wilderness,* 225; André Vachon, "L'eau-de-vie dans la société indienne," Canadian Historical Association, *Report* (1960), 23; R. C. Dailey, "The Role of Alcohol Among North American Indian Tribes as reported in The Jesuit Relations," *Anthropologica,* 10 (1968), 48-50.

53. "Belmont's Brandy," 60; Blair, ed., *Indian Tribes of the Upper Mississippi,* 1:208.

54. Norton, *Fur Trade in Colonial New York,* 32.

55. *The Letters and Papers of Cadwallader Colden,* 10 vols., *Collections of the New-York Historical Society,* 50-56, 67-69 (1918-36), 68:384 (hereafter cited as *Colden Papers*). See Norton, *Fur Trade in Colonial New York,* 32-33, and *The Discoveries of John Lederer* [London, 1670], ed. William P. Cumming (Charlottesville, Va., 1958), 42; "Sometimes you may with Brandy or Strong liquor dispose them to an humour of giving you ten times the value of your commodity; and at other times they are so hide-bound, that they will not offer half the Market-price, especially if they be aware that you have a design to circumvent them with drink."

56. Jennings, "Virgin Land," 540; Gary B. Nash, *Red, White, and Black: The Peoples of Early America* (Englewood Cliffs, N.J., 1974), 252-55; Wallace, *Death and Rebirth of the Seneca,* 180, 183,

199-200; Georgiana C. Nammack, *Fraud, Politics, and the Dispossession of the Indians: The Iroquois Land Frontier in the Colonial Period* (Norman, Okla., 1969), *passim*.

57. *N.Y. Col. Docs.*, 5:796-97. See also Peter Wraxall, *An Abridgment of the Indian Affairs . . . Transacted in the Colony of New York from the Year 1678 to the Year 1751*, ed. Charles Howard McIlwain, Harvard Historical Studies, 21 (Cambridge, Mass., 1915), 160-61.

58. Cadwallader Colden, *The History of the Five Indian Nations of Canada* (London, 1747), 13-14.

59. *William Byrd's Histories of the Dividing Line Betwixt Virginia and North Carolina*, ed. William K. Boyd (New York, 1967), 116.

60. *Ibid.*

61. John Phillip Reid, *A Better Kind of Hatchet: Law, Trade, and Diplomacy in the Cherokee Nation During the Early Years of European Contact* (University Park, Pa., 1976), 38; Harriette S. Arnow, *Seedtime on the Cumberland* (New York, 1960), 89; Carl P. Russell, *Guns on the Early Frontiers* (Berkeley, 1957), ch. 1, esp. pp. 5-6; Patrick M. Malone, "Changing Military Technology Among the Indians of Southern New England, 1600-1677," *American Quarterly*, 25 (1973), 50-53; William Shedrick Willis, "Colonial Conflict and the Cherokee Indians, 1710-1760," unpub. Ph.D. diss., Columbia University, 1955 (University Microfilm 12, 482), 81-86, 99-100.

62. Russell, *Guns on the Early Frontiers*, 6; David B. Quinn and Alison M. Quinn, eds., *Virginia Voyages from Hakluyt* (London, 1973), 10; Bradford, *Plymouth Plantation*, 204; Arthur T. Adams, ed., *The Explorations of Pierre Esprit Radisson* (Minneapolis, 1961), 94; Trigger, *Children of Aataentsic*, 629.

63. Robin F. Wells, "Castoreum and Steel Traps in Eastern North America," *American Anthropologist*, n.s. 74 (1972), 479-83; Christian F. Feest, "More on Castoreum and Traps in Eastern North America," *ibid.*, 77 (1975), 603; Calvin Martin, "The European Impact on the Culture of a Northeastern Algonquian Tribe: An Ecological Interpretation," *WMQ*, 3d ser. 31 (1974), 3-26; Martin, *Keepers of the Game: Indian-Animal Relationships and the Fur Trade* (Berkeley, 1978), which is summarized in Martin, "The War Between Indians and Animals," *Natural History*, 87:6 (June-July 1978), 92-96.

64. George T. Hunt, *The Wars of the Iroquois: A Study in Intertribal Trade Relations* (Madison, Wis., 1940).

65. Allen W. Trelease, "The Iroquois and the Western Fur Trade: A

Problem in Interpretation," *Mississippi Valley Historical Review,* 49 (1962), 32-51; Elisabeth Tooker, "The Iroquois Defeat of the Huron: A Review of Causes," *Pa. Arch.,* 33 (1963), 115-23; Trigger, *Children of Aataentsic,* 617-64; Joseph R. Mayer, "Flintlocks of the Iroquois, 1620-1687," *Research Records of the Rochester Museum of Arts and Sciences,* no. 6 (1943), 7-57.

66. Charles Hudson, *The Southeastern Indians* (Knoxville, Tenn., 1976), 239-57; Jennings, *Invasion of America,* ch. 9; George P. Snyderman, "Behind the Tree of Peace: A Sociological Analysis of Iroquois Warfare," *Pa. Arch.,* 18:3-4 (1948); Bruce G. Trigger, *The Huron: Farmers of the North* (New York, 1969), ch. 4.

67. But see Edward Umfreville, *The Present State of Hudson's Bay* [London, 1790], ed. W. Stewart Wallace (Toronto, 1954), 24, for an account of Indian warfare involving guns and wooden shields as late as 1771.

68. James Sullivan *et al.,* eds., *The Papers of Sir William Johnson,* 14 vols. (Albany, 1921-65), 12:952.

69. The trend toward larger palisaded villages in strategic locations began in most areas of the East during the late-prehistoric period and cannot, therefore, be attributed to European firearms. But the trend was accelerated by the European presence beginning in the sixteenth century, when village clusters and larger palisades became common. The inhabitants of small hamlets still relied on their feet to escape harm. See, for example, Willis, "Colonial Conflict and the Cherokees," 175-88; Hudson, *Southeastern Indians,* 110-13, 210-22; William A. Ritchie and Robert E. Funk, *Aboriginal Settlement Patterns in the Northeast,* New York State Museum and Science Service, Memoir 20 (Albany, 1973), *passim;* Peter P. Pratt, *Archaeology of the Oneida Iroquois,* Vol. 1, Occasional Publications in Northeastern Anthropology, 1 (George's Mills, N.H., 1976), 143-44; Conrad Heidenreich, *Huronia: A History and Geography of the Huron Indians, 1600-1650* (Toronto, 1971), 139-43; Trigger, *Children of Aataentsic,* ch. 3.

70. Willis, "Colonial Conflict and the Cherokees," 157-64; *Lieut. Henry Timberlake's Memoirs, 1756-1765* [London, 1765], ed. Samuel Cole Williams (Johnson City, Tenn., 1927), 82n; John Bartram, *Observations . . . Made . . . In his Travels from Pensilvania to Onondaga . . .* (London, 1751), 78-79.

71. Mary Helms, "Matrilocality, Social Solidarity, and Culture Contact: Three Case Histories," *SWJA,* 26 (1970), 197-212; Trigger, *Children of Aataentsic,* 134-37, 155-56, 418-20; Trigger, "Iroquoian

Matriliny," *Pa. Arch.*, 48 (1978), 55-65; Alexander Spoehr, "Changing Kinship Systems: A Study in the Acculturation of the Creeks, Cherokees, and Choctaws," *Field Museum of Natural History, Anthropology Series,* 33:4 (1947), which should be read in conjunction with William S. Willis, Jr., "Patrilineal Institutions in Southeastern North America," *Ethnohistory,* 10 (1963), 250-69.

72. Bradford, *Plymouth Plantation,* 80, 96-97, 99; *A Journal of the Pilgrims: Mourt's Relation* [London, 1622], ed. Dwight B. Heath (New York, 1963), 56-57, 58, 73, 83; Quinns, eds., *Virginia Voyages,* 4, 10, 29, 39, 72.

73. *Timberlake's Memoirs,* 96-98; Wallace, *Death and Rebirth of the Seneca,* 111-14.

74. Horace P. Beck, *The American Indian as a Sea-Fighter in Colonial Times* (Mystic, Conn., 1959).

75. Richard R. Johnson, "The Search for a Usable Indian: An Aspect of the Defense of Colonial New England," *Journal of American History,* 64 (1977), 623-51.

76. Above, Chapter 2.

77. Wallace, *Death and Rebirth of the Seneca,* chs. 8-10; Wallace, "Revitalization Movements: Some Theoretical Considerations for Their Comparative Study," *American Anthropologist,* n.s. 58 (1956), 264-81; Wallace, *Religion: An Anthropological View* (New York, 1966), 30-39, 157-66, 209-15.

78. The practice of taking Indian debtors' children as servants or slaves was apparently widespread in the English colonies. Traders at Oswego in New York and on Cape Cod were prone to it (*Colden Papers,* 53:167, 68:107; Rev. Gideon Hawley to Andrew Oliver, Dec. 9, 1760, Hawley Manuscripts, Congregational Library, Boston, Mass.; Petition of Mashpee leaders to Governor of Massachusetts, May 24, 1700, Massachusetts Archives, Boston, Mass., vol. 30, 456).

79. Reid, *Better Kind of Hatchet,* chs. 5-6; Verner W. Crane, *The Southern Frontier, 1670-1732* (Ann Arbor, 1929), ch. 7; Richard L. Haan, "The 'Trade Do's Not Flourish as Formerly': The Ecological Origins of the Yamasee War of 1715," *Ethnohistory* (forthcoming). Thanks to Professor Haan for an advance copy of his article.

80. Reid, *Better Kind of Hatchet,* 194-95.

81. Edmund S. Morgan, ed., *The Founding of Massachusetts* (Indianapolis, 1964), 320, 450. See also Merrill Jensen, ed., *American*

Colonial Documents to 1776, in David C. Douglas, ed., *English Historical Documents,* 12 vols. (New York, 1955), 9:65, 82, 85, 93.

82. For an analysis of this puzzling phrase, see above, Chapter 3, pp. 44-61.

83. Rev. East Apthorp, *The Felicity of the Times. A Sermon Preached at Christ-Church, Cambridge* . . . (Boston, 1763), 13.

84. Above, Chapter 3.

85. Anthony Wallace's felicitous phrase (*Death and Rebirth of the Seneca,* ch. 7).

86. Above, Chapter 3; William Kellaway, *The New England Company, 1649-1776* (London, 1961), esp. chs. 5, 9; Jennings, *Invasion of America,* ch. 14; Neal Salisbury, "Red Puritans: The 'Praying Indians' of Massachusetts Bay and John Eliot," *WMQ,* 3d ser. 31 (1974), 27-54.

87. [Anon.], *An Essay towards Propagating the Gospel among the Neighbouring Nations of Indians in North America* (New London, Conn., 1756), 16; R. A. Brock, ed., *The Official Letters of Alexander Spotswood, Lieutenant-Governor of the Colony of Virginia, 1710-1722, Collections of the Virginia Historical Society,* n.s. 1-2 (1882-85), 1:121-22, 124, 134, 281-82; Eleazar Wheelock to the Earl of Dartmouth, Sept. 4, 1766, Wheelock Papers 766504.4, Dartmouth College Library, Hanover, N.H. The English obviously favored the idea of educational hostages before coming to America. In 1572 Humphrey Gilbert wanted the children of the Irish aristocracy paged to the English Crown as hostages for the good behavior of their fathers' followers (David Beers Quinn, ed., *The Voyages and Colonizing Enterprises of Sir Humphrey Gilbert,* Hakluyt Society Publications, 2d ser. 83-84 [London, 1940], 83:126-27).

88. Above, Chapter 4.

89. Frederick L. Weis, "The New England Company of 1649 and Its Missionary Enterprises," *Publications of the Colonial Society of Massachusetts,* 38 (1947-51), 134-218.

90. William Wood, *New England's Prospect,* ed. Nathaniel Rogers (Boston, 1764), 94.

91. Quinn, ed., *Roanoke Voyages,* 104:375-76, 379; Philip L. Barbour, ed., *The Jamestown Voyages under the First Charter, 1606-1609,* Hakluyt Society Publications, 2d ser. 136-37 (Cambridge, 1969), 137:369; Pargellis, ed., "Indians in Virginia," 232-33, 236.

92. Barbour, ed., *Jamestown Voyages,* 137:364.

93. T. J. C. Brasser, "Group Identification along a Moving Frontier,"

Proceedings, 38th International Congress of Americanists (Munich, 1970), 2:261-65.

94. Alden Vaughan is correct in describing the early colonial attitude toward the Indians as cultural rather than racial superiority (*New England Frontier: Puritans and Indians, 1620-1675* [2d ed., New York, 1979], 1, 324, 334, 338). Philip L. Berg, "Racism and the Puritan Mind," *Phylon,* 36 (1975), 1-7, and G. E. Thomas, "Puritans, Indians, and the Concept of Race," *New England Quarterly,* 48 (1975), 3-27, are seriously flawed by lack of precision and a reductionist methodology which ignores chronology, geography, and contact conditions.

95. James Axtell, "Preachers, Priests, and Pagans: Some Thoughts on the Ethnohistory of Missions," paper delivered at the Conference on Iroquois Research, Albany, N.Y., Oct. 2, 1976; James P. Ronda and James Axtell, *Indian Missions: A Critical Bibliography* (Bloomington, 1978), 1-50.

CHAPTER TEN

1. Little has been done since 1952 when Bernard DeVoto scolded American historians for making "disastrously little effort to understand how [Indian culture] affected white men and their societies" (Joseph Kinsey Howard, *Strange Empire* [New York, 1952], 9).

2. Edward Eggleston, "The Aborigines and the Colonists," *Century Magazine* (May 1883), 96-114; Alexander F. Chamberlain, "The Contributions of the American Indian to Civilization," *Proceedings of the American Antiquarian Society,* n.s. 16 (1903-4), 91-126; Clark Wissler, "The Influence of Aboriginal Indian Culture on American Life," in *Some Oriental Influences on Western Culture* (New York: American Council of the Institute of Pacific Relations, 1929); Everett E. Edwards, "American Indians' Contribution to Civilization," *Minnesota History,* 15 (1934), 255-72; Felix S. Cohen, "Americanizing the White Man," *The American Scholar,* 21 (1952), 177-91; E. Russell Carter, *The Gift Is Rich* (New York, 1955); A. Irving Hallowell, "The Impact of the American Indian on American Culture," *American Anthropologist,* n.s. 59 (1957), 201-17; Hallowell, "The Backwash of the Frontier: The Impact of the Indian on American Culture," in Walker D. Wyman and Clifton B. Kroeber, eds., *The Frontier in Perspective* (Madison, Wis., 1957), 229-58; Harold E. Driver, *Indians of North America* (2d rev.

ed., Chicago, 1969), ch. 29; Wilbur R. Jacobs, *Dispossessing the American Indian: Indians and Whites on the Colonial Frontier* (New York, 1972), 151-72; Margaret C. Szasz and Ferenc M. Szasz, "The American Indian and the Classical Past," *The Midwest Quarterly*, 17:1 (Autumn 1975), 58-70.

3. Cohen, "Americanizing the White Man," 178; C. G. Jung, *Contributions to Analytical Psychology*, trans. H. G. and Cary F. Barnes (New York, 1928), 136-40.

4. Roy Harvey Pearce, *Savagism and Civilization: A Study of the Indian and the American Mind* (rev. ed., Baltimore, 1965).

5. William Hubbard, *The History of the Indian Wars in New England* [1677], ed. Samuel G. Drake, 2 vols. (Roxbury, Mass., 1865), 2:256.

6. [Increase Mather], *The Necessity of Reformation* (Boston, 1679), 7.

7. Joseph Easterbrooks, *Abraham the Passenger* (Boston, 1705), 3; J. Hammond Trumbull and C. J. Hoadly, eds., *The Public Records of the Colony of Connecticut*, 15 vols. (Hartford, 1850-90), 2: 328.

8. *Necessity of Reformation*, 5.

9. Cotton Mather, *The Way to Prosperity* (Boston, 1690), 27. See also Kenneth Silverman, ed., *Selected Letters of Cotton Mather* (Baton Rouge, 1971), 398.

10. Franklin B. Dexter, ed., *Diary of David McClure, D.D., 1748-1820* (New York, 1899), 93.

11. Richard J. Hooker, ed., *The Carolina Backcountry on the Eve of the Revolution* (Chapel Hill, 1953), 7, 15, 20, 30-33, 56, 61.

12. Milo Milton Quaife, ed., *John Long's Voyages and Travels in the Years 1768-1788* (Chicago, 1922), 44.

13. Wilbur R. Jacobs, ed., *The Appalachian Indian·Frontier: The Edmond Atkin Report and Plan of 1755* (Lincoln, Neb., 1967), 8, 22.

14. [James] *Adair's History of the American Indians* [London, 1775], ed. Samuel Cole Williams (Kingsport, Tenn., 1930), 306.

15. John Lawson, *A New Voyage to Carolina* [London, 1709], ed. Hugh Talmage Lefler (Chapel Hill, 1967), 190, 192.

16. Ann Maury, ed., *Memoirs of a Huguenot Family* [1852] (New York, 1907), 349-50.

17. Lawson, *New Voyage to Carolina*, 192.

18. Mrs. Anne Grant, *Memoirs of an American Lady*, ed. James Grant Wilson, 2 vols. (New York, 1901), 1:92, 99-109.

19. *Ibid.*, 1:107-8.

20. *Collections of the Massachusetts Historical Society*, 4th ser. 6 (1863), 215, 222, 245.

21. William Hubbard, *The Present State of New-England* (London, 1677), 59 (2d pag.); Charles H. Lincoln, ed., *Narratives of the Indian Wars, 1675-1699*, Original Narratives of Early American History (New York, 1913), 67. See also *Colls. Mass. His. Soc.*, 4th ser. 6 (1863), 307-11. Another renegade, Edward Ashley, drew the fire of Plymouth's William Bradford (*Of Plymouth Plantation, 1620-1647*, ed, Samuel Eliot Morison (New York, 1952), 219, 233).

22. Trumbull and Hoadly, eds., *Pub. Recs. of the Col. of Conn.*, 1:78. Early Virginia also had its share of runaways. See Bernard W. Sheehan, *Savagism and Civility: Indians and Englishmen in Colonial Virginia* (New York, 1980), 110-15.

23. See above, Chapter 6.

24. John Franklin Meginness, *Biography of Frances Slocum, the Lost Sister of Wyoming* (Williamsport, Pa., 1891), 196. See also Felix Renick, "A Trip to the West," *The American Pioneer*, 1 (1842), 79, and Joseph Doddridge, *Notes on the Settlement and Indian Wars, of the Western Parts of Virginia & Pennsylvania . . .* [1763-1783] (Wellsburgh, Va., 1824), 188.

25. [William Smith, D.D.], *An Historical Account of the Expedition Against the Ohio Indians, in the Year 1764 . . .* (Philadelphia, 1765), 29.

26. Silverman, ed., *Selected Letters of Cotton Mather*, 397-99.

27. George W. Corner, ed., *The Autobiography of Benjamin Rush* (Princeton, 1948), 71; J. Hector St. John de Crèvecoeur, *Letters from an American Farmer*, ed. Warren Barton Blake (London: Everyman ed., 1912), 65-66; Samuel Stanhope Smith, *An Essay on the Causes of the Variety of Complexion and Figure in the Human Species*, ed. Winthrop D. Jordan (Cambridge, Mass., 1965), 45n.

28. Smith, *Essay on the Causes*, 12, 17; Crèvecoeur, *Letters from an American Farmer*, 51-52, 222; Alexis de Tocqueville, *Democracy in America*, trans. Henry Reeve and Francis Bowen, ed. Phillips Bradley, 2 vols. (New York, 1945), 1:342-43, 347; Gen. Benjamin Lincoln, in *Colls. Mass. His. Soc.*, 1st ser. 5 (1798), 10. See also Leonard W. Labaree *et al.*, eds., *The Papers of Benjamin Franklin* (New Haven, 1959–), 4:481-82, and L. H. Butterfield, ed., *Letters of Benjamin Rush*, 2 vols. (Princeton, 1951), 1:400-406, 2:1163.

29. Crèvecoeur, *Letters from an American Farmer*, 47, 52, 55; Smith, *Essay on the Causes*, 15, 17-18.

30. Lois M. Feister, "Linguistic Communication Between the Dutch

and Indians in New Netherland, 1609-1664," *Ethnohistory*, 20 (1973), 25-38; James M. Crawford, *The Mobilian Trade Language* (Knoxville, Tenn., 1978); J. Dyneley Prince, "An Ancient New Jersey Indian Jargon," *American Anthropologist*, n.s. 14 (1912), 508-24; Ives Goddard, "Some Early Examples of American Indian Pidgin English from New England," *International Journal of American Linguistics*, 43 (1977), 37-41.

31. Capt. John Smith, *Works 1608-1631*, ed. Edward Arber (Birmingham, Eng., 1884), 102, 449, 528, 564, 569, 599; Eleazar Wheelock, *A plain and faithful Narrative of the . . . Indian Charity-School At Lebanon, in Connecticut* (Boston, 1763), 18, 23-24, 27-28, 34.

32. See the recent edition by John T. Teunissen and Evelyn J. Hinz (Detroit, 1973). For linguistic purposes, the heavily annotated edition by J. Hammond Trumbull (Providence, 1860) is still superior.

33. David B. Quinn, ed., "A List of Books Purchased for the Virginia Company," *Virginia Magazine of History and Biography*, 77 (1969), 347-60.

34. Susie M. Ames, ed. *County Court Records of Accomack-Northampton, Virginia, 1632-1640* (Washington, D.C., 1954), 120.

35. Colonel Norwood, *A Voyage to Virginia* [1649], in Peter Force, ed., *Tracts and Other Papers, Relating Principally to the Origin, Settlement, and Progress of the Colonies in North America, from the Discovery of the Country to the Year 1776*, 4 vols. (Washington, D.C., 1836-47), vol. 3, no. 10, pp. 29-30.

36. Alexander F. Chamberlain, "Algonkian Words in American English: A Study in the Contact of the White Man and the Indian," *Journal of American Folklore*, 15 (1902), 240-67.

37. Jacobs, *Dispossessing the American Indian*, 164; H. L. Mencken, *The American Language* (4th ed., New York, 1936), 104-13, 530-32.

38. Edward Eggleston, *The Transit of Civilization from England to America in the Seventeenth Century* [1900] (Boston, 1959), 106.

39. *Ibid.*, 107; Chamberlain, "Algonkian Words in American English," 244.

40. Bradford, *Of Plymouth Plantation*, 61.

41. Eggleston, "The Aborigines and the Colonists," 100.

42. Christopher Levett, *A Voyage into New England* [London, 1628], in Charles Herbert Levermore, ed., *Forerunners and Competitors of the Pilgrims and Puritans*, 2 vols. (Brooklyn, N.Y., 1912), 2:613.

43. [Edward] *Johnson's Wonder-Working Providence, 1628-1651*, ed. J. Franklin Jameson, Orig. Narrs. of Early Amer. Hist. (New York, 1910), 114.

44. George Francis Dow, *Domestic Life in New England in the Seventeenth Century* (Topsfield, Mass., 1925), 4-5; Fiske Kimball, *Domestic Architecture of the American Colonies and of the Early Republic* (New York, 1922), 3-35; Cary Carson, Norman Barka, William Kelso, Garry Stone, and Dell Upton, "Impermanent Architecture in the Southern American Colonies," *Winterthur Portfolio, 18* (1981).

45. *Johnson's Wonder-Working Providence,* 211.

46. Smith, *Works,* 154-57.

47. Susan Myra Kingsbury, ed., *Records of the Virginia Company of London,* 4 vols. (Washington, D.C., 1906-35), 3:556-57.

48. Bradford, *Of Plymouth Plantation,* 85; William Wood, *New Englands Prospect* (London, 1634), 70.

49. Bradford, *Of Plymouth Plantation,* 85; Dwight B. Heath, ed., *A Journal of the Pilgrims at Plymouth: Mourt's Relation* [1622] (New York, 1963), 82.

50. Lynn Ceci, "Fish Fertilizer: A Native American Practice?" *Science* (April 4, 1975), 26-30; (Sept. 19, 1975), 945-47.

51. *Johnson's Wonder-Working Providence,* 114-15; Edward Everett, ed., *Letters from New England: The Massachusetts Bay Colony, 1629-1638* (Amherst, Mass., 1976), 66, 96; 227; Smith, *Works,* 952; Fulmer Mood, "John Winthrop, Jr. on Indian Corn," *New England Quarterly,* 10 (1937), 121-33 at 127-28.

52. Bradford, *Of Plymouth Plantation,* 178, 181, 202, 380; Darrett B. Rutman, *Husbandmen of Plymouth: Farms and Villages in the Old Colony, 1620-1692* (Boston, 1967), 10-12, 13, 16-17 and n. 33, 37, 42-46, 50-52, 54, 59, 60-61.

53. Charles Hudson, *The Southeastern Indians* (Knoxville, Tenn., 1976), 284.

54. Doddridge, *Notes on the Settlement and Indian Wars,* 156-59; Jeremy Belknap, *The History of New Hampshire,* 3 vols. (2d ed., Boston, 1813), 3:67-69.

55. Rev. Jared Eliot to the Rev. Thomas Prince, June 3, 1729, in *Collections of the Connecticut Historical Society,* 3 (1895), 291-92.

56. Belknap, *History of New Hampshire,* 3:66; Robert Beverley, *The History and Present State of Virginia,* ed. Louis B. Wright (Chapel Hill, 1947), 217-20; Doddridge, *Notes on the Settlement and Indian Wars,* 147-52; Virgil J. Vogel, *American Indian Medicine* (Norman, Okla., 1970), 116-19 and *passim,* esp. Appendix.

57. Dr. Benjamin Gale to Eleazar Wheelock, for Samuel Kirkland,

July 21, 1769, Wheelock Papers 769421.1, Dartmouth College Library, Hanover, N.H.

58. Doddridge, *Notes on the Settlement and Indian Wars*, 114.

59. Williams, *Key into the Language of America*, 120.

60. Doddridge, *Notes on the Settlement and Indian Wars*, 115.

61. Richard Glover, ed., *David Thompson's Narrative, 1784-1812* (Toronto: The Champlain Society, 1962), 304.

62. Doddridge, *Notes on the Settlement and Indian Wars*, 113.

63. Rhys Isaac, "Dramatizing the Ideology of Revolution: Popular Mobilization in Virginia, 1774 to 1776," *William and Mary Quarterly*, 3d ser. 33 (1976), 379-82.

64. Beverley, *History and Present State of Virginia*, 9; Silverman, ed., *Selected Letters of Cotton Mather*, 178, 399; Gottlieb Mittelberger, *Journey to Pennsylvania*, trans. and ed. Oscar Handlin and John Clive (Cambridge, Mass., 1960), 85.

65. George Sheldon, *A History of Deerfield, Massachusetts*, 2 vols. (Deerfield, 1895-96), 1:656.

66. Samuel Penhallow, *The History of the Wars of New-England, with the Eastern Indians* (Boston, 1726), 11.

67. Archibald Kennedy, *Serious Advice to the Inhabitants of the Northern-Colonies* (New York, 1755), 6, 15.

68. Peter E. Russell, "Redcoats in the Wilderness: British Officers and Irregular Warfare in Europe and America, 1740 to 1760," *WMQ*, 3d ser. 35 (1978), 629-52.

69. Harold L. Peterson, "The Military Equipment of the Plymouth and Bay Colonies, 1620-1690," *New Eng. Q.*, 20 (1947), 197-208; Kennedy, *Serious Advice*, 14-15.

70. Archibald Kennedy, *The Importance of Gaining and Preserving the Friendship of the Indians to the British Interest Considered* (London, 1752), 43.

71. Alfred Proctor James, ed., *Writings of General John Forbes* (Menasha, Wis., 1938), 125.

72. John K. Mahon, "Anglo-American Methods of Indian Warfare, 1676-1794," *Mississippi Valley Historical Review*, 45 (1958-59), 254-75; Douglas Edward Leach, *Arms for Empire: A Military History of the British Colonies in North America, 1607-1763* (New York, 1973), chs. 9-10.

73. Mahon, "Anglo-American Methods of Indian Warfare," 254-75; above, Chapter 6, pp. 146-47.

74. Charles Francis Adams, ed., *The Works of John Adams*, 10 vols. (Boston, 1850-56), 10:282-83, 288, 313.

75. See above, Chapter 3, p. 43, and Loren E. Pennington, "The Amerindian in English Promotional Literature, 1575-1625," in K. R. Andrews, N. P. Canny, and P. E. H. Hair, eds., *The Westward Enterprise: English Activities in Ireland, the Atlantic, and America 1480-1650* (Detroit, 1979), 175-94.

76. Edmund S. Morgan, *The Puritan Family: Religion and Domestic Relations in Seventeenth-Century New England* (rev. ed., New York, 1966), ch. 7.

77. David D. Hall, *The Faithful Shepherd: A History of the New England Ministry in the Seventeenth Century* (Chapel Hill, 1972), esp. chs. 7, 11.

78. William Kellaway, *The New England Company, 1649-1776: Missionary Society to the American Indians* (London, 1961), ch. 9; R. Pierce Beaver, ed., *Pioneers in Mission: The Early Missionary Ordination Sermons, Charges, and Instructions* (Grand Rapids, Mich., 1966); John Wolfe Lydekker, *The Faithful Mohawks* (New York, 1938); John C. Guzzardo, "The Superintendent and the Ministers: The Battle for Oneida Allegiances, 1761-75," *New York History*, 57 (1976), 255-83; Cedric B. Cowing, *The Great Awakening and the American Revolution: Colonial Thought in the 18th Century* (Chicago, 1971), 77-86.

79. Lawson, *New Voyage to Carolina*, 240.

80. Mather, *The Way to Prosperity*, 27; Rev. John Heckewelder, *History, Manners, and Customs of the Indian Nations Who Once Inhabited Pennsylvania and the Neighbouring States*, rev. ed. Rev. William C. Reichel (Philadelphia, 1876), 223.

81. Cotton Mather, *A Letter to Ungospellized Plantations* (Boston, 1702), 14.

82. Pearce, *Savagism and Civilization*, 5. See also Robert F. Berkhofer, Jr., *The White Man's Indian: Images of the American Indian from Columbus to the Present* (New York, 1978); Gary B. Nash, "The Image of the Indian in the Southern Colonial Mind," *WMQ*, 3d ser. 29 (1972), 197-230; Sheehan, *Savagism and Civility*; Karen Ordahl Kupperman, *Settling with the Indians: The Meeting of English and Indian Cultures in America, 1580-1640* (Totowa, N.J., 1980); James Axtell, "Through a Glass Darkly: Colonial Attitudes Toward the Native Americans," *American Indian Culture and Research Journal*, 1 (1974), 17-28.

83. Winthrop D. Jordan, *White Over Black: American Attitudes Toward the Negro, 1550-1812* (Chapel Hill, 1968), 40; Michael Zuck-

erman, "The Fabrication of Identity in Early America," *WMQ*, 3d ser. 34 (1977), 183-214 at 204.

84. Daniel Gookin, "Historical Collections of the Indians in New England" [1674], *Colls. Mass. His. Soc.*, 1st ser. 1 (1792), 131.

85. Michael Kammen, *People of Paradox: An Inquiry Concerning the Origins of American Civilization* (New York, 1972). See the perceptive critique by Carl Degler in *Reviews in American History*, 1 (1973), 470-74.

86. Richard P. Johnson, "The Search for a Usable Indian: An Aspect of the Defense of Colonial New England," *Journal of American History*, 64 (1977), 623-51.

87. Richard Slotkin, *Regeneration Through Violence: The Mythology of the American Frontier, 1600-1860* (Middletown, Conn., 1973); Slotkin, "Dreams and Genocide: The American Myth of Regeneration Through Violence," *Journal of Popular History*, 5:1 (Summer 1971), 38-59; Slotkin, "Massacre," *Berkshire Review*, 14 (1979), 112-32; Neal Salisbury, "Inside Out: Perception and Projection in the Puritans' Encounter with Indians," paper delivered at the American Studies Association, San Antonio, Texas, Nov. 7, 1975; Robert Shulman, "Parkman's Indians and American Violence," *Massachusetts Review*, 12 (1971), 221-39.

88. Doddridge, *Notes on the Settlement and Indian Wars*, 207. The style of Indian warfare itself changed as a result of confronting European guns and uninhibited methods. See Francis Jennings, *The Invasion of America: Indians, Colonialism, and the Cant of Conquest* (Chapel Hill, 1975), 165ff., and J. Frederick Fausz, "Fighting 'Fire' with Firearms: The Anglo-Powhatan Arms Race in Early Virginia," *Amer. Indian Cul. and Res. J.*, 3:4 (1979), 34.

89. William J. Eccles, *The Canadian Frontier 1534-1760* (New York, 1969), 42.

90. Diary of Ebenezer Parkman, July 20, 1726, *Proceedings of the American Antiquarian Society*, n.s. 71 (1961), 150-51.

91. Cotton Mather, "A Brand Pluck'd Out of the Burning" [1693], in George Lincoln Burr, ed., *Narratives of the Witchcraft Cases, 1648-1706*, Orig. Narrs. of Early Amer. Hist. (New York, 1914), 255-87.

92. Esther Burr to Sarah Prince, Aug. 3, 1755, Journal of Esther Burr, p. 133, Yale University Library, New Haven, Conn.

93. Journal of Esther Burr, July 19, 1755, pp. 124-25.

94. Doddridge, *Notes on the Settlement and Indian Wars*, 210.

95. See above, Chapter 8.

96. See Chapter 6, pp. 142, 148-49; James Axtell, "The Vengeful Women of Marblehead: Robert Roules's Deposition of 1677," *WMQ*, 3d ser. 31 (1974), 647-52.

97. Samuel Davies, *Religion and Patriotism the Constituents of a Good Soldier* (Philadelphia, 1755), 7.

98. Cotton Mather, *Souldiers Counselled and Comforted* (Boston, 1689), 28.

99. James Sullivan *et al.*, eds., *The Papers of Sir William Johnson*, 14 vols. (Albany, 1921-65), 13:198; Frederick Cook, ed., *Journals of the Military Expedition of Major General John Sullivan Against the Six Nations of Indians in 1779* (Auburn, N.Y., 1887), 8.

100. James K. Hosmer, ed., [John] *Winthrop's Journal 'History of New England' 1630-1649*, Orig. Narrs. of Early Amer. Hist., 2 vols. (New York, 1908), 2:18-19. See also *The Complete Works of Roger Williams*, 7 vols. (New York, 1963), 7:31.

101. *The Poems of Roger Wolcott* (Boston, 1898), 55.

102. R. A. Brock, ed., *The Official Letters of Alexander Spotswood, Collections of the Virginia Historical Society*, n.s. 1 (1882), 134.

103. Bernhard Knollenberg, "General Amherst and Germ Warfare," *Miss. Valley His. Rev.*, 41 (1954-55), 489-94, 762-63.

104. Between 1705 and 1708, Massachusetts's defense bills were £30,000 per year, an amount equal to ten times the whole colony budget in the 1680s (Johnson, "Search for a Usable Indian," *J. of Amer. His.*, 64 (1977), 626 n.5).

105. E. McClung Fleming, "The American Image as Indian Princess, 1765-1783," *Winterthur Portfolio*, 2 (1965), 65-81; Hugh Honour, *The New Golden Land: European Images of America from the Discoveries to the Present Time* (New York, 1975), ch. 6.

Index